50% OFF

Online AFOQT Prep Course!

By Mometrix

Dear Customer,

We consider it an honor and a privilege that you chose our AFOQT Study Guide. As a way of showing our appreciation and to help us better serve you, we are offering **50% off our online AFOQT Prep Course**. Many AFOQT courses are needlessly expensive and don't deliver enough value. With our course, you get access to the best AFOQT prep material, and **you only pay half price**.

We have structured our online course to perfectly complement your printed study guide. The AFOQT Prep Course contains **in-depth lessons** that cover all the most important topics, **50+ video reviews** that explain difficult concepts, over **1,200 practice questions** to ensure you feel prepared.

Online AFOQT Prep Course

Topics Included:

- Verbal Analogies
- Arithmetic Reasoning and Math Knowledge
- Word Knowledge
- Reading Comprehension
- Situational Judgment
- Physical Science
- Table Reading
- Instrumental Comprehension
- Block Counting
- Aviation Information

Course Features:

- AFOQT Study Guide
  - Get content that complements our best-selling study guide.
- Full-Length Practice Tests
  - With over 1,200 practice questions, you can test yourself again and again.
- Mobile Friendly
  - If you need to study on the go, the course is easily accessible from your mobile device.

To receive this discount, visit us at mometrix.com/university/afoqt or simply scan this QR code with your smartphone. At the checkout page, enter the discount code: **afoqt50off**

If you have any questions or concerns, please contact us at support@mometrix.com.

FREE Study Skills Videos/DVD Offer

Dear Customer,

Thank you for your purchase from Mometrix! We consider it an honor and a privilege that you have purchased our product and we want to ensure your satisfaction.

As part of our ongoing effort to meet the needs of test takers, we have developed a set of Study Skills Videos that we would like to give you for FREE. These videos cover our *best practices* for getting ready for your exam, from how to use our study materials to how to best prepare for the day of the test.

All that we ask is that you email us with feedback that would describe your experience so far with our product. Good, bad, or indifferent, we want to know what you think!

To get your FREE Study Skills Videos, you can use the **QR code** below, or send us an **email** at studyvideos@mometrix.com with *FREE VIDEOS* in the subject line and the following information in the body of the email:

- The name of the product you purchased.
- Your product rating on a scale of 1-5, with 5 being the highest rating.
- Your feedback. It can be long, short, or anything in between. We just want to know your impressions and experience so far with our product. (Good feedback might include how our study material met your needs and ways we might be able to make it even better. You could highlight features that you found helpful or features that you think we should add.)

If you have any questions or concerns, please don't hesitate to contact me directly.

Thanks again!

Sincerely,

Jay Willis
Vice President
jay.willis@mometrix.com
1-800-673-8175

AFOQT Study Guide 2022-2023

Air Force Officer Qualifying Test Prep Secrets

2 Full-Length Practice Tests

Step-by-Step Video Tutorials

6th Edition

Written and edited by Mometrix Test Prep

Printed in the United States of America

This paper meets the requirements of ANSI/NISO Z39.48-1992 (Permanence of Paper).

Paperback
ISBN 13: 978-1-5167-1941-9
ISBN 10: 1-5167-1941-7

DEAR FUTURE EXAM SUCCESS STORY

First of all, **THANK YOU** for purchasing Mometrix study materials!

Second, congratulations! You are one of the few determined test-takers who are committed to doing whatever it takes to excel on your exam. **You have come to the right place.** We developed these study materials with one goal in mind: to deliver you the information you need in a format that's concise and easy to use.

In addition to optimizing your guide for the content of the test, we've outlined our recommended steps for breaking down the preparation process into small, attainable goals so you can make sure you stay on track.

We've also analyzed the entire test-taking process, identifying the most common pitfalls and showing how you can overcome them and be ready for any curveball the test throws you.

Standardized testing is one of the biggest obstacles on your road to success, which only increases the importance of doing well in the high-pressure, high-stakes environment of test day. Your results on this test could have a significant impact on your future, and this guide provides the information and practical advice to help you achieve your full potential on test day.

Your success is our success

We would love to hear from you! If you would like to share the story of your exam success or if you have any questions or comments in regard to our products, please contact us at **800-673-8175** or **support@mometrix.com**.

Thanks again for your business and we wish you continued success!

Sincerely,
The Mometrix Test Preparation Team

TABLE OF CONTENTS

Introduction

Thank you for purchasing this resource! You have made the choice to prepare yourself for a test that could have a huge impact on your future, and this guide is designed to help you be fully ready for test day. Obviously, it's important to have a solid understanding of the test material, but you also need to be prepared for the unique environment and stressors of the test, so that you can perform to the best of your abilities.

For this purpose, the first section that appears in this guide is the **Secret Keys**. We've devoted countless hours to meticulously researching what works and what doesn't, and we've boiled down our findings to the five most impactful steps you can take to improve your performance on the test. We start at the beginning with study planning and move through the preparation process, all the way to the testing strategies that will help you get the most out of what you know when you're finally sitting in front of the test.

We recommend that you start preparing for your test as far in advance as possible. However, if you've bought this guide as a last-minute study resource and only have a few days before your test, we recommend that you skip over the first two Secret Keys since they address a long-term study plan.

If you struggle with **test anxiety**, we strongly encourage you to check out our recommendations for how you can overcome it. Test anxiety is a formidable foe, but it can be beaten, and we want to make sure you have the tools you need to defeat it.

Secret Key #1 – Plan Big, Study Small

There's a lot riding on your performance. If you want to ace this test, you're going to need to keep your skills sharp and the material fresh in your mind. You need a plan that lets you review everything you need to know while still fitting in your schedule. We'll break this strategy down into three categories.

Information Organization

Start with the information you already have: the official test outline. From this, you can make a complete list of all the concepts you need to cover before the test. Organize these concepts into groups that can be studied together, and create a list of any related vocabulary you need to learn so you can brush up on any difficult terms. You'll want to keep this vocabulary list handy once you actually start studying since you may need to add to it along the way.

Time Management

Once you have your set of study concepts, decide how to spread them out over the time you have left before the test. Break your study plan into small, clear goals so you have a manageable task for each day and know exactly what you're doing. Then just focus on one small step at a time. When you manage your time this way, you don't need to spend hours at a time studying. Studying a small block of content for a short period each day helps you retain information better and avoid stressing over how much you have left to do. You can relax knowing that you have a plan to cover everything in time. In order for this strategy to be effective though, you have to start studying early and stick to your schedule. Avoid the exhaustion and futility that comes from last-minute cramming!

Study Environment

The environment you study in has a big impact on your learning. Studying in a coffee shop, while probably more enjoyable, is not likely to be as fruitful as studying in a quiet room. It's important to keep distractions to a minimum. You're only planning to study for a short block of time, so make the most of it. Don't pause to check your phone or get up to find a snack. It's also important to **avoid multitasking**. Research has consistently shown that multitasking will make your studying dramatically less effective. Your study area should also be comfortable and well-lit so you don't have the distraction of straining your eyes or sitting on an uncomfortable chair.

The time of day you study is also important. You want to be rested and alert. Don't wait until just before bedtime. Study when you'll be most likely to comprehend and remember. Even better, if you know what time of day your test will be, set that time aside for study. That way your brain will be used to working on that subject at that specific time and you'll have a better chance of recalling information.

Finally, it can be helpful to team up with others who are studying for the same test. Your actual studying should be done in as isolated an environment as possible, but the work of organizing the information and setting up the study plan can be divided up. In between study sessions, you can discuss with your teammates the concepts that you're all studying and quiz each other on the details. Just be sure that your teammates are as serious about the test as you are. If you find that your study time is being replaced with social time, you might need to find a new team.

Secret Key #2 – Make Your Studying Count

You're devoting a lot of time and effort to preparing for this test, so you want to be absolutely certain it will pay off. This means doing more than just reading the content and hoping you can remember it on test day. It's important to make every minute of study count. There are two main areas you can focus on to make your studying count.

Retention

It doesn't matter how much time you study if you can't remember the material. You need to make sure you are retaining the concepts. To check your retention of the information you're learning, try recalling it at later times with minimal prompting. Try carrying around flashcards and glance at one or two from time to time or ask a friend who's also studying for the test to quiz you.

To enhance your retention, look for ways to put the information into practice so that you can apply it rather than simply recalling it. If you're using the information in practical ways, it will be much easier to remember. Similarly, it helps to solidify a concept in your mind if you're not only reading it to yourself but also explaining it to someone else. Ask a friend to let you teach them about a concept you're a little shaky on (or speak aloud to an imaginary audience if necessary). As you try to summarize, define, give examples, and answer your friend's questions, you'll understand the concepts better and they will stay with you longer. Finally, step back for a big picture view and ask yourself how each piece of information fits with the whole subject. When you link the different concepts together and see them working together as a whole, it's easier to remember the individual components.

Finally, practice showing your work on any multi-step problems, even if you're just studying. Writing out each step you take to solve a problem will help solidify the process in your mind, and you'll be more likely to remember it during the test.

Modality

Modality simply refers to the means or method by which you study. Choosing a study modality that fits your own individual learning style is crucial. No two people learn best in exactly the same way, so it's important to know your strengths and use them to your advantage.

For example, if you learn best by visualization, focus on visualizing a concept in your mind and draw an image or a diagram. Try color-coding your notes, illustrating them, or creating symbols that will trigger your mind to recall a learned concept. If you learn best by hearing or discussing information, find a study partner who learns the same way or read aloud to yourself. Think about how to put the information in your own words. Imagine that you are giving a lecture on the topic and record yourself so you can listen to it later.

For any learning style, flashcards can be helpful. Organize the information so you can take advantage of spare moments to review. Underline key words or phrases. Use different colors for different categories. Mnemonic devices (such as creating a short list in which every item starts with the same letter) can also help with retention. Find what works best for you and use it to store the information in your mind most effectively and easily.

Secret Key #3 – Practice the Right Way

Your success on test day depends not only on how many hours you put into preparing, but also on whether you prepared the right way. It's good to check along the way to see if your studying is paying off. One of the most effective ways to do this is by taking practice tests to evaluate your progress. Practice tests are useful because they show exactly where you need to improve. Every time you take a practice test, pay special attention to these three groups of questions:

- The questions you got wrong
- The questions you had to guess on, even if you guessed right
- The questions you found difficult or slow to work through

This will show you exactly what your weak areas are, and where you need to devote more study time. Ask yourself why each of these questions gave you trouble. Was it because you didn't understand the material? Was it because you didn't remember the vocabulary? Do you need more repetitions on this type of question to build speed and confidence? Dig into those questions and figure out how you can strengthen your weak areas as you go back to review the material.

Additionally, many practice tests have a section explaining the answer choices. It can be tempting to read the explanation and think that you now have a good understanding of the concept. However, an explanation likely only covers part of the question's broader context. Even if the explanation makes perfect sense, **go back and investigate** every concept related to the question until you're positive you have a thorough understanding.

As you go along, keep in mind that the practice test is just that: practice. Memorizing these questions and answers will not be very helpful on the actual test because it is unlikely to have any of the same exact questions. If you only know the right answers to the sample questions, you won't be prepared for the real thing. **Study the concepts** until you understand them fully, and then you'll be able to answer any question that shows up on the test.

It's important to wait on the practice tests until you're ready. If you take a test on your first day of study, you may be overwhelmed by the amount of material covered and how much you need to learn. Work up to it gradually.

On test day, you'll need to be prepared for answering questions, managing your time, and using the test-taking strategies you've learned. It's a lot to balance, like a mental marathon that will have a big impact on your future. Like training for a marathon, you'll need to start slowly and work your way up. When test day arrives, you'll be ready.

Start with the strategies you've read in the first two Secret Keys—plan your course and study in the way that works best for you. If you have time, consider using multiple study resources to get different approaches to the same concepts. It can be helpful to see difficult concepts from more than one angle. Then find a good source for practice tests. Many times, the test website will suggest potential study resources or provide sample tests.

Practice Test Strategy

If you're able to find at least three practice tests, we recommend this strategy:

Untimed and Open-Book Practice

Take the first test with no time constraints and with your notes and study guide handy. Take your time and focus on applying the strategies you've learned.

Timed and Open-Book Practice

Take the second practice test open-book as well, but set a timer and practice pacing yourself to finish in time.

Timed and Closed-Book Practice

Take any other practice tests as if it were test day. Set a timer and put away your study materials. Sit at a table or desk in a quiet room, imagine yourself at the testing center, and answer questions as quickly and accurately as possible.

Keep repeating timed and closed-book tests on a regular basis until you run out of practice tests or it's time for the actual test. Your mind will be ready for the schedule and stress of test day, and you'll be able to focus on recalling the material you've learned.

Secret Key #4 – Pace Yourself

Once you're fully prepared for the material on the test, your biggest challenge on test day will be managing your time. Just knowing that the clock is ticking can make you panic even if you have plenty of time left. Work on pacing yourself so you can build confidence against the time constraints of the exam. Pacing is a difficult skill to master, especially in a high-pressure environment, so **practice is vital**.

Set time expectations for your pace based on how much time is available. For example, if a section has 60 questions and the time limit is 30 minutes, you know you have to average 30 seconds or less per question in order to answer them all. Although 30 seconds is the hard limit, set 25 seconds per question as your goal, so you reserve extra time to spend on harder questions. When you budget extra time for the harder questions, you no longer have any reason to stress when those questions take longer to answer.

Don't let this time expectation distract you from working through the test at a calm, steady pace, but keep it in mind so you don't spend too much time on any one question. Recognize that taking extra time on one question you don't understand may keep you from answering two that you do understand later in the test. If your time limit for a question is up and you're still not sure of the answer, mark it and move on, and come back to it later if the time and the test format allow. If the testing format doesn't allow you to return to earlier questions, just make an educated guess; then put it out of your mind and move on.

On the easier questions, be careful not to rush. It may seem wise to hurry through them so you have more time for the challenging ones, but it's not worth missing one if you know the concept and just didn't take the time to read the question fully. Work efficiently but make sure you understand the question and have looked at all of the answer choices, since more than one may seem right at first.

Even if you're paying attention to the time, you may find yourself a little behind at some point. You should speed up to get back on track, but do so wisely. Don't panic; just take a few seconds less on each question until you're caught up. Don't guess without thinking, but do look through the answer choices and eliminate any you know are wrong. If you can get down to two choices, it is often worthwhile to guess from those. Once you've chosen an answer, move on and don't dwell on any that you skipped or had to hurry through. If a question was taking too long, chances are it was one of the harder ones, so you weren't as likely to get it right anyway.

On the other hand, if you find yourself getting ahead of schedule, it may be beneficial to slow down a little. The more quickly you work, the more likely you are to make a careless mistake that will affect your score. You've budgeted time for each question, so don't be afraid to spend that time. Practice an efficient but careful pace to get the most out of the time you have.

Secret Key #5 – Have a Plan for Guessing

When you're taking the test, you may find yourself stuck on a question. Some of the answer choices seem better than others, but you don't see the one answer choice that is obviously correct. What do you do?

The scenario described above is very common, yet most test takers have not effectively prepared for it. Developing and practicing a plan for guessing may be one of the single most effective uses of your time as you get ready for the exam.

In developing your plan for guessing, there are three questions to address:

- When should you start the guessing process?
- How should you narrow down the choices?
- Which answer should you choose?

When to Start the Guessing Process

Unless your plan for guessing is to select C every time (which, despite its merits, is not what we recommend), you need to leave yourself enough time to apply your answer elimination strategies. Since you have a limited amount of time for each question, that means that if you're going to give yourself the best shot at guessing correctly, you have to decide quickly whether or not you will guess.

Of course, the best-case scenario is that you don't have to guess at all, so first, see if you can answer the question based on your knowledge of the subject and basic reasoning skills. Focus on the key words in the question and try to jog your memory of related topics. Give yourself a chance to bring the knowledge to mind, but once you realize that you don't have (or you can't access) the knowledge you need to answer the question, it's time to start the guessing process.

It's almost always better to start the guessing process too early than too late. It only takes a few seconds to remember something and answer the question from knowledge. Carefully eliminating wrong answer choices takes longer. Plus, going through the process of eliminating answer choices can actually help jog your memory.

Summary: Start the guessing process as soon as you decide that you can't answer the question based on your knowledge.

How to Narrow Down the Choices

The next chapter in this book (**Test-Taking Strategies**) includes a wide range of strategies for how to approach questions and how to look for answer choices to eliminate. You will definitely want to read those carefully, practice them, and figure out which ones work best for you. Here though, we're going to address a mindset rather than a particular strategy.

Your odds of guessing an answer correctly depend on how many options you are choosing from.

Number of options left	5	4	3	2	1
Odds of guessing correctly	20%	25%	33%	50%	100%

You can see from this chart just how valuable it is to be able to eliminate incorrect answers and make an educated guess, but there are two things that many test takers do that cause them to miss out on the benefits of guessing:

- Accidentally eliminating the correct answer
- Selecting an answer based on an impression

We'll look at the first one here, and the second one in the next section.

To avoid accidentally eliminating the correct answer, we recommend a thought exercise called **the $5 challenge**. In this challenge, you only eliminate an answer choice from contention if you are willing to bet $5 on it being wrong. Why $5? Five dollars is a small but not insignificant amount of money. It's an amount you could afford to lose but wouldn't want to throw away. And while losing $5 once might not hurt too much, doing it twenty times will set you back $100. In the same way, each small decision you make—eliminating a choice here, guessing on a question there—won't by itself impact your score very much, but when you put them all together, they can make a big difference. By holding each answer choice elimination decision to a higher standard, you can reduce the risk of accidentally eliminating the correct answer.

The $5 challenge can also be applied in a positive sense: If you are willing to bet $5 that an answer choice *is* correct, go ahead and mark it as correct.

Summary: Only eliminate an answer choice if you are willing to bet $5 that it is wrong.

Which Answer to Choose

You're taking the test. You've run into a hard question and decided you'll have to guess. You've eliminated all the answer choices you're willing to bet $5 on. Now you have to pick an answer. Why do we even need to talk about this? Why can't you just pick whichever one you feel like when the time comes?

The answer to these questions is that if you don't come into the test with a plan, you'll rely on your impression to select an answer choice, and if you do that, you risk falling into a trap. The test writers know that everyone who takes their test will be guessing on some of the questions, so they intentionally write wrong answer choices to seem plausible. You still have to pick an answer though, and if the wrong answer choices are designed to look right, how can you ever be sure that you're not falling for their trap? The best solution we've found to this dilemma is to take the decision out of your hands entirely. Here is the process we recommend:

Once you've eliminated any choices that you are confident (willing to bet $5) are wrong, select the first remaining choice as your answer.

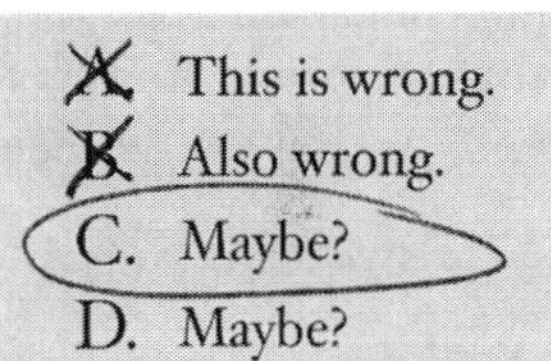

Whether you choose to select the first remaining choice, the second, or the last, the important thing is that you use some preselected standard. Using this approach guarantees that you will not be enticed into selecting an answer choice that looks right, because you are not basing your decision on how the answer choices look.

This is not meant to make you question your knowledge. Instead, it is to help you recognize the difference between your knowledge and your impressions. There's a huge difference between thinking an answer is right because of what you know, and thinking an answer is right because it looks or sounds like it should be right.

Summary: To ensure that your selection is appropriately random, make a predetermined selection from among all answer choices you have not eliminated.

Test-Taking Strategies

This section contains a list of test-taking strategies that you may find helpful as you work through the test. By taking what you know and applying logical thought, you can maximize your chances of answering any question correctly!

It is very important to realize that every question is different and every person is different: no single strategy will work on every question, and no single strategy will work for every person. That's why we've included all of them here, so you can try them out and determine which ones work best for different types of questions and which ones work best for you.

Question Strategies

✓ Read Carefully

Read the question and the answer choices carefully. Don't miss the question because you misread the terms. You have plenty of time to read each question thoroughly and make sure you understand what is being asked. Yet a happy medium must be attained, so don't waste too much time. You must read carefully and efficiently.

✓ Contextual Clues

Look for contextual clues. If the question includes a word you are not familiar with, look at the immediate context for some indication of what the word might mean. Contextual clues can often give you all the information you need to decipher the meaning of an unfamiliar word. Even if you can't determine the meaning, you may be able to narrow down the possibilities enough to make a solid guess at the answer to the question.

✓ Prefixes

If you're having trouble with a word in the question or answer choices, try dissecting it. Take advantage of every clue that the word might include. Prefixes can be a huge help. Usually, they allow you to determine a basic meaning. *Pre-* means before, *post-* means after, *pro-* is positive, *de-* is negative. From prefixes, you can get an idea of the general meaning of the word and try to put it into context.

✓ Hedge Words

Watch out for critical hedge words, such as *likely, may, can, sometimes, often, almost, mostly, usually, generally, rarely*, and *sometimes*. Question writers insert these hedge phrases to cover every possibility. Often an answer choice will be wrong simply because it leaves no room for exception. Be on guard for answer choices that have definitive words such as *exactly* and *always*.

✓ Switchback Words

Stay alert for *switchbacks*. These are the words and phrases frequently used to alert you to shifts in thought. The most common switchback words are *but, although*, and *however*. Others include *nevertheless, on the other hand, even though, while, in spite of, despite*, and *regardless of*. Switchback words are important to catch because they can change the direction of the question or an answer choice.

✅ Face Value

When in doubt, use common sense. Accept the situation in the problem at face value. Don't read too much into it. These problems will not require you to make wild assumptions. If you have to go beyond creativity and warp time or space in order to have an answer choice fit the question, then you should move on and consider the other answer choices. These are normal problems rooted in reality. The applicable relationship or explanation may not be readily apparent, but it is there for you to figure out. Use your common sense to interpret anything that isn't clear.

Answer Choice Strategies

✅ Answer Selection

The most thorough way to pick an answer choice is to identify and eliminate wrong answers until only one is left, then confirm it is the correct answer. Sometimes an answer choice may immediately seem right, but be careful. The test writers will usually put more than one reasonable answer choice on each question, so take a second to read all of them and make sure that the other choices are not equally obvious. As long as you have time left, it is better to read every answer choice than to pick the first one that looks right without checking the others.

✅ Answer Choice Families

An answer choice family consists of two (in rare cases, three) answer choices that are very similar in construction and cannot all be true at the same time. If you see two answer choices that are direct opposites or parallels, one of them is usually the correct answer. For instance, if one answer choice says that quantity *x* increases and another either says that quantity *x* decreases (opposite) or says that quantity *y* increases (parallel), then those answer choices would fall into the same family. An answer choice that doesn't match the construction of the answer choice family is more likely to be incorrect. Most questions will not have answer choice families, but when they do appear, you should be prepared to recognize them.

✅ Eliminate Answers

Eliminate answer choices as soon as you realize they are wrong, but make sure you consider all possibilities. If you are eliminating answer choices and realize that the last one you are left with is also wrong, don't panic. Start over and consider each choice again. There may be something you missed the first time that you will realize on the second pass.

✅ Avoid Fact Traps

Don't be distracted by an answer choice that is factually true but doesn't answer the question. You are looking for the choice that answers the question. Stay focused on what the question is asking for so you don't accidentally pick an answer that is true but incorrect. Always go back to the question and make sure the answer choice you've selected actually answers the question and is not merely a true statement.

✅ Extreme Statements

In general, you should avoid answers that put forth extreme actions as standard practice or proclaim controversial ideas as established fact. An answer choice that states the "process should be used in certain situations, if…" is much more likely to be correct than one that states the "process should be discontinued completely." The first is a calm rational statement and doesn't even make a definitive, uncompromising stance, using a hedge word *if* to provide wiggle room, whereas the second choice is far more extreme.

☑ Benchmark

As you read through the answer choices and you come across one that seems to answer the question well, mentally select that answer choice. This is not your final answer, but it's the one that will help you evaluate the other answer choices. The one that you selected is your benchmark or standard for judging each of the other answer choices. Every other answer choice must be compared to your benchmark. That choice is correct until proven otherwise by another answer choice beating it. If you find a better answer, then that one becomes your new benchmark. Once you've decided that no other choice answers the question as well as your benchmark, you have your final answer.

☑ Predict the Answer

Before you even start looking at the answer choices, it is often best to try to predict the answer. When you come up with the answer on your own, it is easier to avoid distractions and traps because you will know exactly what to look for. The right answer choice is unlikely to be word-for-word what you came up with, but it should be a close match. Even if you are confident that you have the right answer, you should still take the time to read each option before moving on.

General Strategies

☑ Tough Questions

If you are stumped on a problem or it appears too hard or too difficult, don't waste time. Move on! Remember though, if you can quickly check for obviously incorrect answer choices, your chances of guessing correctly are greatly improved. Before you completely give up, at least try to knock out a couple of possible answers. Eliminate what you can and then guess at the remaining answer choices before moving on.

☑ Check Your Work

Since you will probably not know every term listed and the answer to every question, it is important that you get credit for the ones that you do know. Don't miss any questions through careless mistakes. If at all possible, try to take a second to look back over your answer selection and make sure you've selected the correct answer choice and haven't made a costly careless mistake (such as marking an answer choice that you didn't mean to mark). This quick double check should more than pay for itself in caught mistakes for the time it costs.

☑ Pace Yourself

It's easy to be overwhelmed when you're looking at a page full of questions; your mind is confused and full of random thoughts, and the clock is ticking down faster than you would like. Calm down and maintain the pace that you have set for yourself. Especially as you get down to the last few minutes of the test, don't let the small numbers on the clock make you panic. As long as you are on track by monitoring your pace, you are guaranteed to have time for each question.

☑ Don't Rush

It is very easy to make errors when you are in a hurry. Maintaining a fast pace in answering questions is pointless if it makes you miss questions that you would have gotten right otherwise. Test writers like to include distracting information and wrong answers that seem right. Taking a little extra time to avoid careless mistakes can make all the difference in your test score. Find a pace that allows you to be confident in the answers that you select.

⊘ Keep Moving

Panicking will not help you pass the test, so do your best to stay calm and keep moving. Taking deep breaths and going through the answer elimination steps you practiced can help to break through a stress barrier and keep your pace.

Final Notes

The combination of a solid foundation of content knowledge and the confidence that comes from practicing your plan for applying that knowledge is the key to maximizing your performance on test day. As your foundation of content knowledge is built up and strengthened, you'll find that the strategies included in this chapter become more and more effective in helping you quickly sift through the distractions and traps of the test to isolate the correct answer.

Now that you're preparing to move forward into the test content chapters of this book, be sure to keep your goal in mind. As you read, think about how you will be able to apply this information on the test. If you've already seen sample questions for the test and you have an idea of the question format and style, try to come up with questions of your own that you can answer based on what you're reading. This will give you valuable practice applying your knowledge in the same ways you can expect to on test day.

Good luck and good studying!

Verbal Analogies

What Are Analogy Questions?

Analogies are pairs of terms that have a common relationship. Analogy questions are presented in the format, "A is to B as C is to D," meaning that terms A and B are related to one another in the same or similar way that terms C and D are related to each other. Terms A and B do not have to be related to terms C and D at all, though they usually will be.

Usually in the question, you will be given terms A, B, and C, and will have to supply term D from the choices given. Occasionally, you may be given only terms A and B, and you will have to select a pair of terms for C and D.

What Sort of Relationships Will There Be?

Below are some examples of the types of analogies that may appear on the exam. Most of the questions you encounter will be relatively simple relationships, but here is an extensive list of the types of analogies that might show up.

Characteristic

Some characteristic analogies will focus on a characteristic of something else.

- DOG is to PAW—The foot of a dog is its paw.
- LADY is to LOVELY—A lady has a lovely personality.
- OUTRAGEOUS is to LIES—Lies can be described as being outrageous.

Some characteristic analogies will focus on something that is NOT a characteristic of something else.

- DESERT is to HUMIDITY—A desert does not have humidity.
- JOB is to UNEMPLOYED—A person without a job is unemployed.
- QUICK is to CONSIDERED—A quick decision is often not very considered.

Source

- CASTING is to METAL—A casting is made from metal.
- FOREST is to TREES—A forest is composed of trees.
- SLOGANS is to BANNERS—A slogan is printed on banners.

Location

- EIFFEL TOWER is to PARIS—The Eiffel Tower is a structure in Paris.
- WELSH is to WALES—The Welsh are the inhabitants of Wales.
- POUND is to ENGLAND—The pound is the monetary unit of England.

Sequential

- ONE is to TWO—These are consecutive numbers.
- BIRTH is to DEATH—These are the first and last events of a life or project.
- SPRING is to SUMMER—The season of spring immediately precedes summer.

Cause/Effect

- STORM is to HAIL—Hail can be caused by a storm.
- HEAT is to FIRE—Heat results from a fire.
- MONOTONY is to BOREDOM—Boredom is a consequence of monotony.

Creator/Creation

- CARPENTER is to HOUSE—A carpenter builds a house.
- PAINTER is to PORTRAIT—A painter makes a portrait.
- BURROUGHS is to TARZAN—Edgar Rice Burroughs wrote the novel Tarzan.

Provider/Provision

- JOB is to SALARY—A job provides a salary.
- THERAPIST is to TREATMENT—A therapist treats patients.
- ARMY is to DEFENSE—An army enables national defense.

Object/Function

- PENCIL is to WRITE—A pencil is used to write.
- PRESSURE is to BAROMETER—A barometer measures pressure.
- FROWN is to UNHAPPY—A frown shows unhappiness.

User/Tool

- CARPENTER is to HAMMER—A carpenter uses a hammer.
- TEACHER is to CHALK—A teacher uses chalk.
- FARMER is to TRACTOR—A farmer drives a tractor.

Whole/Part

- DOOR is to HOUSE—A door is part of a house.
- STATE is to COUNTRY—A country is made up of states.
- DAY is to MONTH—A month consists of many days.

Grammatical Transformation

- RAN is to RUN—These are different tenses of the same verb.
- DIE is to DICE—These are singular and plural forms.
- WE is to OUR—These are pronouns related to groups.

Translation

- SATAN is to LUCIFER—These are both names for the devil.
- BON VOYAGE is to FAREWELL—These are the French and English words for goodbye.
- JAPAN is to NIPPON—These are two names for the same country.

Category

- DOOR is to WINDOW—Both a door and a window are parts of a house.
- THIGH is to SHIN—Both a thigh and a shin are parts of a leg.
- MEASLES is to MUMPS—Both measles and mumps are types of diseases.

Synonym or Definition

These are analogies in which both terms have a similar meaning.

- CHASE is to PURSUE—Both of these terms mean to "go after."
- ACHIEVE is to ACCOMPLISH—Both of these terms refer to the successful attainment of a goal.
- SATIATE is to SATISFY—Both of these terms mean to gratify a desire.

Antonym or Contrast

These are analogies in which both terms have an opposite meaning.

- DISGUISE is to REVEAL—To disguise something is not to reveal it, but to conceal it.
- PEACE is to WAR—Peace is a state in which there is no war.
- FORGET is to REMEMBER—The word "remember" means not to forget something.

Intensity

These are analogies in which either one term expresses a higher degree of something than the other term.

- EXUBERANT is to HAPPY—To be exuberant is to be extremely happy.
- BREAK is to SHATTER—To shatter is to break violently into many pieces.
- DELUGE is to RAIN—A deluge is a heavy rain.

What Strategies Can I Use?

A huge vocabulary is not necessary to succeed on analogy questions (though it certainly doesn't hurt). In most cases though, you can determine the answer even if you don't recognize all the words. The strategies listed here will help you develop the ability to recognize basic relationships and apply simple steps and methods to solving them.

Determine the Relationship

Don't focus on the meanings, but rather the relationship between the two words.

To understand the relationship, first create a sentence that links the two words and puts them into perspective. The sentence that you use to connect the words can be simple at first.

- Example:
    - WOOD is to FIRE
    - *Wood* feeds a *fire*.

Then go through each answer choice and replace the words with the answer choices. If the question is easy, then that may be all that is necessary. If the question is hard, you might have to fine-tune your sentence.

- Example:
    - FIRE is to WOOD as COW is to (*a*. GRASS, *b*. FARMER)

Using the initial sentence, you would state "Grass feeds a cow." This is correct, but then so is the next answer choice "Farmer feeds a cow." So which is right? Modify the sentence to be more specific.

- Example: "Wood feeds a fire and is consumed."

This modified sentence makes answer choice B incorrect and answer choice A clearly correct, because while "grass feeds a cow and is consumed" is correct, "farmer feeds a cow and is consumed" is definitely wrong.

If your initial sentence seems correct with more than one answer choice, then keep modifying it until only one answer choice makes sense.

Similar Choices

If you don't know the word, don't worry. Start by looking at the answer choices and trying them out. Remember that three of the answer choices will always be wrong. If you can find a common relationship between any three answer choices, then you know they are all wrong. Find the answer choice that does not have a common relationship to the other answer choices and it will be the correct answer.

- Example:
  - TOUGH is to RUGGED as HARD is to (*a.* SOFT, *b.* EASY, *c.* DELICATE, *d.* RIGID)

In this example the first three choices are all opposites of the term "hard". Even if you don't know that rigid means the same as hard, you know it must be correct, because the other three all had the same relationship. They were all opposites, so they must all be wrong. The one that has a different relationship from the other three must be correct. So don't worry if you don't know a word. Focus on the answer choices that you do understand and see if you can identify common relationships. Even identifying two word pairs with the same relationship (for example, two word pairs that are both opposites) will allow you to eliminate those two answer choices, for they are both wrong.

A simple way to remember this is that if you have two or more answer choices with the exact same relationship, then they are both or all wrong.

- Example: (*a.* NEAT, *b.* ORDERLY)

Since the two answer choices above are synonyms and therefore have the same relationship with the matching term, then you know that they both must be wrong, because they both can't be correct, and for all intents and purposes they are the same word.

Be sure to read all of the choices. You may find an answer choice that seems right at first, but you may find a better choice if you continue reading.

Difficult words are usually synonyms or antonyms (opposites). Whenever you have extremely difficult words that you don't understand, look at the answer choices. Try and identify whether two or more of the answer choices are either synonyms or antonyms. Remember that if you can find two word pairs that have the same relationship (for example, they are both synonyms) then you can eliminate them both.

Eliminate Answers

Eliminate choices as soon as you realize they are wrong, but be careful! Make sure you consider all of the possible answer choices. Don't worry if you are stuck between two that seem right. By

reading them carefully. Yet a happy medium must be attained, so don't waste too much time. You must read carefully, but efficiently.

Brainstorm

If you get stuck on a difficult analogy, spend a few seconds quickly brainstorming. Run through the complete list of possible relationships. Break down each answer choice into all of the potential combinations with the two possible analogous terms. Since there are four answer choices and each answer choice could form a pair with one of two terms, there are only eight possible relationships to test. Look at each relationship and see if it would make sense. Test with sentences to determine if any relationship can be established. By systematically going through all possibilities, you may find something that you would otherwise overlook.

Practice Questions

1. STIRRUP is to EAR as ATRIUM is to

a. BLOOD
b. VENTRICLE
c. VESTIBULE
d. HEART
e. CHAMBER

2. DWELLING is to CONDOMINIUM as MEAL is to

a. ENTREE
b. BRUNCH
c. APPETIZER
d. PLATE
e. DESSERT

3. FRAGRANT is to SMELL as MELLIFLUOUS is to

a. SOUND
b. PLEASANT
c. FLUID
d. TASTE
e. SOOTHING

4. BRACELET is to JEWELRY as POMEGRANATE is to

a. SEEDS
b. EDIBLE
c. FRUIT
d. ACIDIC
e. CITRUS

5. LOUD is to DEAFENING as HAPPY is to

a. ECSTATIC
b. GLAD
c. MOROSE
d. CONTENT
e. DEPRESSED

6. FACILE is to EASY as LOQUACIOUS is to

a. SILENT
b. DIFFICULT
c. FRIENDLY
d. LACKING
e. TALKATIVE

7. ABATE is to INCREASE as ABHOR

a. DESPISE
b. LOVE
c. TOLERATE
d. ABDICATE
e. HATE

8. QUILLS is to PORCUPINE as TUSKS is to

a. PROBOSCIS
b. HORN
c. IVORY
d. ELEPHANT
e. NOSE

9. DUPLICITY is to DECEPTION as AVARICE is to

a. GREED
b. MONEY
c. AVERAGE
d. ACCUMULATE
e. BENEVOLENT

10. WHISPER is to YELL as TAP is to

a. WATER
b. PAT
c. DANCE
d. JAB
e. JUMP

11. EUCALYPTUS is to TREE as IRIS is to

a. TULIP
b. PURPLE
c. EYE
d. FACE
e. FLOWER

12. IRKSOME is to TEDIOUS as INTRIGUING is to

a. FASCINATING
b. SILLY
c. UNLIKELY
d. IMPOSSIBLE
e. IRRITATING

Practice Answers

1. D: This is a "part to whole" analogy. Just as the *stirrup* is a part of the *ear*, so is the *atrium* a part of the *heart*.

2. B: In "type" analogies, one word in the stem names a category that encompasses the other. Just as a *condominium* is a type of *dwelling*, so is *brunch* a type of *meal*.

3. A: This analogy is that of adjective to noun. *Fragrant* is an adjective modifying the noun *smell* in a positive way. *Mellifluous* is an adjective modifying the noun *sound* in a positive way.

4. C: In this "type" analogy, one word in the stem names a category that encompasses the other. A *bracelet* is a type of *jewelry*, just as a *pomegranate* is a type of *fruit*.

5. A: In this analogy of relative degree, the second term in each pair indicates a more intense degree of the first term. *Deafening* is a more intense version of *loud*, just as *ecstatic* is a more intense version of *happy*.

6. E: This analogy is based on synonyms. Just as *facile* and *easy* mean about the same thing, so do *loquacious* and *talkative*.

7. B: This analogy is based on antonyms. Just as *abate* means the opposite of *increase*, so does *abhor* mean the opposite of *love*.

8. D: This analogy names prominent features of each animal. *Quills* are a prominent feature of a *porcupine*, just as *tusks* are a prominent feature of an *elephant*.

9. A: This is another synonym-based analogy. *Duplicity* and *deception* mean about the same thing, just as *avarice* and *greed* do. You might have been tempted to choose D, which suggests something that an avaricious person might do, but *greed* is the better answer since it is a noun, like *avarice* is.

10. D: This is an analogy of relative degree. A *yell* is a much louder version of a *whisper*, just as a *jab* is a much harder version of a *tap*.

11. E: This is an analogy indicating types, since a *eucalyptus* is one type of *tree*, and an *iris* is one type of *flower*.

12. A: In this analogy based on synonyms, *irksome* means about the same as *tedious*, just as *intriguing* means about the same as *fascinating*.

Arithmetic Reasoning and Math Knowledge

What Do the Arithmetic Reasoning Questions Look Like?

Arithmetic questions will generally take the form of a simple word problem. You will be posed an everyday situation that requires arithmetic to solve and asked to select the correct answer from the choices given. You may be asked to calculate rates, percentages, averages, or some other practical math quantity, and you may have to convert between different units. It is usually obvious what the question is asking for.

How Can I Prepare?

Since the math needed for these questions is not complicated, that means that you only need to learn or refresh your memory of a few simple operations. Then it's just a matter of practicing them. One of the biggest mistakes people make when trying to learn math is that they read about a concept, look at a worked-out example problem, and when it makes sense, they assume they understand it well enough and move on. Then when the test comes, they don't remember how to solve the problems. Math skills must be practiced in order to be remembered.

What Do the Math Knowledge Questions Look Like?

Math knowledge questions are much less predictable than arithmetic questions. Math knowledge questions may test your knowledge of anything covered in the arithmetic section, plus square roots, exponents, factors, multiples, equations, geometric properties, and more.

How Can I Prepare?

The questions may be more difficult, but the preparation process should be the same: learn the concepts and facts you need to know, then practice them.

What Math Do I Need to Know?

All of the major concepts you will need to excel on the arithmetic and math knowledge sections are covered in the remainder of this chapter.

Foundational Math Concepts

Classifications of Numbers

Numbers are the basic building blocks of mathematics. Specific features of numbers are identified by the following terms:

Integer – any positive or negative whole number, including zero. Integers do not include fractions $\left(\frac{1}{3}\right)$, decimals (0.56), or mixed numbers $\left(7\frac{3}{4}\right)$.

Prime number – any whole number greater than 1 that has only two factors, itself and 1; that is, a number that can be divided evenly only by 1 and itself.

Composite number – any whole number greater than 1 that has more than two different factors; in other words, any whole number that is not a prime number. For example: The composite number 8 has the factors of 1, 2, 4, and 8.

Even number – any integer that can be divided by 2 without leaving a remainder. For example: 2, 4, 6, 8, and so on.

Odd number – any integer that cannot be divided evenly by 2. For example: 3, 5, 7, 9, and so on.

Decimal number – any number that uses a decimal point to show the part of the number that is less than one. Example: 1.234.

Decimal point – a symbol used to separate the ones place from the tenths place in decimals or dollars from cents in currency.

Decimal place – the position of a number to the right of the decimal point. In the decimal 0.123, the 1 is in the first place to the right of the decimal point, indicating tenths; the 2 is in the second place, indicating hundredths; and the 3 is in the third place, indicating thousandths.

The **decimal**, or base 10, system is a number system that uses ten different digits (0, 1, 2, 3, 4, 5, 6, 7, 8, 9). An example of a number system that uses something other than ten digits is the **binary**, or base 2, number system, used by computers, which uses only the numbers 0 and 1. It is thought that the decimal system originated because people had only their 10 fingers for counting.

Rational numbers include all integers, decimals, and fractions. Any terminating or repeating decimal number is a rational number.

Irrational numbers cannot be written as fractions or decimals because the number of decimal places is infinite and there is no recurring pattern of digits within the number. For example, pi (π) begins with 3.141592 and continues without terminating or repeating, so pi is an irrational number.

Real numbers are the set of all rational and irrational numbers.

Review Video and Practice: Classification of Numbers
Visit mometrix.com/academy and enter code: 461071

Review Video and Practice: Rational and Irrational Numbers
Visit mometrix.com/academy and enter code: 280645

Review Video and Practice: Prime and Composite Numbers
Visit mometrix.com/academy and enter code: 565581

THE NUMBER LINE

A number line is a graph to see the distance between numbers. Basically, this graph shows the relationship between numbers. So a number line may have a point for zero and may show negative numbers on the left side of the line. Any positive numbers are placed on the right side of the line. For example, consider the points labeled on the following number line:

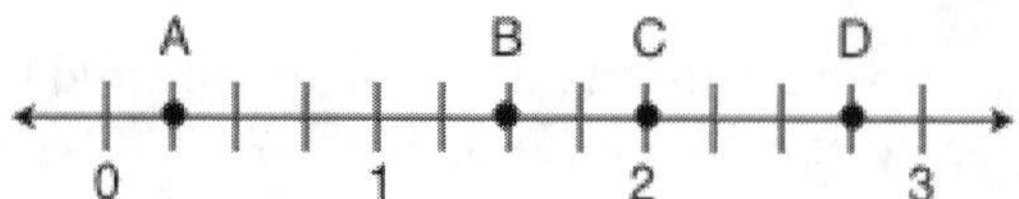

We can use the dashed lines on the number line to identify each point. Each dashed line between two whole numbers is $\frac{1}{4}$. The line halfway between two numbers is $\frac{1}{2}$.

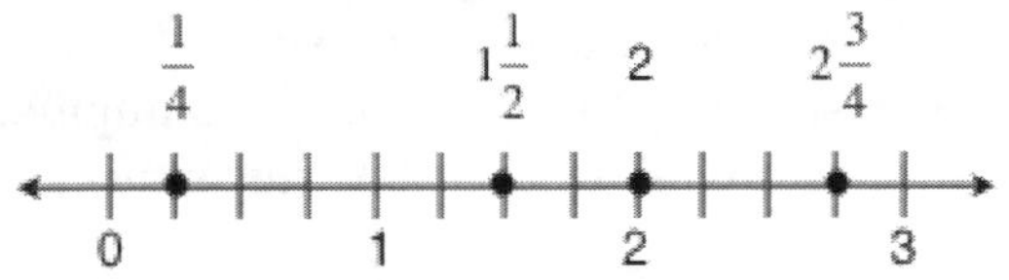

Review Video: The Number Line
Visit mometrix.com/academy and enter code: 816439

Numbers in Word Form and Place Value

When writing numbers out in word form or translating word form to numbers, it is essential to understand how a place value system works. In the decimal or base-10 system, each digit of a number represents how many of the corresponding place value—a specific factor of 10—are contained in the number being represented. To make reading numbers easier, every three digits to the left of the decimal place is preceded by a comma. The following table demonstrates some of the place values:

Power of 10	10^3	10^2	10^1	10^0	10^{-1}	10^{-2}	10^{-3}
Value	1,000	100	10	1	0.1	0.01	0.001
Place	thousands	hundreds	tens	ones	tenths	hundredths	thousandths

For example, consider the number 4,546.09, which can be separated into each place value like this:

4: thousands
5: hundreds
4: tens
6: ones
0: tenths
9: hundredths

This number in word form would be *four thousand five hundred forty-six and nine hundredths.*

Review Video: Place Value
Visit mometrix.com/academy and enter code: 205433

ABSOLUTE VALUE

A precursor to working with negative numbers is understanding what **absolute values** are. A number's absolute value is simply the distance away from zero a number is on the number line. The absolute value of a number is always positive and is written $|x|$. For example, the absolute value of 3, written as $|3|$, is 3 because the distance between 0 and 3 on a number line is three units. Likewise, the absolute value of -3, written as $|-3|$, is 3 because the distance between 0 and -3 on a number line is three units. So $|3| = |-3|$.

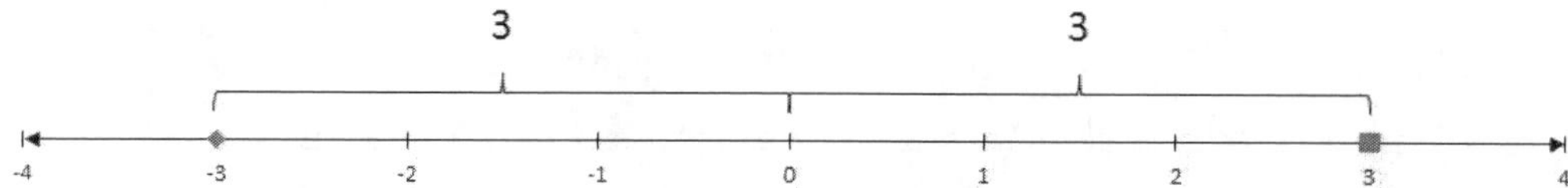

Review Video: Absolute Value
Visit mometrix.com/academy and enter code: 314669

PRACTICE

P1. Write the place value of each digit in 14,059.826

P2. Write out each of the following in words:

(a) 29
(b) 478
(c) 98,542
(d) 0.06
(e) 13.113

P3. Write each of the following in numbers:

(a) nine thousand four hundred thirty-five
(b) three hundred two thousand eight hundred seventy-six
(c) nine hundred one thousandths
(d) nineteen thousandths
(e) seven thousand one hundred forty-two and eighty-five hundredths

Practice Solutions

P1. The place value for each digit would be as follows:

Digit	Place Value
1	ten-thousands
4	thousands
0	hundreds
5	tens
9	ones
8	tenths
2	hundredths
6	thousandths

P2. Each written out in words would be:

(a) twenty-nine
(b) four hundred seventy-eight
(c) ninety-eight thousand five hundred forty-two
(d) six hundredths
(e) thirteen and one hundred thirteen thousandths

P3. Each in numeric form would be:

(a) 9,435
(b) 302, 876
(c) 0.901
(d) 0.019
(e) 7,142.85

Measurement Principles

Rounding and Estimation

Rounding is reducing the digits in a number while still trying to keep the value similar. The result will be less accurate but in a simpler form and easier to use. Whole numbers can be rounded to the nearest ten, hundred, or thousand.

When you are asked to estimate the solution to a problem, you will need to provide only an approximate figure or **estimation** for your answer. In this situation, you will need to round each number in the calculation to the level indicated (nearest hundred, nearest thousand, etc.) or to a level that makes sense for the numbers involved. When estimating a sum **all numbers must be rounded to the same level**. You cannot round one number to the nearest thousand while rounding another to the nearest hundred.

Review Video: Rounding and Estimation
Visit mometrix.com/academy and enter code: 126243

Scientific Notation

Scientific notation is a way of writing large numbers in a shorter form. The form $a \times 10^n$ is used in scientific notation, where a is greater than or equal to 1 but less than 10, and n is the number of places the decimal must move to get from the original number to a. Example: The number 230,400,000 is cumbersome to write. To write the value in scientific notation, place a decimal point between the first and second numbers and include all digits through the last non-zero digit ($a = 2.304$). To find the appropriate power of 10, count the number of places the decimal point had to move ($n = 8$). The number is positive if the decimal moved to the left and negative if it moved to the right. We can then write 230,400,000 as 2.304×10^8. If we look instead at the number 0.00002304, we have the same value for a, but this time the decimal moved 5 places to the right ($n = -5$). Thus, 0.00002304 can be written as 2.304×10^{-5}. Using this notation makes it simple to compare very large or very small numbers. By comparing exponents, it is easy to see that 3.28×10^4 is smaller than 1.51×10^5, because 4 is less than 5.

Review Video: Scientific Notation
Visit mometrix.com/academy and enter code: 976454

Practice

P1. Round each number to the indicated degree:

(a) Round to the nearest ten: 11; 47; 118

(b) Round to the nearest hundred: 78; 980; 248

(c) Round each number to the nearest thousand: 302; 1,274; 3,756

P2. Estimate the solution to $345,932 + 96,369$ by rounding each number to the nearest ten thousand.

P3. A runner's heart beats 422 times over the course of six minutes. About how many times did the runner's heart beat during each minute?

Practice Solutions

P1. (a) When rounding to the nearest ten, anything ending in 5 or greater rounds up. So, 11 rounds to 10, 47 rounds to 50, and 118 rounds to 120.

(b) When rounding to the nearest hundred, anything ending in 50 or greater rounds up. So, 78 rounds to 100, 980 rounds to 1000, and 248 rounds to 200.

(c) When rounding to the nearest thousand, anything ending in 500 or greater rounds up. So, 302 rounds to 0, 1,274 rounds to 1,000, and 3,756 rounds to 4,000.

P2. Start by rounding each number to the nearest ten thousand: 345,932 becomes 350,000, and 96,369 becomes 100,000. Then, add the rounded numbers: $350,000 + 100,000 = 450,000$. So, the answer is approximately 450,000. The exact answer would be $345,932 + 96,369 = 442,301$. So, the estimate of 450,000 is a similar value to the exact answer.

P3. "About how many" indicates that you need to estimate the solution. In this case, look at the numbers you are given. 422 can be rounded down to 420, which is easily divisible by 6. A good estimate is $420 \div 6 = 70$ beats per minute. More accurately, the patient's heart rate was just over 70 beats per minute since his heart actually beat a little more than 420 times in six minutes.

Units of Measurement

Measurement Conversion

When converting between units, the goal is to maintain the same meaning but change the way it is displayed. In order to go from a larger unit to a smaller unit, multiply the number of the known amount by the equivalent amount. When going from a smaller unit to a larger unit, divide the number of the known amount by the equivalent amount.

For complicated conversions, it may be helpful to set up conversion fractions. In these fractions, one fraction is the **conversion factor**. The other fraction has the unknown amount in the numerator. So, the known value is placed in the denominator. Sometimes, the second fraction has the known value from the problem in the numerator and the unknown in the denominator. Multiply the two fractions to get the converted measurement. Note that since the numerator and the denominator of the factor are equivalent, the value of the fraction is 1. That is why we can say that the result in the new units is equal to the result in the old units even though they have different numbers.

It can often be necessary to chain known conversion factors together. As an example, consider converting 512 square inches to square meters. We know that there are 2.54 centimeters in an inch and 100 centimeters in a meter, and we know we will need to square each of these factors to achieve the conversion we are looking for.

$$\frac{512\text{ in}^2}{1} \times \left(\frac{2.54\text{ cm}}{1\text{ in}}\right)^2 \times \left(\frac{1\text{ m}}{100\text{ cm}}\right)^2 = \frac{512\text{ }\cancel{\text{in}^2}}{1} \times \left(\frac{6.4516\text{ }\cancel{\text{cm}^2}}{1\text{ }\cancel{\text{in}^2}}\right) \times \left(\frac{1\text{ m}^2}{10{,}000\text{ }\cancel{\text{cm}^2}}\right) = 0.330\text{ m}^2$$

Review Video: Measurement Conversions
Visit mometrix.com/academy and enter code: 316703

Metric Measurement Prefixes

Giga-	One billion	1 *giga*watt is one billion watts
Mega-	One million	1 *mega*hertz is one million hertz
Kilo-	One thousand	1 *kilo*gram is one thousand grams
Deci-	One-tenth	1 *deci*meter is one-tenth of a meter
Centi-	One-hundredth	1 *centi*meter is one-hundredth of a meter
Milli-	One-thousandth	1 *milli*liter is one-thousandth of a liter
Micro-	One-millionth	1 *micro*gram is one-millionth of a gram

Review Video: Metric System Conversions
Visit mometrix.com/academy and enter code: 163709

Common Units and Equivalents

Metric Equivalents

1000 μg (microgram)	1 mg
1000 mg (milligram)	1 g
1000 g (gram)	1 kg
1000 kg (kilogram)	1 metric ton
1000 mL (milliliter)	1 L
1000 μm (micrometer)	1 mm
1000 mm (millimeter)	1 m
100 cm (centimeter)	1 m
1000 m (meter)	1 km

Distance and Area Measurement

Unit	Abbreviation	US equivalent	Metric equivalent
Inch	in	1 inch	2.54 centimeters
Foot	ft	12 inches	0.305 meters
Yard	yd	3 feet	0.914 meters
Mile	mi	5280 feet	1.609 kilometers
Acre	ac	4840 square yards	0.405 hectares
Square Mile	sq. mi. or $mi.^2$	640 acres	2.590 square kilometers

Capacity Measurements

Unit	Abbreviation	US equivalent	Metric equivalent
Fluid Ounce	fl oz	8 fluid drams	29.573 milliliters
Cup	c	8 fluid ounces	0.237 liter
Pint	pt.	16 fluid ounces	0.473 liter
Quart	qt.	2 pints	0.946 liter
Gallon	gal.	4 quarts	3.785 liters
Teaspoon	t or tsp.	1 fluid dram	5 milliliters
Tablespoon	T or tbsp.	4 fluid drams	15 or 16 milliliters
Cubic Centimeter	cc or cm^3	0.271 drams	1 milliliter

Weight Measurements

Unit	Abbreviation	US equivalent	Metric equivalent
Ounce	oz	16 drams	28.35 grams
Pound	lb	16 ounces	453.6 grams
Ton	tn.	2,000 pounds	907.2 kilograms

Volume and Weight Measurement Clarifications

Always be careful when using ounces and fluid ounces. They are not equivalent.

1 pint = 16 fluid ounces	1 fluid ounce $\neq$ 1 ounce
1 pound = 16 ounces	1 pint $\neq$ 1 pound

In the United States, the word "ton" by itself refers to a short ton or a net ton. Do not confuse this with a long ton (also called a gross ton) or a metric ton (also spelled *tonne*), which have different measurements.

1 US ton = 2000 pounds $\neq$ 1 metric ton = 1000 kilograms

Practice

P1. Perform the following conversions:

(a) 1.4 meters to centimeters

(b) 218 centimeters to meters

(c) 42 inches to feet

(d) 15 kilograms to pounds

(e) 80 ounces to pounds

(f) 2 miles to kilometers

(g) 5 feet to centimeters

(h) 15.14 liters to gallons

(i) 8 quarts to liters

(j) 13.2 pounds to grams

Practice Solutions

P1. (a) $\frac{100 \text{ cm}}{1 \text{ m}} = \frac{x \text{ cm}}{1.4 \text{ m}}$ Cross multiply to get $x = 140$

(b) $\frac{100 \text{ cm}}{1 \text{ m}} = \frac{218 \text{ cm}}{x \text{ m}}$ Cross multiply to get $100x = 218$, or $x = 2.18$

(c) $\frac{12 \text{ in}}{1 \text{ ft}} = \frac{42 \text{ in}}{x \text{ ft}}$ Cross multiply to get $12x = 42$, or $x = 3.5$

(d) $15 \text{ kilograms} \times \frac{2.2 \text{ pounds}}{1 \text{ kilogram}} = 33 \text{ pounds}$

(e) $80 \text{ ounces} \times \frac{1 \text{ pound}}{16 \text{ ounces}} = 5 \text{ pounds}$

(f) $2 \text{ miles} \times \frac{1.609 \text{ kilometers}}{1 \text{ mile}} = 3.218 \text{ kilometers}$

(g) $5 \text{ feet} \times \frac{12 \text{ inches}}{1 \text{ foot}} \times \frac{2.54 \text{ centimeters}}{1 \text{ inch}} = 152.4 \text{ centimeters}$

(h) $15.14 \text{ liters} \times \frac{1 \text{ gallon}}{3.785 \text{ liters}} = 4 \text{ gallons}$

(i) $8 \text{ quarts} \times \frac{1 \text{ gallon}}{4 \text{ quarts}} \times \frac{3.785 \text{ liters}}{1 \text{ gallon}} = 7.57 \text{ liters}$

(j) $13.2 \text{ pounds} \times \frac{1 \text{ kilogram}}{2.2 \text{ pounds}} \times \frac{1{,}000 \text{ grams}}{1 \text{ kilogram}} = 6{,}000 \text{ grams}$

Operations

Operations

An **operation** is simply a mathematical process that takes some value(s) as input(s) and produces an output. Elementary operations are often written in the following form: *value operation value*. For instance, in the expression $1 + 2$ the values are 1 and 2 and the operation is addition. Performing the operation gives the output of 3. In this way we can say that $1 + 2$ and 3 are equal, or $1 + 2 = 3$.

Addition

Addition increases the value of one quantity by the value of another quantity (both called **addends**). For example, $2 + 4 = 6$ or $8 + 9 = 17$. The result is called the **sum**. With addition, the order does not matter, $4 + 2 = 2 + 4$.

When adding signed numbers, if the signs are the same simply add the absolute values of the addends and apply the original sign to the sum. For example, $(+4) + (+8) = +12$ and $(-4) + (-8) = -12$. When the original signs are different, take the absolute values of the addends and subtract the smaller value from the larger value, then apply the original sign of the larger value to the difference. For instance, $(+4) + (-8) = -4$ and $(-4) + (+8) = +4$.

Subtraction

Subtraction is the opposite operation to addition; it decreases the value of one quantity (the **minuend**) by the value of another quantity (the **subtrahend**). For example, $6 - 4 = 2$ or $17 - 8 = 9$. The result is called the **difference**. Note that with subtraction, the order does matter, $6 - 4 \neq 4 - 6$.

For subtracting signed numbers, change the sign of the subtrahend and then follow the same rules used for addition. For example, $(+4) - (+8) = (+4) + (-8) = -4$.

Multiplication

Multiplication can be thought of as repeated addition. One number (the **multiplier**) indicates how many times to add the other number (the **multiplicand**) to itself. For example, $3 \times 2 = 2 + 2 + 2 = 6$. With multiplication, the order does not matter: $2 \times 3 = 3 \times 2$ or $3 + 3 = 2 + 2 + 2$, either way the result (the **product**) is the same.

If the signs are the same, the product is positive when multiplying signed numbers. For example, $(+4) \times (+8) = +32$ and $(-4) \times (-8) = +32$. If the signs are opposite, the product is negative. For example, $(+4) \times (-8) = -32$ and $(-4) \times (+8) = -32$. When more than two factors are multiplied together, the sign of the product is determined by how many negative factors are present. If there are an odd number of negative factors then the product is negative, whereas an even number of negative factors indicates a positive product. For instance, $(+4) \times (-8) \times (-2) = +64$ and $(-4) \times (-8) \times (-2) = -64$.

Division

Division is the opposite operation to multiplication; one number (the **divisor**) tells us how many parts to divide the other number (the **dividend**) into. The result of division is called the **quotient**. For example, $20 \div 4 = 5$; if 20 is split into 4 equal parts, each part is 5. With division, the order of the numbers does matter, $20 \div 4 \neq 4 \div 20$.

The rules for dividing signed numbers are similar to multiplying signed numbers. If the dividend and divisor have the same sign, the quotient is positive. If the dividend and divisor have opposite signs, the quotient is negative. For example, $(-4) \div (+8) = -0.5$.

Review Video: Mathematical Operations
Visit mometrix.com/academy and enter code: 208095

PARENTHESES

Parentheses are used to designate which operations should be done first when there are multiple operations. Example: $4 - (2 + 1) = 1$; the parentheses tell us that we must add 2 and 1, and then subtract the sum from 4, rather than subtracting 2 from 4 and then adding 1 (this would give us an answer of 3).

Review Video: Mathematical Parentheses
Visit mometrix.com/academy and enter code: 978600

EXPONENTS

An **exponent** is a superscript number placed next to another number at the top right. It indicates how many times the base number is to be multiplied by itself. Exponents provide a shorthand way to write what would be a longer mathematical expression, for example: $2^4 = 2 \times 2 \times 2 \times 2$. A number with an exponent of 2 is said to be "squared," while a number with an exponent of 3 is said to be "cubed." The value of a number raised to an exponent is called its power. So 8^4 is read as "8 to the 4th power," or "8 raised to the power of 4."

The properties of exponents are as follows:

Property	Description
$a^1 = a$	Any number to the power of 1 is equal to itself.
$1^n = 1$	The number 1 raised to any power is equal to 1.
$a^0 = 1$	Any number raised to the power of 0 is equal to 1.
$a^n \times a^m = a^{n+m}$	Add exponents to multiply powers of the same base number.
$a^n \div a^m = a^{n-m}$	Subtract exponents to divide powers of the same base number.
$(a^n)^m = a^{n \times m}$	When a power is raised to a power, the exponents are multiplied.
$(a \times b)^n = a^n \times b^n$ $(a \div b)^n = a^n \div b^n$	Multiplication and division operations inside parentheses can be raised to a power. This is the same as each term being raised to that power.
$a^{-n} = \frac{1}{a^n}$	A negative exponent is the same as the reciprocal of a positive exponent.

Note that exponents do not have to be integers. Fractional or decimal exponents follow all the rules above as well. Example: $5^{\frac{1}{4}} \times 5^{\frac{3}{4}} = 5^{\frac{1}{4}+\frac{3}{4}} = 5^1 = 5$.

Review Video: What is an Exponent?
Visit mometrix.com/academy and enter code: 600998

Review Video: Laws of Exponents
Visit mometrix.com/academy and enter code: 532558

ROOTS

A **root**, such as a square root, is another way of writing a fractional exponent. Instead of using a superscript, roots use the radical symbol ($\sqrt{\ }$) to indicate the operation. A radical will have a number underneath the bar, and may sometimes have a number in the upper left: $\sqrt[n]{a}$, read as "the nth root of a." The relationship between radical notation and exponent notation can be described by this equation:

$$\sqrt[n]{a} = a^{\frac{1}{n}}$$

The two special cases of $n = 2$ and $n = 3$ are called square roots and cube roots. If there is no number to the upper left, the radical is understood to be a square root ($n = 2$). Nearly all of the roots you encounter will be square roots. A square root is the same as a number raised to the one-half power. When we say that a is the square root of b ($a = \sqrt{b}$), we mean that a multiplied by itself equals b: ($a \times a = b$).

A **perfect square** is a number that has an integer for its square root. There are 10 perfect squares from 1 to 100: 1, 4, 9, 16, 25, 36, 49, 64, 81, 100 (the squares of integers 1 through 10).

Review Video: Roots
Visit mometrix.com/academy and enter code: 795655

Review Video: Square Root and Perfect Squares
Visit mometrix.com/academy and enter code: 648063

ORDER OF OPERATIONS

The **order of operations** is a set of rules that dictates the order in which we must perform each operation in an expression so that we will evaluate it accurately. If we have an expression that includes multiple different operations, the order of operations tells us which operations to do first. The most common mnemonic for the order of operations is **PEMDAS**, or "Please Excuse My Dear Aunt Sally." PEMDAS stands for parentheses, exponents, multiplication, division, addition, and subtraction. It is important to understand that multiplication and division have equal precedence, as do addition and subtraction, so those pairs of operations are simply worked from left to right in order.

For example, evaluating the expression $5 + 20 \div 4 \times (2 + 3)^2 - 6$ using the correct order of operations would be done like this:

- **P:** Perform the operations inside the parentheses: $(2 + 3) = 5$
- **E:** Simplify the exponents: $(5)^2 = 5 \times 5 = 25$
  - The equation now looks like this: $5 + 20 \div 4 \times 25 - 6$
- **MD:** Perform multiplication and division from left to right: $20 \div 4 = 5$; then $5 \times 25 = 125$
  - The equation now looks like this: $5 + 125 - 6$
- **AS:** Perform addition and subtraction from left to right: $5 + 125 = 130$; then $130 - 6 = 124$

Review Video: Order of Operations
Visit mometrix.com/academy and enter code: 259675

SUBTRACTION WITH REGROUPING

A great way to make use of some of the features built into the decimal system would be regrouping when attempting longform subtraction operations. When subtracting within a place value, sometimes the minuend is smaller than the subtrahend; **regrouping** enables you to 'borrow' a unit from a place value to the left in order to get a positive difference. For example, consider subtracting 189 from 525 with regrouping.

Review Video: Subtracting Large Numbers
Visit mometrix.com/academy and enter code: 603350

First, set up the subtraction problem in vertical form:

$$\begin{array}{r} 525 \\ -\ 189 \\ \hline \end{array}$$

Notice that the numbers in the ones and tens columns of 525 are smaller than the numbers in the ones and tens columns of 189. This means you will need to use regrouping to perform subtraction:

$$\begin{array}{cccc} & 5 & 2 & 5 \\ - & 1 & 8 & 9 \\ \hline \end{array}$$

To subtract 9 from 5 in the ones column you will need to borrow from the 2 in the tens columns:

$$\begin{array}{cccc} & 5 & 1 & 15 \\ - & 1 & 8 & 9 \\ \hline & & & 6 \end{array}$$

Next, to subtract 8 from 1 in the tens column you will need to borrow from the 5 in the hundreds column:

$$\begin{array}{cccc} & 4 & 11 & 15 \\ - & 1 & 8 & 9 \\ \hline & & 3 & 6 \end{array}$$

Last, subtract the 1 from the 4 in the hundreds column:

$$\begin{array}{cccc} & 4 & 11 & 15 \\ - & 1 & 8 & 9 \\ \hline & 3 & 3 & 6 \end{array}$$

Word Problems and Mathematical Symbols

When working on word problems, you must be able to translate verbal expressions or "math words" into math symbols. This chart contains several "math words" and their appropriate symbols:

Phrase	Symbol
equal, is, was, will be, has, costs, gets to, is the same as, becomes	$=$
times, of, multiplied by, product of, twice, doubles, halves, triples	$\times$
divided by, per, ratio of/to, out of	$\div$
plus, added to, sum, combined, and, more than, totals of	$+$
subtracted from, less than, decreased by, minus, difference between	$-$
what, how much, original value, how many, a number, a variable	x, n, etc.

Examples of Translated Mathematical Phrases

- The phrase four more than twice a number can be written algebraically as $2x + 4$.
- The phrase half a number decreased by six can be written algebraically as $\frac{1}{2}x - 6$.
- The phrase the sum of a number and the product of five and that number can be written algebraically as $x + 5x$.

You may see a test question that reads something like this:

> Olivia is constructing a bookcase from seven boards. Two of them are for vertical supports and five are for shelves. The height of the bookcase is twice the width of the bookcase. If the seven boards total 36 feet in length, what will be the height of Olivia's bookcase?

You would need to make a sketch and then create the equation to determine the width of the shelves. The height can be represented as double the width. (If x represents the width of the shelves in feet, then the height of the bookcase is $2x$. Since the seven boards total 36 feet, $2x + 2x + x + x + x + x + x = 36$ or $9x = 36$; $x = 4$. The height is twice the width, or 8 feet.)

PRACTICE

P1. Demonstrate how to subtract 477 from 620 using regrouping.

P2. Simplify the following expressions with exponents:

> **(a)** 37^0
> **(b)** 1^{30}
> **(c)** $2^3 \times 2^4 \times 2^x$
> **(d)** $(3^x)^3$
> **(e)** $(12 \div 3)^2$

Practice Solutions

P1. First, set up the subtraction problem in vertical form:

$$\begin{array}{rrrr} & 6 & 2 & 0 \\ - & 4 & 7 & 7 \\ \hline \end{array}$$

To subtract 7 from 0 in the ones column you will need to borrow from the 2 in the tens column:

$$\begin{array}{rrrr} & 6 & 1 & 10 \\ - & 4 & 7 & 7 \\ \hline & & & 3 \end{array}$$

Next, to subtract 7 from the 1 that's still in the tens column you will need to borrow from the 6 in the hundreds column:

$$\begin{array}{rrrr} & 5 & 11 & 10 \\ - & 4 & 7 & 7 \\ \hline & & 4 & 3 \end{array}$$

Lastly, subtract 4 from the 5 remaining in the hundreds column:

$$\begin{array}{rrrr} & 5 & 11 & 10 \\ - & 4 & 7 & 7 \\ \hline & 1 & 4 & 3 \end{array}$$

P2. Using the properties of exponents and the proper order of operations:

> **(a)** Any number raised to the power of 0 is equal to 1: $37^0 = 1$
> **(b)** The number 1 raised to any power is equal to 1: $1^{30} = 1$
> **(c)** Add exponents to multiply powers of the same base: $2^3 \times 2^4 \times 2^x = 2^{(3+4+x)} = 2^{(7+x)}$
> **(d)** When a power is raised to a power, the exponents are multiplied: $(3^x)^3 = 3^{3x}$
> **(e)** Perform the operation inside the parentheses first: $(12 \div 3)^2 = 4^2 = 16$

Rational Numbers

Fractions

A **fraction** is a number that is expressed as one integer written above another integer, with a dividing line between them $\left(\frac{x}{y}\right)$. It represents the **quotient** of the two numbers "x divided by y." It can also be thought of as x out of y equal parts.

The top number of a fraction is called the **numerator**, and it represents the number of parts under consideration. The 1 in $\frac{1}{4}$ means that 1 part out of the whole is being considered in the calculation. The bottom number of a fraction is called the **denominator**, and it represents the total number of equal parts. The 4 in $\frac{1}{4}$ means that the whole consists of 4 equal parts. A fraction cannot have a denominator of zero; this is referred to as "*undefined*."

Fractions can be manipulated, without changing the value of the fraction, by multiplying or dividing (but not adding or subtracting) both the numerator and denominator by the same number. If you divide both numbers by a common factor, you are **reducing** or simplifying the fraction. Two fractions that have the same value but are expressed differently are known as **equivalent fractions**. For example, $\frac{2}{10}, \frac{3}{15}, \frac{4}{20}$, and $\frac{5}{25}$ are all equivalent fractions. They can also all be reduced or simplified to $\frac{1}{5}$.

When two fractions are manipulated so that they have the same denominator, this is known as finding a **common denominator**. The number chosen to be that common denominator should be the least common multiple of the two original denominators. Example: $\frac{3}{4}$ and $\frac{5}{6}$; the least common multiple of 4 and 6 is 12. Manipulating to achieve the common denominator: $\frac{3}{4} = \frac{9}{12}; \frac{5}{6} = \frac{10}{12}$.

Proper Fractions and Mixed Numbers

A fraction whose denominator is greater than its numerator is known as a **proper fraction**, while a fraction whose numerator is greater than its denominator is known as an **improper fraction**. Proper fractions have values *less than one* and improper fractions have values *greater than one.*

A **mixed number** is a number that contains both an integer and a fraction. Any improper fraction can be rewritten as a mixed number. Example: $\frac{8}{3} = \frac{6}{3} + \frac{2}{3} = 2 + \frac{2}{3} = 2\frac{2}{3}$. Similarly, any mixed number can be rewritten as an improper fraction. Example: $1\frac{3}{5} = 1 + \frac{3}{5} = \frac{5}{5} + \frac{3}{5} = \frac{8}{5}$.

Review Video: Improper Fractions and Mixed Numbers
Visit mometrix.com/academy and enter code: 211077

Review Video: Overview of Fractions
Visit mometrix.com/academy and enter code: 262335

Adding and Subtracting Fractions

If two fractions have a common denominator, they can be added or subtracted simply by adding or subtracting the two numerators and retaining the same denominator. If the two fractions do not already have the same denominator, one or both of them must be manipulated to achieve a common denominator before they can be added or subtracted. Example: $\frac{1}{2}+\frac{1}{4}=\frac{2}{4}+\frac{1}{4}=\frac{3}{4}$.

> **Review Video: Adding and Subtracting Fractions**
> Visit mometrix.com/academy and enter code: 378080

Multiplying Fractions

Two fractions can be multiplied by multiplying the two numerators to find the new numerator and the two denominators to find the new denominator. Example: $\frac{1}{3}\times\frac{2}{3}=\frac{1\times2}{3\times3}=\frac{2}{9}$.

Dividing Fractions

Two fractions can be divided by flipping the numerator and denominator of the second fraction and then proceeding as though it were a multiplication problem. Example: $\frac{2}{3}\div\frac{3}{4}=\frac{2}{3}\times\frac{4}{3}=\frac{8}{9}$.

> **Review Video: Multiplying and Dividing Fractions**
> Visit mometrix.com/academy and enter code: 473632

Multiplying a Mixed Number by a Whole Number or a Decimal

When multiplying a mixed number by something, it is usually best to convert it to an improper fraction first. Additionally, if the multiplicand is a decimal, it is most often simplest to convert it to a fraction. For instance, to multiply $4\frac{3}{8}$ by 3.5, begin by rewriting each quantity as a whole number plus a proper fraction. Remember, a mixed number is a fraction added to a whole number and a decimal is a representation of the sum of fractions, specifically tenths, hundredths, thousandths, and so on:

$$4\frac{3}{8}\times 3.5=\left(4+\frac{3}{8}\right)\times\left(3+\frac{1}{2}\right)$$

Next, the quantities being added need to be expressed with the same denominator. This is achieved by multiplying and dividing the whole number by the denominator of the fraction. Recall that a whole number is equivalent to that number divided by 1:

$$=\left(\frac{4}{1}\times\frac{8}{8}+\frac{3}{8}\right)\times\left(\frac{3}{1}\times\frac{2}{2}+\frac{1}{2}\right)$$

When multiplying fractions, remember to multiply the numerators and denominators separately:

$$=\left(\frac{4\times 8}{1\times 8}+\frac{3}{8}\right)\times\left(\frac{3\times 2}{1\times 2}+\frac{1}{2}\right)$$
$$=\left(\frac{32}{8}+\frac{3}{8}\right)\times\left(\frac{6}{2}+\frac{1}{2}\right)$$

Now that the fractions have the same denominators, they can be added and then multiplied out:

$$=\frac{35}{8}\times\frac{7}{2}=\frac{245}{16}=\frac{240}{16}+\frac{5}{16}=15\frac{5}{16}$$

DECIMALS

Decimals are one way to represent parts of a whole. Using the place value system, each digit to the right of a decimal point denotes the number of units of a corresponding *negative* power of ten. For example, consider the decimal 0.24. We can use a model to represent the decimal. Since a dime is worth one-tenth of a dollar and a penny is worth one-hundredth of a dollar, one possible model to represent this fraction is to have 2 dimes representing the 2 in the tenths place and 4 pennies representing the 4 in the hundredths place:

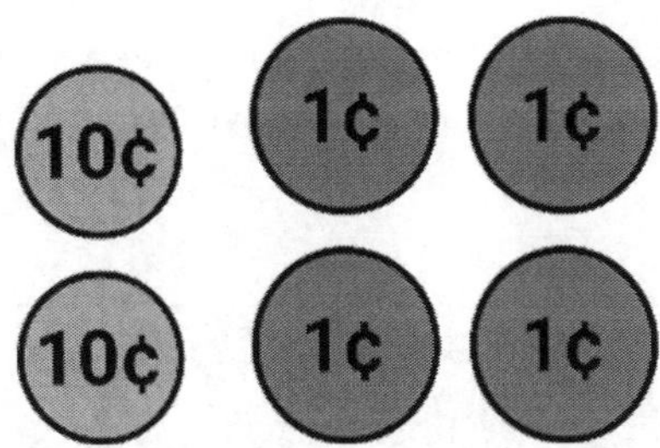

To write the decimal as a fraction, put the decimal in the numerator with 1 in the denominator. Multiply the numerator and denominator by tens until there are no more decimal places. Then simplify the fraction to lowest terms. For example, converting 0.24 to a fraction:

$$0.24 = \frac{0.24}{1} = \frac{0.24 \times 100}{1 \times 100} = \frac{24}{100} = \frac{6}{25}$$

Review Video: Decimals
Visit mometrix.com/academy and enter code: 837268

OPERATIONS WITH DECIMALS

ADDING AND SUBTRACTING DECIMALS

When adding and subtracting decimals, the decimal points must always be aligned. Adding decimals is just like adding regular whole numbers. Example: $4.5 + 2.0 = 6.5$.

If the problem-solver does not properly align the decimal points, an incorrect answer of 4.7 may result. An easy way to add decimals is to align all of the decimal points in a vertical column visually. This will allow you to see exactly where the decimal should be placed in the final answer. Begin adding from right to left. Add each column in turn, making sure to carry the number to the left if a column adds up to more than 9. The same rules apply to the subtraction of decimals.

Review Video: Adding and Subtracting Decimals
Visit mometrix.com/academy and enter code: 381101

MULTIPLYING DECIMALS

A simple multiplication problem has two components: a **multiplicand** and a **multiplier**. When multiplying decimals, work as though the numbers were whole rather than decimals. Once the final product is calculated, count the number of places to the right of the decimal in both the multiplicand and the multiplier. Then, count that number of places from the right of the product and place the decimal in that position.

For example, 12.3×2.56 has a total of three places to the right of the respective decimals. Multiply 123×256 to get 31,488. Now, beginning on the right, count three places to the left and insert the decimal. The final product will be 31.488.

Review Video: Multiplying Decimals
Visit mometrix.com/academy and enter code: 731574

Dividing Decimals

Every division problem has a **divisor** and a **dividend**. The dividend is the number that is being divided. In the problem $14 \div 7$, 14 is the dividend and 7 is the divisor. In a division problem with decimals, the divisor must be converted into a whole number. Begin by moving the decimal in the divisor to the right until a whole number is created. Next, move the decimal in the dividend the same number of spaces to the right. For example, 4.9 into 24.5 would become 49 into 245. The decimal was moved one space to the right to create a whole number in the divisor, and then the same was done for the dividend. Once the whole numbers are created, the problem is carried out normally: $245 \div 49 = 5$.

Review Video: Dividing Decimals
Visit mometrix.com/academy and enter code: 560690

Review Video: Dividing Decimals by Whole Numbers
Visit mometrix.com/academy and enter code: 535669

Percentages

Percentages can be thought of as fractions that are based on a whole of 100; that is, one whole is equal to 100%. The word **percent** means "per hundred." Percentage problems are often presented in three main ways:

- Find what percentage of some number another number is.
  - Example: What percentage of 40 is 8?
- Find what number is some percentage of a given number.
  - Example: What number is 20% of 40?
- Find what number another number is a given percentage of.
  - Example: What number is 8 20% of?

There are three components in each of these cases: a **whole** (W), a **part** (P), and a **percentage** (%). These are related by the equation: $P = W \times \%$. This can easily be rearranged into other forms that may suit different questions better: $\% = \frac{P}{W}$ and $W = \frac{P}{\%}$. Percentage problems are often also word problems. As such, a large part of solving them is figuring out which quantities are what. For example, consider the following word problem:

In a school cafeteria, 7 students choose pizza, 9 choose hamburgers, and 4 choose tacos. What percentage of student choose tacos?

To find the whole, you must first add all of the parts: $7 + 9 + 4 = 20$. The percentage can then be found by dividing the part by the whole $\left(\% = \frac{P}{W}\right)$: $\frac{4}{20} = \frac{20}{100} = 20\%$.

Review Video: Computation with Percentages
Visit mometrix.com/academy and enter code: 693099

Converting Between Percentages, Fractions, and Decimals

Converting decimals to percentages and percentages to decimals is as simple as moving the decimal point. To *convert from a decimal to a percentage*, move the decimal point **two places to the right**. To *convert from a percentage to a decimal*, move it **two places to the left**. It may be helpful to remember that the percentage number will always be larger than the equivalent decimal number. For example:

$$0.23 = 23\% \quad 5.34 = 534\% \quad 0.007 = 0.7\%$$
$$700\% = 7.00 \quad 86\% = 0.86 \quad 0.15\% = 0.0015$$

To convert a fraction to a decimal, simply divide the numerator by the denominator in the fraction. To convert a decimal to a fraction, put the decimal in the numerator with 1 in the denominator. Multiply the numerator and denominator by tens until there are no more decimal places. Then simplify the fraction to lowest terms. For example, converting 0.24 to a fraction:

$$0.24 = \frac{0.24}{1} = \frac{0.24 \times 100}{1 \times 100} = \frac{24}{100} = \frac{6}{25}$$

Fractions can be converted to a percentage by finding equivalent fractions with a denominator of 100. For example,

$$\frac{7}{10} = \frac{70}{100} = 70\% \quad \frac{1}{4} = \frac{25}{100} = 25\%$$

To convert a percentage to a fraction, divide the percentage number by 100 and reduce the fraction to its simplest possible terms. For example,

$$60\% = \frac{60}{100} = \frac{3}{5} \quad 96\% = \frac{96}{100} = \frac{24}{25}$$

Review Video: Converting Fractions to Percentages and Decimals
Visit mometrix.com/academy and enter code: 306233

Review Video: Converting Percentages to Decimals and Fractions
Visit mometrix.com/academy and enter code: 287297

Review Video: Converting Decimals to Fractions and Percentages
Visit mometrix.com/academy and enter code: 986765

Review Video: Converting Decimals, Improper Fractions, and Mixed Numbers
Visit mometrix.com/academy and enter code: 696924

Rational Numbers

The term **rational** means that the number can be expressed as a ratio or fraction. That is, a number, r, is rational if and only if it can be represented by a fraction $\frac{a}{b}$ where a and b are integers and b does not equal 0. The set of rational numbers includes integers and decimals. If there is no finite way to represent a value with a fraction of integers, then the number is **irrational**. Common examples of irrational numbers include: $\sqrt{5}$, $(1 + \sqrt{2})$, and π.

Review Video: Rational and Irrational Numbers
Visit mometrix.com/academy and enter code: 280645

PRACTICE

P1. What is 30% of 120?

P2. What is 150% of 20?

P3. What is 14.5% of 96?

P4. Simplify the following expressions:

(a) $\frac{2}{5} \div \frac{4}{7}$
(b) $\frac{7}{8} - \frac{8}{16}$
(c) $\frac{1}{2} + \left(3\left(\frac{3}{4}\right) - 2\right) + 4$
(d) $0.22 + 0.5 - (5.5 + 3.3 \div 3)$
(e) $\frac{3}{2} + (4(0.5) - 0.75) + 2$

P5. Convert the following to a fraction and to a decimal: **(a)** 15%; **(b)** 24.36%

P6. Convert the following to a decimal and to a percentage. **(a)** $\frac{4}{5}$; **(b)** $3\frac{2}{5}$

P7. A woman's age is thirteen more than half of 60. How old is the woman?

P8. A patient was given pain medicine at a dosage of 0.22 grams. The patient's dosage was then increased to 0.80 grams. By how much was the patient's dosage increased?

P9. At a hotel, $\frac{3}{4}$ of the 100 rooms are occupied today. Yesterday, $\frac{4}{5}$ of the 100 rooms were occupied. On which day were more of the rooms occupied and by how much more?

P10. At a school, 40% of the teachers teach English. If 20 teachers teach English, how many teachers work at the school?

P11. A patient was given blood pressure medicine at a dosage of 2 grams. The patient's dosage was then decreased to 0.45 grams. By how much was the patient's dosage decreased?

P12. Two weeks ago, $\frac{2}{3}$ of the 60 customers at a skate shop were male. Last week, $\frac{3}{6}$ of the 80 customers were male. During which week were there more male customers?

P13. Jane ate lunch at a local restaurant. She ordered a $4.99 appetizer, a $12.50 entrée, and a $1.25 soda. If she wants to tip her server 20%, how much money will she spend in all?

P14. According to a survey, about 82% of engineers were highly satisfied with their job. If 145 engineers were surveyed, how many reported that they were highly satisfied?

P15. A patient was given 40 mg of a certain medicine. Later, the patient's dosage was increased to 45 mg. What was the percent increase in his medication?

P16. Order the following rational numbers from least to greatest: 0.55, 17%, $\sqrt{25}$, $\frac{64}{4}$, $\frac{25}{50}$, 3.

P17. Order the following rational numbers from greatest to least: 0.3, 27%, $\sqrt{100}$, $\frac{72}{9}$, $\frac{1}{9}$, 4.5

P18. Perform the following multiplication. Write each answer as a mixed number.

(a) $\left(1\frac{11}{16}\right) \times 4$

(b) $\left(12\frac{1}{3}\right) \times 1.1$

(c) $3.71 \times \left(6\frac{1}{5}\right)$

P19. Suppose you are making doughnuts and you want to triple the recipe you have. If the following list is the original amounts for the ingredients, what would be the amounts for the tripled recipe?

$1\frac{3}{4}$	cup	Flour	$1\frac{1}{2}$	Tbsp	Butter
$1\frac{1}{4}$	tsp	Baking powder	2	large	Eggs
$\frac{3}{4}$	tsp	Salt	$\frac{3}{4}$	tsp	Vanilla extract
$\frac{3}{8}$	cup	Sugar	$\frac{3}{8}$	cup	Sour cream

Practice Solutions

P1. The word *of* indicates multiplication, so 30% of 120 is found by multiplying 120 by 30%. Change 30% to a decimal, then multiply: $120 \times 0.3 = 36$

P2. The word *of* indicates multiplication, so 150% of 20 is found by multiplying 20 by 150%. Change 150% to a decimal, then multiply: $20 \times 1.5 = 30$

P3. Change 14.5% to a decimal before multiplying. $0.145 \times 96 = 13.92$.

P4. Follow the order of operations and utilize properties of fractions to solve each:

(a) Rewrite the problem as a multiplication problem: $\frac{2}{5} \times \frac{7}{4} = \frac{2\times7}{5\times4} = \frac{14}{20}$. Make sure the fraction is reduced to lowest terms. Both 14 and 20 can be divided by 2.

$$\frac{14}{20} = \frac{14 \div 2}{20 \div 2} = \frac{7}{10}$$

(b) The denominators of $\frac{7}{8}$ and $\frac{8}{16}$ are 8 and 16, respectively. The lowest common denominator of 8 and 16 is 16 because 16 is the least common multiple of 8 and 16. Convert the first fraction to its equivalent with the newly found common denominator of 16: $\frac{7 \times 2}{8 \times 2} = \frac{14}{16}$. Now that the fractions have the same denominator, you can subtract them.

$$\frac{14}{16} - \frac{8}{16} = \frac{6}{16} = \frac{3}{8}$$

(c) When simplifying expressions, first perform operations within groups. Within the set of parentheses are multiplication and subtraction operations. Perform the multiplication first to get $\frac{1}{2} + \left(\frac{9}{4} - 2\right) + 4$. Then, subtract two to obtain $\frac{1}{2} + \frac{1}{4} + 4$. Finally, perform addition from left to right:

$$\frac{1}{2} + \frac{1}{4} + 4 = \frac{2}{4} + \frac{1}{4} + \frac{16}{4} = \frac{19}{4} = 4\frac{3}{4}$$

(d) First, evaluate the terms in the parentheses $(5.5 + 3.3 \div 3)$ using order of operations. $3.3 \div 3 = 1.1$, and $5.5 + 1.1 = 6.6$. Next, rewrite the problem: $0.22 + 0.5 - 6.6$. Finally, add and subtract from left to right: $0.22 + 0.5 = 0.72$; $0.72 - 6.6 = -5.88$. The answer is -5.88.

(e) First, simplify within the parentheses, then change the fraction to a decimal and perform addition from left to right:

$$\frac{3}{2} + (2 - 0.75) + 2 =$$
$$\frac{3}{2} + 1.25 + 2 =$$
$$1.5 + 1.25 + 2 = 4.75$$

P5. (a) 15% can be written as $\frac{15}{100}$. Both 15 and 100 can be divided by 5: $\frac{15 \div 5}{100 \div 5} = \frac{3}{20}$

When converting from a percentage to a decimal, drop the percent sign and move the decimal point two places to the left: $15\% = 0.15$

(b) 24.36% written as a fraction is $\frac{24.36}{100}$, or $\frac{2436}{10{,}000}$, which reduces to $\frac{609}{2500}$. 24.36% written as a decimal is 0.2436. Recall that dividing by 100 moves the decimal two places to the left.

P6. (a) Recall that in the decimal system the first decimal place is one tenth: $\frac{4 \times 2}{5 \times 2} = \frac{8}{10} = 0.8$

Percent means "per hundred." $\frac{4 \times 20}{5 \times 20} = \frac{80}{100} = 80\%$

(b) The mixed number $3\frac{2}{5}$ has a whole number and a fractional part. The fractional part $\frac{2}{5}$ can be written as a decimal by dividing 5 into 2, which gives 0.4. Adding the whole to the part gives 3.4.

To find the equivalent percentage, multiply the decimal by 100. $3.4(100) = 340\%$. Notice that this percentage is greater than 100%. This makes sense because the original mixed number $3\frac{2}{5}$ is greater than 1.

P7. "More than" indicates addition, and "of" indicates multiplication. The expression can be written as $\frac{1}{2}(60) + 13$. So, the woman's age is equal to $\frac{1}{2}(60) + 13 = 30 + 13 = 43$. The woman is 43 years old.

P8. The first step is to determine what operation (addition, subtraction, multiplication, or division) the problem requires. Notice the keywords and phrases "by how much" and "increased."

"Increased" means that you go from a smaller amount to a larger amount. This change can be found by subtracting the smaller amount from the larger amount: 0.80 grams– 0.22 grams = 0.58 grams.

Remember to line up the decimal when subtracting:

$$\begin{array}{r} 0.80 \\ -\ 0.22 \\ \hline 0.58 \end{array}$$

P9. First, find the number of rooms occupied each day. To do so, multiply the fraction of rooms occupied by the number of rooms available:

$$\text{Number occupied} = \text{Fraction occupied} \times \text{Total number}$$

$$\text{Number of rooms occupied today} = \frac{3}{4} \times 100 = 75$$

$$\text{Number of rooms occupied} = \frac{4}{5} \times 100 = 80$$

The difference in the number of rooms occupied is: $80 - 75 = 5$ rooms

P10. To answer this problem, first think about the number of teachers that work at the school. Will it be more or less than the number of teachers who work in a specific department such as English? More teachers work at the school, so the number you find to answer this question will be greater than 20.

40% of the teachers are English teachers. "Of" indicates multiplication, and words like "is" and "are" indicate equivalence. Translating the problem into a mathematical sentence gives $40\% \times t = 20$, where t represents the total number of teachers. Solving for t gives $t = \frac{20}{40\%} = \frac{20}{0.40} = 50$. Fifty teachers work at the school.

P11. The decrease is represented by the difference between the two amounts:

$$2 \text{ grams} - 0.45 \text{ grams} = 1.55 \text{ grams}.$$

Remember to line up the decimal point before subtracting.

$$\begin{array}{r} 2.00 \\ -\ 0.45 \\ \hline 1.55 \end{array}$$

P12. First, you need to find the number of male customers that were in the skate shop each week. You are given this amount in terms of fractions. To find the actual number of male customers, multiply the fraction of male customers by the number of customers in the store.

$$\text{Actual number of male customers} = \text{fraction of male customers} \times \text{total customers}$$

$$\text{Number of male customers two weeks ago} = \frac{2}{3} \times 60 = \frac{120}{3} = 40$$

$$\text{Number of male customers last week} = \frac{3}{6} \times 80 = \frac{1}{2} \times 80 = \frac{80}{2} = 40$$

The number of male customers was the same both weeks.

P13. To find total amount, first find the sum of the items she ordered from the menu and then add 20% of this sum to the total.

$$\$4.99 + \$12.50 + \$1.25 = \$18.74$$

$$\$18.74 \times 20\% = (0.20)(\$18.74) = \$3.748 \approx \$3.75$$

$$\text{Total} = \$18.74 + \$3.75 = \$22.49$$

P14. 82% of 145 is $0.82 \times 145 = 118.9$. Because you can't have 0.9 of a person, we must round up to say that 119 engineers reported that they were highly satisfied with their jobs.

P15. To find the percent increase, first compare the original and increased amounts. The original amount was 40 mg, and the increased amount is 45 mg, so the dosage of medication was increased by 5 mg ($45 - 40 = 5$). Note, however, that the question asks not by how much the dosage increased but by what percentage it increased.

$$\begin{aligned}\text{Percent increase} &= \frac{\text{new amount} - \text{original amount}}{\text{original amount}} \times 100\% \\ &= \frac{45\text{ mg} - 40\text{ mg}}{40\text{ mg}} \times 100\% = \frac{5}{40} \times 100\% = 0.125 \times 100\% = 12.5\%\end{aligned}$$

P16. Recall that the term rational simply means that the number can be expressed as a ratio or fraction. Notice that each of the numbers in the problem can be written as a decimal or integer:

$$\begin{aligned}17\% &= 0.17 \\ \sqrt{25} &= 5 \\ \frac{64}{4} &= 16 \\ \frac{25}{50} &= \frac{1}{2} = 0.5\end{aligned}$$

So, the answer is 17%, $\frac{25}{50}$, 0.55, 3, $\sqrt{25}$, $\frac{64}{4}$.

P17. Converting all the numbers to integers and decimals makes it easier to compare the values:

$$\begin{aligned}27\% &= 0.27 \\ \sqrt{100} &= 10 \\ \frac{72}{9} &= 8 \\ \frac{1}{9} &\approx 0.11\end{aligned}$$

So, the answer is $\sqrt{100}$, $\frac{72}{9}$, 4.5, 0.3, 27%, $\frac{1}{9}$.

Review Video: Ordering Rational Numbers
Visit mometrix.com/academy and enter code: 419578

P18. For each, convert improper fractions, adjust to a common denominator, perform the operations, and then simplify:

(a) Sometimes, you can skip converting the denominator and just distribute the multiplication.

$$\left(1\frac{11}{16}\right) \times 4 = \left(1 + \frac{11}{16}\right) \times 4$$
$$= 1 \times 4 + \frac{11}{16} \times 4$$
$$= 4 + \frac{11}{16} \times \frac{4}{1}$$
$$= 4 + \frac{44}{16} = 4 + \frac{11}{4} = 4 + 2\frac{3}{4} = 6\frac{3}{4}$$

(b)

$$\left(12\frac{1}{3}\right) \times 1.1 = \left(12 + \frac{1}{3}\right) \times \left(1 + \frac{1}{10}\right)$$
$$= \left(\frac{12}{1} \times \frac{3}{3} + \frac{1}{3}\right) \times \left(\frac{10}{10} + \frac{1}{10}\right)$$
$$= \left(\frac{36}{3} + \frac{1}{3}\right) \times \frac{11}{10}$$
$$= \frac{37}{3} \times \frac{11}{10}$$
$$= \frac{407}{30} = \frac{390}{30} + \frac{17}{30} = 13\frac{17}{30}$$

(c)

$$3.71 \times \left(6\frac{1}{5}\right) = \left(3 + \frac{71}{100}\right) \times \left(6 + \frac{1}{5}\right)$$
$$= \left(\frac{300}{100} + \frac{71}{100}\right) \times \left(\frac{6}{1} \times \frac{5}{5} + \frac{1}{5}\right)$$
$$= \frac{371}{100} \times \left(\frac{30}{5} + \frac{1}{5}\right)$$
$$= \frac{371}{100} \times \frac{31}{5}$$
$$= \frac{11501}{500} = \frac{11500}{500} + \frac{1}{500} = 23\frac{1}{500}$$

P19. Fortunately, some of the amounts are duplicated, so we do not need to convert every amount.

$$1\frac{3}{4}\times 3 = (1\times 3) + \left(\frac{3}{4}\times 3\right) = 3 + \frac{9}{4} = 3 + 2\frac{1}{4} = 5\frac{1}{4}$$

$$1\frac{1}{4}\times 3 = (1\times 3) + \left(\frac{1}{4}\times 3\right) = 3 + \frac{3}{4} = 3\frac{3}{4}$$

$$\frac{3}{4}\times 3 = \frac{3}{4}\times 3 = \frac{9}{4} = 2\frac{1}{4}$$

$$\frac{3}{8}\times 3 = \frac{3}{8}\times 3 = \frac{9}{8} = 1\frac{1}{8}$$

$$1\frac{1}{2}\times 3 = 1\times 3 + \frac{1}{2}\times 3 = 3 + \frac{3}{2} = 3 + 1\frac{1}{2} = 4\frac{1}{2}$$

$$2\times 3 = 6$$

So, the result for the triple recipe is:

$5\frac{1}{4}$	cup	Flour	$4\frac{1}{2}$	Tbsp	Butter
$3\frac{3}{4}$	tsp	Baking powder	6	large	Eggs
$2\frac{1}{4}$	tsp	Salt	$2\frac{1}{4}$	tsp	Vanilla extract
$1\frac{1}{8}$	cup	Sugar	$1\frac{1}{8}$	cup	Sour cream

Factoring

Factors and Greatest Common Factor

Factors are numbers that are multiplied together to obtain a **product**. For example, in the equation $2 \times 3 = 6$, the numbers 2 and 3 are factors. A **prime number** has only two factors (1 and itself), but other numbers can have many factors.

A **common factor** is a number that divides exactly into two or more other numbers. For example, the factors of 12 are 1, 2, 3, 4, 6, and 12, while the factors of 15 are 1, 3, 5, and 15. The common factors of 12 and 15 are 1 and 3.

A **prime factor** is also a prime number. Therefore, the prime factors of 12 are 2 and 3. For 15, the prime factors are 3 and 5.

The **greatest common factor** (GCF) is the largest number that is a factor of two or more numbers. For example, the factors of 15 are 1, 3, 5, and 15; the factors of 35 are 1, 5, 7, and 35. Therefore, the greatest common factor of 15 and 35 is 5.

Review Video: Factors
Visit mometrix.com/academy and enter code: 920086

Review Video: Greatest Common Factor (GCF)
Visit mometrix.com/academy and enter code: 838699

Multiples and Least Common Multiple

Often listed out in multiplication tables, **multiples** are integer increments of a given factor. In other words, dividing a multiple by the factor will result in an integer. For example, the multiples of 7 include: $1 \times 7 = 7, 2 \times 7 = 14, 3 \times 7 = 21, 4 \times 7 = 28, 5 \times 7 = 35$. Dividing 7, 14, 21, 28, or 35 by 7 will result in the integers 1, 2, 3, 4, and 5, respectively.

The least common multiple (**LCM**) is the smallest number that is a multiple of two or more numbers. For example, the multiples of 3 include 3, 6, 9, 12, 15, etc.; the multiples of 5 include 5, 10, 15, 20, etc. Therefore, the least common multiple of 3 and 5 is 15.

Review Video: Multiples
Visit mometrix.com/academy and enter code: 626738

Proportions and Ratios

PROPORTIONS

A proportion is a relationship between two quantities that dictates how one changes when the other changes. A **direct proportion** describes a relationship in which a quantity increases by a set amount for every increase in the other quantity or decreases by that same amount for every decrease in the other quantity. Example: Assuming a constant driving speed, the time required for a car trip increases as the distance of the trip increases. The distance to be traveled and the time required to travel are directly proportional.

An **inverse proportion** is a relationship in which an increase in one quantity is accompanied by a decrease in the other, or vice versa. Example: the time required for a car trip decreases as the speed increases and increases as the speed decreases, so the time required is inversely proportional to the speed of the car.

Review Video: Proportions
Visit mometrix.com/academy and enter code: 505355

RATIOS

A **ratio** is a comparison of two quantities in a particular order. Example: If there are 14 computers in a lab, and the class has 20 students, there is a student to computer ratio of 20 to 14, commonly written as 20: 14. Ratios are normally reduced to their smallest whole number representation, so 20: 14 would be reduced to 10: 7 by dividing both sides by 2.

Review Video: Ratios
Visit mometrix.com/academy and enter code: 996914

CONSTANT OF PROPORTIONALITY

When two quantities have a proportional relationship, there exists a **constant of proportionality** between the quantities. The product of this constant and one of the quantities is equal to the other quantity. For example, if one lemon costs $0.25, two lemons cost $0.50, and three lemons cost $0.75, there is a proportional relationship between the total cost of lemons and the number of lemons purchased. The constant of proportionality is the **unit price**, namely $0.25/lemon. Notice that the total price of lemons, t, can be found by multiplying the unit price of lemons, p, and the number of lemons, n: $t = pn$.

WORK/UNIT RATE

Unit rate expresses a quantity of one thing in terms of one unit of another. For example, if you travel 30 miles every two hours, a unit rate expresses this comparison in terms of one hour: in one hour you travel 15 miles, so your unit rate is 15 miles per hour. Other examples are how much one ounce of food costs (price per ounce) or figuring out how much one egg costs out of the dozen (price per 1 egg, instead of price per 12 eggs). The denominator of a unit rate is always 1. Unit rates are used to compare different situations to solve problems. For example, to make sure you get the best deal when deciding which kind of soda to buy, you can find the unit rate of each. If soda #1 costs $1.50 for a 1-liter bottle, and soda #2 costs $2.75 for a 2-liter bottle, it would be a better deal to buy soda #2, because its unit rate is only $1.375 per 1-liter, which is cheaper than soda #1. Unit rates can also help determine the length of time a given event will take. For example, if you can paint 2 rooms in 4.5 hours, you can determine how long it will take you to paint 5 rooms by solving for the unit rate per room and then multiplying that by 5.

Review Video: Rates and Unit Rates
Visit mometrix.com/academy and enter code: 185363

SLOPE

On a graph with two points, (x_1, y_1) and (x_2, y_2), the **slope** is found with the formula $m = \frac{y_2 - y_1}{x_2 - x_1}$; where $x_1 \neq x_2$ and m stands for slope. If the value of the slope is **positive**, the line has an *upward direction* from left to right. If the value of the slope is **negative**, the line has a *downward direction* from left to right. Consider the following example:

A new book goes on sale in bookstores and online stores. In the first month, 5,000 copies of the book are sold. Over time, the book continues to grow in popularity. The data for the number of copies sold is in the table below.

# of Months on Sale	1	2	3	4	5
# of Copies Sold (In Thousands)	5	10	15	20	25

So, the number of copies that are sold and the time that the book is on sale is a proportional relationship. In this example, an equation can be used to show the data: $y = 5x$, where x is the number of months that the book is on sale, and y is the number of copies sold. So, the slope of the corresponding line is $\frac{\text{rise}}{\text{run}} = \frac{5}{1} = 5$.

Review Video: Finding the Slope of a Line
Visit mometrix.com/academy and enter code: 766664

FINDING AN UNKNOWN IN EQUIVALENT EXPRESSIONS

It is often necessary to apply information given about a rate or proportion to a new scenario. For example, if you know that Jedha can run a marathon (26.2 miles) in 3 hours, how long would it take her to run 10 miles at the same pace? Start by setting up equivalent expressions:

$$\frac{26.2\text{ mi}}{3\text{ hr}} = \frac{10\text{ mi}}{x\text{ hr}}$$

Now, cross multiply and solve for x:

$$26.2x = 30$$
$$x = \frac{30}{26.2} = \frac{15}{13.1}$$
$$x \approx 1.15\text{ hrs } or\text{ 1 hr 9 min}$$

So, at this pace, Jedha could run 10 miles in about 1.15 hours or about 1 hour and 9 minutes.

Review Video: Cross Multiply Fractions
Visit mometrix.com/academy and enter code: 893904

PRACTICE

P1. Solve the following for x.

(a) $\frac{45}{12} = \frac{15}{x}$

(b) $\frac{0.50}{2} = \frac{1.50}{x}$

(c) $\frac{40}{8} = \frac{x}{24}$

P2. At a school, for every 20 female students there are 15 male students. This same student ratio happens to exist at another school. If there are 100 female students at the second school, how many male students are there?

P3. In a hospital emergency room, there are 4 nurses for every 12 patients. What is the ratio of nurses to patients? If the nurse-to-patient ratio remains constant, how many nurses must be present to care for 24 patients?

P4. In a bank, the banker-to-customer ratio is 1: 2. If seven bankers are on duty, how many customers are currently in the bank?

P5. Janice made $40 during the first 5 hours she spent babysitting. She will continue to earn money at this rate until she finishes babysitting in 3 more hours. Find how much money Janice earns per hour and the total she earned babysitting.

P6. The McDonalds are taking a family road trip, driving 300 miles to their cabin. It took them 2 hours to drive the first 120 miles. They will drive at the same speed all the way to their cabin. Find the speed at which the McDonalds are driving and how much longer it will take them to get to their cabin.

P7. It takes Andy 10 minutes to read 6 pages of his book. He has already read 150 pages in his book that is 210 pages long. Find how long it takes Andy to read 1 page and also find how long it will take him to finish his book if he continues to read at the same speed.

Practice Solutions

P1. Cross multiply, then solve for x:

(a)

$$45x = 12 \times 15$$
$$45x = 180$$
$$x = \frac{180}{45} = 4$$

(b)

$$0.5x = 1.5 \times 2$$
$$0.5x = 3$$
$$x = \frac{3}{0.5} = 6$$

(c)

$$8x = 40 \times 24$$
$$8x = 960$$
$$x = \frac{960}{8} = 120$$

P2. One way to find the number of male students is to set up and solve a proportion.

$$\frac{\text{number of female students}}{\text{number of male students}} = \frac{20}{15} = \frac{100}{\text{number of male students}}$$

Represent the unknown number of male students as the variable x: $\frac{20}{15} = \frac{100}{x}$

Cross multiply and then solve for x:

$$20x = 15 \times 100$$
$$x = \frac{1500}{20}$$
$$x = 75$$

P3. The ratio of nurses to patients can be written as 4 to 12, 4: 12, or $\frac{4}{12}$. Because four and twelve have a common factor of four, the ratio should be reduced to 1: 3, which means that there is one nurse present for every three patients. If this ratio remains constant, there must be eight nurses present to care for 24 patients.

P4. Use proportional reasoning or set up a proportion to solve. Because there are twice as many customers as bankers, there must be fourteen customers when seven bankers are on duty. Setting up and solving a proportion gives the same result:

$$\frac{\text{number of bankers}}{\text{number of customers}} = \frac{1}{2} = \frac{7}{\text{number of customers}}$$

Represent the unknown number of customers as the variable x: $\frac{1}{2} = \frac{7}{x}$.

To solve for x, cross multiply: $1 \times x = 7 \times 2$, so $x = 14$.

P5. Janice earns \$8 per hour. This can be found by taking her initial amount earned, \$40, and dividing it by the number of hours worked, 5. Since $\frac{40}{5} = 8$, Janice makes \$8 in one hour. This can also be found by finding the unit rate, money earned per hour: $\frac{40}{5} = \frac{x}{1}$. Since cross multiplying yields $5x = 40$, and division by 5 shows that $x = 8$, Janice earns \$8 per hour.

Janice will earn \$64 babysitting in her 8 total hours (adding the first 5 hours to the remaining 3 gives the 8-hour total). Since Janice earns \$8 per hour and she worked 8 hours, $\frac{\$8}{\text{hr}} \times 8 \text{ hrs} = \$64$. This can also be found by setting up a proportion comparing money earned to babysitting hours. Since she earns \$40 for 5 hours and since the rate is constant, she will earn a proportional amount in 8 hours: $\frac{40}{5} = \frac{x}{8}$. Cross multiplying will yield $5x = 320$, and division by 5 shows that $x = 64$.

P6. The McDonalds are driving 60 miles per hour. This can be found by setting up a proportion to find the unit rate, the number of miles they drive per one hour: $\frac{120}{2} = \frac{x}{1}$. Cross multiplying yields $2x = 120$ and division by 2 shows that $x = 60$.

Since the McDonalds will drive this same speed for the remaining miles, it will take them another 3 hours to get to their cabin. This can be found by first finding how many miles the McDonalds have left to drive, which is $300 - 120 = 180$. The McDonalds are driving at 60 miles per hour, so a proportion can be set up to determine how many hours it will take them to drive 180 miles: $\frac{180}{x} = \frac{60}{1}$. Cross multiplying yields $60x = 180$, and division by 60 shows that $x = 3$. This can also be found by using the formula $D = r \times t$ (or distance = rate × time), where $180 = 60 \times t$, and division by 60 shows that $t = 3$.

P7. It takes Andy 10 minutes to read 6 pages, $\frac{10}{6} = 1\frac{2}{3}$ minutes, which is 1 minute and 40 seconds.

Next, determine how many pages Andy has left to read, $210 - 150 = 60$. Since it is now known that it takes him $1\frac{2}{3}$ minutes to read each page, that rate must be multiplied by however many pages he has left to read (60) to find the time he'll need: $60 \times 1\frac{2}{3} = 100$, so it will take him 100 minutes, or 1 hour and 40 minutes, to read the rest of his book.

Probability

PROBABILITY

Probability is the likelihood of a certain outcome occurring for a given event. An **event** is any situation that produces a result. It could be something as simple as flipping a coin or as complex as launching a rocket. Determining the probability of an outcome for an event can be equally simple or complex. As such, there are specific terms used in the study of probability that need to be understood:

- **Compound event**—an event that involves two or more independent events (rolling a pair of dice and taking the sum)
- **Desired outcome** (or success)—an outcome that meets a particular set of criteria (a roll of 1 or 2 if we are looking for numbers less than 3)
- **Independent events**—two or more events whose outcomes do not affect one another (two coins tossed at the same time)
- **Dependent events**—two or more events whose outcomes affect one another (two cards drawn consecutively from the same deck)
- **Certain outcome**—probability of outcome is 100% or 1
- **Impossible outcome**—probability of outcome is 0% or 0
- **Mutually exclusive outcomes**—two or more outcomes whose criteria cannot all be satisfied in a single event (a coin coming up heads and tails on the same toss)
- **Random variable**—refers to all possible outcomes of a single event which may be discrete or continuous.

Review Video: Intro to Probability
Visit mometrix.com/academy and enter code: 212374

THEORETICAL AND EXPERIMENTAL PROBABILITY

Theoretical probability can usually be determined without actually performing the event. The likelihood of an outcome occurring, or the probability of an outcome occurring, is given by the formula:

$$P(A) = \frac{\text{Number of acceptable outcomes}}{\text{Number of possible outcomes}}$$

Note that $P(A)$ is the probability of an outcome A occurring, and each outcome is just as likely to occur as any other outcome. If each outcome has the same probability of occurring as every other possible outcome, the outcomes are said to be equally likely to occur. The total number of acceptable outcomes must be less than or equal to the total number of possible outcomes. If the two are equal, then the outcome is certain to occur, and the probability is 1. If the number of acceptable outcomes is zero, then the outcome is impossible, and the probability is 0. For example, if there are 20 marbles in a bag and 5 are red, then the theoretical probability of randomly selecting a red marble is 5 out of 20, $\left(\frac{5}{20} = \frac{1}{4}, 0.25, \text{or } 25\%\right)$.

If the theoretical probability is unknown or too complicated to calculate, it can be estimated by an experimental probability. **Experimental probability**, also called empirical probability, is an estimate of the likelihood of a certain outcome based on repeated experiments or collected data. In other words, while theoretical probability is based on what *should* happen, experimental probability is based on what *has* happened. Experimental probability is calculated in the same way as theoretical probability, except that actual outcomes are used instead of possible outcomes. The more experiments performed or datapoints gathered, the better the estimate should be.

Theoretical and experimental probability do not always line up with one another. Theoretical probability says that out of 20 coin-tosses, 10 should be heads. However, if we were actually to toss 20 coins, we might record just 5 heads. This doesn't mean that our theoretical probability is incorrect; it just means that this particular experiment had results that were different from what was predicted. A practical application of empirical probability is the insurance industry. There are no set functions that define lifespan, health, or safety. Insurance companies look at factors from hundreds of thousands of individuals to find patterns that they then use to set the formulas for insurance premiums.

Review Video: Empirical Probability
Visit mometrix.com/academy and enter code: 513468

Expected Value

Expected value is a method of determining the expected outcome in a random situation. It is a sum of the weighted probabilities of the possible outcomes. Multiply the probability of an event occurring by the weight assigned to that probability (such as the amount of money won or lost). A practical application of the expected value is to determine whether a game of chance is really fair. If the sum of the weighted probabilities is equal to zero, the game is generally considered fair because the player has a fair chance to at least break even. If the expected value is less than zero, then players are expected to lose more than they win. For example, a lottery drawing might allow the player to choose any three-digit number, 000–999. The probability of choosing the winning number is 1:1000. If it costs \$1 to play, and a winning number receives \$500, the expected value is $\left(-\$1 \times \frac{999}{1{,}000}\right) + \left(\$499 \times \frac{1}{1{,}000}\right) = -\$0.50$. You can expect to lose on average 50 cents for every dollar you spend.

Review Video: Expected Value
Visit mometrix.com/academy and enter code: 643554

Practice

P1. Determine the theoretical probability of the following events:

(a) Rolling an even number on a regular 6-sided die.

(b) Not getting a red ball when selecting one from a bag of 3 red balls, 4 black balls, and 2 green balls.

(c) Rolling a standard die and then selecting a card from a standard deck that is less than the value rolled.

Practice Solutions

P1. (a). The values on the faces of a regular die are 1, 2, 3, 4, 5, and 6. Since three of these are even numbers (2, 4, 6), the probability of rolling an even number is $\frac{3}{6} = \frac{1}{2} = 0.5 = 50\%$.

(b) The bag contains a total of 9 balls, 6 of which are not red, so the probability of selecting one non-red ball would be $\frac{6}{9} = \frac{2}{3} \cong 0.667 \cong 66.7\%$.

(c) In this scenario, we need to determine how many cards could satisfy the condition for each possible value of the die roll. If a one is rolled, there is no way to achieve the desired outcome, since no cards in a standard deck are less than 1. If a two is rolled, then any of the four aces would achieve the desired result. If a three is rolled, then either an ace or a two would satisfy the condition, and so on. Note that any value on the die is equally likely to occur, meaning that the probability of each roll is $\frac{1}{6}$. Putting all this in a table can help:

Roll	Cards < Roll	Probability of Card	Probability of Event
1	-	$\frac{0}{52} = 0$	$\frac{1}{6} \times 0 = 0$
2	1	$\frac{4}{52} = \frac{1}{13}$	$\frac{1}{6} \times \frac{1}{13} = \frac{1}{78}$
3	1,2	$\frac{8}{52} = \frac{2}{13}$	$\frac{1}{6} \times \frac{2}{13} = \frac{2}{78}$
4	1,2,3	$\frac{12}{52} = \frac{3}{13}$	$\frac{1}{6} \times \frac{3}{13} = \frac{3}{78}$
5	1,2,3,4	$\frac{16}{52} = \frac{4}{13}$	$\frac{1}{6} \times \frac{4}{13} = \frac{4}{78}$
6	1,2,3,4,5	$\frac{20}{52} = \frac{5}{13}$	$\frac{1}{6} \times \frac{5}{13} = \frac{5}{78}$

Assuming that each value of the die is equally likely, then the probability of selecting a card less than the value of the die is the sum of the probabilities of each way to achieve the desired outcome: $\frac{0+1+2+3+4+5}{78} = \frac{15}{78} = \frac{5}{26} \cong 0.192 \cong 19.2\%$.

Statistical Analysis

Measures of Central Tendency

A **measure of central tendency** is a statistical value that gives a reasonable estimate for the center of a group of data. There are several different ways of describing the measure of central tendency. Each one has a unique way it is calculated, and each one gives a slightly different perspective on the data set. Whenever you give a measure of central tendency, always make sure the units are the same. If the data has different units, such as hours, minutes, and seconds, convert all the data to the same unit, and use the same unit in the measure of central tendency. If no units are given in the data, do not give units for the measure of central tendency.

Mean

The **statistical mean** of a group of data is the same as the arithmetic average of that group. To find the mean of a set of data, first convert each value to the same units, if necessary. Then find the sum of all the values, and count the total number of data values, making sure you take into consideration each individual value. If a value appears more than once, count it more than once. Divide the sum of the values by the total number of values and apply the units, if any. Note that the mean does not have to be one of the data values in the set, and may not divide evenly.

$$\text{mean} = \frac{\text{sum of the data values}}{\text{quantity of data values}}$$

For instance, the mean of the data set $\{88, 72, 61, 90, 97, 68, 88, 79, 86, 93, 97, 71, 80, 84, 89\}$ would be the sum of the fifteen numbers divided by 15:

$$\frac{88 + 72 + 61 + 90 + 97 + 68 + 88 + 79 + 86 + 93 + 97 + 71 + 80 + 84 + 88}{15} = \frac{1242}{15} = 82.8$$

While the mean is relatively easy to calculate and averages are understood by most people, the mean can be very misleading if it is used as the sole measure of central tendency. If the data set has outliers (data values that are unusually high or unusually low compared to the rest of the data values), the mean can be very distorted, especially if the data set has a small number of values. If unusually high values are countered with unusually low values, the mean is not affected as much. For example, if five of twenty students in a class get a 100 on a test, but the other 15 students have an average of 60 on the same test, the class average would appear as 70. Whenever the mean is skewed by outliers, it is always a good idea to include the median as an alternate measure of central tendency.

A **weighted mean**, or weighted average, is a mean that uses "weighted" values. The formula is weighted mean $= \frac{w_1x_1+w_2x_2+w_3x_3...+w_nx_n}{w_1+w_2+w_3+\cdots+w_n}$. Weighted values, such as $w_1, w_2, w_3, \dots w_n$ are assigned to each member of the set $x_1, x_2, x_3, \dots x_n$. When calculating the weighted mean, make sure a weight value for each member of the set is used.

Median

The **statistical median** is the value in the middle of the set of data. To find the median, list all data values in order from smallest to largest or from largest to smallest. Any value that is repeated in the set must be listed the number of times it appears. If there are an odd number of data values, the median is the value in the middle of the list. If there is an even number of data values, the median is the arithmetic mean of the two middle values.

For example, the median of the data set {88, 72, 61, 90, 97, 68, 88, 79, 86, 93, 97, 71, 80, 84, 88} is 86 since the ordered set is {61, 68, 71, 72, 79, 80, 84, **86**, 88, 88, 88, 90, 93, 97, 97}.

The big disadvantage of using the median as a measure of central tendency is that is relies solely on a value's relative size as compared to the other values in the set. When the individual values in a set of data are evenly dispersed, the median can be an accurate tool. However, if there is a group of rather large values or a group of rather small values that are not offset by a different group of values, the information that can be inferred from the median may not be accurate because the distribution of values is skewed.

MODE

The **statistical mode** is the data value that occurs the greatest number of times in the data set. It is possible to have exactly one mode, more than one mode, or no mode. To find the mode of a set of data, arrange the data like you do to find the median (all values in order, listing all multiples of data values). Count the number of times each value appears in the data set. If all values appear an equal number of times, there is no mode. If one value appears more than any other value, that value is the mode. If two or more values appear the same number of times, but there are other values that appear fewer times and no values that appear more times, all of those values are the modes.

For example, the mode of the data set {**88**, 72, 61, 90, 97, 68, **88**, 79, 86, 93, 97, 71, 80, 84, **88**} is 88.

The main disadvantage of the mode is that the values of the other data in the set have no bearing on the mode. The mode may be the largest value, the smallest value, or a value anywhere in between in the set. The mode only tells which value or values, if any, occurred the greatest number of times. It does not give any suggestions about the remaining values in the set.

Review Video: Mean, Median, and Mode
Visit mometrix.com/academy and enter code: 286207

Lines and Angles

Points and Lines

A **point** is a fixed location in space, has no size or dimensions, and is commonly represented by a dot. A **line** is a set of points that extends infinitely in two opposite directions. It has length, but no width or depth. A line can be defined by any two distinct points that it contains. A **line segment** is a portion of a line that has definite endpoints. A **ray** is a portion of a line that extends from a single point on that line in one direction along the line. It has a definite beginning, but no ending.

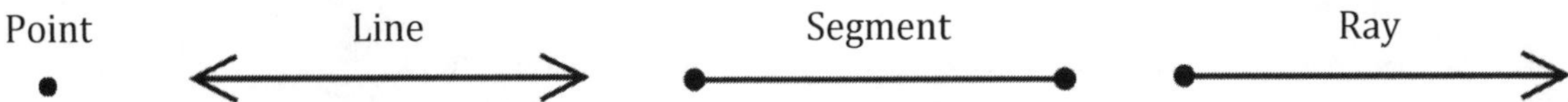

Interactions between Lines

Intersecting lines are lines that have exactly one point in common. **Concurrent lines** are multiple lines that intersect at a single point. **Perpendicular lines** are lines that intersect at right angles. They are represented by the symbol ⊥. The shortest distance from a line to a point not on the line is a perpendicular segment from the point to the line. **Parallel lines** are lines in the same plane that have no points in common and never meet. It is possible for lines to be in different planes, have no points in common, and never meet, but they are not parallel because they are in different planes.

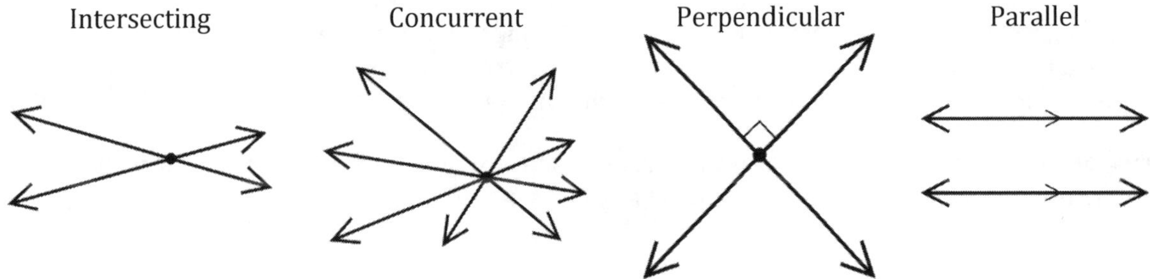

A **transversal** is a line that intersects at least two other lines, which may or may not be parallel to one another. A transversal that intersects parallel lines is a common occurrence in geometry. A **bisector** is a line or line segment that divides another line segment into two equal lengths. A **perpendicular bisector** of a line segment is composed of points that are equidistant from the endpoints of the segment it is dividing.

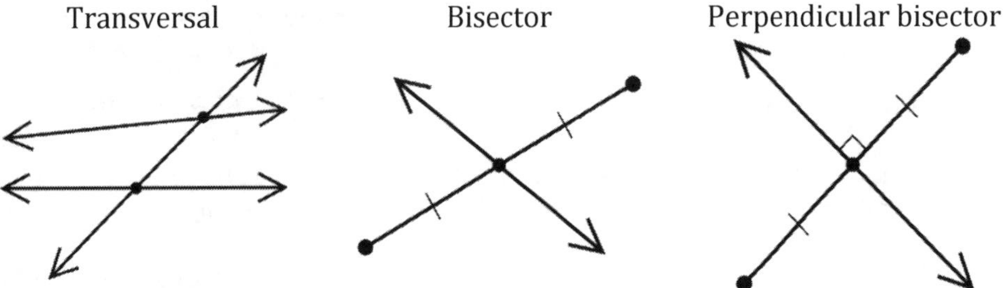

ANGLES AND VERTICES

An **angle** is formed when two lines or line segments meet at a common point. It may be a common starting point for a pair of segments or rays, or it may be the intersection of lines. Angles are represented by the symbol ∠.

The **vertex** is the point at which two segments or rays meet to form an angle. If the angle is formed by intersecting rays, lines, and/or line segments, the vertex is the point at which four angles are formed. The pairs of angles opposite one another are called vertical angles, and their measures are equal.

- An **acute** angle is an angle with a degree measure less than 90°.
- A **right** angle is an angle with a degree measure of exactly 90°.
- An **obtuse** angle is an angle with a degree measure greater than 90° but less than 180°.
- A **straight angle** is an angle with a degree measure of exactly 180°. This is also a semicircle.
- A **reflex angle** is an angle with a degree measure greater than 180° but less than 360°.
- A **full angle** is an angle with a degree measure of exactly 360°. This is also a circle.

RELATIONSHIPS BETWEEN ANGLES

Two angles whose sum is exactly 90° are said to be **complementary**. The two angles may or may not be adjacent. In a right triangle, the two acute angles are complementary.

Two angles whose sum is exactly 180° are said to be **supplementary**. The two angles may or may not be adjacent. Two intersecting lines always form two pairs of supplementary angles. Adjacent supplementary angles will always form a straight line.

Two angles that have the same vertex and share a side are said to be **adjacent**. Vertical angles are not adjacent because they share a vertex but no common side.

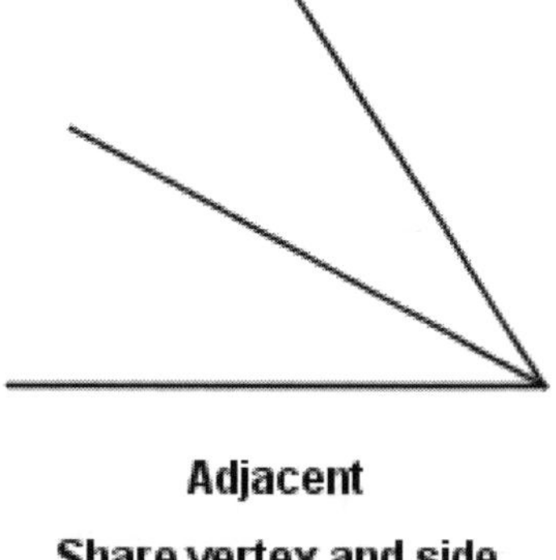

Adjacent

Share vertex and side

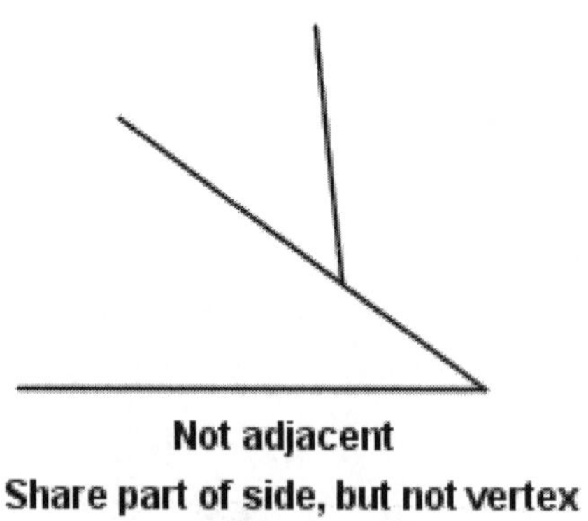

Not adjacent

Share part of side, but not vertex

When two parallel lines are cut by a transversal, the angles that are between the two parallel lines are **interior angles**. In the diagram below, angles 3, 4, 5, and 6 are interior angles.

When two parallel lines are cut by a transversal, the angles that are outside the parallel lines are **exterior angles**. In the diagram below, angles 1, 2, 7, and 8 are exterior angles.

When two parallel lines are cut by a transversal, the angles that are in the same position relative to the transversal and a parallel line are **corresponding angles**. The diagram below has four pairs of corresponding angles: angles 1 and 5, angles 2 and 6, angles 3 and 7, and angles 4 and 8. Corresponding angles formed by parallel lines are congruent.

When two parallel lines are cut by a transversal, the two interior angles that are on opposite sides of the transversal are called **alternate interior angles**. In the diagram below, there are two pairs of alternate interior angles: angles 3 and 6, and angles 4 and 5. Alternate interior angles formed by parallel lines are congruent.

When two parallel lines are cut by a transversal, the two exterior angles that are on opposite sides of the transversal are called **alternate exterior angles**.

Review Video: Angles
Visit mometrix.com/academy and enter code: 264624

In the diagram below, there are two pairs of alternate exterior angles: angles 1 and 8, and angles 2 and 7. Alternate exterior angles formed by parallel lines are congruent.

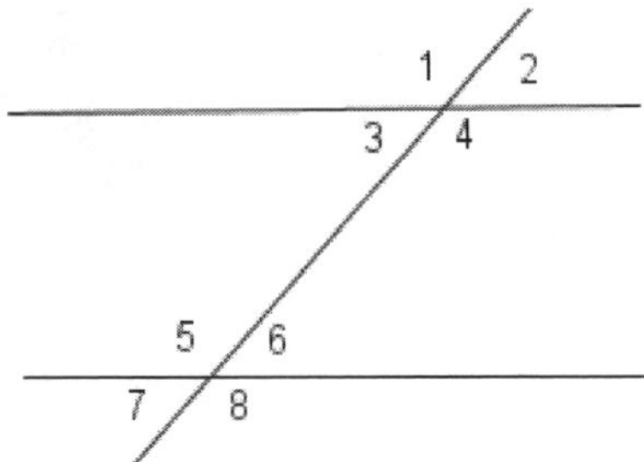

When two lines intersect, four angles are formed. The non-adjacent angles at this vertex are called vertical angles. Vertical angles are congruent. In the diagram, $\angle ABD \cong \angle CBE$ and $\angle ABC \cong \angle DBE$.

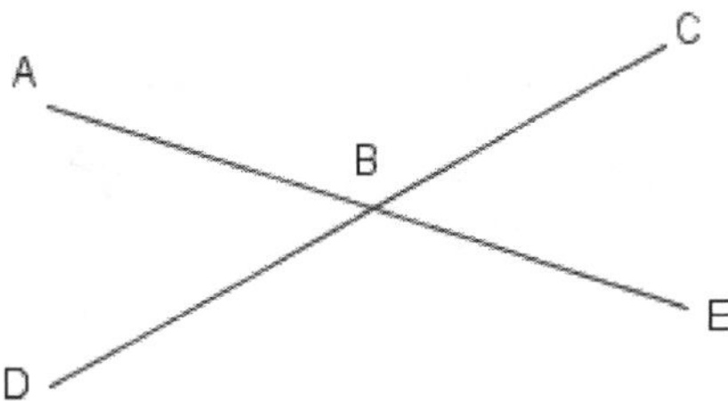

Practice

P1. Find the measure of angles $\angle a$, $\angle b$, and $\angle c$ based on the figure with two parallel lines, two perpendicular lines, and one transversal:

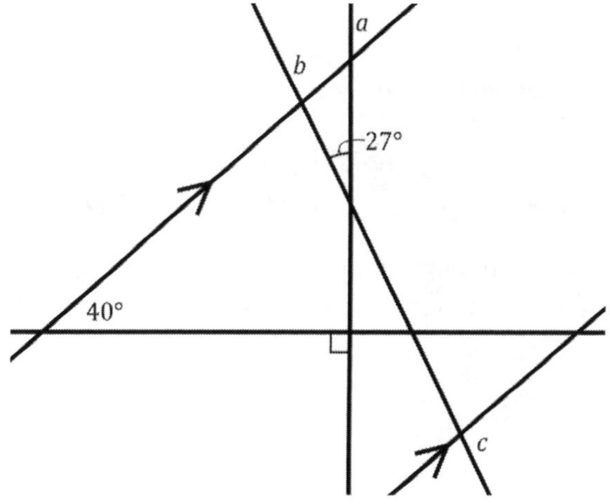

Practice Solutions

P1. (a) The vertical angle paired with $\angle a$ is part of a right triangle with the 40° angle. Thus the measure can be found:

$$90° = 40° + a$$
$$a = 50°$$

(b) The triangle formed by the supplementary angle to $\angle b$ is part of a triangle with the vertical angle paired with $\angle a$ and the given angle of 27°. Since $\angle a = 50°$:

$$180° = (180° - b) + 50° + 27°$$
$$103° = 180° - b$$
$$-77° = -b$$
$$77° = b$$

(c) As they are part of a transversal crossing parallel lines, angles $\angle b$ and $\angle c$ are supplementary. Thus $\angle c = 103°$.

Two-Dimensional Shapes

TRIANGLES

A triangle is a three-sided figure with the sum of its interior angles being 180°. The **perimeter of any triangle** is found by summing the three side lengths; $P = a + b + c$. For an equilateral triangle, this is the same as $P = 3a$, where a is any side length, since all three sides are the same length.

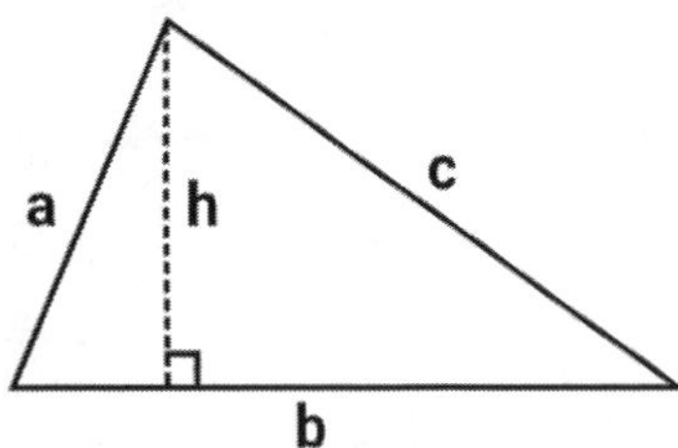

The **area of any triangle** can be found by taking half the product of one side length, referred to as the base and often given the variable b, and the perpendicular distance from that side to the opposite vertex, called the altitude or height and given the variable h. In equation form that is $A = \frac{1}{2}bh$.

Review Video: Area and Perimeter of a Triangle
Visit mometrix.com/academy and enter code: 853779

CLASSIFICATIONS OF TRIANGLES

A **scalene triangle** is a triangle with no congruent sides. A scalene triangle will also have three angles of different measures. The angle with the largest measure is opposite the longest side, and the angle with the smallest measure is opposite the shortest side. An **acute triangle** is a triangle whose three angles are all less than 90°. If two of the angles are equal, the acute triangle is also an **isosceles triangle**. An isosceles triangle will also have two congruent angles opposite the two congruent sides. If the three angles are all equal, the acute triangle is also an **equilateral triangle**. An equilateral triangle will also have three congruent angles, each 60°. All equilateral triangles are also acute triangles. An **obtuse triangle** is a triangle with exactly one angle greater than 90°. The other two angles may or may not be equal. If the two remaining angles are equal, the obtuse triangle is also an isosceles triangle. A **right triangle** is a triangle with exactly one angle equal to 90°. All right triangles follow the Pythagorean theorem. A right triangle can never be acute or obtuse.

The table below illustrates how each descriptor places a different restriction on the triangle:

Angles / Sides	Acute: All angles < 90°	Obtuse: One angle > 90°	Right: One angle = 90°
Scalene: No equal side lengths	$90° > \angle a > \angle b > \angle c$ $x > y > z$	$\angle a > 90° > \angle b > \angle c$ $x > y > z$	$90° = \angle a > \angle b > \angle c$ $x > y > z$
Isosceles: Two equal side lengths	$90° > \angle a, \angle b, or\ \angle c$ $\angle b = \angle c, \quad y = z$	$\angle a > 90° > \angle b = \angle c$ $x > y = z$	$\angle a = 90°$ $\angle b = \angle c = 45°$ $x > y = z$
Equilateral: Three equal side lengths	$60° = \angle a = \angle b = \angle c$ $x = y = z$		

Review Video: Introduction to Types of Triangles
Visit mometrix.com/academy and enter code: 511711

QUADRILATERALS

A **quadrilateral** is a closed two-dimensional geometric figure that has four straight sides. The sum of the interior angles of any quadrilateral is 360°.

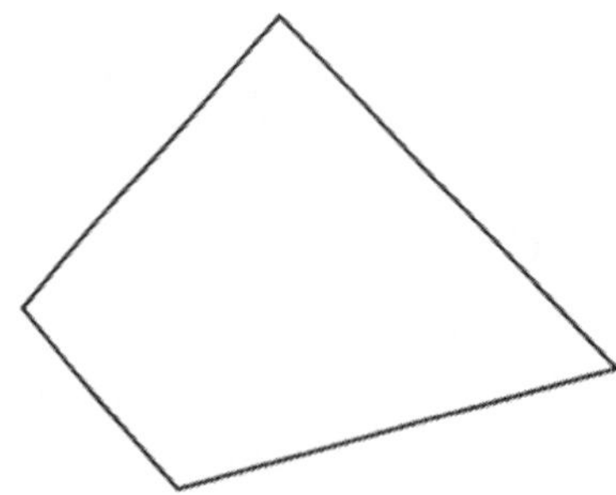

PARALLELOGRAM

A **parallelogram** is a quadrilateral that has two pairs of opposite parallel sides. As such it is a special type of trapezoid. The sides that are parallel are also congruent. The opposite interior angles are always congruent, and the consecutive interior angles are supplementary. The diagonals of a parallelogram divide each other. Each diagonal divides the parallelogram into two congruent triangles. A parallelogram has no line of symmetry, but does have 180-degree rotational symmetry about the midpoint.

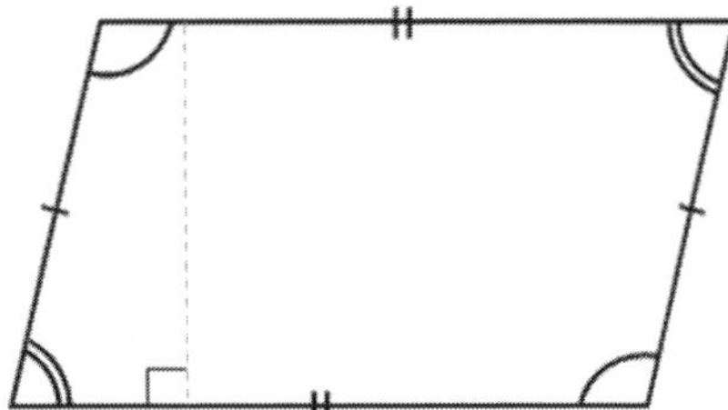

The **area of a parallelogram** is found by the formula $A = bh$, where b is the length of the base, and h is the height. Note that the base and height correspond to the length and width in a rectangle, so this formula would apply to rectangles as well. Do not confuse the height of a parallelogram with the length of the second side. The two are only the same measure in the case of a rectangle.

The **perimeter of a parallelogram** is found by the formula $P = 2a + 2b$ or $P = 2(a + b)$, where a and b are the lengths of the two sides.

Review Video: How to Find the Area and Perimeter of a Parallelogram
Visit mometrix.com/academy and enter code: 718313

RECTANGLE

A **rectangle** is a quadrilateral with four right angles. All rectangles are parallelograms and trapezoids, but not all parallelograms or trapezoids are rectangles. The diagonals of a rectangle are congruent. Rectangles have two lines of symmetry (through each pair of opposing midpoints) and 180-degree rotational symmetry about the midpoint.

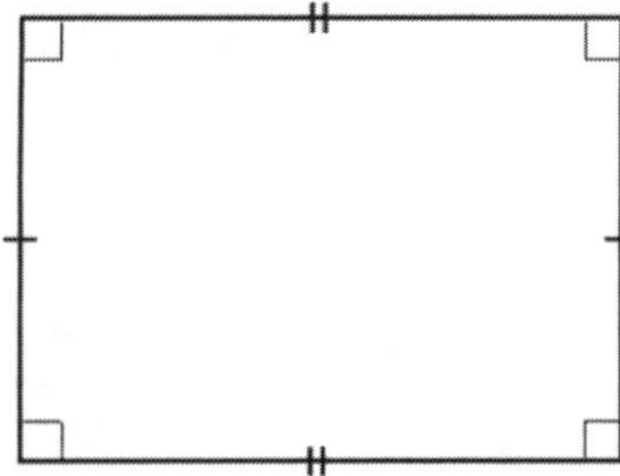

The **area of a rectangle** is found by the formula $A = lw$, where A is the area of the rectangle, l is the length (usually considered to be the longer side) and w is the width (usually considered to be the shorter side). The numbers for l and w are interchangeable.

The **perimeter of a rectangle** is found by the formula $P = 2l + 2w$ or $P = 2(l + w)$, where l is the length, and w is the width. It may be easier to add the length and width first and then double the result, as in the second formula.

SQUARE

A **square** is a quadrilateral with four right angles and four congruent sides. Squares satisfy the criteria of all other types of quadrilaterals. The diagonals of a square are congruent and perpendicular to each other. Squares have four lines of symmetry (through each pair of opposing midpoints and along each of the diagonals) as well as 90° rotational symmetry about the midpoint.

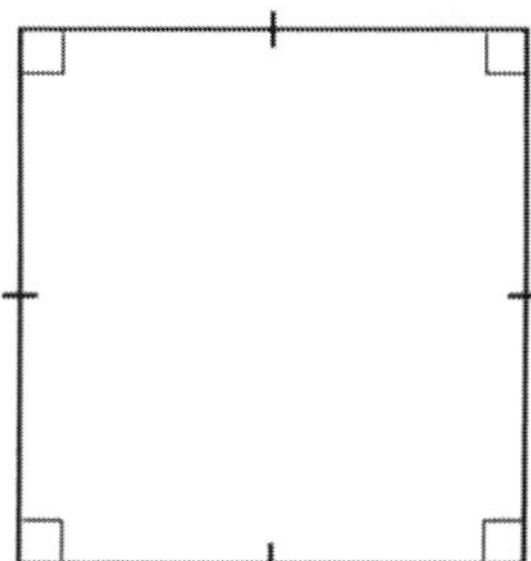

The **area of a square** is found by using the formula $A = s^2$, where s is the length of one side. The **perimeter of a square** is found by using the formula $P = 4s$, where s is the length of one side. Because all four sides are equal in a square, it is faster to multiply the length of one side by 4 than to add the same number four times. You could use the formulas for rectangles and get the same answer.

CIRCLES

The **center** of a circle is the single point from which every point on the circle is **equidistant**. The **radius** is a line segment that joins the center of the circle and any one point on the circle. All radii of a circle are equal. Circles that have the same center but not the same length of radii are **concentric**. The **diameter** is a line segment that passes through the center of the circle and has both endpoints on the circle. The length of the diameter is exactly twice the length of the radius. Point O in the diagram below is the center of the circle, segments $\overline{OX}$, $\overline{OY}$, and $\overline{OZ}$ are radii; and segment $\overline{XZ}$ is a diameter.

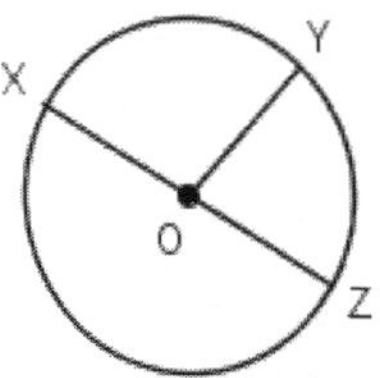

Review Video: Points of a Circle
Visit mometrix.com/academy and enter code: 420746

Review Video: The Diameter, Radius, and Circumference of Circles
Visit mometrix.com/academy and enter code: 448988

The **area of a circle** is found by the formula $A = \pi r^2$, where r is the length of the radius. If the diameter of the circle is given, remember to divide it in half to get the length of the radius before proceeding.

The **circumference** of a circle is found by the formula $C = 2\pi r$, where r is the radius. Again, remember to convert the diameter if you are given that measure rather than the radius.

Review Video: Area and Circumference of a Circle
Visit mometrix.com/academy and enter code: 243015

Practice

P1. Find the area and perimeter of the following quadrilaterals:

(a) A square with side length 2.5 cm

(b) A parallelogram with height 3 m, base 4 m, and other side 6 m

(c) A rhombus with diagonals 15 in and 20 in

Practice Solutions

P1. (a) $A = s^2 = (2.5 \text{ cm})^2 = 6.25 \text{ cm}^2$; $P = 4s = 4 \times 2.5 \text{ cm} = 10 \text{ cm}$

(b) $A = bh = (3 \text{ m})(4 \text{ m}) = 12 \text{ m}^2$; $P = 2a + 2b = 2 \times 6 \text{ m} + 2 \times 4 \text{ m} = 20 \text{ m}$

(c) $A = \frac{d_1 d_2}{2} = \frac{(15 \text{ in})(20 \text{ in})}{2} = 150 \text{ in}^2$;
$P = 2\sqrt{(d_1)^2 + (d_2)^2} = 2\sqrt{(15 \text{ in})^2 + (20 \text{ in})^2} = 2\sqrt{625 \text{ in}^2} = 50 \text{ in}$

Three-Dimensional Shapes

SOLIDS

The **surface area of a solid object** is the area of all sides or exterior surfaces. For objects such as prisms and pyramids, a further distinction is made between base surface area (B) and lateral surface area (LA). For a prism or cylinder, the total surface area (SA) is $SA = LA + 2B$.

Review Video: How to Calculate the Volume of 3D Objects
Visit mometrix.com/academy and enter code: 163343

The **surface area of a sphere** can be found by the formula $A = 4\pi r^2$, where r is the radius. The **volume** is given by the formula $V = \frac{4}{3}\pi r^3$, where r is the radius. Both quantities are generally given in terms of π.

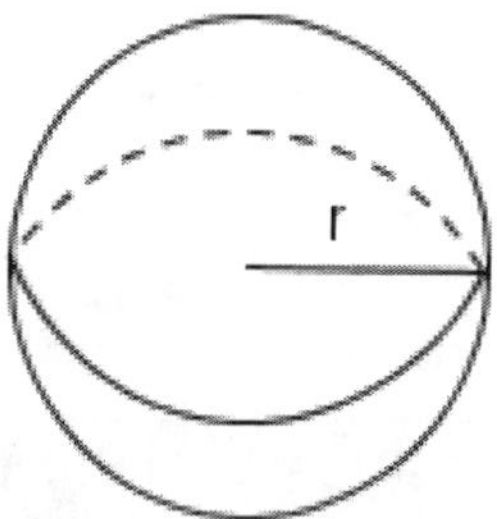

Review Video: Volume and Surface Area of a Sphere
Visit mometrix.com/academy and enter code: 786928

The **volume of any prism** is found by the formula $V = Bh$, where B is the area of the base, and h is the height (perpendicular distance between the bases). The **surface area of any prism** is the sum of the areas of both bases and all sides. It can be calculated as $SA = 2B + Ph$, where P is the perimeter of the base.

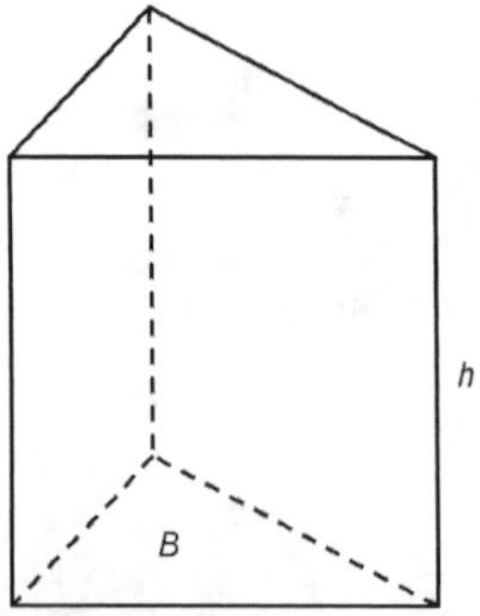

Review Video: Volume and Surface Area of a Prism
Visit mometrix.com/academy and enter code: 420158

For a rectangular prism, the **volume** can be found by the formula $V = lwh$, where V is the volume, l is the length, w is the width, and h is the height. The **surface area** can be calculated as $SA = 2lw + 2hl + 2wh$ or $SA = 2(lw + hl + wh)$.

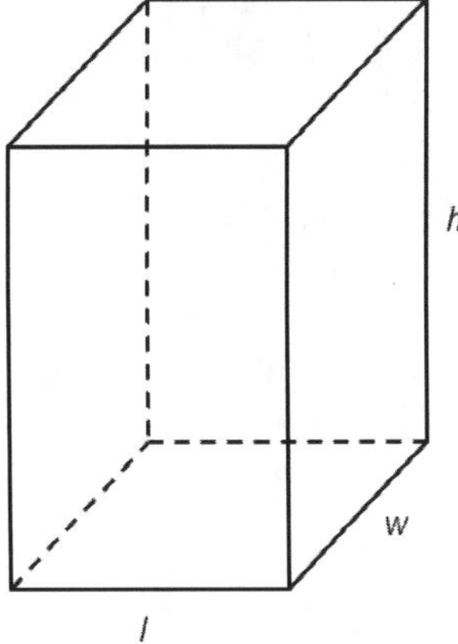

Review Video: Volume and Surface Area of a Rectangular Prism
Visit mometrix.com/academy and enter code: 282814

The **volume of a cube** can be found by the formula $V = s^3$, where s is the length of a side. The **surface area of a cube** is calculated as $SA = 6s^2$, where SA is the total surface area and s is the length of a side. These formulas are the same as the ones used for the volume and surface area of a rectangular prism, but simplified since all three quantities (length, width, and height) are the same.

Review Video: Volume and Surface Area of a Cube
Visit mometrix.com/academy and enter code: 664455

The **volume of a cylinder** can be calculated by the formula $V = \pi r^2 h$, where r is the radius, and h is the height. The **surface area of a cylinder** can be found by the formula $SA = 2\pi r^2 + 2\pi rh$. The first term is the base area multiplied by two, and the second term is the perimeter of the base multiplied by the height.

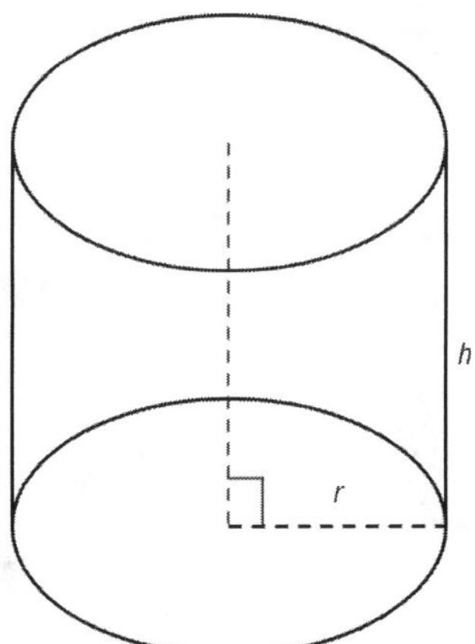

Review Video: Volume and Surface Area of a Right Circular Cylinder
Visit mometrix.com/academy and enter code: 226463

Practice

P1. Find the surface area and volume of the following solids:

(a) A cylinder with radius 5 m and height 0.5 m.

(b) A trapezoidal prism with base area of 254 mm^2, base perimeter 74 mm, and height 10 mm.

Practice Solutions

P1. (a) $SA = 2\pi r^2 + 2\pi rh = 2\pi(5\text{ m})^2 + 2\pi(5\text{ m})(0.5\text{ m}) = 55\pi\text{ m}^2 \approx 172.79\text{ m}^2$;
$V = \pi r^2 h = \pi(5\text{ m})^2(0.5\text{ m}) = 12.5\pi\text{ m}^3 \approx 39.27\text{ m}^3$

(b) $SA = 2B + Ph = 2(254\text{ mm}^2) + (74\text{ mm})(10\text{ mm}) = 1{,}248\text{ mm}^2$;
$V = Bh = (254\text{ mm}^2)(10\text{ mm}) = 2{,}540\text{ mm}^3$

Arithmetic Reasoning Practice Questions

1. A couple plans to buy a car. They have $569 in a joint bank account. The man has $293 in additional cash and the woman has $189. What is the most expensive down payment they will be able to afford?

a. $482
b. $758
c. $862
d. $1051
e. $1121

2. The temperature of a cup of coffee is 98 degrees. If its temperature decreases by 2 degrees per minute, what will its temperature be after 4 minutes?

a. 100 degrees
b. 98 degrees
c. 94 degrees
d. 90 degrees
e. 88 degrees

3. A man's lawn grass is 3 inches high. He mows the lawn and cuts off 30% of its height. How tall will the grass be after the lawn is mowed?

a. 0.9 inches
b. 2.1 inches
c. 2.7 inches
d. 2.9 inches
e. 3.3 inches

4. Three outlets are selling concert tickets. One ticket outlet sells 432; another outlet sells 238; the third outlet sells 123. How many concert tickets were sold in total?

a. 361
b. 555
c. 670
d. 793
e. 823

5. A boy has a bag with 26 pieces of candy inside. He eats 8 pieces of candy, then divides the rest evenly between two friends. How many pieces of candy will each friend get?

a. 7
b. 9
c. 11
d. 13
e. 18

Practice Answers

1. D: Calculate the total amount of money the couple has available to spend, which is the amount in the joint bank account and the amount that each has:

$$\$569 + \$293 + \$189 = \$1{,}051$$

2. D: First, find out what the total temperature decrease will be after 4 minutes:

$$2 \times 4 = 8 \text{ degrees}$$

Then, subtract that from the original temperature: $98 - 8 = 90$ degrees

3. B: First, calculate 30% of 3 inches: $3 \times 0.3 = 0.9$ inches

Then, subtract this value from the original length: $3 - 0.9 = 2.1$

4. D: Add the number of tickets that were sold at each location to get the total number of tickets sold: $432 + 238 + 123 = 793$

5. B: First, figure out how many pieces of candy are in the bag before they are divided:

$$26 - 8 = 18$$

Then, figure out how many pieces each friend will get by dividing by 2: $\frac{18}{2} = 9$

Math Knowledge Practice Questions

1. If the volume of a cube is 8 cm^3, what is the length of one side of the cube?

a. 1 cm
b. 2 cm
c. 3 cm
d. 4 cm
e. 8 cm

2. Simplify the following expression:

$$(2x^2 + 3)(2x - 1)$$

a. $4x^3 - 2x^2 + 6x - 3$
b. $2x^2 + 6x - 3$
c. $4x^3 - 2x^2 + 6x + 3$
d. $4x^3 - 2x^2 - 6x - 3$
e. $2x^2 - 6x + 3$

3. Simplify the following expression

$$(2x^4y^7m^2z) \times (5x^2y^3m^8)$$

a. $10x^6y^9m^{10}z$
b. $7x^6y^{10}m^{10}z$
c. $10x^5y^{10}m^{10}z$
d. $10x^6y^{10}m^{10}z$
e. $7x^5y^9m^{10}z$

4. A classroom contains 13 boys and 18 girls. If a student's name is chosen randomly, what is the probability it will be a girl's name?

a. 36%
b. 42%
c. 58%
d. 72%
e. 84%

5. If $x - 9 = 2x + 10$, what is the value of x?

a. -19
b. 19
c. 6.3
d. -6.3
e. None of the above

Practice Answers

1. B: The volume of a cube is calculated by cubing the length of any one side of the cube (All sides have the same length). Therefore, the volume of a cube equals s^3, where s is the length of any side.

In this case, we can say that $s \times s \times s = 8$, so we must determine which number cubed equals 8.

The answer is 2 cm: $2 \times 2 \times 2 = 8$, or $2 \text{ cm} \times 2 \text{ cm} \times 2 \text{ cm} = 8 \text{ cm}^3$.

2. A: Use the FOIL (first, outside, inside, last) to expand the expression:

$$4x^3 - 2x^2 + 6x - 3$$

There are no like terms, so the expression cannot be simplified any further.

3. D: To simplify this expression, recall that the law of exponents states that $x^m x^n = x^{m+n}$. Take each variable in turn and apply this law:

$$x^4x^2 = x^6; y^7y^3 = y^{10}; m^2m^8 = m^{10}$$

Putting these all together along with the constants and the unaltered variable z yields the full simplified expression:

$$10x^6y^{10}m^{10}z$$

4. C: First, find the total number of students in the classroom:

$$13 + 18 = 31$$

There is an 18 in 31 chance that a name chosen randomly will be a girl's name. To express this as a percentage, divide 18 by 31 and multiply the result by 100%:

$$\frac{18}{31} = 0.58 \times 100\% = 58\%$$

5. A: First, gather all of the terms that contain an x on the left side of the equation to make it easier to solve:

$$x - 2x - 9 = 10$$

$$-x - 9 = 10$$

Then, add nine to both sides to isolate the x:

$$-x - 9 + 9 = 10 + 9$$

$$-x = 19$$

Finally, divide by -1 to solve for x:

$$\frac{-x}{-1} = \frac{19}{-1}$$

$$x = -19$$

Word Knowledge

What Do Word Knowledge Questions Look Like?

Word knowledge questions follow a very simple format. You will be given a word and you must select the word that is closest in meaning to the given word, from the choices given.

How Can I Prepare?

Unfortunately, there is no easy way to prepare for this section. The questions test your vocabulary and if you don't have a very large vocabulary, this will probably be one of your harder sections to prepare for. The best way to build a large, long-lasting vocabulary is to read extensively, but you may not have time for that if your test is soon. Cramming with vocabulary lists is one way to build up a short-term vocabulary. Learning common prefixes and suffixes is another valuable use of your limited time. Whether or not you decide you need to add to your vocabulary before the test, there are a few strategies you can use to get the most out of the words you already know.

What Strategies Can I Use?

Nearly and Perfect Synonyms

You must determine which of the provided choices has the best similar definition as a certain word. **Nearly similar** may often be more correct, because the goal is to test your understanding of the nuances, or little differences, between words. A perfect match may not exist, so don't be concerned if your answer choice is not a complete synonym. Focus upon edging closer to the word. Eliminate the words that you know aren't correct first. Then narrow your search. Cross out the words that are the least similar to the main word until you are left with the one that is the most similar.

Prefixes

Take advantage of every clue that the word might include. Prefixes and suffixes can be a huge help. Usually, they allow you to determine a word's basic meaning. *Pre-* means before, *post-* means after, *pro-* is positive, *de-* is negative. From these prefixes and suffixes, you can get an idea of the general meaning of the word and look for its opposite. Be sure to watch out for traps, though. Just because *con* is the opposite of *pro*, doesn't necessarily mean *congress* is the opposite of *progress*!

Positive vs. Negative

Many words can be easily determined to be a positive word or a negative word. Words such as despicable, gruesome, and bleak are all **negative**. Words such as ecstatic, praiseworthy, and magnificent are all **positive**. You will be surprised at how many words can be viewed as either positive or negative. Once that is determined, you can quickly eliminate any other words with an opposite meaning and focus on those that have the same characteristic, whether positive or negative.

Word Strength

Part of the challenge is determining the most nearly similar word. This is particularly true when two words seem to be similar. When analyzing a word, determine how strong it is. For example, stupendous and good are both positive words.

However, stupendous is a much stronger positive adjective than good. Also, towering or gigantic are stronger words than tall or large. Search for an answer choice that is similar and also has the same strength. If the main word is weak, look for similar words that are also weak. If the main word is strong, look for similar words that are also strong.

Type and Topic

Another key is what type of word is the main word. If the main word is an adjective describing height, then look for the answer to be an adjective describing height as well. Match both the type and topic of the main word. The **type** refers to the parts of speech, whether the word is an adjective, adverb, noun, or verb. The **topic** refers to what sort of definition or thing the word refers to, such as sizes or fashion styles.

Form a Sentence

Many words seem more natural in a sentence. *Specious* reasoning, *irresistible* force, and *uncanny* resemblance are just a few of the word combinations that usually go together. When faced with an uncommon word that you barely understand, try to put the word in a sentence that makes sense. It will help you to understand the word's meaning. Once you have a good descriptive sentence that utilizes the main word properly, plug in the answer choices and see if the sentence still has the same meaning with each answer choice. The answer choice that maintains the meaning of the sentence is correct!

Use Replacements

Using a sentence is a great help because it puts the word into a proper perspective. Since the exam actually gives you a sentence, you don't always have to create your own (though in many cases the sentence won't be helpful). Read the provided sentence, picking out the main word. Then read the sentence again and again, each time replacing the main word with one of the answer choices. The correct answer should "sound" right and fit.

Example: The desert landscape was desolate. Desolate means

a. Cheerful
b. Creepy
c. Excited
d. Forlorn

After reading the example sentence, begin replacing "desolate" with each of the answer choices. Does "the desert landscape was cheerful, creepy, excited, or forlorn" sound right? Deserts are typically hot, empty, and rugged environments, probably not *cheerful*, or *excited*. While *creepy* might sound right, that word would be more appropriate for a haunted house. But "the desert landscape was forlorn" has a certain ring to it and would be correct. *Forlorn* means abandoned or lonely, *desolate* similarly means empty, bleak, or barren. Both of these words make sense when used to convey the lonely feeling one may experience when looking at an empty desert landscape.

Eliminate Similar Choices

If you don't know the word, don't worry. Remember that there is only one correct answer choice. If you can find a common relationship between a set of answer choices, then you know they are wrong. Find the answer choice that does not have a common relationship to the other answer choices and it will be the correct answer.

Example: Laconic most nearly means

a. Wordy
b. Talkative
c. Expressive
d. Quiet

In this example, the first three choices are all similar. Even if you don't know that laconic means the same as quiet, you know that "quiet" must be correct, because the other three choices are all virtually the same. They are all the same, so they must all be wrong. The one that is different must be correct. So, don't worry if you don't know a word. Focus on the answer choices that you do understand and see if you can identify similarities. Even identifying two words that are similar will allow you to eliminate those two answer choices. Because they are similar, they are either both right or both wrong, and since they can't both be right, they must both be wrong.

Example: He worked slowly, moving the leather back and forth until it was ____.

a. Rough
b. Hard
c. Stiff
d. Pliable

In this example the first three choices are all similar. *Hard* and *stiff* are both synonyms, and *rough*, while not quite a synonym, is not the opposite of *hard* or *stiff*. Even without knowing what pliable means, it has to be correct, because you know the other three answer choices mean similar things.

Adjectives Give it Away

Words mean things and are added to sentences for a reason. Adjectives in particular may be the clue to determining which answer choice is correct.

Example: The brilliant scientist made several discoveries that were

a. Dull
b. Dazzling

Look at the adjectives first to help determine what makes sense. A "brilliant" or smart scientist would make dazzling discoveries, rather than dull ones. Without that simple adjective, no answer choice is clear.

Use Logic

Ask yourself questions about each answer choice to see if they are logical.

Example: In the distance, the deep pounding resonance of the drums could be

a. Seen
b. Heard

Would resonating pounding be seen or would resonating pounding be heard?

The Trap of Familiarity

Don't just choose a word because you recognize it. On difficult questions, you may only recognize one or two words. The exam doesn't have "make-believe words" on it, so don't think that just because you only recognize one word means that word must be correct. If you don't recognize most of the words, then focus on the ones that you do recognize. Are any of them correct? Try your best to determine if they fit the sentence. If any of them do, you have your answer, but if not, eliminate them and guess from among the remaining options.

Practice Questions

1. <u>Sketch</u> most nearly means

a. Skip
b. Scope
c. Draw
d. Drain
e. Drip

2. The child was <u>frightened</u> by the movie.

a. Scared
b. Entertained
c. Amused
d. Saddened
e. Delighted

3. <u>Sever</u> most nearly means

a. Hard
b. Cut
c. Add
d. Soft
e. Change

4. Her prediction was <u>accurate</u>.

a. False
b. Funny
c. Planned
d. Assumed
e. Correct

5. <u>Taunt</u> most nearly means

a. Truant
b. Tried
c. Tight
d. Tease
e. Tired

6. Her concern for him was <u>sincere.</u>

a. Intense
b. Genuine
c. Brief
d. Misunderstood
e. Repetitive

7. <u>Disclose</u> most nearly means

a. Reveal
b. Return
c. Near
d. Hide
e. Conceal

8. He <u>sprinted</u> down the road.

a. Crawled
b. Walked
c. Hurried
d. Ran
e. Drove

9. The naughty child was <u>disciplined</u>.

a. Upset
b. Punished
c. Hidden
d. Bad
e. Surprised

10. <u>Seize</u> most nearly means

a. Grab
b. Release
c. Tell
d. Fight
e. Give

Practice Answers

1. C: To sketch something is to draw something. Saying somebody was planning to sketch a landscape and saying they were going to draw a landscape conveys the same meaning.

2. A: To say somebody is frightened is the same as saying they are scared or afraid.

3. B: To sever something is to cut something. For example, to say that somebody severed all ties with someone else means that they have cut those ties. It can also be used to describe the cutting of objects. For example, saying someone severed a rope with a knife means they cut the rope.

4. E: Describing something as accurate and describing it as correct conveys the same meaning. For example, saying somebody accurately predicted something is the same as saying they correctly predicted something.

5. D: To taunt somebody is to tease them. To say somebody taunted another person conveys the same meaning as saying somebody teased another person. Usually, teasing and taunting is understood to be a mean practice.

6. B: To say something is sincere means that it is genuine or real. For example, saying someone showed sincere concern means that their concern was genuine, not fake.

7. A: To disclose something is to reveal something. For example, saying somebody disclosed something they had been hiding is the same as saying they revealed it.

8. D: To sprint is to run. Saying that somebody sprinted to their destination and saying they ran to their destination conveys the same meaning.

9. B: To discipline someone for their undesirable actions or behaviors is to punish them. Saying a child was disciplined for his actions and saying he was punished conveys the same meaning.

10. A: To seize something is to take hold of it or grab it. For example, saying the woman seized the man's arm is the same as saying she grabbed it.

Reading Comprehension

What Do Reading Comprehension Questions Look Like?

The questions in this section will follow the typical format of reading comprehension questions on standardized tests. You'll be given a passage to read, several paragraphs in length, and then be shown several questions about the passage. Each question will have five possible answers to choose from; only one answer will be correct.

What Are They Testing?

The questions in this section are testing your ability to read and understand written material. Most people taking the AFOQT will have a level of reading ability that's quite a bit higher than the reading ability of the average American, and the passages in this section will reflect that fact. They will tend to be written on the level of articles in academic and scientific publications, and not at the level of articles one reads in most magazines or newspapers, or on most websites.

However, don't take this to mean that you'll need any specialized scientific or technical knowledge to do well on these questions; you won't. Each passage, while written on a higher level than average, and possibly on a scientific or technical subject, will assume no specialized knowledge on the part of the reader about the subject matter.

Some questions will test your ability to remember or quickly locate facts in the passage, and these questions will generally not use the same words or phrases used in the passage. Other questions will require you to make judgments about what you've read, such as choosing a statement the author would agree or disagree with, perceiving the author's main point, or detecting the author's purpose in writing the passage.

How Can I Prepare?

The vast majority of Americans engage in very little reading these days, beyond texts and social media. Needless to say, that kind of reading won't suffice to prepare you for the AFOQT. Even if you do some legitimate reading from time to time, odds are that you read much less than the average aspiring Air Force officer of 30 years ago did, and you too likely need to brush up on your reading comprehension skills.

In either case, you'll want to set aside regular practice sessions where you read higher level reading passages than you're used to and ask yourself a lot of questions after each passage.

- What is the author's main point?
- What kind of statements would the author be likely to agree with or disagree with?
- Is the passage educational, persuasive, argumentative, etc.?
- What are some of the secondary points the author makes?
- Is the article fact based, or merely stating an opinion?
- Has the author made a good case?
- If you think he has, what do you base this on?
- If not, where is his argument or article weak?

Libraries have a lot of great resources you can take advantage of to help you improve your reading comprehension skills.

Practice Questions

Sample Passage

Historically, the term pilot error has been used to describe an accident in which an action or decision made by the pilot was the cause or a contributing factor that led to the accident. This definition also includes the pilot's failure to make a correct decision or take proper action. From a broader perspective, the phrase human factors related more aptly describes these accidents. A single decision or event does not lead to an accident, but a series of events, and the resultant decisions together form a chain of events leading to an outcome.

In his article *Accident-Prone Pilots*, Dr. Patrick R. Veillette uses the history of Captain Everyman to demonstrate how aircraft accidents are caused more by a chain of poor choices rather than one single poor choice. In the case of Captain Everyman, after a gear-up landing accident, he became involved in another accident while taxiing a Beech 58P Baron out of the ramp. Interrupted by a radio call from the 17-11 dispatcher, Everyman neglected to complete the fuel crossfeed check before taking off. Everyman, who was flying solo, left the right-fuel selector in the cross-feed position. Once aloft and cruising, he noticed a right roll tendency and corrected with aileron trim. He did not realize that both engines were feeding off the left wing's tank, making the wing lighter.

After two hours of flight, the right engine quit when Everyman was flying along a deep canyon gorge. While he was trying to troubleshoot the cause of the right engine's failure, the left engine quit. Everyman landed the aircraft on a river sand bar but it sank into ten feet of water.

Several years later, Everyman flew a de Havilland Twin Otter to deliver supplies to a remote location. When he returned to home base and landed, the aircraft veered sharply to the left, departed the runway, and ran into a marsh 375 feet from the runway. The airframe and engines sustained considerable damage. Upon inspecting the wreck, accident investigators found the nose wheel steering tiller in the fully deflected position. Both the after-takeoff and before-landing checklists required the tiller to be placed in the neutral position. Everyman had overlooked this item.

Now, is Everyman accident prone or just unlucky? Skipping details on a checklist appears to be a common theme in the preceding accidents. While most pilots have made similar mistakes, these errors were probably caught prior to a mishap due to extra margin, good warning systems, a sharp copilot, or just good luck. What makes a pilot less prone to accidents?

The successful pilot possesses the ability to concentrate, manage workloads, and monitor and perform several simultaneous tasks. Some of the latest psychological screenings used in aviation test applicants for their ability to multitask, measuring both accuracy and the individual's ability to focus attention on several subjects simultaneously. The FAA oversaw an extensive research study on the similarities and dissimilarities of accident-free pilots and those who were not. The project surveyed over 4,000 pilots, half of whom had clean records while the other half had been involved in an accident.

Five traits were discovered in pilots prone to having accidents. These pilots:

- Have disdain toward rules.
- Have very high correlation between accidents on their flying records and safety violations on their driving records.
- Frequently fall into the thrill and adventure seeking personality category.
- Are impulsive rather than methodical and disciplined, both in information gathering and in speed and selection of actions to be taken.
- Show a disregard for or under-utilization of outside sources of information, including copilots, flight attendants, flight service personnel, flight instructors, and air traffic controllers.

(Questions on the following page)

1. The primary purpose of the passage is to

a. Criticize Captain Everyman.
b. Advocate for more comprehensive pilot training.
c. Reduce flight accidents.
d. Entertain the reader with a story of pilot incompetence.
e. Describe some characteristics that correlate with flight accidents.

2. Which of the following statements about Captain Everyman is NOT supported by the passage?

a. Captain Everyman is a reckless thrill-seeker.
b. Captain Everyman is easily distracted.
c. Captain Everyman is not methodical in his work.
d. Captain Everyman can fly a variety of aircraft.
e. Captain Everyman does not double-check his work.

3. Why does the author prefer to describe the main cause of accidents as human factors rather than pilot error?

a. Because most accidents are caused by multiple poor decisions rather than a single error.
b. Because most accidents are caused by faulty equipment.
c. Because most accidents can be traced to a single mistake.
d. Because many accidents are caused by miscommunication with the control tower.
e. Because pilots can be subject to criminal charges of negligence.

4. In the fifth paragraph, *prone* most nearly means

a. Immobile
b. Supine
c. Likely to have
d. Lying down
e. Encouraging

5. With which one of the following claims about pilots would the author most likely agree?

a. Pilots should not be allowed to fly solo until they are thirty years old.
b. A good pilot must be able to keep track of many different things simultaneously.
c. Pilots should be restricted to flying one type of plane.
d. Pilots should never fly solo.
e. Some pilots never make mistakes.

Practice Answers

1. E: Describing some characteristics that correlate with flight accidents is the primary purpose of the passage. The author explains how most flight accidents are the result of several mistakes in sequence, and how inattention, inability to multi-task, and carelessness are common characteristics of the accident-prone pilot.

2. A: The passage presents a critical portrait of Captain Everyman, but it never directly suggests that he is a reckless thrill-seeker. The passage does state that this personality type is correlated with flight accidents, but, in the example scenarios, the causes of Captain Everyman's accidents are carelessness and distraction rather than recklessness.

3. A: The author prefers saying that the main cause of accidents is human factors, not simply pilot error, because accidents are rarely the result of a single mistake, but rather are typically caused by a series of mistakes, oversights, or general carelessness over a period of time. The author makes this point in the first paragraph of the passage.

4. C: In the fifth paragraph, *prone* most nearly means *likely to have*. The author is discussing pilots who are accident prone, meaning that they are more likely to have accidents. Prone can also mean *lying down*, or *supine*, but it does not have that meaning in this context.

5. B: The author would most likely agree that a good pilot must be able to keep track of many different things simultaneously. Specifically, the author emphasizes the importance of multi-tasking as a pilot. There is no indication in the passage that age or flying different types of aircraft is correlated with accidents, and there is no argument that pilots should never fly solo. Finally, the author explicitly states that all pilots make mistakes, though some are better than others at correcting them.

Situational Judgment

What Do Situational Judgment Questions Look Like?

All situational judgment questions will have a similar format. Test takers will be given a scenario which requires some action to be taken to solve a problem that has come up, usually involving interpersonal and/or official relationships between an officer and his subordinates and/or his superiors. The test taker will then be shown several possible actions that could be taken, and will be told to select both the **most effective** and the **least effective** of the actions listed.

What Are Situational Judgment Questions Testing?

This is a newer section of the AFOQT, added to make the test a better predictor of success as an Air Force officer. These questions are primarily focused on testing a person in the areas of judgment and self-sufficient decision-making abilities. In order to do well on this section, test takers will need to show that they can lead subordinates and solve problems independently by using their core competencies of resource management, communication, innovation, mentoring, leadership, professionalism, and integrity.

How Can I Prepare?

Situational judgment questions aren't the kind of questions that lend themselves easily to preparation, as there really isn't any material for a person to review and memorize. However, you should keep in mind the qualities listed above (resource management, communication, innovation, mentoring, leadership, professionalism, and integrity) when answering questions. Your answers should reflect these qualities as much as possible. Also, you should avoid choosing any answer which involves going to a superior for advice or help unless there are no other viable options, or discussing a person's shortcomings behind their back no matter their rank. Officers are expected to be resourceful men and women of character.

Physical Science

What Do Physical Science Questions Look Like?

Physical science questions primarily test your understanding of scientific terms. You won't be asked to perform complex physics calculations or balance a chemical reaction. The purpose of this section is to make sure you paid attention in high school science and retained some of the general concepts.

How Can I Prepare?

The best way to prepare for these questions is to brush up on your science terminology and concepts. We've included a glossary of terms here to give you head start, but it's a good idea to find a high school physical science textbook and look through the full glossary in there if you want a more thorough review.

A

Absolute zero: The lowest possible temperature (−273.15 °C).

Atmospheric pressure: The pressure exerted by the gases in the air. Units of measurement are kilopascals (kPa), atmospheres (atm), millimeters of mercury (mmHg) and Torr. Standard atmospheric pressure is 100 kPa, 1atm, 760 mmHg, or 760 Torr.

Atom: The smallest particle of an element; a nucleus and its surrounding electrons.

Atomic mass: The mass of an atom measured in atomic mass units (amu). An atomic mass unit is equal to one-twelfth of the atom of carbon-12. Atomic mass is now more generally used instead of atomic weight. Example: the atomic mass of chlorine is about 35 amu.

Atomic number: Also known as the proton number, it is the number of electrons or the number of protons in an atom. Example: the atomic number of gold is 79.

Atomic weight: A common term used to mean the average molar mass of an element. This is the mass per mole of atoms. Example: the atomic weight of chlorine is about 35 g/mol.

B

Boiling point: The temperature at which a substance undergoes a phase change from a liquid to a gas.

C

Celsius scale (°C): A temperature scale on which the freezing point of water is at 0 degrees and the normal boiling point at standard atmospheric pressure is 100 degrees.

Change of state: A change between two of the three states of matter, solid, liquid and gas. Example: when water evaporates it changes from a liquid to a gaseous state.

Compound: A chemical consisting of two or more elements chemically bonded together. Example: Calcium can combine with carbon and oxygen to make calcium carbonate ($CaCO_3$), a compound of all three elements.

Condensation: The formation of a liquid from a gas. This is a change of state, also called a phase change.

Conduction: (1) the exchange of heat (heat conduction) by contact with another object, or (2) allowing the flow of electrons (electrical conduction).

Convection: The exchange of heat energy with the surroundings produced by the flow of a fluid due to being heated or cooled.

D

Decay (radioactive decay): The way that a radioactive element changes into another element due to loss of mass through radiation. Example: uranium 238 decays with the loss of an alpha particle to form thorium 234.

Density: The mass per unit volume (e.g., g/cm^3).

Diffusion: The slow mixing of one substance with another until the two substances are evenly mixed. Mixing occurs because of differences in concentration within the mixture. Diffusion works rapidly with gases, very slowly with liquids.

Dissolve: To break down a substance in a solution without causing a reaction.

E

Electrical potential: The energy produced by an electrochemical cell and measured by the voltage or electromotive force (emf).

Electron: A tiny, negatively charged particle that is part of an atom. The flow of electrons through a solid material such as a wire produces an electric current.

Element: A substance that cannot be decomposed into a simpler substance by chemical means. Examples: calcium, iron, gold.

Explosive: A substance which, when a shock is applied to it, decomposes very rapidly, releasing a very large amount of heat and creating a large volume of gases as a shock wave.

F

Fluid: Able to flow; either a liquid or a gas.

Freezing point: The temperature at which a substance undergoes a phase change from a liquid to a solid. It is the same temperature as the melting point. At any temperature below this point the substance will freeze.

G

Gamma rays: Waves of radiation produced as the nucleus of a radioactive element rearranges itself into a tighter cluster of protons and neutrons. Gamma rays carry enough energy to damage living cells.

Gas/gaseous phase: A form of matter in which the molecules form no definite shape and are free to move about to uniformly fill any vessel they are put in. A gas can easily be compressed into a much smaller volume.

Group: A vertical column in the Periodic Table. There are eight groups in the table. Their numbers correspond to the number of electrons in the outer shell of the atoms in the group. Example: Group 2 contains beryllium, magnesium, calcium, strontium, barium, and radium.

H

Half-life: The time it takes for the radiation coming from a sample of a radioactive element to decrease by half.

Heat: The energy that is transferred when a substance is at a different temperature to that of its surroundings.

Heat capacity: The ratio of the heat supplied to a substance, compared with the rise in temperature that is produced.

Heat of combustion: The amount of heat given off by a mole of a substance during combustion. This heat is a property of the substance and is the same no matter what kind of combustion is involved. Example: The heat of combustion of carbon is $94.14 \text{ kcal} \times -4.18 \text{ kJ/kcal} = -393.5 \text{ kJ}$.

I

Ion: An atom, or group of atoms, that has gained or lost one or more electrons and so developed an electrical charge. Ions behave differently from electrically neutral atoms and molecules. They can move in an electric field, and they can also bind strongly to solvent molecules such as water. Positively charged ions are called cations; negatively charged ions are called anions. Ions can carry an electrical current through solutions.

Isotope: One of two or more atoms of the same element that have the same number of protons in their nucleus (atomic number), but which have a different number of neutrons (atomic mass). Example: carbon-12 and carbon-14.

K

Kinetic energy: The energy an object has by virtue of its being in motion.

L

Latent heat: The amount of heat that is absorbed or released during the process of changing state between gas, liquid, or solid. For example, heat is absorbed when a substance melts, and it is released again when the substance solidifies.

Liquid/liquid phase: A form of matter that has a fixed volume but no fixed shape.

M

Mass: The amount of matter in an object. In everyday use the word *weight* is often used (somewhat incorrectly) to mean mass.

Matter: Anything that has mass and takes up space.

Melting point: The temperature at which a substance changes state from a solid phase to a liquid phase. It is the same as freezing point. At any temperature above this point the substance will melt.

Metal: A class of elements that is a good conductor of electricity and heat, has a metallic luster, is malleable and ductile, forms cations and has oxides that are bases. Metals are formed as cations held together by a sea of electrons. A metal may also be an alloy of these elements. Example: sodium, calcium, gold.

Mixture: A material that can be separated into two or more substances using physical means. Example: a mixture of copper (II) sulfate and cadmium sulfide can be separated by filtration.

Mole: 1 mole is the amount of a substance which contains Avogadro's number (about 6×10^{23}) of particles. Example: 1 mole of carbon-12 weighs exactly 12 g.

Molecule: A group of two or more atoms held together by chemical bonds. Example: O_2.

N

Neutron: A particle inside the nucleus of an atom that is neutral and has no charge.

Newton (N): The unit of force required to give one kilogram an acceleration of one meter per second every second ($1\ m/s^2$).

Noble gases: The members of Group 8 of the Periodic Table: helium, neon, argon, krypton, xenon, and radon. These gases are almost entirely unreactive.

Nucleus: The small, positively charged particle at the center of an atom. The nucleus is responsible for most of the mass of an atom.

P

Period: A row in the Periodic Table.

Periodic Table: A chart organizing elements by atomic number and chemical properties into groups and periods.

Phase: A particular state of matter. A substance may exist as a solid, liquid or gas and may change between these phases with addition or removal of energy. Examples: ice, liquid and vapor are the three phases of water. Ice undergoes a phase change to water when heat energy is added.

Photon: A parcel of light energy.

Potential energy: The energy an object has by virtue of its position or orientation, most commonly its height above some reference point, or amount of compression as with a spring.

Pressure: The force per unit area measured in Pascals.

Proton: A positively charged particle in the nucleus of an atom that balances out the charge of the surrounding electrons.

R

Radiation: The exchange of energy with the surroundings through the transmission of waves or particles of energy. Radiation is a form of energy transfer that can happen through space; no intervening medium is required (as would be the case for conduction and convection).

S

Solid/solid phase: A rigid form of matter which maintains its shape, whatever its container.

Table Reading

What Are These Questions Testing?

The table reading section tests your ability to quickly and accurately locate information stored in a table. The questions require you to find a particular number in a table given a set of coordinates.

What Is the Question Format?

The questions will be given in groups of around 5 questions, where each group will refer to a table of numbers, with column and row headers. Each question will give an ordered pair of numbers that indicate the location in the table where the correct answer can be found. The ordered pair is given in the form (x, y), where x is the column number and y is the row number.

The questions will be presented like this:

	-3	**-2**	**-1**	**0**	**1**	**2**	**3**
3	41	39	84	77	35	42	37
2	75	57	95	16	93	16	15
1	34	54	50	89	26	19	94
0	66	89	65	23	13	42	20
-1	15	97	86	76	76	58	92
-2	80	92	78	52	90	11	56
-3	88	81	61	79	35	64	52

1. $(3, -2)$

a. 56
b. 39
c. 64
d. 11
e. 92

To answer the question, look at the ordered pair. It indicates that the number you are looking for is in the column labeled 3, and the row labeled -2. In this table, that number is 56, answer choice A.

What Strategies Can I Use to Answer the Questions Quickly and Accurately?

The best way to approach these questions is methodically. Take the first number in the ordered pair and find it on the column headers. Keep your finger on that number while you take the second number of the ordered pair and locate it on the row headers. Put another finger on that number. Drag the first finger straight down the column until you get to the row that your other finger is on. The number at the intersection of the indicated column and row is your answer.

If you find yourself staring at the table for too long trying to be sure that you've selected the right number, you may find it helpful to draw lines on the graph, or take two pieces of scratch paper and line up their edges with the column and row numbers given in the question so that the number you are looking for appears at the corner where the two pieces of paper come together.

WHAT ARE THE COMMON MISTAKES TO AVOID?

Since the process for answering these questions is very straightforward, most errors are the result of trying to go too quickly. The more you practice these sorts of questions, the faster you will be able to accurately answer them. Once you've practiced for a while, you'll be able to get a feel for how fast you can go while accurately answering all the questions. On test day, force yourself to go no faster than this.

One common mistake made on these questions is taking the ordered pair in the question to be ordinal coordinates rather than numbers referencing the column and row labels. For example, suppose a question asks for the ordered pair (1,2). Under the pressure of the test, many people will instinctively go to the first column and second row, and take that number. Don't succumb to pressure on the test. Just follow the procedure and work through the questions at your ideal speed.

Practice Questions

For each question, select the number that appears in the table at the given coordinates. Recall that the first number in the ordered pair gives the column number, and the second gives the row number. For instance, the ordered pair $(0, -2)$ refers to the number in column 0, row -2, which is 84 in the table below.

Use the table below to answer questions 1-5.

	-3	-2	-1	0	1	2	3
3	89	57	70	68	11	95	40
2	85	28	75	82	63	42	58
1	85	20	16	52	62	87	87
0	25	83	78	21	73	11	31
-1	30	72	73	51	91	30	70
-2	16	82	32	84	28	91	63
-3	74	19	96	38	49	17	25

1. $(-1, 1)$

a. 63
b. 84
c. 16
d. 51
e. 87

2. $(-2, 3)$

a. 57
b. 21
c. 25
d. 58
e. 51

3. $(3, -3)$

a. 58
b. 25
c. 89
d. 16
e. 21

4. $(-2, 2)$

a. 28
b. 96
c. 11
d. 72
e. 49

5. $(-1,-2)$

a. 17
b. 95
c. 32
d. 42
e. 25

Use the table below to answer questions 6-10.

	-3	-2	-1	0	1	2	3
3	94	49	12	84	91	92	33
2	23	79	99	97	33	51	22
1	50	92	16	12	74	86	53
0	59	11	55	72	86	29	65
-1	14	66	14	34	16	97	17
-2	27	37	82	52	18	39	43
-3	79	39	96	22	87	98	54

6. $(1,1)$

a. 28
b. 16
c. 42
d. 73
e. 74

7. $(-2,1)$

a. 49
b. 92
c. 28
d. 91
e. 57

8. $(0,2)$

a. 30
b. 25
c. 20
d. 91
e. 97

9. $(3,-3)$

a. 54
b. 82
c. 87
d. 95
e. 20

10. $(-2, -1)$

a. 82
b. 63
c. 52
d. 72
e. 66

Practice Answers

1. C
2. A
3. B
4. A
5. C
6. E
7. B
8. E
9. A
10. E

Instrument Comprehension

What Are These Questions Testing?

These questions are designed to test your familiarity with and understanding of common instruments.

What Is the Question Format?

The question format will vary depending on the types of instruments that the test covers. This section of the book will focus on the compass and the artificial horizon, two instruments commonly used in airplanes.

Test questions related to these instruments will illustrate a compass and an artificial horizon inside an airplane cockpit. Based on the readings of both of these instruments, you will have to determine the position and orientation of the airplane.

How Do I Read the Compass and Artificial Horizon Instruments?

The compass, a relatively intuitive instrument with which many people are familiar, shows which direction a person or vehicle is facing. When a person is facing north, for example, the needle on the compass points toward the "N." If the person is facing a direction between south and southeast, the needle will point between "S" and "SE."

The artificial horizon is an instrument that shows how the nose and wings of a plane are tilted. For most people, the artificial horizon is less intuitive and less familiar than the compass. However, if you imagine yourself actually flying in a plane, the artificial horizon becomes easier to read and understand.

The artificial horizon has two components that illustrate how the nose of an airplane is tilted with respect to the ground: the miniature wings and the horizon bar. The miniature wings represent the actual wings of the aircraft, and the horizon bar represents the horizon, the imaginary line that divides the ground and the sky from the pilot's point of view. When the miniature wings are level with the horizon bar, the plane is level. When the miniature wings are above the horizon bar, the plane is tilted upward, and when the miniature wings are below the horizon bar, the plane is tilted downward. These categories of nose tilt are shown in the drawing below.

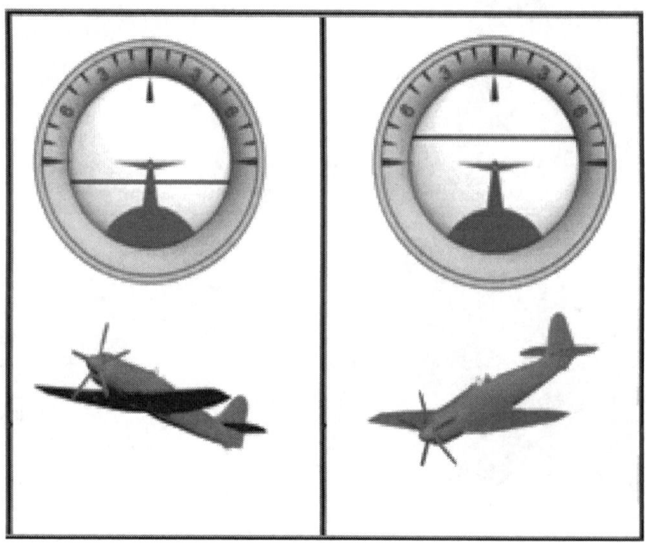

To illustrate how the wings are tilted from side to side, the artificial horizon instrument also has a dial with degree marks representing the bank angle. A needle on the dial indicates the exact bank angle, and the horizon bar is tilted accordingly, as shown in the picture below. If the left wing of the plane is tilted downward, the needle will be to the right of the center of the dial; if the right wing is tilted downward; the needle will be to the left of the center. Note that the tilted horizon bar reflects the pilot's point of view: if the left wing of the plane is tilted downward, the horizon will appear to be tilted in the opposite direction.

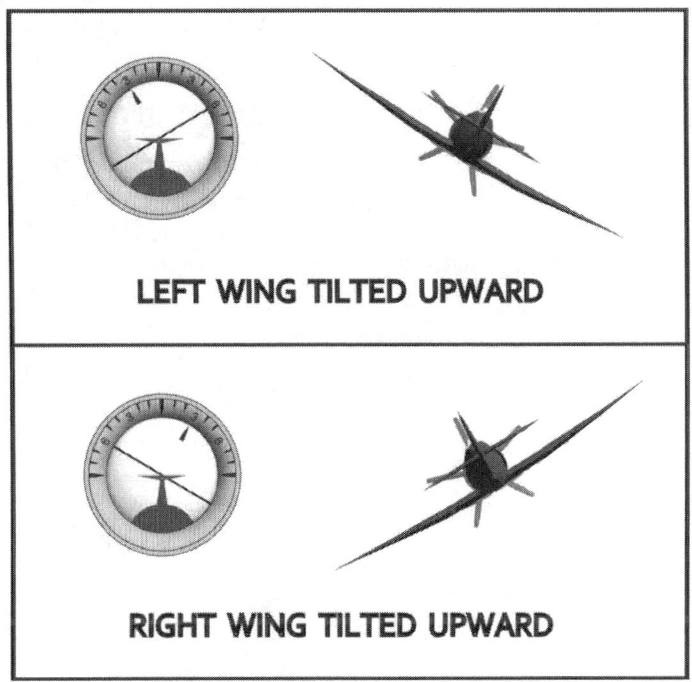

To answer the questions on this test, you will have to use information from both the compass and artificial horizon to determine how the plane is oriented. If the plane is flying north, it will appear to fly into the page in the illustrations.

For example, based on the compass and artificial horizon shown below, which of the answer choices represents the orientation of the plane?

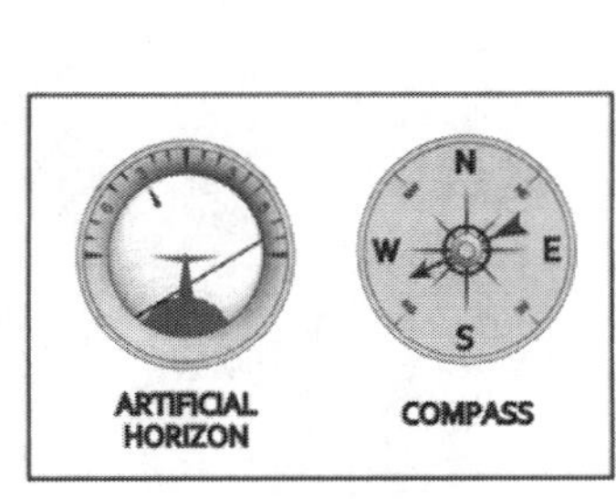

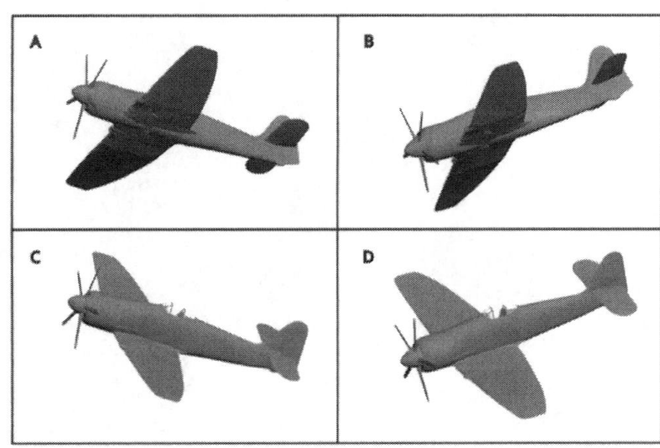

ANSWER: The answer is A. First, notice that the compass is pointing in a west-southwest direction. If a north-flying plane is facing into the page, then a westbound plane will be facing left. The compass indicates that the plane is flying somewhere between west and southwest, so the illustration will show a plane that appears to be facing left and just slightly out of the page.

Second, notice that the miniature wings in the artificial horizon are above the horizon line, and the needle on the dial is to the left of the center. From this information, you know that 1) the nose of the plane is tilted upward, and 2) the left wing of the plane is tilted upward, and the right wing is tilted downward. Because only the plane illustrated in choice A fits this description, it is the correct answer.

How Can I Improve My Ability to Read the Compass and Artificial Horizon?

Most people don't encounter these instruments on an everyday basis, so the best way to improve your ability to read them is simply to do the practice question in this section. However, although the artificial horizon is not commonly found outside of aircraft, you might want to practice using a real compass if you are still having trouble with these questions. You can find a reasonably-priced compass at most outdoor or sporting goods stores.

Practice Questions

1. Which of the answer choices represents the orientation of the plane?

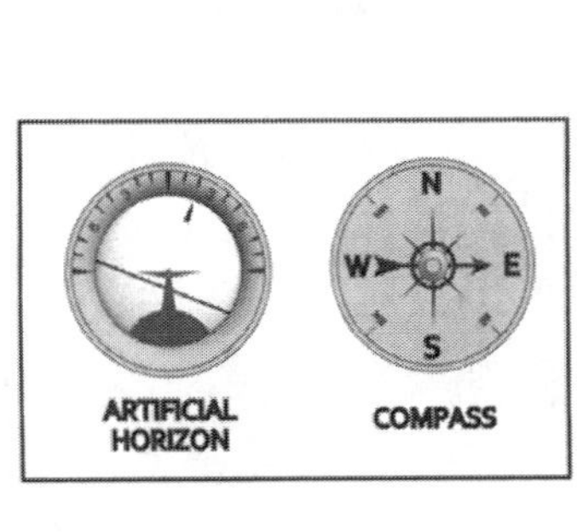

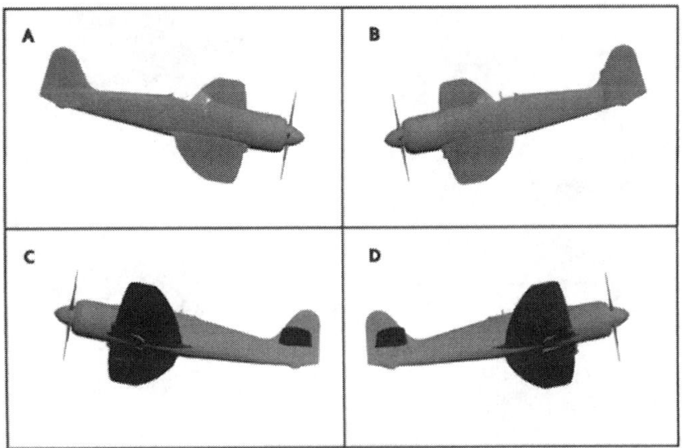

2. Which of the answer choices represents the orientation of the plane?

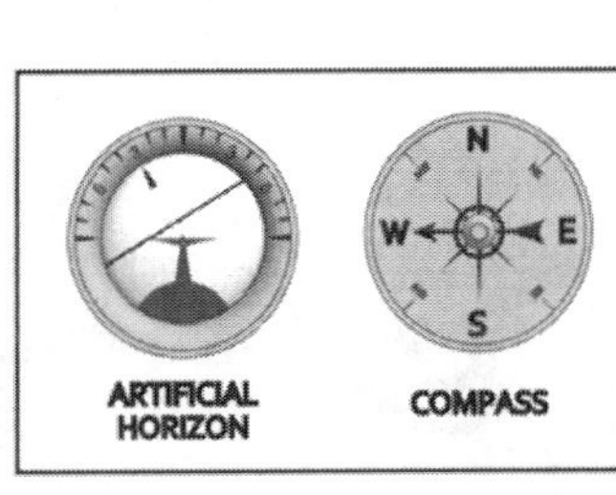

3. Which of the answer choices represents the orientation of the plane?

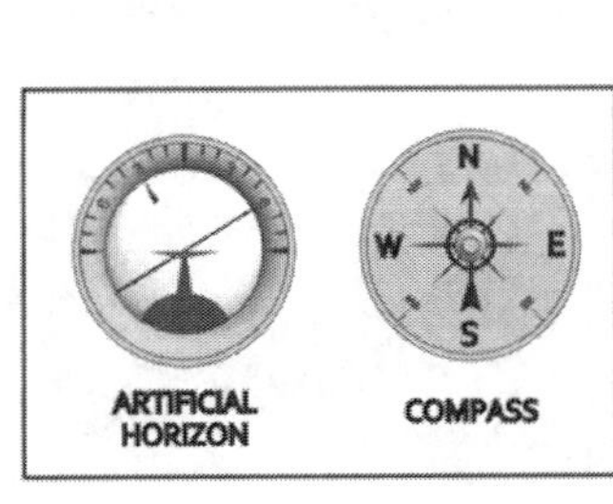

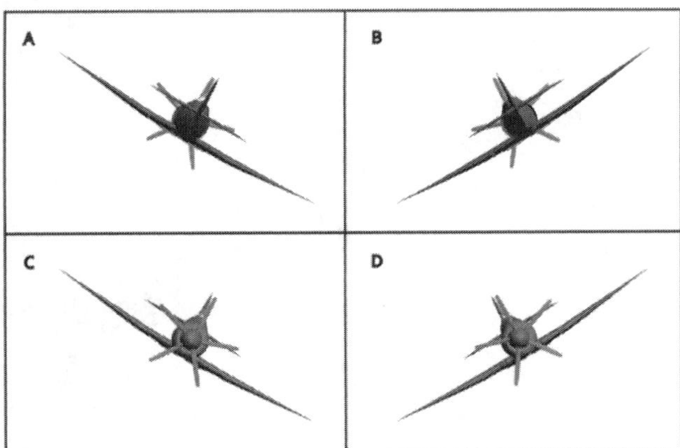

4. **Which of the answer choices represents the orientation of the plane?**

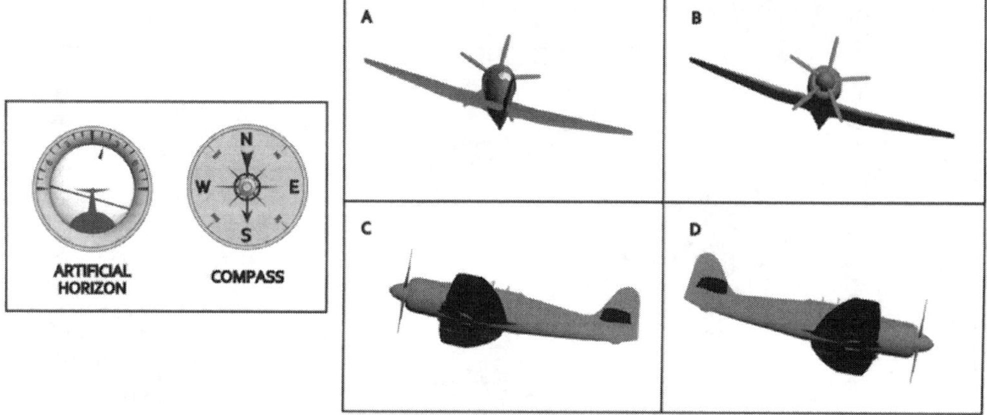

5. **Which of the answer choices represents the orientation of the plane?**

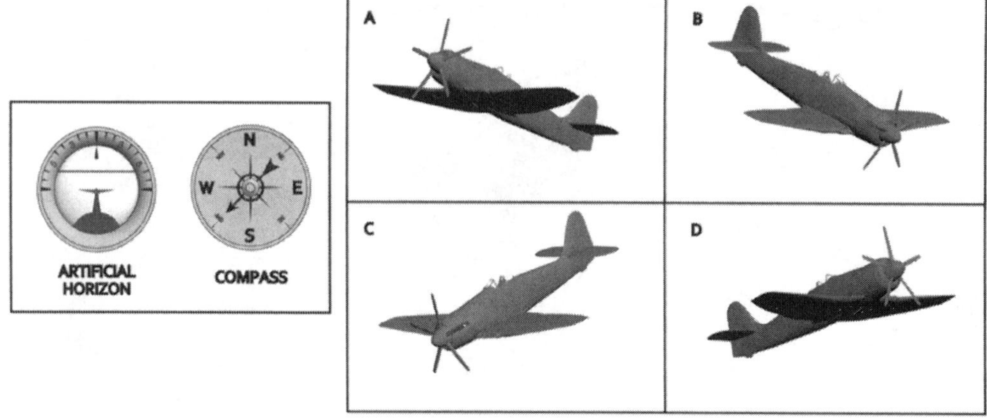

6. **Which of the answer choices represents the orientation of the plane?**

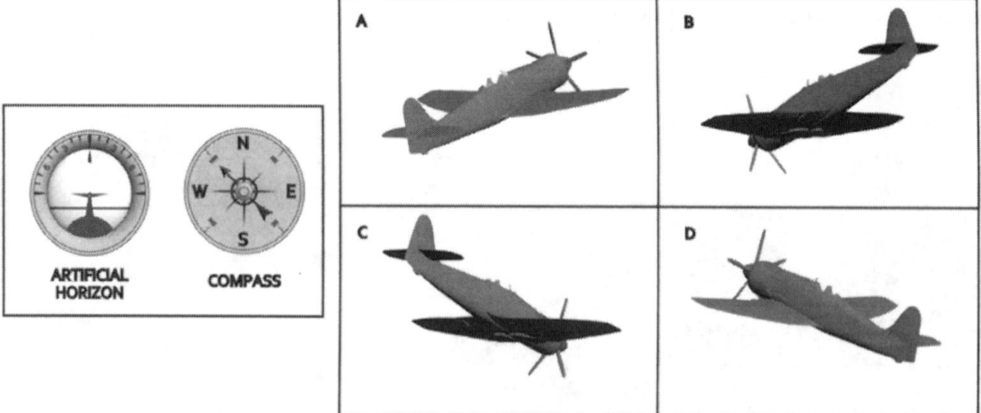

7. Which of the answer choices represents the orientation of the plane?

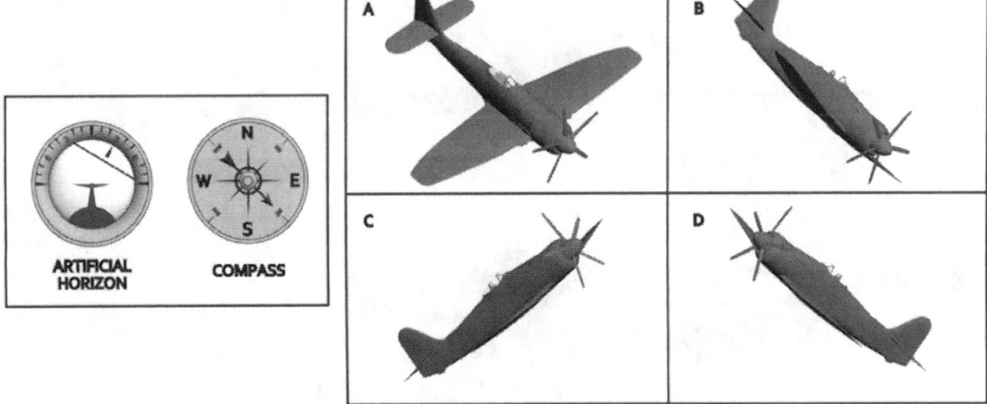

8. Which of the answer choices represents the orientation of the plane?

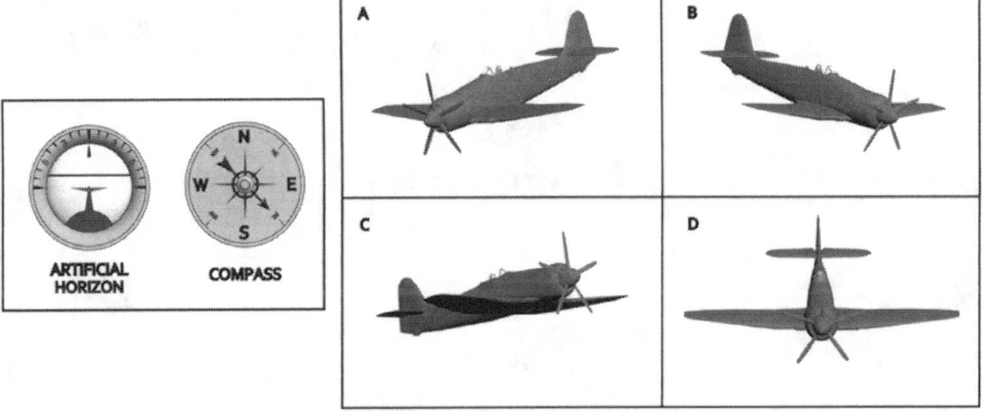

9. Which of the answer choices represents the orientation of the plane?

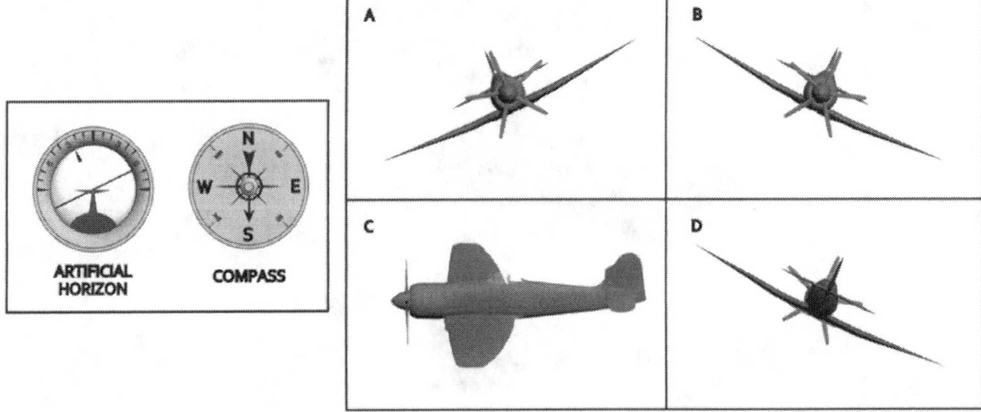

10. Which of the answer choices represents the orientation of the plane?

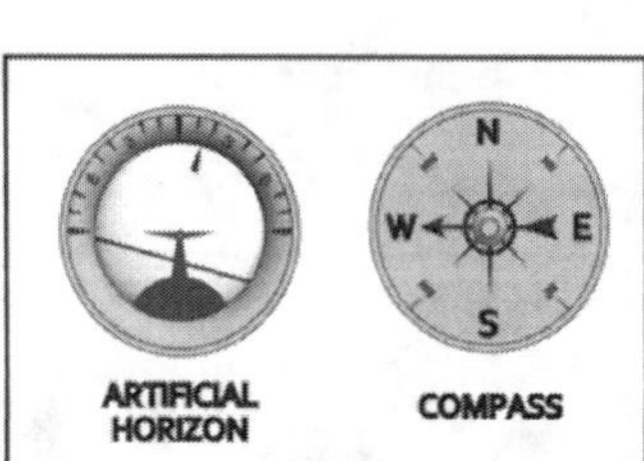

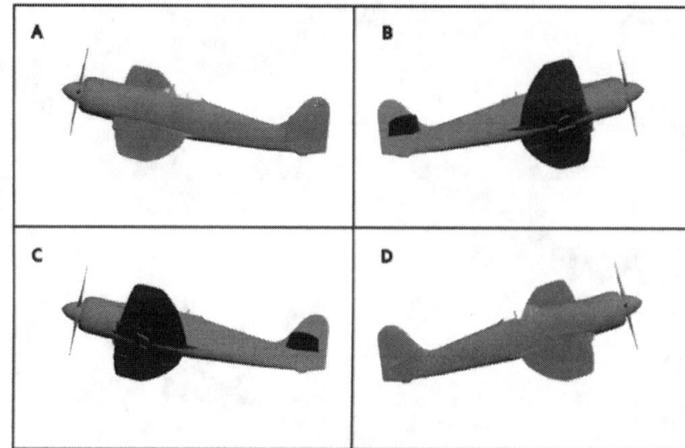

Practice Answers

1. D: The plane is flying east, which eliminates choices B and C. The artificial horizon indicates that the right wing of the plane is tilted upward. Only choice D meets this requirement.

2. C: The plane is facing west, which eliminates choice B. The artificial horizon indicates that the left wing of the plane is facing upward, so the answer is choice C.

3. A: The plane is facing north, which eliminates choices C and D. The artificial horizon indicates that the left wing is tilted upward, so the answer is choice A.

4. B: The answer is B because this is the only answer choice in which the plane is facing south.

5. C: The miniature wings indicate that the nose is tilted downward, which eliminates choices A and D. Of the two remaining choices, the answer must be C because the plane is flying southwest.

6. D: The artificial horizon indicates that the nose is tilted upward, which eliminates choices B and C. In addition, the compass is pointing northwest. Only choice D meets both requirements.

7. B: The compass shows that the plane is flying southeast, so you can eliminate choice D. In addition, the artificial horizon indicates that the nose of the plane is tilted downward, and the right wing of the plane is tilted upward. The only choice that meets both requirements is B.

8. B: The miniature wings in the artificial horizon are below the horizon bar, so the nose of the plane is tilted downward. As explained earlier, a plane that is traveling north is facing into the page. Therefore, a plane that is going southeast will have the orientation shown in choice B.

9. A: Because the compass is pointing south, the plane must appear to fly out of the page, so you can eliminate choices C and D. In addition, the artificial horizon indicates that the plane's left wing is tilted upward. Thus, A is the correct answer.

10. A: The compass indicates that the plane is flying west, which eliminates choices B and D. Also, the artificial horizon indicates that the right wing of the plane is tilted upward. Thus, A is the correct answer.

Block Counting

What Are These Questions Testing?

These questions are designed to test your spatial, geometric, and logical abilities.

What Is the Question Format?

The test will show a drawing of a three-dimensional arrangement of blocks with the same size and shape and ask you to identify how many other blocks a particular block is touching. Typically, the blocks are arranged in irregular shapes, and some of the blocks are hidden. You will have to use spatial intuition and reasoning to determine how many blocks are touching the block in question.

How Do I Know How Many Blocks Are Touching the Particular Block?

First, it is important to know which blocks qualify as "touching" the other block. If at least part of a face of one block touches at least part of a face of another block, those blocks are considered to touch each other. However, if a block shares only a corner or an edge with another block, the two blocks do not touch.

The example below illustrates the difference between touching and non-touching blocks. Block A is touching blocks 1, 2, and 3 because part of a face of block A is touching each of these blocks. However, blocks 4 and 5 do *not* touch block A because they only contact block A at an edge; that is, they share no area with any faces of block A. Therefore, block A is touching three blocks in this picture.

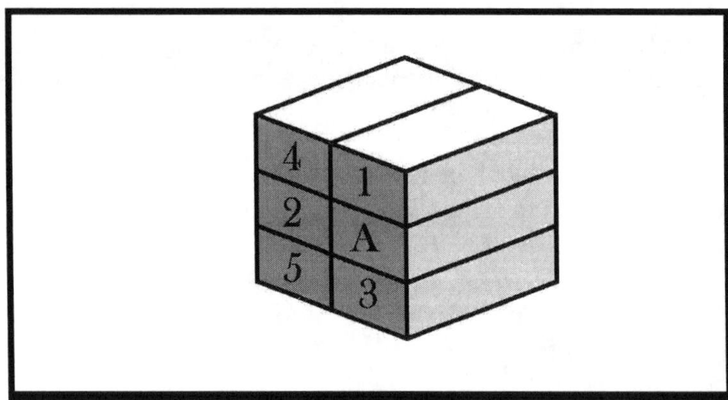

Sometimes, the blocks may be positioned so that certain blocks are hidden from view. In these cases, you will have to use basic spatial intuition and logic to determine the number of blocks touching a particular block.

In the example below, try to figure out how many blocks are touching block A.

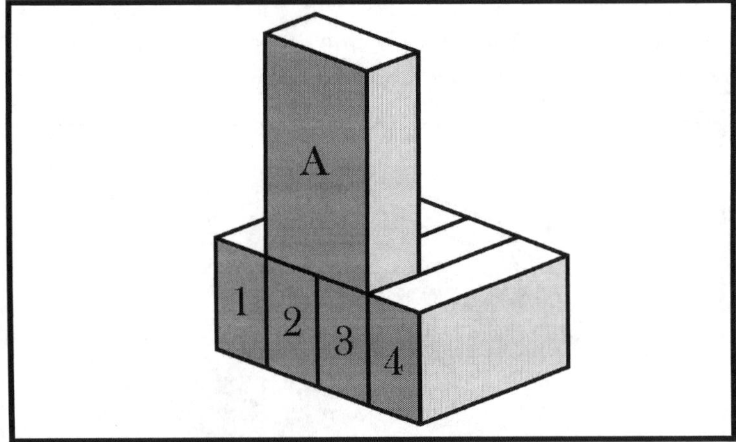

Answer: There are two blocks touching block A. Even though blocks 1 and 4 each share an edge with block A, they do not "touch" block A, as the word is used in the context of the test. Only blocks 2 and 3 actually touch a face of block A, so block A is only touching two blocks.

Are There Any Ways to Make It Easier to Count the Number of Touching Blocks?

Remember that for a block to count as "touching," it must contact a face of that block. Therefore, it might help to count the number of blocks that are touching each face of the block in question.

Try to apply this strategy to the example below, in order to count the number of blocks touching block A.

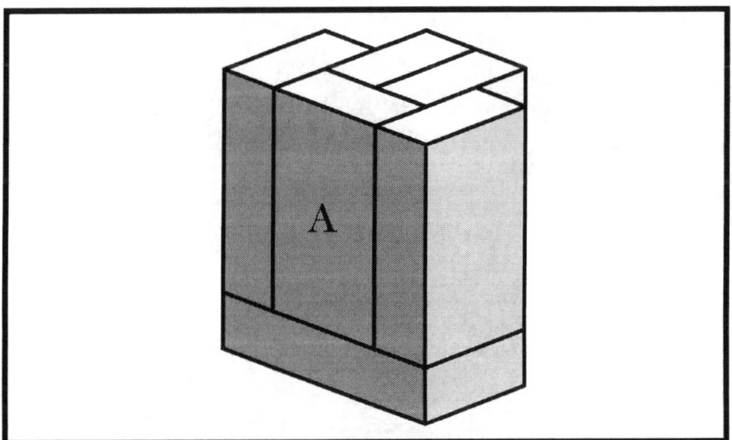

Answer: The back face of block A is touching two blocks. The left face of block A is touching one block, as is the right side. The bottom face is touching one block. Therefore, block A is touching a total of five blocks.

If you are still having trouble with the practice questions, it might help to try to re-create the example problems with a set of rectangular blocks. Practicing with physical blocks will make it easier to visualize hidden blocks when the blocks are drawn on paper.

Practice Questions

The explanations to these problems use terms like "top," "left," and "front" to refer to the faces of the blocks. Because this terminology can be confusing due to the angled view of the block arrangements, the illustration below is provided to help you keep these terms straight.

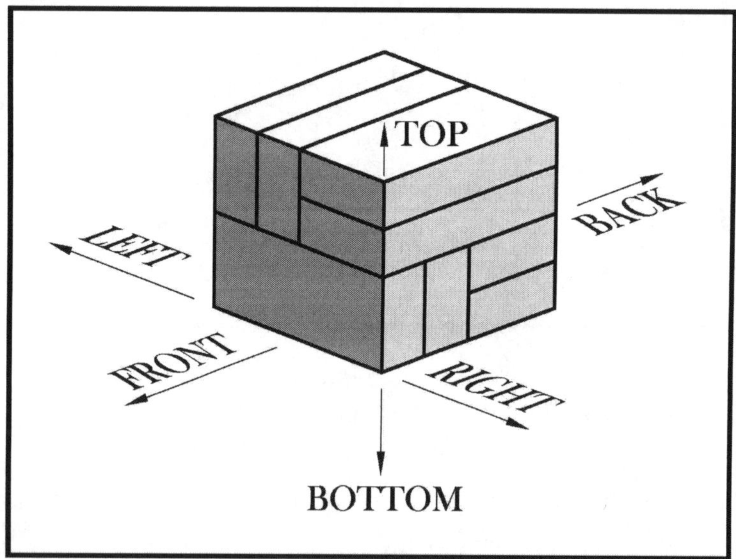

Once you understand these terms, proceed to the practice problems below.

1. How many blocks are touching block 1 in the arrangement below?

2. How many blocks are touching block 2 in the arrangement below?

3. How many blocks are touching block 8 in the arrangement below?

4. How many blocks are touching block 14 in the arrangement below?

5. How many blocks are touching block 18 in the arrangement below?

Practice Answers

1. There are a total of six blocks touching block 1. One block (block #4) is touching the top face of block 1, two blocks are touching the left face, and three blocks are touching the bottom face.

2. There are a total of seven blocks touching block 2. Two blocks are touching the left face of block 2, one block (block 4) is touching the right face, and four blocks are touching the bottom face.

Note that the picture only directly shows two blocks (block 5 and the block in front of it) touching the bottom face of block 2. However, you can deduce from the picture that block 3 and the block in front of it must also touch block 2. Because the width of each block is twice the thickness, the width of block 3 and the block next to it must extend underneath block 2. Therefore, block 2 touches both of these blocks, even if it isn't explicitly shown in the picture.

3. A total of eight blocks are touching block 8. One block is touching the left face, one block is touching the right face, three blocks are touching the bottom face, one block is touching the top face, and two blocks are touching the back face.

4. A total of five blocks are touching block 14. One block (block 11) is touching the left face, and four blocks are touching the top face.

5. A total of nine blocks are touching block 18. Four blocks, including blocks 19 and 17, are touching the front face of block 18, four blocks are touching the back face, and one block is touching the bottom face.

Aviation Information

What Are These Questions Testing?

The aviation information section tests your knowledge of basic aviation information. This includes a variety of things including aircraft terminology, the basic physics involved in flight, and common airport information.

How Can I Improve My Ability to Answer These Questions?

Since these are all knowledge-based questions, you can improve your success rate here by reading up on aircraft operation and airport information. The section below is an overview of the basics in these areas.

Fixed-Wing Aircraft

There are six basic components of a fixed-wing aircraft: wings, fuselage, tail assembly, landing gear, powerplant, and flight controls and control surfaces.

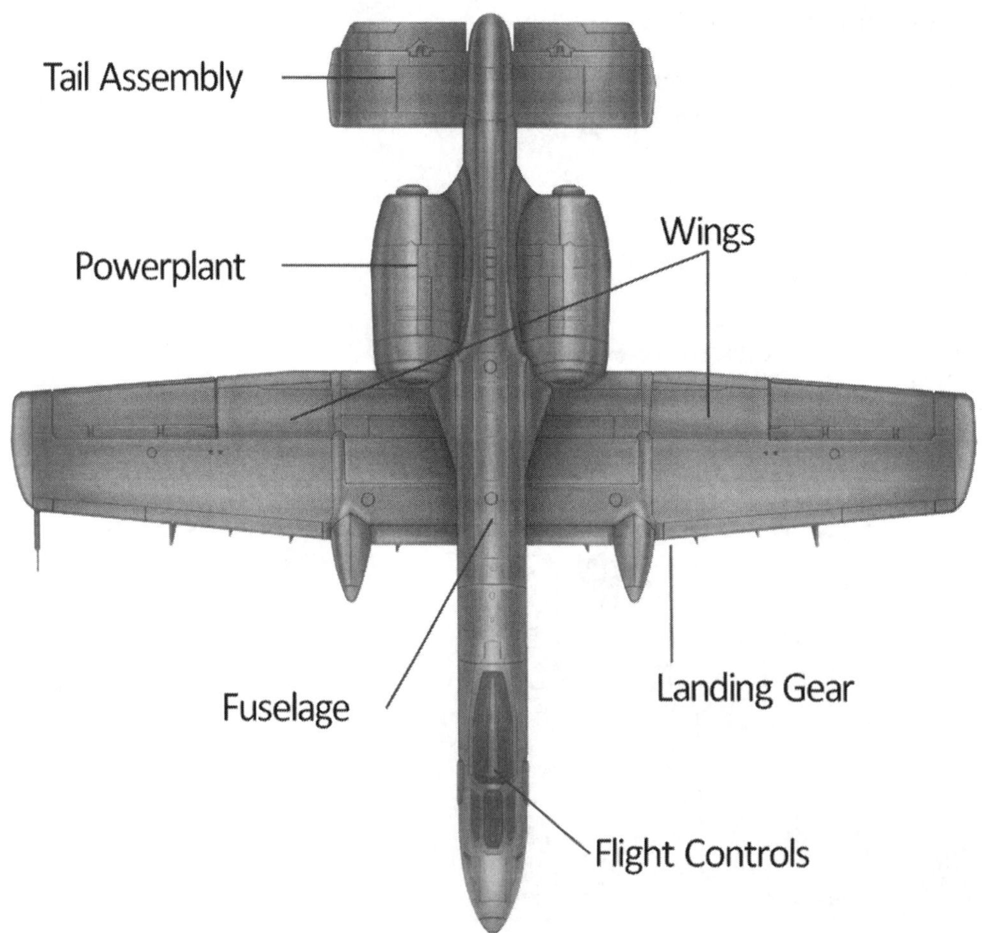

Wings

The **wings** are the primary airfoils of the plane. An airfoil is anything designed to produce lift when it moves through the air. The leading edge of an airfoil is thicker and rounder than the trailing edge, and the top surface of the airfoil has a greater curve than the bottom. The result is that air flows more quickly over the top of the wing, and the greater air pressure beneath pushes the wing, and thus the plane, upwards.

The wings connect to either side of the fuselage. Planes are designated as high-, mid-, and low-wing, depending on where the wings are attached. The wings themselves are described as either cantilever or semi-cantilever. A **cantilever wing** has sufficient internal support structures to keep it steady in its location. A **semi-cantilever wing**, on the other hand, requires additional external support structures. The trailing edge of a wing typically has two control surfaces attached by means of a hinge: **flaps** run from the fuselage to the middle of the wing, and **ailerons** run from the middle of the wing to the tip. By raising and lowering the ailerons, the pilot can roll the plane. The plane will roll when the ailerons are pointed in opposite directions. When the plane is cruising, however, these control surfaces are aligned with the rest of the wing. During takeoff and landing, both surfaces are extended, which increases the lift.

The distance from one wingtip to the other is the **wingspan**, and the distance from the leading edge to the trailing edge is called the **chord**. The chord line runs through the wing from leading edge to trailing edge: it divides the wing into upper and lower surfaces. The **mean camber** line runs along the inside of the wing, such that the parts of the wing above and below it are equal in thickness. The camber is the curvature of the airfoil: if an airfoil is heavily curved, it has a **high camber**. The thickness of a wing is measured at its greatest point. The shape of the wings when viewed from overhead is known as the **planform**.

When the wings are not attached parallel to the horizontal plane, the angle they make with the horizontal plane is called the **dihedral angle**. A positive dihedral wing angle (wings angling above the horizontal plane) keeps the plane stable when it rolls, as it will encourage the plane to return to its original position. This does diminish the maneuverability of the plane, which is why the wings of fighter jets are usually horizontal or even pointed slightly downwards (**anhedral**).

The shape of the wings has a major influence on the handling, maneuverability, and speed of the plane. Today's planes generally have a straight, sweep, or delta shape. **Straight wings** may be rectangular, elliptical (rounded), or tapered. They are commonly found on sailplanes, gliders, and other low-speed aircraft.

A **swept wing** provides better handling at high speeds, but makes the plane slightly less stable at low speeds. Since most modern aircraft are designed to operate at high speeds, this is the most commonly used wing style. Wings may be swept forward or back, though forward-swept wings are rarely seen. In general, a higher angle of sweep is used for planes that are meant to travel faster and be more maneuverable; however, more extreme sweeps require much greater speeds for takeoff and landing.

The **delta wing** shape is triangular, so that the leading edge of the wing has a high sweep angle while the trailing edge is mostly, if not completely, straight. A delta shape enables the plane to travel but also requires very high takeoff and landing speeds. Many of the earliest supersonic aircraft used the delta wing shape, as did the space shuttles.

Fuselage

The **fuselage** is the main body of the airplane. The basic features of the fuselage are the cockpit, cabin, cargo area, and attachment points for external components, like the wings and landing gear. Some planes designed for specific purposes may not have all of these components; for instance, a fighter jet will not have a cabin for passengers or a cargo area, since it needs to be light and maneuverable. The fuselage may be described as either **truss** or **monocoque**, depending on whether its strength is created by triangular arrangements of steel or aluminum tubing or by bulkheads, stringers, and formers. A **stringer** is a support structure that runs the length of the fuselage, while a **former** runs perpendicular.

Tail Assembly

The **tail assembly**, or empennage, includes the vertical and horizontal stabilizers, elevators, rudders, and trim tabs. The **stabilizers** are fixed (non-adjustable) surfaces that extend from the back end of the fuselage. The **elevators** are positioned along the trailing edges of the horizontal stabilizers; the pilot can move them to raise or lower the nose of the plane. The **rudders** are connected to the trailing edge of the vertical stabilizer and are used to move the nose of the plane to the left or right, typically in combination with the ailerons. The **trim tabs** are movable surfaces that extend off the trailing edges of the rudder, elevators, and ailerons and are used to make smaller adjustments.

Landing Gear

The **landing gear** usually consists of three sets of wheels used for takeoffs and landings, though some planes have special non-wheel landing gear for landing on snow or water. Landing gear is commonly retractable, meaning that it is pulled up inside the plane during flight to reduce drag. In a typical arrangement, wheel sets are positioned either under each wing or on the sides of the fuselage, with the third wheel set being under the nose or the tail. The most common arrangement on modern aircraft is the **tricycle** arrangement, which has the third wheel set under the nose, but having the third wheel set under the tail is still known as the **conventional** arrangement. Whether located under the tail or the nose, the third wheel will typically be able to rotate so that the plane can turn while traveling on the ground. The addition of extra wheels to each set allows the plane to handle a greater weight.

Powerplant

In aviation, the **powerplant** is the part of the plane that supplies the thrust. A jet engine operates by compressing the air that comes in the front, burning it along with fuel, and then blasting it out the back. There are different methods for compressing the air, but most jet engines do so by slowing it down with a set of small rotating blades. This greatly increases the air pressure at the front of the engine. The compressed air is then forced into a different section, where it is mixed with fuel and burned. As it then expands, it is pushed at great force through a series of turbines, the turning of which moves the compressor blades at the front of the engine, supplying both power and air. The exhausted air then passes out the back of the engine, which propels the plane forward. Some jet engines have afterburners, which feed extra fuel into the area between the turbines and the rear exhaust, increasing forward thrust.

In a propeller plane, on the other hand, the powerplant is the propellers and the engine. The propellers have tilted blades, which push air backwards and thereby push the plane forward. There are two types of propeller: fixed-pitch or variable-pitch. The blade angle of a **fixed-pitch propeller** cannot be adjusted by the pilot. **Variable-pitch propellers** allow the pilot, usually indirectly via the plane's control systems, to adjust the pitch of the propeller blades to alter the amount of thrust being generated. Some variable-pitch propellers are designed to operate only at a single rotational speed, allowing the engine to be much simpler and more efficient, so the amount of thrust is controlled entirely by the pitch of the blades. These are known as **constant-speed propellers**.

The engines of a propeller plane turn the **crankshafts**, which turn the propellers. The engines also are responsible for powering the plane's electrical system. The location of the engines on a propeller plane may vary. Single-engine planes typically have their engines in front of the fuselage, while multi-engine planes usually have their engines underneath the wings. Some multi-engine planes have engines in both locations.

Flight Envelope

During flight, there are four forces a pilot must manage: lift, gravity, thrust, and drag. These forces act downward (gravity), upward (lift), forward (thrust), and backward (drag). The collective input of these forces is known as the **flight envelope**.

Gravity

The weight of a plane is the primary force that must be overcome for flight to take place. The force of **gravity** on a given object is the same, regardless of orientation, though it varies slightly with large changes in altitude.

Aviation experts distinguish between different types of weight. The basic weight includes the aircraft and any internal or external equipment that will remain a part of the plane during flight. The **operating weight** is the basic weight plus the crew and any other nonexpendable items not included in the basic weight. The **gross weight** is the total weight of the aircraft and all contents at any given time. The weight of the airplane when it has no usable fuel is called the **zero-fuel weight**.

Lift

In order to overcome gravity, the plane must generate **lift**. Lift is the upward force of air pressure on the aircraft, primarily the wings, that allows it to achieve and maintain altitude. In order to generate lift, the plane typically must be traveling forward at considerable speed.

If the wing tilts too far back the airflow may stop over the wing's upper surface, which will result in a rapid loss of altitude and often control of the plane. This is known as a stall, and it may be avoided by decreasing the angle of attack, so that normal airflow over the top of the wing is not interrupted.

Thrust

The speed required for generating lift is provided by the aircraft's **thrust**. It ensures that the aircraft is able to continue moving forward at sufficient speed to generate lift. As was discussed in the previous section, thrust is generated by the powerplant of the aircraft, usually one or more jet engines or propellers.

Drag

An aircraft's thrust is countered by **drag**, the resistance to forward movement provided by the air that the aircraft is traveling through. At anything above normal walking or running speeds, air resistance is a noticeable hindrance to motion, and it only increases as airspeed goes up. The primary implication that this has on aircraft is that the faster the aircraft goes, the more thrust is required just to overcome the drag and maintain a constant speed.

There are two types of drag: profile drag and induced drag. **Profile drag** is the drag that exists when any object moves through the air. It is the result of the plane pushing air aside as it moves. Profile drag can be minimized by designing the aircraft to have a better wind profile. **Induced drag**, on the other hand, is drag that results from the wings generating lift. Part of the process of generating lift involves the wings redirecting the oncoming air downward (think Newton's third law), and this causes additional drag.

Atmospheric Conditions

The flight envelope is significantly affected by the atmospheric conditions, primarily the density of the surrounding air and the speed and direction of any wind. The density is in turn determined by the temperature, pressure, and humidity of the air. Lower temperatures, higher pressures, and lower humidity are all associated with higher density air. Denser air will produce greater lift, but will also produce more drag. Air pressure is most closely associated with altitude. In general, pressure decreases with altitude, so as you go higher up, the pressure of the surrounding air decreases.

With regard to wind, flying into the wind (**headwind**) has a similar type of impact to flying in denser air, though of much greater magnitude. In a headwind, the aircraft will have a higher speed relative to the surrounding air, which means it will experience greater drag and lift forces. Similarly, if the aircraft is flying the same direction as the wind (**tailwind**), it will have a lower speed relative to the surrounding air, and will experience reduced drag and lift.

Flight Concepts and Terminology

Flight Attitude

The flight attitude is described in terms of three axes, all of which meet at the plane's center of mass.

The **longitudinal** axis is the axis that extends from the center forward toward the nose and rearward toward the tail. The **lateral** axis extends from the center out to the right and left, perpendicular to the longitudinal axis. Typically, the lateral axis passes through (over/under) the wings. Both of these axes are in the horizontal plane when the aircraft is level. The **vertical** axis meanwhile extends straight upward and downward from the aircraft's center, perpendicular to the horizontal plane of the other two axes. The motion of the aircraft can be described in relation to these axes: Rotation about the longitudinal axis is called **roll**; rotation about the lateral axis is called **pitch**; rotation about the vertical axis is called **yaw**. In turn, these three types of motion are controlled by three sets of flight control surfaces. Roll is controlled by the ailerons, pitch by the elevators, and yaw by the rudder. This information is summarized in the table below, and is expanded upon in the following section.

Axis	Motion	Control surface
Longitudinal	Roll	Ailerons
Lateral	Pitch	Elevators
Vertical	Yaw	Rudder

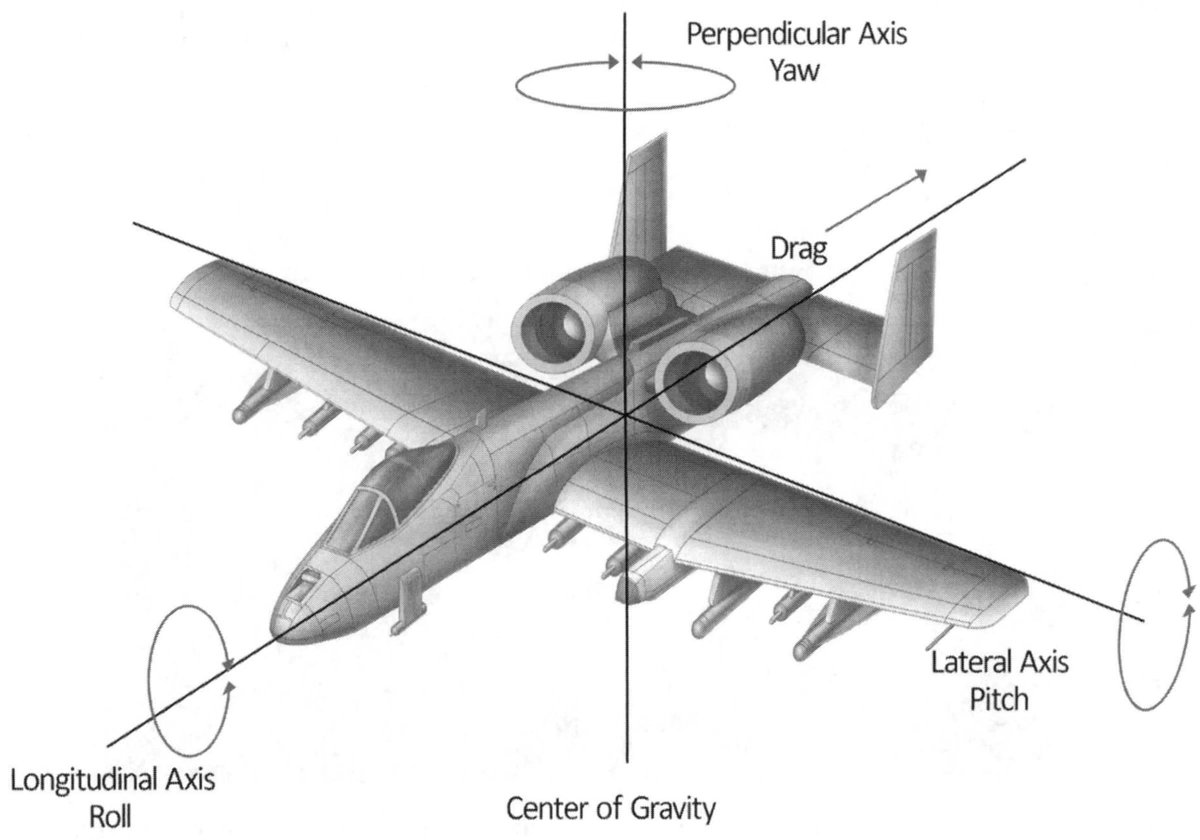

Flight Controls

Flight controls are divided into primary and secondary groups.

Primary

The **primary flight control surfaces** are the ailerons, rudder, and elevator.

The **ailerons** are responsible for the roll, or movement around the longitudinal axis. The ailerons extend from the trailing edges of the wings as shown in the figure below. They can be manipulated by the pilot to cause the wing to either dip below or elevate above the horizontal plane.

The joystick (or control wheel) controls the roll of the aircraft. By pushing the stick (or turning the wheel) to the left, the pilot raises the left aileron and lowers the right aileron, causing the left wing to dip and the right wing to elevate.

The **elevators** control the plane's pitch, or movement around the lateral axis. They are attached to the trailing edges of the horizontal stabilizers at the rear of the aircraft. Depending on the design of the plane, there may be one elevator that extends across the length of the horizontal stabilizer, or there may be two elevators, divided by the vertical stabilizer, as shown in the figure below. When the elevators are undivided, they are sometimes referred to as a **stabilator**.

The joystick also controls the pitch of the aircraft. By pulling the stick back, the pilot raises the elevators, causing the tail of the plane to experience downward force, thus raising the nose of the plane. Pushing the stick forward will have the opposite effect on the elevators and will result in the nose of the plane dropping as the tail is pushed upward.

The **rudder** is a large flap attached by a hinge to the vertical stabilizer. It controls the motion of the plane around its vertical axis. The rudder can swing to the right or the left, causing the plane to turn (yaw) in either direction.

The rudder is controlled with two pedals: when the pilot pushes on the right pedal, the rudder swings out to the right, causing leftward pressure on the tail of the aircraft. This results in the nose of the plane turning to the right. Similarly, if the pilot pushes on the left pedal, the rudder will swing to the left, causing the tail to move right, and the nose to turn left.

The pilot also controls the amount of power or thrust being produced by the engines by manipulating the **throttle**. It is considered a primary flight control because the pilot must manage the thrust to ensure that the plane will be able to accomplish its intended maneuvers. With all three of the primary control surfaces, it is important to remember that the speed of the aircraft relative to the surrounding air determines the magnitude of the aircraft's response to the control. A plane that is traveling at 300 mph will roll much more quickly than one that is traveling at 200 mph in response to the same amount of aileron manipulation. The same is true of the other two types of motion.

Flight maneuvers usually involve the use of multiple controls. To make a proper turn, for instance, the pilot will need to employ the rudder, ailerons, and elevators. The bank is established by raising and lowering the ailerons, and the rudder pedals counteract any adverse yaw that occurs. Adverse yaw is the drifting of the nose caused by the extra drag on the downward-pointing aileron. Also, because extra lift is needed during a turn, the pilot must increase the angle of attack by applying downward elevator pressure. The amount of back elevator pressure required will be in proportion to the sharpness of the turn. This will be discussed in greater detail in the section on flight maneuvers.

SECONDARY

The **secondary flight control surfaces** include the flaps and leading-edge devices, spoilers, and trim systems.

The **flaps** are connected to the trailing edges of the wings; they are raised or lowered to adjust the lift or drag. The retractable flaps on modern airplanes make it possible to cruise at a high speed and land at a low speed. On the opposite end of the wing, **leading-edge devices** accomplish much the same purpose, they can increase camber, lift, or airflow, depending on the device. Both flaps and leading-edge devices reduce stall speed. There are a number of different leading-edge devices: fixed slats, moveable slats, and leading-edge flaps.

Spoilers are attached to the wings of some airplanes in order to diminish the lift and increase the drag. Spoilers can also be useful for roll control, in part because they reduce adverse yaw. This is accomplished by raising the spoiler on the side of the turn. This reduces the lift and creates more drag on that side, which causes that wing to drop and the plane to bank and yaw to that side. If both of the spoilers are raised at the same time, the plane can descend without increasing its speed. Raising the spoilers also improves the performance of the brakes, because they eliminate lift and push the plane down onto its wheels.

Trim systems exist mainly to ease the work of the pilot. They are attached to the trailing edges of one or more of the primary control surfaces. Small aircraft often have a single trim tab attached to the elevator. This tab is adjusted with a small wheel or crank, and its position is displayed in the cockpit. When the tab is deflected upwards, the trailing edge of the elevator is forced downward and the tail is pushed up, which lowers the nose of the plane.

Typically, a pilot first will achieve the desired pitch, power, attitude, and configuration, and then use the trim tabs to resolve the remaining control pressures. There are control pressures generated by any change in the flight condition, so trimming is necessary after any change. Trimming is complete when the pilot has eliminated any heaviness in the nose or tail of the plane.

Flight Maneuvers

The four basic maneuvers in flight are straight-and-level flight, turning, climbing, and descending. As the name suggests, **straight-and-level flight** involves keeping the aircraft headed in a particular direction at a particular altitude. Maintaining straight-and-level flight requires frequent adjustment, much the same way as the driver of a car has to make frequent adjustments to maintain a straight path on a windy day or when driving on a rough uneven road.

Making a smooth **turn** requires the use of all four primary controls: the throttle is set to achieve a speed suitable to the desired type of turn, the ailerons bank the wings and the elevators raise the nose to establish the rate of turn, and the rudder is employed to counter any undesired yaw resulting from the effects of the other controls or to introduce desired yaw.

There are three classes of turn: shallow, medium, and deep. A **shallow turn** has a bank of less than 20 degrees. At angles this shallow, most planes will tend to try to stabilize themselves back to a level angle, so the pilot must maintain some pressure on the stick to ensure that the plane doesn't pull out of the bank prematurely. A **medium turn** has a bank of roughly 20 to 45 degrees. Most planes will tend to stay in a medium bank until the pilot makes an adjustment. Finally, a **steep turn** is one in which the bank is greater than 45 degrees. For angles this steep, most planes will tend to try to increase the banking angle even further unless the pilot counters that tendency by maintaining some pressure on the stick in a stabilizing direction.

While the pilot is getting the plane to the desired bank angle, he will also be pulling back on the stick to ensure that the nose of the plane does not dip during the bank. This also serves to increase the rate at which the plane turns its heading. In general, the steeper the bank, the more sharply the pilot must pull back on the stick to maintain altitude. Because the lowered aileron on the raised wing generally creates more drag than the raised aileron on the lowered wing, the airplane tends to yaw in the direction opposite to the turn. For this reason, the pilot must at the same time apply rudder pressure in the direction of the turn.

To initiate a **climb**, an aircraft's nose is angled upward so that it gains altitude. Several things that remain constant while the aircraft is flying level change when the nose of the plane is raised. The two most significant are the effective angle of gravity and the angle of attack of the wings.

When the aircraft is level, gravity acts entirely in the direction of the vertical axis of the plane. When the plane angles upward, the force of gravity, which still acts straight down like before, now has a component in the longitudinal direction, since the rear of the plane is now pointed slightly toward the ground. Additionally, since raising the noise of the aircraft increases the angle of attack of the wings, the amount of drag the aircraft experiences goes up considerably during a climb. This means that, in order to maintain flight, the thrust must now overcome both an increased amount of drag and part of the force of gravity.

If the nose of the aircraft is raised too quickly or without a sufficient increase in thrust to account for the changing flight conditions, the aircraft may **stall**. The most common cause of a stall is the plane not generating enough thrust to maintain air speed, which means that the lift being generated by the wings is not sufficient to keep the plane in the air, so the plane ceases to fly in a practical sense and instead begins to fall. To correct a stall, the pilot must angle the nose of the aircraft steeply downward and increase the throttle to generate enough airspeed in the forward direction so that the control surfaces are effective in controlling the flight of the plane again, and pull out of the dive. As should be apparent from this description, recovering from a stall involves significant loss of altitude, which makes stalling at low altitudes extremely dangerous.

There are a few different styles of controlled **descent**, but they all involve manipulation of the same two factors: pitch and thrust. By angling the nose of the plane downward, the pilot reduces the angle of attack of the wings and consequently reduces the amount of lift generated by the wings. This causes the plane to lose altitude. Similarly, by pulling back on the throttle, the pilot reduces the amount of thrust being generated, which in turn reduces the plane's air speed and the amount of lift generated by the wings, also resulting in a loss of altitude.

A **glide** is a controlled descent in which little or no engine power is used, and the plane drifts downward at a regular pace. The pilot manages a glide by balancing the forces of lift and gravity as they act on the plane.

When a pilot is executing a **landing**, the nose of the plane will actually be angled upward, but the throttle will be pulled far back to ensure that the plane continues its descent all the way to the ground.

HELICOPTERS

In many ways, the operation of a helicopter is based on the same fundamentals as airplane flight. A helicopter is subject to the same four fundamental forces of lift, weight, thrust, and drag. Unlike an airplane, however, a helicopter applies most of its thrust vertically. When a helicopter flies at a constant speed in a stable horizontal path, the lift is equal to the weight and the forward thrust is equal to the drag. The helicopter will increase its horizontal speed if the thrust is greater than the drag, and will increase its altitude if the lift is greater than the weight. If the helicopter is hovering (i.e., not moving at all), there is no drag or forward thrust; only gravity and vertical thrust or lift, which are balanced.

The manner in which a helicopter generates lift is considerably different from that of an airplane. Whereas a plane derives its lift from the natural flow of air over the wing, the helicopter spins its "wing" rapidly and at a variable angle, giving it a variety of options for angles of attack. Because the main rotor of the helicopter is being torqued with such great force, it exerts the same amount of torque back on the fuselage of the helicopter but in the opposite direction (Newton's third law again). This necessitates a tail rotor to provide the force required to the keep the fuselage from spinning around while in flight. This function of the tail rotor is called **torque control**. Manipulation of the tail rotor is also used to change the heading of the helicopter.

HELICOPTER CONTROLS

Piloting a helicopter requires the use of three controls: the cyclic (stick), the collective, and the directional control system. The **cyclic** controls the longitudinal and lateral movement of the helicopter by adjusting the tilt of the main rotor. Moving the stick forward tilts the rotor forward, which in turn pushes the helicopter forward.

The **collective** is a tube running up from the cockpit floor to the left of the pilot. It has a handle that may be raised or lowered to affect the pitch, as well as a throttle that wraps around the handle and can be used to alter the engine torque. The collective controls the angle of the main rotor blades. If the handle is pulled up, the leading edge of the rotor blade lifts relative to the trailing edge.

The **directional control system** is a pair of pedals the pilot uses to alter the pitch of the tail rotor blades. Pressing one or the other of the pedals will cause the tail rotor to exert more or less force on the fuselage, which will in turn affect the heading of the helicopter.

A helicopter pilot must use all three of the controls at the same time. The cyclic and collective adjust the action of the main rotor, which must be compensated for with adjustment to the tail rotor. For instance, if the speed of the main rotor increases during a climb, the pilot will need to increase the amount of force generated by the tail rotor to ensure the fuselage does not begin to rotate.

If the helicopter loses engine power for some reason, the pilot will need to rely on **autorotation**, or the spinning of the rotors that is generated by airflow rather than the engine. The amount of torque on the fuselage will be smaller during autorotation, but it will still be enough to require the use of the tail rotor.

Unique Forces

A helicopter generates some other forces that distinguish it from an airplane. **Translational lift** is extra lift a helicopter experiences when traveling in a forward direction.

The **Coriolis force** is another physical phenomenon related to helicopters. The Coriolis force is the increase in rotational speed that occurs when the weight of a spinning object moves closer to the rotation center. In the case of a helicopter, having a greater portion of the weight closer to the base of the blade will cause the rotor to move faster, or to require less power to move at the same rotational speed.

If the main rotor increases the flow of air over the rear part of the main rotor disc, then the rear part will have a smaller angle of attack. The result of this will be less lift in the rear part of the rotor disc. This is called the **transverse flow effect**. However, when a force is applied to a spinning disc, the effects will occur ninety degrees later. This phenomenon is known as **gyroscopic precession**.

Airport Information

At an **airport**, the areas controlled by the aircraft traffic controller are called the **movement areas** (or maneuvering areas). These include the runways and taxiways. **Runways** may be composed of all different materials, ranging from grass and dirt to asphalt and concrete. At a general aviation airport, the runways may be as little as 800 feet long and 26 feet wide, while an international airport may have runways that are 18,000 feet long and 260 feet across. The markings on a runway are white and usually outlined in black so that they may be better seen. **Taxiways** and areas not meant to be traveled by aircraft are marked in yellow.

There are three basic types of runways: visual, nonprecision instrument, and precision instrument. **Visual runways** are typical of small airports: they have no markings, though the boundaries and center lines may be indicated in some way. They are called visual runways because the pilot must be able to see the ground in order to land. It is not possible to land a plane on a visual runway with only the use of instruments.

With a **nonprecision instrument runway**, a pilot may be able to make his approach using instruments. Specifically, this sort of runway can provide feedback on the horizontal position of the plane as it nears. Nonprecision instrument runways are commonly found at small and medium airports. These runways may have threshold markings, centerlines, and designators. These runways may also have a special mark, called an aiming point, between 1000 and 1500 feet long along the centerline of the runway.

Medium and large airports will have **precision instrument runways**, which give the pilot feedback on both horizontal and vertical position when the plane is on instrument approach. A precision instrument runway includes thresholds, designators, centerlines, aiming points, blast pads, stopways, and touchdown zone marks every 500 feet from the 500-foot to the 3000-foot mark.

Runways are named according to their **direction** on the compass, ranging from 01 to 36. So, for instance, due south would be runway 18 ("one-eight"), and due west would be runway 27 ("two-seven"). In North America, the runways are named in accordance with geographic (grid) north, rather than magnetic north. Of course, a runway may have two names, one for each direction in which it is used. The same runway may be referred to as runway 05 ("zero-five") or runway 23 ("two-three") depending on the direction it is being used on a given day. In most cases, fixed-wing aircraft take off and land against the wind, because the extra amount of air over the wing will increase lift (and reduce the required ground speed).

In the event that **multiple runways** travel in the same direction, they will be distinguished from each other by their relative positions according to an observer on approach from the appropriate direction: left or right runway if there are only two; left, right, or center runway if there are three. Of course, a runway that is on the right when travelling in one direction will be on the left when it is being used in the opposite direction.

In most cases, **runway lights** are operated by the airport control tower. There are a number of different components to a runway lighting system. A Runway Centerline Lighting System is a line of white lights mounted every fifty feet along the centerline. When the approaching plane gets within 3000 feet of the runway, the lights begin to blink red and white; when the plane gets within 1000 feet, the lights become solid red. Precision instrument runways have runway end lights and edge lights. Runway end lights run the width of both ends of the runway: from the ground these lights appear red, while they appear green from above. Runway edge lights run the length of the runway on both sides. This lighting typically changes color as well when the plane gets within a certain distance of the front end of the runway. There are similar lights marking the boundaries of taxiways. An Approach Lighting System is a set of strobe lights and/or lightbars that indicate the end of the runway from which descending aircraft should arrive. Runway end identification lights are synchronized lights that flash at the runway thresholds. At some airports these lights face in every direction, while at others they only face the direction from which planes approach. Runway end identification lights are useful when the runway doesn't stand out from the surrounding area, or when visibility is poor.

Some big airports also have **Visual Approach Slope Indicators**, which give the incoming pilot useful information. In a typical VASI system, white lights indicate the lower glide path limits, and red lights indicate the upper. The VASI should be visible for twenty miles at night and for three to five miles during the day under normal conditions. An effective VASI should keep the plane clear of obstructions so long as it remains within approximately ten degrees of the extended runway centerline and within four nautical miles of the runway threshold.

Practice Questions

1. What would be the name of a runway that the pilot approaches while heading due east?

a. Runway 01
b. Runway 09
c. Runway 27
d. Runway E
e. Runway B

2. Which part of a fixed-wing airplane supplies the thrust?

a. Tail assembly
b. Control surfaces
c. Fuselage
d. Landing gear
e. Powerplant

3. What is the path of the chord line on a wing?

a. From leading edge to trailing edge, through the wing
b. From leading edge to trailing edge, along the surface of the wing
c. Along the inside of the wing, such that the upper and lower wings are equal in thickness
d. From one wingtip to the other
e. From wingtip to fuselage

4. Which of the following statements about a medium bank is true?

a. A plane will tend to level out from a medium bank unless there is input from the pilot.
b. A plane that is put into a medium bank will tend to increase its bank unless the ailerons are applied.
c. A medium bank is between ten and thirty degrees.
d. A medium bank is between thirty and fifty degrees.
e. A plane will tend to remain in a medium bank until the pilot makes an adjustment.

5. Which of the following is NOT one of the four basic maneuvers in flight?

a. Turn
b. Spin
c. Straight-and-level flight
d. Climb
e. Descent

Practice Answers

1. B: The name of a runway pointing due east would be Runway 9. The names of runways are based on the compass. A runway pointing due south would be Runway 18, and a runway pointing due west would be Runway 27. Of course, every runway will be called by two names, depending on which direction planes are traveling on it. Runway 9 will become Runway 27 when the planes travel west rather than east. When the names of runways are spoken, each number in the name is stated individually. So, Runway 24 would be spoken, "Runway Two-Four" rather than "Runway Twenty-four."

2. E: The powerplant supplies the thrust for a fixed-wing aircraft. The powerplant may be a jet engine or an engine and a set of propellers. Thrust is the force that propels the plane forward.

3. A: The chord line runs through the wing from the leading edge to the trailing edge. This line divides the upper and lower surfaces of the wing. This is one of the key elements of wing design. The distance from one wingtip to the other, meanwhile, is called the wingspan. The mean camber line runs along the inside of the wing, such that the upper and lower wings are equal in thickness.

4. E: A plane will tend to remain in a medium bank until the pilot makes an adjustment. A medium bank is between 20 and 45 degrees. A shallow bank, on the other hand, is less than 20 degrees, and requires the assistance of the ailerons to maintain itself. A steep bank is greater than 45 degrees. When a plane enters a steep bank, it will tend to increase the bank unless the ailerons are used to prevent this. Turning occurs because of the forces that act on a banked wing. The plane will be pushed in a direction perpendicular to the wings.

5. B: Spin is not one of the four basic maneuvers in flight. Straight-and-level flight, turn, climb, and descent are the four basic flight maneuvers. Straight-and-level flight occurs when the plane maintains a constant altitude and is pointed in the same direction. Of course, maintaining the same altitude and direction requires a number of adjustments. Turns are made by banking the wings in the direction of the turn. For example, turning to the right requires lowering the right wing. A climb requires raising the nose of the plane and increasing the power from the engine. Finally, there are a few types of descent. A plane may descend with its nose up, down, or level.

Self-Description Inventory

The final section of the AFOQT is a self-description inventory, or basically a personality test. You will be shown a series of statements and you will have to decide how well those statements describe you. There are no right or wrong answers to the questions in this section, so don't spend a lot of thinking about them. Your first instinct will usually be the most accurate assessment of yourself.

AFOQT Practice Test #1

Want to take this practice test in an online interactive format?
Check out the bonus page, which includes interactive practice questions and much more: **https://www.mometrix.com/bonus948/afoqt**

Verbal Analogies

1. CHASTISE is to REPRIMAND as IMPETUOUS is to

a. PUNISH
b. RASH
c. CONSIDERED
d. POOR
e. CALM

2. ARM is to HUMERUS as LEG is to

a. ULNA
b. CLAVICLE
c. FEMUR
d. MANDIBLE
e. METACARPAL

3. MULTIPLICATION is to DIVISION as PRODUCT is to

a. QUOTIENT
b. DIVISOR
c. INTEGER
d. DIVIDEND
e. MULTIPLIER

4. WEAR is to SWEATER as EAT is to

a. SHIRT
b. TOP HAT
c. ASPARAGUS
d. LOOKS
e. MOUTH

5. MONEY is to IMPECUNIOUS as FOOD is to

a. FAMISHED
b. NAUSEATED
c. DISTRACTED
d. ANTAGONISTIC
e. IMPOVERISHED

6. DENIGRATE is to MALIGN as DEMUR is to

a. PROTEST
b. DEFER
c. SLANDER
d. BENUMB
e. BELITTLE

7. OBEISANCE is to DEFERENCE as MUNIFICENT is to

a. BENEVOLENT
b. MAGNIFICENT
c. SQUALID
d. GENEROUS
e. AVARICE

8. GOAT is to NANNY as PIG is to

a. SHOAT
b. EWE
c. CUB
d. SOW
e. CALF

9. CACHE is to RESERVE as DEARTH is to

a. STOCKPILE
b. PAUCITY
c. CUDGEL
d. DIRGE
e. SOMBER

10. ARABLE is to FARMABLE as ASYLUM is to

a. FAMINE
b. DANGER
c. ARID
d. FERTILE
e. REFUGE

11. MYRIAD is to FEW as STATIONARY is to

a. PERIPATETIC
b. MANY
c. SEVERAL
d. HALTED
e. PARKED

12. HOUSE is to MANSION as BOTTLE is to

a. FLAGON
b. CONTAINER
c. VESSEL
d. POT
e. FLASK

13. DICTIONARY is to DEFINITIONS as THESAURUS is to

a. PRONUNCIATIONS
b. SYNONYMS
c. EXPLANATIONS
d. PRONOUNS
e. DEFINITIONS

14. ABSTRUSE is to ESOTERIC as ADAMANT is to

a. YIELDING
b. STUBBORN
c. KEEN
d. FORTHRIGHT
e. FLEXIBLE

15. BEES is to HIVE as CATTLE is to

a. SWARM
b. POD
c. HERD
d. FLOCK
e. PACK

16. LATITUDE is to LONGITUDE as PARALLEL is to

a. STRAIT
b. LINE
c. EQUATOR
d. AQUIFER
e. MERIDIAN

17. PREVENTION is to DETERRENCE as INCITEMENT is to

a. EXCITEMENT
b. PROVOCATION
c. REQUEST
d. DISREGARD
e. DISGUST

18. VALUE is to WORTH as MEASURE is to

a. GAUGE
b. ALLOWANCE
c. DEMERIT
d. INSIGNIFICANCE
e. LARGE

19. ENERVATE is to ENERGIZE as ESPOUSE is to

a. OPPOSE
b. WED
c. EQUINE
d. EPISTOLARY
e. MARRY

20. HAMMER is to CARPENTER as STETHOSCOPE is to

a. PATIENT
b. HEARING
c. HEARTBEAT
d. DOCTOR
e. PEDOMETER

21. ARMOIRE is to BEDROOM as DESK is to

a. CHAIR
b. OFFICE
c. COMPUTER
d. WORK
e. BUILDING

22. PLANKTON is to WHALES as BAMBOO is to

a. PREDATORS
b. GRASSES
c. PANDAS
d. FAST-GROWING
e. CHINA

23. TUNDRA is to ARCTIC as SAVANNA is to

a. PRAIRIE
b. LUSH
c. TROPIC
d. GEORGIA
e. JUNGLE

24. THIRSTY is to PARCHED as HUNGRY is to

a. FAMISHED
b. FED
c. SATIATED
d. SATISFIED
e. FULL

25. FELICITY is to SADNESS as IGNOMINY is to

a. SHAME
b. SLANDER
c. CRIME
d. INDICT
e. HONOR

Arithmetic Reasoning

1. A man buys two shirts. One is $7.50 and the other is $3.00. A 6% tax is added to his total. How much does he pay in all?

a. $10.50
b. $11.13
c. $14.58
d. $16.80
e. $18.21

2. If a chef can make 25 pastries in a day, how many can he make in a week?

a. 32
b. 74
c. 126
d. 175
e. 250

3. A woman must earn $250 in the next four days to pay a traffic ticket. How much will she have to earn each day?

a. $45.50
b. $62.50
c. $75.50
d. $100.50
e. $125.00

4. A car lot has an inventory of 476 cars. If 36 people bought cars in the week after the inventory was taken, how many cars will remain in inventory at the end of that week?

a. 440
b. 476
c. 484
d. 512
e. 536

5. A woman has $450 in a bank account. She earns 0.5% interest on her end-of-month balance. How much interest will she earn for the month?

a. $0.50
b. $2.25
c. $4.28
d. $4.73
e. $6.34

6. Three children decide to buy a gift for their father. The gift costs $78. One child contributes $24. The second contributes $15 less than the first. How much will the third child have to contribute?

a. $15
b. $39
c. $45
d. $62
e. $69

7. Two women have credit cards. One earns 3 points for every dollar she spends. The other earns 6 points for every dollar she spends. If they each spend $5.00, how many combined total points will they earn?

a. 15
b. 30
c. 45
d. 60
e. 75

8. A company employing 540 individuals plans to increase its workforce by 13%. How many people will the company employ after the expansion? Round to the nearest whole number.

a. 527
b. 547
c. 553
d. 570
e. 610

9. A 13-story building has 65 apartments. If each floor has an equal number of apartments, how many apartments are on each floor?

a. 2
b. 3
c. 4
d. 5
e. 6

10. If 5 people buy 3 pens each and 3 people buy 7 pencils each, what is the ratio of the total number of pens sold to the total number of pencils sold?

a. 7:3
b. 3:7
c. 5:7
d. 1:1
e. 5:3

11. A man earns $15.23 per hour and gets a raise of $2.34 per hour. What is his new hourly rate of pay?

a. $12.89
b. $15.46
c. $17.57
d. $23.40
e. $35.64

12. How many people can travel on 6 planes if each carries 300 passengers?

a. 1,800
b. 1,200
c. 600
d. 350
e. 300

13. In a town, the ratio of men to women is 2: 1. If the number of women in the town is doubled, what will be the new ratio of men to women?

a. 1: 2
b. 1: 1
c. 2: 1
d. 3: 1
e. 4: 1

14. A woman weighing 250 pounds goes on a diet. During the first week, she loses 3% of her body weight. During the second week, she loses 2% of her new body weight. At the end of the second week, how many pounds has she lost in all?

a. 12.5
b. 10
c. 12.35
d. 15
e. 17.5

15. A woman is traveling to a destination 600 km away. If she drives 80 km every hour, how many hours will it take for her to reach her destination?

a. 2.0
b. 3.5
c. 5.0
d. 7.5
e. 8.5

16. If one gallon of paint can paint 3 rooms, how many rooms can be painted with 28 gallons of paint?

a. 10
b. 25
c. 56
d. 84
e. 92

17. Five workers each earn $135/day. What is the total amount earned by the five workers?

a. $675
b. $700
c. $725
d. $750
e. $775

18. A girl scores a 99 on her math test. On her second test, her score drops by 15. On the third test, she scores 5 points higher than she did on her second. What was the girl's score on the third test?

a. 79
b. 84
c. 89
d. 99
e. 104

19. A man goes to the mall with $50.00. He spends $15.64 in one store and $7.12 in a second store. How much does he have left?

a. $27.24
b. $32.76
c. $34.36
d. $42.80
e. $57.12

20. 600 students must share a school that has 20 classrooms. How many students will each classroom contain if there are an equal number of students in each class?

a. 10
b. 15
c. 20
d. 25
e. 30

21. Four workers at a shelter agree to care for the dogs over a holiday. If there are 48 dogs, how many must each worker look after?

a. 8
b. 10
c. 12
d. 14
e. 16

22. One worker has an office that is 20 feet long. Another has an office that is 6 feet longer. What is the combined length of both offices?

a. 26 feet
b. 36 feet
c. 46 feet
d. 56 feet
e. 66 feet

23. Four friends go shopping. They purchase items that cost $6.65 and $159.23. If they split the cost evenly, how much will each friend have to pay?

a. $26.64
b. $39.81
c. $41.47
d. $55.30
e. $82.95

24. A 140-acre forest is cut in half to make way for development. What is the size of the new forest's acreage?

a. 70
b. 80
c. 90
d. 100
e. 120

25. A farmer has 360 cows. He decides to sell 45. Shortly after, he purchases 85 more cows. How many cows does he have?

a. 230
b. 315
c. 400
d. 490
e. 530

Word Knowledge

Select the answer choice that is closest in meaning to the given word.

1. SPOILED

a. Ruined
b. Splendid
c. Told
d. Believed
e. Hated

2. OATH

a. Delivery
b. Promise
c. Statement
d. Criticism
e. Threat

3. INQUIRE

a. Invest
b. Ask
c. Tell
d. Release
e. Inquest

4. COMPREHEND

a. Learn
b. Speak
c. Understand
d. Appreciate
e. Commemorate

5. APPARENT

a. Clear
b. Occasional
c. Angry
d. Applied
e. Father

6. SILENCE

a. Darkness
b. Excitement
c. Quiet
d. Mood
e. Quaint

7. ABSOLUTELY

a. Assuredly
b. Rapidly
c. Never
d. Weakly
e. completely

8. MODIFIED

a. Checked
b. Shortened
c. Considered
d. Changed
e. Lengthened

9. DELICATE

a. Fragile
b. Sturdy
c. Loud
d. Soft
e. Lovely

10. FESTIVITIES

a. Commitments
b. Celebrations
c. Crowds
d. Dates
e. Funeral

11. EXHAUSTED

a. Excited
b. Tired
c. Worried
d. Energized
e. Animated

12. CLEANSED

a. Examined
b. Washed
c. Touched
d. Dried
e. Motivated

13. BATTLED

a. Fought
b. Attempt
c. Bold
d. Saw
e. Excited

14. WANDERED

a. Looked
b. Shopped
c. Roamed
d. Searched
e. Lived

15. ABRUPTLY

a. Homely
b. Commonly
c. Wisely
d. Ugly
e. Suddenly

16. TRICKED

a. Conned
b. Begged
c. Convinced
d. Nagged
e. Criticized

17. EXTREMELY

a. Almost
b. Slightly
c. Very
d. Clearly
e. Happily

18. DOUBTFUL

a. Uncertain
b. Panicked
c. Pondering
d. Indifferent
e. Confused

19. PECULIAR

a. Original
b. Novel
c. Dull
d. Strange
e. Awesome

20. COURTEOUS

a. Handsome
b. Polite
c. Inconsiderate
d. Odd
e. Unrelenting

21. TROUBLED

a. Relieved
b. Satisfied
c. Bothered
d. Relaxed
e. Persistent

22. PERSPIRATION

a. Sweat
b. Work
c. Help
d. Advice
e. Job

23. TREMBLED

a. Spoke
b. Shook
c. Wept
d. Ducked
e. Cowered

24. ADHERED

a. Stuck
b. Went
c. Spoke
d. Altered
e. Stunk

25. TIDY

a. Furnished
b. Warm
c. Locked
d. Neat
e. Inviting

Mathematics Knowledge

1. A rectangle has a width of 7 cm and a length of 9 cm. What is its perimeter?

a. 16 cm
b. 32 cm
c. 48 cm
d. 62 cm
e. 63 cm

2. In the following inequality, solve for q.

$$-3q + 12 \geq 4q - 30$$

a. $q \geq 6$
b. $q = 6$
c. $q \neq 6$
d. $q \leq 6$
e. q does not exist

3. If $x - 6 = 0$, then x is equal to

a. 0
b. 3
c. 6
d. 9
e. 12

4. If $x = -3$, calculate the value of the following expression:

$$3x^3 + (3x + 4) - 2x^2$$

a. -104
b. -58
c. 58
d. 104
e. 0

5. If $3x - 30 = 45 - 2x$, what is the value of x?

a. 5
b. 10
c. 15
d. 20
e. 25

6. Solve for x in the following inequality.

$$\frac{1}{4}x - 25 \geq 75$$

a. $x \geq 400$
b. $x \leq 400$
c. $x \geq 25$
d. $x \leq 25$
e. $x \geq 50$

7. If $x^2 - 5 = 20$, what is one possible value of x?

a. 5
b. 10
c. 12.5
d. 15
e. 25

8. What is the area of a square that has a perimeter of 8 cm?

a. 2 cm^2
b. 4 cm^2
c. 32 cm^2
d. 64 cm^2
e. 160 cm^2

9. If $x = 4$ and $y = 2$, what is the value of the following expression:

$$3xy - 12y + 5x$$

a. -4
b. 10
c. 12
d. 20
e. 24

10. If $\frac{2}{3}x + 10 = 16$, what is the value of x?

a. 6
b. 7
c. 8
d. 9
e. 10

11. Simplify the following:

$$(3x + 5)(4x - 6)$$

a. $12x^2 - 38x - 30$
b. $12x^2 + 2x - 30$
c. $12x^2 - 2x - 1$
d. $12x^2 + 2x + 30$
e. $12x^2 + 7x - 30$

12. Simplify the following expression:

$$\frac{50x^{18}t^6w^3z^{20}}{5x^5t^2w^2z^{19}}$$

a. $10x^{13}t^3wz$
b. $10x^{13}t^4wz$
c. $10x^{12}t^4wz$
d. $10x^{13}t^4wz^2$
e. $10x^{12}t^3w^2z^2$

13. The quantity $n!$ (n-factorial) is defined as the product of all positive integers between n and zero. (i.e., $n \times (n-1) \times (n-2) \times \ldots \times 3 \times 2 \times 1$). The quantity $4!$ (four-factorial) is equal to

a. 4
b. 12
c. 16
d. 20
e. 24

14. If one side of a cube is 5 cm long, what is the volume of the cube?

a. 15 cm^3
b. 65 cm^3
c. 105 cm^3
d. 125 cm^3
e. 225 cm^3

15. Solve for x by factoring:

$$x^2 - 13x + 42 = 0$$

a. $x = 6,7$
b. $x = -6,-7$
c. $x = 6,-7$
d. $x = -6,7$
e. $x = 7$ only

16. A triangle has a base measuring 12 cm and a height of 12 cm. What is its area?

a. 24 cm^2
b. 56 cm^2
c. 72 cm^2
d. 144 cm^2
e. 288 cm^2

17. Simplify the following expression:

$$(3x^2 7x^7) + (2y^3 9y^{12})$$

a. $21x^{14} + 18y^{26}$
b. $10x^9 + 11y^{15}$
c. $21x^{14} + 18y^{15}$
d. $21x^9 + 18y^{15}$
e. $10x^{14} + 11y^{26}$

18. If $\frac{x}{3} + 27 = 30$, what is the value of x?

a. 3
b. 6
c. 9
d. 12
e. 27

19. What is the slope of a line with points A $(4, 1)$ and B $(-13, 8)$?

a. $\frac{7}{17}$
b. $-\frac{7}{17}$
c. $-\frac{17}{7}$
d. $\frac{17}{7}$
e. None of the above

20. If x is 20% of 200, what is the value of x?

a. 40
b. 80
c. 100
d. 150
e. 180

21. If a bag of balloons consists of 37 white balloons, 8 yellow balloons, and 15 black balloons, what is the probability that a balloon chosen randomly from the bag will be black?

a. 29%
b. 25%
c. 21%
d. 17%
e. 13%

22. A raffle game has a single grand prize that will be drawn randomly from among all the tickets. A total of 500 tickets are sold. If a man buys 25 tickets, what is the probability that he will win the grand prize?

a. 1 in 2
b. 1 in 5
c. 1 in 10
d. 1 in 20
e. 1 in 40

23. What is the volume of a rectangular prism with a height of 10 cm, a length of 5 cm, and a width of 6 cm?

a. 30 cm^3
b. 60 cm^3
c. 150 cm^3
d. 240 cm^3
e. 300 cm^3

24. What is the midpoint of a line segment that runs from point A $(6, 20)$ to point B $(10, 40)$?

a. $(30, 8)$
b. $(16, 60)$
c. $(8, 30)$
d. $(7, 15)$
e. $(15, 8)$

25. If $5x + 60 = 75$, what is the value of x?

a. 3
b. 4
c. 5
d. 6
e. 7

Reading Comprehension

Passage 1

Air is a gas which means it can be compressed or expanded. When air is compressed, a greater amount of air can occupy a fixed volume. Conversely, when pressure on a fixed amount of air is decreased, the air expands and occupies a greater volume. That is, the original column of air at a lower pressure has a lower density. In fact, density is directly proportional to pressure. If the pressure is doubled, the density is doubled, and if the pressure is lowered, so is the density. This statement is true only at a constant temperature.

Increasing the temperature of a substance decreases its density. Conversely, decreasing the temperature increases the density. Thus, the density of air varies inversely with temperature. This statement is true only at a constant pressure. In the atmosphere, both temperature and pressure decrease with altitude and have conflicting effects upon density. However, the fairly rapid drop in pressure as altitude is increased usually has the dominant effect. Hence, pilots can expect the density to decrease with altitude.

The preceding paragraphs are based on the presupposition of perfectly dry air. In reality, it is never completely dry. The small amount of water vapor suspended in the atmosphere is typically considered negligible under most circumstances, but in certain tropical conditions, it can make a measurable difference. Water vapor is lighter than air; consequently, moist air is lighter than dry air. Therefore, as the water content of the air increases, the air becomes less dense, increasing density altitude and decreasing performance. It is lightest or least dense when, in a given set of conditions, it contains the maximum amount of water vapor.

Humidity, also called relative humidity, refers to the amount of water vapor contained in the atmosphere and is expressed as a percentage of the maximum amount of water vapor the air can hold. This amount varies with the temperature; warm air can hold more water vapor, while colder air can hold less. Perfectly dry air that contains no water vapor has a relative humidity of zero percent, while saturated air that cannot hold any more water vapor has a relative humidity of 100 percent. Humidity alone is usually not considered an essential factor in calculating density altitude and aircraft performance; however, it does contribute.

The higher the temperature, the greater amount of water vapor that the air can hold. When comparing two separate air masses, the first warm and moist (both qualities making air lighter) and the second cold and dry (both qualities making it heavier), the first must be less dense than the second. Pressure and temperature have a great influence on aircraft performance because of their effect upon density. There is no rule-of-thumb or chart used to compute the effects of humidity on density altitude, but expect a decrease in overall performance in high humidity conditions.

1. The primary purpose of the passage is to

a. Explain the qualities of air that may affect flight
b. Explain g-force and how it works
c. Describe the constituent elements of air
d. Explain humidity
e. Describe the ideal air conditions for flight

2. In the second paragraph, *inversely* most nearly means

a. Severely
b. Incredibly
c. In the opposite direction
d. In an unrelated fashion
e. Concurrently

3. If the air temperature drops while a plane is gaining altitude, the pilot can expect

a. The density of the air to increase
b. The humidity of the air to increase
c. The air pressure to increase
d. The density of the air to decrease
e. Aircraft performance to decrease

4. With which one of the following claims about air quality would the author most likely agree?

a. Pilots never need to pay attention to relative humidity.
b. For a pilot, the density of air is more important than the relative humidity.
c. Completely dry air is very rare.
d. Aircraft performance is unrelated to humidity.
e. The best conditions for flying are very hot and humid.

5. What is the most likely reason why there is no chart for assessing the effects of humidity on density altitude?

a. Humidity does not affect density altitude.
b. It is impossible to measure humidity.
c. Humidity does not affect flight performance very much.
d. Humidity varies a great deal in relatively small areas.
e. Density altitude never varies.

Passage 2

The climb performance of an aircraft is affected by certain variables. The conditions of the aircraft's maximum climb angle or maximum climb rate occur at specific speeds, and variations in speed will produce variations in climb performance. There is sufficient latitude in most aircraft that small variations in speed from the optimum do not produce large changes in climb performance, and certain operational considerations may require speeds slightly different from the optimum. Of course, climb performance would be most critical with high gross weight, at high altitude, in obstructed takeoff areas, or during malfunction of a powerplant. Then, optimum climb speeds are necessary.

Weight has a very pronounced effect on aircraft performance. If weight is added to an aircraft, it must fly at a higher angle of attack (AOA) to maintain a given altitude and speed. This increases the induced drag of the wings, as well as the parasite drag of the aircraft. Increased drag means that additional thrust is needed to overcome it, which in turn means that less reserve thrust is available for climbing. Aircraft designers go to great effort to minimize the weight since it has such a marked effect on the factors pertaining to performance.

A change in an aircraft's weight produces a twofold effect on climb performance. First, a change in weight will change the drag and the power required. This alters the reserve power available, which in turn, affects both the climb angle and the climb rate. Secondly, an increase in weight will reduce the maximum rate of climb, but the aircraft must be operated at a higher climb speed to achieve the smaller peak climb rate.

An increase in altitude also will increase the power required and decrease the power available. Therefore, the climb performance of an aircraft diminishes with altitude. The speeds for maximum rate of climb, maximum angle of climb, and maximum and minimum level flight airspeeds vary with altitude. As altitude is increased, these various speeds finally converge at the absolute ceiling of the aircraft. At the absolute ceiling, there is no excess of power and only one speed will allow steady, level flight. Consequently, the absolute ceiling of an aircraft produces zero rate of climb. The service ceiling is the altitude at which the aircraft is unable to climb at a rate greater than 100 feet per minute (fpm). Usually, these specific performance reference points are provided for the aircraft at a specific design configuration.

In discussing performance, it frequently is convenient to use the terms power loading, wing loading, blade loading, and disk loading. Power loading is expressed in pounds per horsepower and is obtained by dividing the total weight of the aircraft by the rated horsepower of the engine. It is a significant factor in an aircraft's takeoff and climb capabilities. Wing loading is expressed in pounds per square foot and is obtained by dividing the total weight of an airplane in pounds by the wing area (including ailerons) in square feet. It is the airplane's wing loading that determines the landing speed. Blade loading is expressed in pounds per square foot and is obtained by dividing the total weight of a helicopter by the area of the rotor blades. Blade loading is not to be confused with disk loading, which is the total weight of a helicopter divided by the area of the disk swept by the rotor blades.

6. Which of the following would be the best title for this passage?

a. The Importance of Weight
b. Climb Performance and You
c. Power Loading, Wing Loading, and Disk Loading
d. Influences on Climb Performance
e. Achieving Maximum Climb Angle

7. In the second paragraph, *pronounced* most nearly means

a. Selective
b. Intoned
c. Detrimental
d. Spoken
e. Noticeable

8. Which of the following is NOT one of the effects of increased weight on flight performance?

a. Diminished reserve power
b. Decreased climb rate
c. Lower angle of attack required to maintain altitude
d. Diminished maximum rate of climb
e. Increased drag

9. With which one of the following claims about climb performance would the author most likely agree?

a. Optimal climb performance can be achieved even with heavy cargo.
b. At the end of a long journey, a plane will have a higher maximum rate of climb.
c. A plane can handle any amount of weight, though climb performance will be affected.
d. Pilots have no influence over climb performance.
e. The climb performance of a two-engine plane will remain the same even if one engine fails.

10. If a helicopter weighs two tons and its rotor blades cover an area of five hundred square feet, what is its disc loading measure?

a. 8 pounds per square foot
b. 125 square foot-pounds
c. 0.125 tons per square foot
d. 4 metric tons
e. 8 ton-feet

Passage 3

The aerodynamic properties of an aircraft generally determine the power requirements at various conditions of flight, while the powerplant capabilities generally determine the power available at various conditions of flight. When an aircraft is in steady, level flight, a condition of equilibrium must prevail. An unaccelerated condition of flight is achieved when lift equals weight, and the powerplant is set for thrust equal to drag. The power required to achieve equilibrium in constant-altitude flight at various airspeeds is depicted on a power required curve. The power required curve illustrates the fact that at low airspeeds near the stall or minimum controllable airspeed, the power setting required for steady, level flight is quite high.

Flight in the region of normal command means that while holding a constant altitude, a higher airspeed requires a higher power setting, and a lower airspeed requires a lower power setting. The majority of aircraft flying (climb, cruise, and maneuvers) is conducted in the region of normal command.

Flight in the region of reversed command means flight in which a higher airspeed requires a lower power setting, and a lower airspeed requires a higher power setting to hold altitude. It does not imply that a decrease in power will produce lower airspeed. The region of reversed command is encountered in the low speed phases of flight. Flight speeds below the speed for maximum endurance (lowest point on the power curve) require higher power settings with a decrease in airspeed. Since the need to increase the required power setting with decreased speed is contrary to the normal command of flight, the regime of flight speeds between the speed for minimum required power setting and the stall speed (or minimum control speed) is termed the region of reversed command. In the region of reversed command, a decrease in airspeed must be accompanied by an increased power setting in order to maintain steady flight.

An airplane performing a low airspeed, high pitch attitude power approach for a short-field landing is an example of operating in the region of reversed command. If an unacceptably high sink rate should develop, it may be possible for the pilot to reduce or stop the descent by applying power. But without further use of power, the airplane would probably stall or be incapable of flaring for the landing. Merely lowering the nose of the airplane to regain flying speed in this situation, without the use of power, would result in a rapid sink rate and corresponding loss of altitude.

If during a soft-field takeoff and climb, for example, the pilot attempts to climb out of ground effect without first attaining normal climb pitch attitude and airspeed, the airplane may inadvertently enter the region of reversed command at a dangerously low altitude. Even with full power, the airplane may be incapable of climbing or even maintaining altitude. The pilot's only recourse in this situation is to lower the pitch attitude in order to increase airspeed, which will inevitably result in a loss of altitude. Airplane pilots must give particular attention to precise control of airspeed when operating in the low flight speeds of the region of reversed command.

11. The primary purpose of the passage is to

a. Instruct pilots on proper airspeed.
b. Discuss the interrelationships of airspeed, power, and pitch attitude.
c. Explain reversed command.
d. Discuss the physics of flight at low airspeeds.
e. Persuade the reader to fly faster aircraft.

12. In the fifth paragraph, *inadvertently* most nearly means

a. Unintentionally
b. Indirectly
c. Sequentially
d. Primarily
e. Eventually

13. In which region of command does most flight occur?

a. Inverse command
b. Normal command
c. Direct command
d. Reverse command
e. Decreased command

14. With which one of the following statements about flight would the author most likely agree?

a. As speed increases, the power required to descend decreases.
b. As speed increases, the power required to descend remains constant.
c. As speed decreases, the power required to climb remains constant.
d. As speed increases, the power required to maintain altitude increases.
e. As speed decreases, the power required to maintain altitude increases.

15. Which of the following would be the best title for this passage?

a. How to Avoid Reversed Command
b. Normal Command Flight
c. Learning to Fly
d. Power Requirements During Flight
e. Reversed Command and the Modern Pilot

Passage 4

In many cases, the landing distance of an aircraft will define the runway requirements for flight operations. The minimum landing distance is obtained by landing at some minimum safe speed, which allows sufficient margin above stall and provides satisfactory control and capability for a go-around. Generally, the landing speed is some fixed percentage of the stall speed or minimum control speed for the aircraft in the landing configuration. As such, the landing will be accomplished at some particular value of lift coefficient and angle of attack (AOA). The exact values will depend on the aircraft characteristics but, once defined, the values are independent of weight, altitude, and wind.

To obtain minimum landing distance at the specified landing speed, the forces that act on the aircraft must provide maximum deceleration during the landing roll. The forces acting on the aircraft during the landing roll may require various procedures to maintain landing deceleration at the peak value.

A distinction should be made between the procedures for minimum landing distance and an ordinary landing roll with considerable excess runway available. Minimum landing distance will be obtained by creating a continuous peak deceleration of the aircraft; that is, extensive use of the brakes for maximum deceleration. On the other hand, an ordinary landing roll with considerable excess runway may allow extensive use of aerodynamic drag to minimize wear and tear on the tires and brakes. If aerodynamic drag is sufficient to cause deceleration, it can be used in deference to the brakes in the early stages of the landing roll; i.e., brakes and tires suffer from continuous hard use, but aircraft aerodynamic drag is free and does not wear out with use.

The use of aerodynamic drag is applicable only for deceleration to 60 or 70 percent of the touchdown speed. At speeds less than 60 to 70 percent of the touchdown speed, aerodynamic drag is so slight as to be of little use, and braking must be utilized to produce continued deceleration. Since the objective during the landing roll is to decelerate, the powerplant thrust should be the smallest possible positive value (or largest possible negative value in the case of thrust reversers). In addition to the important factors of proper procedures, many other variables affect the landing performance. Any item that alters the landing speed or deceleration rate during the landing roll will affect the landing distance.

The effect of gross weight on landing distance is one of the principal items determining the landing distance. One effect of an increased gross weight is that a greater speed will be required to support the aircraft at the landing AOA and lift coefficient. For an example of the effect of a change in gross weight, a 21 percent increase in landing weight will require a ten percent increase in landing speed to support the greater weight.

When minimum landing distances are considered, braking friction forces predominate during the landing roll and, for the majority of aircraft configurations, braking friction is the main source of deceleration.

The minimum landing distance will vary in direct proportion to the gross weight. For example, a ten percent increase in gross weight at landing would cause a:

- Five percent increase in landing velocity
- Ten percent increase in landing distance

A contingency of this is the relationship between weight and braking friction force.

The effect of wind on landing distance is large and deserves proper consideration when predicting landing distance. Since the aircraft will land at a particular airspeed independent of the wind, the principal effect of wind on landing distance is the change in the groundspeed at which the aircraft touches down. The effect of wind on deceleration during the landing is identical to the effect on acceleration during the takeoff.

The effect of pressure altitude and ambient temperature is to define density altitude and its effect on landing performance. An increase in density altitude increases the landing speed but does not alter the net retarding force. Thus, the aircraft at altitude lands at the same indicated airspeed as at sea level but, because of the reduced density, the true airspeed is greater. Since the aircraft lands at altitude with the same weight and dynamic pressure, the drag and braking friction throughout the landing roll have the same values as at sea level. As long as the condition is within the capability of the brakes, the net retarding force is unchanged, and the deceleration is the same as with the landing at sea level. Since an increase in altitude does not alter deceleration, the effect of density altitude on landing distance is due to the greater true airspeed.

16. The main purpose of the passage is to

a. Give some examples of near accidents during landing.
b. Improve landing skills.
c. Explain the effects of varying pressure altitudes.
d. Advocate safer protocols for landing.
e. Describe the factors that influence landing distance.

17. Why will a pilot rely on aerodynamic drag when making a normal landing?

a. To increase the rate of deceleration
b. To avoid wearing down the brakes and tires
c. To avoid unnecessary turbulence
d. To mitigate a large gross weight
e. To simplify landing procedures

18. In the fifth paragraph, *principal* most nearly means

a. Most important
b. Easiest
c. Moral
d. First
e. Value

19. Why must a heavier plane land at a higher speed?

a. To diminish fuel supplies and thereby decrease gross weight
b. To encourage a stall just before landing
c. To avoid hitting the runway with too much force
d. To improve handling on the runway
e. To allow for the longest landing distance

20. With which one of the following claims about landing performance would the author most likely agree?

a. Many landings occur without any use of the brakes.
b. Ambient temperature has no effect on minimum landing distance.
c. Gross weight and minimum landing distance are positively correlated.
d. Runway length is less important than gross weight in determining the appropriate airspeed during landing.
e. Minimum landing distance is generally consistent for aircraft of the same size.

Passage 5

For over 25 years, the importance of good pilot judgment, or aeronautical decision-making (ADM), has been recognized as critical to the safe operation of aircraft, as well as accident avoidance. The airline industry, motivated by the need to reduce accidents caused by human factors, developed the first training programs based on improving ADM. Crew resource management (CRM) training for flight crews is focused on the effective use of all available resources: human resources, hardware, and information supporting ADM to facilitate crew cooperation and improve decision-making. The goal of all flight crews is good ADM and the use of CRM is one way to make good decisions.

Research in this area prompted the Federal Aviation Administration (FAA) to produce training directed at improving the decision-making of pilots and led to current FAA regulations that require that decision-making be taught as part of the pilot training curriculum. ADM research, development, and testing culminated in 1987 with the publication of six manuals oriented to the decision-making needs of variously rated pilots.

These manuals provided multifaceted materials designed to reduce the number of decision-related accidents. The effectiveness of these materials was validated in independent studies where student pilots received such training in conjunction with the standard flying curriculum. When tested, the pilots who had received ADM training made fewer inflight errors than those who had not received ADM training. The differences were statistically significant and ranged from about 10 to 50 percent fewer judgment errors. In the operational environment, an operator flying about 400,000 hours annually demonstrated a 54 percent reduction in accident rate after using these materials for recurrency training.

Contrary to popular opinion, good judgment can be taught. Tradition held that good judgment was a natural by-product of experience, but as pilots continued to log accident-free flight hours, a corresponding increase of good judgment was assumed. Building upon the foundation of conventional decision-making, ADM enhances the process to decrease the probability of human error and increase the probability of a safe flight. ADM provides a structured, systematic approach to analyzing changes that occur during a flight and how these changes might affect a flight's safe outcome. The ADM process addresses all aspects of decision-making in the flight deck and identifies the steps involved in good decision-making.

Steps for good decision-making are:

1. Identifying personal attitudes hazardous to safe flight
2. Learning behavior modification techniques
3. Learning how to recognize and cope with stress
4. Developing risk assessment skills
5. Using all resources
6. Evaluating the effectiveness of one's ADM skills

Risk management is an important component of ADM. When a pilot follows good decision-making practices, the inherent risk in a flight is reduced or even eliminated. The ability to make good decisions is based upon direct or indirect experience and education.

Consider automotive seat belt use. In just two decades, seat belt use has become the norm, placing those who do not wear seat belts outside the norm, but this group may learn to wear a seat belt by either direct or indirect experience.

For example, a driver learns through direct experience about the value of wearing a seat belt when he or she is involved in a car accident that leads to a personal injury. An indirect learning experience occurs when a loved one is injured during a car accident because he or she failed to wear a seat belt.

While poor decision-making in everyday life does not always lead to tragedy, the margin for error in aviation is thin. Since ADM enhances management of an aeronautical environment, all pilots should become familiar with and employ ADM.

21. The primary purpose of the passage is to

a. List the steps in good decision-making.
b. Improve the decision-making abilities of the reader.
c. Outline the relationship between aeronautical decision-making and crew resource management.
d. Discuss aeronautical decision-making.
e. Inspire the reader to make better decisions.

22. According to the passage, how is aviation safety distinguished from other forms of safety?

a. Aviation safety is much simpler than most other areas of safety.
b. Aviation safety is no different than most other areas of safety.
c. Aviation safety is only important to a small percentage of the population.
d. There is a smaller margin for error in aviation.
e. Aviation safety can be systematized.

23. In the second paragraph, *conjunction* most nearly means

a. Combination
b. Linking word
c. Opposition
d. Collection
e. Organization

24. With which one of the following claims about aeronautical decision-making would the author most likely agree?

a. The body of knowledge about ADM is increasing, and this will have a positive effect on flight safety.
b. Aeronautical decision-making is the responsibility of the pilot alone.
c. Eventually, researchers will establish a perfect set of decision-making tools for pilots.
d. Aeronautical decision-making is the only tool required for flight safety.
e. Aeronautical decision-making has no applications in areas other than flight.

25. When a pilot reads the account of a recent aviation accident, this is an opportunity for a(n)

a. Recertification
b. Direct learning experience
c. Implicit learning experience
d. Reorientation of learning
e. Indirect learning experience

Situational Judgment

SITUATION 1:

You are approached by a senior officer, who requests a private meeting with you. He asks you for your candid opinion on your immediate supervisor, who is a subordinate to the senior officer. You have a generally favorable opinion of the supervisor, but you do have a few complaints about her performance. Specifically, you feel that she does a poor job of running staff meetings.

Possible actions:

a. Decline to meet with the senior officer.
b. Meet with the senior officer, and focus on the ways your supervisor could improve staff meetings.
c. Give your candid opinion of your supervisor, including your criticisms, but emphasizing your overall positive opinion.
d. Write a letter to the senior officer, explaining your opinions about your supervisor.
e. Give the senior officer a glowing report of the supervisor, without mentioning your complaints.

1. Select the MOST EFFECTIVE action in response to the situation.

2. Select the LEAST EFFECTIVE action in response to the situation.

SITUATION 2:

While performing administrative work with another officer, you notice that he is manipulating the numbers on some reports. Specifically, the officer is inflating the amounts of time spent on certain training exercises. These reports are sent on to senior officers, who use them to assess the readiness of the airmen for more sophisticated and complicated missions. If men and women are unprepared for these more difficult missions, there is a greater risk of accident or injury, to themselves or others.

Possible actions:

a. Immediately report this infraction to your superior.
b. Wait until you can acquire clear proof of the data manipulation.
c. Say nothing at present, but keep an eye on this other officer.
d. Write an anonymous letter to the other officer, encouraging him to stop manipulating the data.
e. Go back over the other officer's work, correcting the data as necessary.

3. Select the MOST EFFECTIVE action in response to the situation.

4. Select the LEAST EFFECTIVE action in response to the situation.

Situation 3:

You and two of your fellow officers have been selected to interview candidates for a promotion. One of the three candidates (Candidate A) is known to be an old family friend of your commanding officer. During the interviews, Candidate A is, in your opinion, the most impressive. However, Candidate B also seems like an excellent choice for the position. Candidate C performs poorly. One of the other judges votes for Candidate A, and the other votes for Candidate B.

Possible actions:

a. Vote for Candidate B to avoid the appearance of favoritism.
b. Vote for Candidate C so that the decision will be passed on to another round of deliberation.
c. Abstain from voting.
d. Request a new set of candidates.
e. Vote for Candidate A because you feel he is the most qualified.

5. Select the MOST EFFECTIVE action in response to the situation.

6. Select the LEAST EFFECTIVE action in response to the situation.

Situation 4:

You attend a meeting with two other officers. During the meeting, these officers get into a heated conflict over a possible change in policy. You have heard that they have a personal antipathy, though you are not aware of its origins. They ask you to settle their dispute.

Possible actions:

a. Ignore the request, and instead lecture the two officers on the need for cooperation and goodwill in the military.
b. Take the side of the officer who you believe will be the most help to you in the future.
c. Refuse to take a side, citing the obvious personal differences between the two officers.
d. Select the option that you think is best, leaving aside everything you know about their personal conflict.
e. Take the side of the officer you like better.

7. Select the MOST EFFECTIVE action in response to the situation.

8. Select the LEAST EFFECTIVE action in response to the situation.

Situation 5:

You are asked to collaborate on an important project with an officer from a different unit. This officer is very close to retirement and appears to have lost interest in his work. Consequently, he puts very little effort into the work you two are supposed to be sharing.

Possible actions:

a. Request a different partner for the project.
b. Inform your senior officer of the situation.
c. Do your best on your work, but accept that the project probably will fail because of the poor attitude of your collaborator.
d. Do your work and the work that was supposed to be done by your partner, since the most important thing is the successful completion of the project.
e. Express your frustrations directly to your collaborator, emphasizing that the success of this project is very important to you, and agree upon a fair division of labor.

9. Select the MOST EFFECTIVE action in response to the situation.

10. Select the LEAST EFFECTIVE action in response to the situation.

Situation 6:

While working in a field office, you observe that one of your colleagues is being severely overworked. Despite doing an excellent job and working more than the required number of hours, she is unable to keep up with the amount of paperwork being sent to her by other offices. Her commanding officers do not seem to be aware that she is being asked to do an unfair amount of work.

Possible actions:

a. Assign one of your subordinates to assist your overworked colleague.
b. Request a meeting with your overworked colleague's commanding officer, and describe the problem to him.
c. Ignore the problem, since it does not relate to your work.
d. Express your sympathy with your overworked colleague.
e. Help your overworked colleague whenever you finish your own work.

11. Select the MOST EFFECTIVE action in response to the situation.

12. Select the LEAST EFFECTIVE action in response to the situation.

Situation 7:

You have become suspicious that one of your junior officers is trying to undermine your work. This junior officer is very competent and very ambitious. You have even heard from other officers that this junior officer wants to take over your job. You have not yet mentioned your suspicion directly to the junior officer.

Possible actions:

a. Meet with the junior officer and explain that you expect his full cooperation and support.
b. Publicly reprimand and humiliate the junior officer.
c. Ignore the situation, in the hopes that it will resolve itself.
d. Report this insubordination to your commanding officer.
e. Ask one of your fellow officers to talk with the junior officer and try to improve the situation.

13. Select the MOST EFFECTIVE action in response to the situation.

14. Select the LEAST EFFECTIVE action in response to the situation.

Situation 8:

You are extremely busy with paperwork, but a senior officer asks you to complete a set of special reports in addition to your normal work. You do not think it will be possible for you to complete this extra assignment without sacrificing the quality of your work. However, you would like to impress your senior officer by fulfilling his request.

Possible actions:

a. Tell the senior officer that you are too busy to complete extra projects.
b. Accept the extra work and resolve to complete it quickly no matter what.
c. Ask the senior officer if you can have a few days to decide whether you will complete the extra work.
d. Accept the extra work, but have a junior staff member complete it for you.
e. Decline the extra work, but offer to pass it along to another qualified member of your team.

15. Select the MOST EFFECTIVE action in response to the situation.

16. Select the LEAST EFFECTIVE action in response to the situation.

SITUATION 9:

Over the past few months, you have noticed that office supplies are being used at a much greater pace than is usual. There is no clear reason for this, but you have begun to suspect that one of your fellow officers is taking office supplies home with her at night. You have no specific evidence to support your claims, but the office supplies seem to be disappearing after shifts in which this officer is alone with access to the supply closet.

Possible actions:

a. Ignore the situation, since you know that you are not personally responsible for the thefts.
b. Tell a senior officer about your suspicions.
c. Confront the officer with your suspicions and ask for an explanation.
d. Set up a hidden surveillance camera so that you can catch the officer stealing supplies.
e. Ask some of your fellow officers if they have noticed any suspicious behavior.

17. Select the MOST EFFECTIVE action in response to the situation.

18. Select the LEAST EFFECTIVE action in response to the situation.

SITUATION 10:

You have been working in the same unit for the past two years. Although you have been successful, you are beginning to get burnt out, and you are thinking about requesting a transfer. You contact some friends and colleagues in other units, trying to determine whether you would like it there. After a few weeks, you realize that rumors about your interest in a transfer have begun to spread throughout your unit.

Possible actions:

a. In a letter to your senior officer, acknowledge the truth of the rumors and request a transfer.
b. Deny the rumors publicly, but continue to pursue a transfer.
c. Ignore the rumors, but refocus on your work with your current unit.
d. Acknowledge the rumors and refocus on your work with your current unit.
e. Request a leave of absence so that you can decide how to handle the situation.

19. Select the MOST EFFECTIVE action in response to the situation.

20 Select the LEAST EFFECTIVE action in response to the situation.

Situation 11:

You have been asked to attend a meeting between the senior officers in your unit and a group of local community leaders. The meeting has been called because of rumors that your military base will be shut down due to budgetary constraints. The community leaders are willing to lobby on behalf of the base, so long as they receive assurances that the military leadership will cooperate with them on some local initiatives. Specifically, the community leaders would like the airmen to help coordinate disaster relief efforts when necessary. At one point, a community leader turns to you and asks for your opinion on the subject.

Possible actions:

a. Answer the question, but mention only the potential positive consequences of the proposal.
b. Try to answer the question as honestly and completely as possible, but remind the community leader that you are only a junior officer.
c. Answer the question thoroughly, even though you have little direct knowledge of the situation.
d. Remind the community leader that you are a junior officer and cannot give your opinion.
e. Decline to answer the question, and instead refer it to one of the senior officers.

21. Select the MOST EFFECTIVE action in response to the situation.

22. Select the LEAST EFFECTIVE action in response to the situation.

Situation 12:

Another officer in your section is granted a week-long leave to visit his sick grandmother. However, during this period you discover through social media that the officer is actually on a beach vacation with his girlfriend, hundreds of miles from the hospital where his grandmother was supposedly being treated.

Possible actions:

a. Tell the officer that he has been dishonest and unethical, and that you will have to report any future episodes of this nature.
b. Ignore the situation, since it does not really involve you.
c. Tell the officer that you will agree to keep his misbehavior a secret if he will do your weekly reports.
d. Immediately notify your commanding officer in person.
e. Anonymously forward the evidence of the officer's misbehavior to your commanding officer.

23. Select the MOST EFFECTIVE action in response to the situation.

24. Select the LEAST EFFECTIVE action in response to the situation.

Situation 13:

One of the airmen in your unit has displayed a marked decline in her performance over the past month. She appears frustrated and burnt out with her normal duties. She is one of the more popular members of the unit, so her negative attitude has a bad influence on her fellow airmen.

Possible actions:

a. Convene a meeting of the entire unit, and use this as a chance to single out the airman for her poor performance.
b. Meet with the airman and offer whatever help you can give to improve her performance, while emphasizing the effect that her behavior has on the other airmen.
c. Reassign the airman to a different unit so that her bad attitude doesn't continue to affect the other airmen.
d. Do nothing, in the hopes that the situation will improve without your influence.
e. Inform your senior officer about the situation.

25. Select the MOST EFFECTIVE action in response to the situation.

26. Select the LEAST EFFECTIVE action in response to the situation.

Situation 14:

You are about to transfer to a new unit, where you will have duties in areas where you have little experience. A week before you are due to make the transfer, you receive an email from the senior officer in charge of your new unit. She reminds you that you will be entering her unit at a very important time for them, because they will be leading a set of training exercises for highly-skilled airmen. She wants to make sure that you are ready to contribute immediately to the success of the unit, and that you will not need a great deal of assistance to complete your work.

Possible actions:

a. Do not respond to the email, and assume that you will be able to move into your new role seamlessly.
b. Thank the senior officer for her message, and do some internet research on your new duties.
c. Request that the transfer be canceled, and remain with your original unit.
d. Email the senior officer back, requesting a personal meeting where you can get more information about how to make a good transition to your new role.
e. Ask one of the other officers in your new unit if he will quietly bring you up to speed when you arrive.

27. Select the MOST EFFECTIVE action in response to the situation.

28. Select the LEAST EFFECTIVE action in response to the situation.

Situation 15:

One of your responsibilities is to keep a set of officers briefed on some confidential activities that are taking place at your base. One day, you accidentally send an email containing some information about these confidential activities to an officer who has not received the security clearance.

Possible actions:

a. Notify your supervisor of your mistake and let him resolve the situation.
b. Immediately send a second email to the improper recipient, requesting that he or she destroy the email. Inform your supervisors of your mistake.
c. Send a second email to the improper recipient, claiming that your email account has been hacked and that he should disregard any earlier messages.
d. Wait to see if there will be any negative consequences of your mistake.
e. Ask your supervisor if the improper recipient could be given the security clearance retroactively.

29. Select the MOST EFFECTIVE action in response to the situation.

30. Select the LEAST EFFECTIVE action in response to the situation.

Situation 16:

After completing your work at the base, you return to your living quarters for the evening. An hour later, you realize that you failed to affix your signature to a set of papers that are to be forwarded on to a different unit for completion. Without your signature, the papers cannot be sent. The content of the papers is not particularly urgent, but the delay will require the other unit officer to stay later than normal at his post.

Possible actions:

a. Wait until your next shift to sign the papers, since they are not considered urgent.
b. Call the base and ask a junior officer to forge your signature so the paperwork can be sent.
c. Call the officer at the other base and explain that the papers will be arriving a little later than expected.
d. Arrive for your next shift a little early and sign the papers first.
e. Return to the base and sign the necessary papers.

31. Select the MOST EFFECTIVE action in response to the situation.

32. Select the LEAST EFFECTIVE action in response to the situation.

SITUATION 17:

Several of the airmen in your unit have yet to complete a basic training module at a nearby base. They have asked to participate in the next training session, but instead, a group of airmen from another unit have been selected. The selected airmen have not been waiting nearly as long as your airmen to complete this training module. You suspect that the director of the training session dislikes you personally, though you have no specific evidence of this.

Possible actions:

a. Request a meeting with the training director, and ask why your airmen have been passed over, emphasizing the importance of this module for their development.
b. Do nothing, in the hopes that the situation will improve on its own.
c. Ask the officer in charge of the other unit if your airmen can attend the training session instead of his.
d. Write a critical letter to the training director and your senior officer, outlining what you perceive as the injustice of the situation.
e. Ask the training director if your airmen can attend the next training session along with the selected airmen.

33. Select the MOST EFFECTIVE action in response to the situation.

34. Select the LEAST EFFECTIVE action in response to the situation.

SITUATION 18:

You have been assigned to draft an important report along with another officer in your unit. It is expected that the report will take approximately one month to complete. However, after about a week of work, the other officer falls ill and is required to go on leave. He is only supposed to be gone for about ten days, but at the end of this period he has not returned and there is no definitive word on when he will. You need the expertise of this officer in order to finish the report.

Possible actions:

a. Wait until the other officer returns from leave, even if it means delaying the report.
b. Ask for an extension, without making excuses for your failure to complete the report on time.
c. Work extra hours to complete the report as best as you can.
d. Tell your commanding officer the situation, and request assistance in completing the report.
e. Order a junior officer to assist you in the completion of the report.

35. Select the MOST EFFECTIVE action in response to the situation.

36. Select the LEAST EFFECTIVE action in response to the situation.

Situation 19:

Two months ago, you joined a new unit. The leader of this unit was very welcoming to you and made sure to give you as much assistance as you needed in learning your new duties and responsibilities. However, you are now feeling more comfortable in your role and would like more independence in your work.

Possible actions:

a. Request a meeting with the unit leader, thank him for his assistance, and indicate that you would like to work on your own a bit more.
b. Request that another officer be transferred to your unit so that the unit leader will divert his attention to training this new arrival.
c. Without saying anything directly, try to avoid the unit leader as much as possible.
d. Tell the unit leader's commanding officer that you need the unit leader to give you more space.
e. Keep extensive records of your work so that you can demonstrate your competence to the unit leader.

37. Select the MOST EFFECTIVE action in response to the situation.

38. Select the LEAST EFFECTIVE action in response to the situation.

Situation 20:

One of the other officers in your division is going to make an important presentation at the end of the week. He is nervous, but he has done good work in the past and has spent a great deal of time preparing the report. He asks you to look over his work in advance. You notice a few things that need to be changed, but the other officer disagrees with your corrections. You are certain that you are right and that the other officer will be sorry he did not listen to you.

Possible actions:

a. Let your coworker go ahead with the uncorrected presentation, but make yourself look better by mentioning the errors to a senior officer before the presentation.
b. Allow your coworker to go ahead with the presentation as is, without trying to convince him to make the corrections.
c. Discuss the matter with your senior officer, and ask him or her to mandate the corrections.
d. Contrive an excuse to be absent from the presentation.
e. Make every effort to convince your colleague to make the necessary corrections.

39. Select the MOST EFFECTIVE action in response to the situation.

40. Select the LEAST EFFECTIVE action in response to the situation.

Situation 21:

You have been working with a new unit for the past six weeks. During that time, you have noticed some inefficiencies in the unit's operations, and you have developed a set of proposals for eliminating them. The majority of your coworkers agree with your proposals, but the senior officer in charge of the unit does not. The senior officer believes that implementing your proposals would be too risky and would undermine the stability of the unit.

Possible actions:

a. Confront your senior officer, using the support of your coworkers as a reason to implement your proposals.
b. Create a detailed and comprehensive report outlining the potential benefits of your proposals. Deliver the report and then obey the senior officer's final decision.
c. Implement your proposals anyway, on the assumption that your senior officer will change his mind once he sees their success.
d. Accept the senior officer's decision and try to succeed within the agreed-upon structure.
e. Accept the senior officer's decision, but keep a running list of the ways your proposals could have improved performance, had they been implemented.

41. Select the MOST EFFECTIVE action in response to the situation.

42. Select the LEAST EFFECTIVE action in response to the situation.

Situation 22:

Six months ago, you were assigned a new assistant. Although you have been able to work successfully together, you have developed a personal dislike for this person. In your opinion, he is arrogant and too critical of the other officers. During a meeting with your senior officer, she mentions that she is considering transferring your assistant to another unit. This would represent a step up for him and would make it possible for him to achieve even more promotions in a relatively short time.

Possible actions:

a. Recommend that your assistant receive the promotion, if only to get him away from you.
b. Strongly discourage the senior officer from choosing your assistant so that he will not get a professional reward.
c. Write an anonymous letter to the senior officer, outlining your complaints about your assistant.
d. Strongly discourage the senior officer from choosing your assistant, with an emphasis on his personality flaws.
e. Avoid interfering in the senior officer's decision, but make sure that she is aware of your opinion of your assistant.

43. Select the MOST EFFECTIVE action in response to the situation.

44. Select the LEAST EFFECTIVE action in response to the situation.

SITUATION 23:

Your base uses a computer program to determine the logistics related to supply deliveries. One day, while you are coordinating the arrival and unloading of several concurrent deliveries, the computer system crashes. The computer technician tells you that it could be an hour before the system is up and running again. You can see that there is a long line of trucks waiting to deliver their goods and that the drivers are becoming impatient.

Possible actions:

a. Ask one of your assistants to inform the drivers of the situation and the likely wait time. Offer whatever accommodations you can in the interim.
b. Receive the deliveries despite the computer problems, and keep paper records so you can update the system later.
c. Call your senior officer and ask for advice.
d. Use this opportunity to take your lunch break, somewhere you are unlikely to meet any of the drivers.
e. Encourage the drivers to make any other deliveries they have and then come back later.

45. Select the MOST EFFECTIVE action in response to the situation.

46. Select the LEAST EFFECTIVE action in response to the situation.

SITUATION 24:

You have developed an idea that you believe will improve the performance of your unit. However, some of the airmen in your unit disagree with this idea, and one has gone so far as to write a letter of complaint to your senior officer without notifying you. You have not yet implemented your idea.

Possible actions:

a. Meet with the letter-writer and other critics, emphasizing that going above your head will not be tolerated in the future.
b. Abandon your idea and ask for suggestions from the airmen who were critical of it.
c. Ignore the critics in you unit, and implement your idea anyway.
d. Harshly punish the letter writer, as a warning to the other airmen.
e. Implement your idea without acknowledging the letter or the criticism of other airmen in the unit.

47. Select the MOST EFFECTIVE action in response to the situation.

48. Select the LEAST EFFECTIVE action in response to the situation.

SITUATION 25:

You received a promotion six months ago and have been excelling in your new job. However, due to forces beyond your control, the quality of your work has decreased over the past few weeks. In part, you have been undermined by recent budget cuts. Unfortunately, your commanding officer does not fully understand the consequences of the budget cuts and has expressed her displeasure with your recent work. She has even suggested that problems in your unit may be a result of poor management on your part.

Possible actions:

a. Ask the commanding officer if you can take a brief leave to refocus.
b. Do not make any excuses, but ask the advice of other officers who are dealing with the same budget constraints.
c. Ask your commanding officer for a list of her specific complaints.
d. Shift the blame for your unit's performance to your subordinates.
e. Remind the commanding officer of the budget constraints, and defend your management style to her.

49. Select the MOST EFFECTIVE action in response to the situation.

50. Select the LEAST EFFECTIVE action in response to the situation.

Physical Science

1. A long nail is heated at one end. After a few seconds, the other end of the nail becomes equally hot. What type of heat transfer does this represent?

a. Advection
b. Conduction
c. Convection
d. Entropy
e. Radiation

2. The measure of energy within a system is called

a. Temperature
b. Convection
c. Entropy
d. Thermodynamics
e. Heat

3. How do two isotopes of the same element differ?

a. They have different numbers of protons.
b. They have different numbers of neutrons.
c. They have different numbers of electrons.
d. They have different charges.
e. They have different atomic numbers.

4. Which type of nuclear process features atomic nuclei splitting apart to form smaller nuclei?

a. Fission
b. Fusion
c. Decay
d. Ionization
e. Chain reaction

5. The process whereby a radioactive element releases energy slowly over a long period of time to lower its energy and become more stable is best described as

a. Combustion
b. Fission
c. Fusion
d. Decay
e. Radioactivity

6. What property of light explains why a pencil in a glass of water appears to be bent?

a. Reflection
b. Refraction
c. The angle of incidence equals the angle of reflection
d. Constructive interference
e. Destructive interference

7. What unit describes the frequency of a wave?

a. Hertz (Hz)
b. Decibels (dB)
c. Meters (m)
d. Meters per second (m/s)
e. Meters per second squared (m/s^2)

8. Which of the following is an example of kinetic energy being converted to potential energy?

a. A child sliding down a slide
b. A cyclist coasting on his way up a hill
c. A pilot deploying airbrakes on approach to land
d. A motorist swerving to avoid a deer
e. A pair of billiard balls colliding and rebounding off each other

9. The boiling of water is an example of

a. Sublimation
b. Condensation
c. Neutralization
d. Chemical change
e. Physical change

10. The center of an atom is called the

a. Nucleus
b. Nuclide
c. Neutrino
d. Electron cloud
e. Electrolyte

11. When a solid is heated and transforms directly to the gaseous phases, this process is called

a. Sublimation
b. Fusion
c. Diffusion
d. Condensation
e. Fission

12. Which scientist was responsible for developing the format of the modern periodic table?

a. Faraday
b. Einstein
c. Hess
d. Mendeleev
e. Oppenheimer

13. The density of a material refers to its:

a. Mass per unit volume
b. Mass per unit length
c. Mass per unit surface area
d. Volume per unit surface area
e. Volume per unit length

14. The precision of a set of experimentally obtained data points refers to

a. How accurate the data points are
b. How many errors the data points contain
c. How close the data points are to the mean of the data
d. How close the data points are to the predicted result
e. How close the set of data is to a normal distribution

15. Current, or the amount of electricity that is flowing, is measured in

a. Volts
b. Watts
c. Ohms
d. Farads
e. Amperes

16. A solar eclipse can only occur if

a. The earth and the sun are on the same side of the moon.
b. The earth is between the sun and the moon.
c. The moon is between the earth and the sun.
d. The sun is between the earth and the moon.
e. The moon is full.

17. What property of motion explains why passengers in a turning car feel pulled toward the outside of the turn?

a. Centripetal force
b. Inertia
c. Normal force
d. Impulse
e. Torque

18. According to the ideal gas law, if a certain amount of gas is being held at a constant volume, and the temperature is increased, what will happen?

a. The mass of the gas will increase
b. The pressure of the gas will increase
c. The density of the gas will decrease
d. The mass of the gas will decrease
e. The pressure of the gas will decrease

19. What wave characteristic is related to the loudness of a sound?

a. Frequency
b. Amplitude
c. Wavelength
d. Velocity
e. Period

20. Which of the following scenarios is NOT an example of a person applying work to a book?

a. A book is picked up from the floor and put on a shelf.
b. A book is pushed across a table top.
c. A backpack holding a book is carried across the room.
d. A book is held and then released so that it falls to the ground.
e. A book is thrown vertically into the air.

Table Reading

For each question, select the number that appears in the table at the given coordinates. Recall that the first number in the ordered pair gives the column number, and the second gives the row number. For instance, the ordered pair $(2, -1)$ refers to the number in column 2, row -1, which is 732 in the table.

Use the table below to answer questions 1-40.

	-12	-11	-10	-9	-8	-7	-6	-5	-4	-3	-2	-1	0	1	2	3	4	5	6	7	8	9	10	11	12
-12	987	972	433	251	462	338	836	424	131	773	809	602	261	569	550	952	216	808	891	232	316	623	986	141	488
-11	337	740	563	587	510	138	491	654	775	261	528	986	212	387	837	100	241	114	536	568	673	833	610	398	578
-10	639	122	374	648	229	692	250	767	803	337	725	838	725	144	863	542	928	232	908	809	296	852	284	963	991
-9	280	271	269	575	696	649	637	750	161	366	151	226	577	995	494	106	819	390	618	557	191	993	438	850	751
-8	586	970	977	677	988	166	748	340	833	710	631	207	464	524	279	596	990	621	752	365	355	920	544	122	185
-7	728	206	273	437	636	394	813	161	731	219	494	278	349	423	325	409	631	538	918	134	151	867	624	920	733
-6	714	817	929	377	264	974	300	999	982	348	166	859	667	762	441	226	734	692	302	688	550	589	143	169	860
-5	780	511	934	814	538	712	832	165	315	637	252	800	205	290	557	713	629	764	228	585	594	912	473	651	957
-4	278	232	882	615	475	795	492	763	943	798	519	682	314	471	338	666	996	118	712	879	663	111	593	380	907
-3	576	534	470	835	886	318	738	322	739	284	890	397	683	356	177	839	679	496	344	613	268	179	951	292	204
-2	597	806	779	782	137	601	669	599	486	562	119	331	497	848	701	602	476	253	787	785	212	734	357	810	356
-1	266	142	405	779	792	514	369	731	663	422	328	529	754	122	732	319	332	927	665	438	342	698	714	637	262
0	836	881	121	327	431	710	702	742	966	902	562	733	522	486	608	810	432	843	413	179	219	556	235	330	776
1	928	271	938	525	554	176	714	402	992	199	870	962	595	959	800	851	823	561	568	647	245	652	669	953	121
2	201	464	830	565	678	748	176	382	161	598	909	610	483	902	512	435	607	119	111	710	331	105	430	958	838
3	955	181	865	766	989	835	207	894	836	533	907	137	339	693	166	619	247	882	948	913	701	130	259	361	754
4	258	997	209	333	331	773	987	354	436	837	269	650	263	813	345	137	861	442	394	456	616	521	870	139	974
5	818	390	866	177	144	937	368	823	703	862	512	545	414	571	713	766	818	268	116	494	936	678	237	401	604
6	165	464	708	301	825	992	526	975	649	450	527	507	455	581	287	528	414	338	779	729	284	247	341	972	443
7	206	217	571	346	566	921	741	462	106	647	464	743	480	700	222	139	947	963	392	826	106	661	917	228	502
8	516	409	120	796	838	721	852	106	226	704	231	187	115	827	434	548	683	138	848	824	957	304	998	617	121
9	779	812	809	702	596	844	261	136	301	227	582	378	683	735	910	620	367	483	826	518	905	563	596	521	751
10	477	320	645	916	438	150	787	578	236	734	393	396	156	507	176	236	886	161	676	226	179	812	999	853	167
11	273	514	137	670	965	886	919	657	775	420	354	146	610	639	181	293	476	150	192	558	729	160	955	780	293
12	675	164	725	723	196	262	436	496	880	663	650	765	851	848	620	743	615	248	536	881	122	642	440	307	846

1. $(\mathbf{0}, -\mathbf{1})$
a. 529
b. 754
c. 733
d. 536
e. 486

2. $(\mathbf{7}, -\mathbf{11})$
a. 568
b. 138
c. 348
d. 809
e. 232

3. $(\mathbf{1}, -\mathbf{2})$
a. 122
b. 356
c. 848
d. 331
e. 497

4. $(-\mathbf{9}, -\mathbf{11})$
a. 648
b. 510
c. 587
d. 216
e. 563

5. $(\mathbf{11}, \mathbf{5})$
a. 139
b. 972
c. 237
d. 511
e. 401

6. $(-\mathbf{9}, -\mathbf{1})$
a. 792
b. 782
c. 405
d. 779
e. 327

7. $(\mathbf{6}, \mathbf{9})$
a. 848
b. 138
c. 826
d. 261
e. 618

8. $(-\mathbf{4}, -\mathbf{3})$
a. 739
b. 322
c. 284
d. 943
e. 679

9. $(\mathbf{2}, -\mathbf{5})$
a. 557
b. 441
c. 290
d. 762
e. 382

10. $(-\mathbf{7}, -\mathbf{10})$
a. 649
b. 692
c. 250
d. 510
e. 273

11. $(\mathbf{11}, -\mathbf{12})$
a. 398
b. 578
c. 488
d. 972
e. 141

12. $(\mathbf{4}, -\mathbf{10})$
a. 241
b. 100
c. 803
d. 882
e. 928

13. $(-\mathbf{8}, \mathbf{9})$
a. 596
b. 844
c. 702
d. 566
e. 438

14. $(\mathbf{10}, \mathbf{7})$
a. 661
b. 917
c. 341
d. 998
e. 571

15. $(-\mathbf{5}, -\mathbf{11})$
a. 424
b. 654
c. 803
d. 114
e. 511

16. $(-\mathbf{6}, -\mathbf{11})$
a. 836
b. 536
c. 169
d. 491
e. 817

17. $(\mathbf{3}, -\mathbf{5})$
a. 713
b. 226
c. 637
d. 511
e. 496

18. $(-\mathbf{7}, \mathbf{7})$
a. 741
b. 462
c. 721
d. 992
e. 921

19. $(-\mathbf{4}, -\mathbf{5})$
a. 999
b. 982
c. 315
d. 763
e. 629

20. $(-\mathbf{4}, -\mathbf{1})$
a. 663
b. 422
c. 486
d. 731
e. 471

21. $(-\mathbf{5}, \mathbf{8})$
a. 852
b. 462
c. 138
d. 166
e. 106

22. $(8, -1)$
a. 212
b. 219
c. 792
d. 207
e. 342

23. $(-11, 9)$
a. 409
b. 809
c. 812
d. 320
e. 141

24. $(8, -2)$
a. 268
b. 212
c. 342
d. 137
e. 678

25. $(5, -2)$
a. 253
b. 787
c. 927
d. 599
e. 557

26. $(12, -11)$
a. 568
b. 578
c. 991
d. 398
e. 337

27. $(0, -10)$
a. 725
b. 151
c. 337
d. 838
e. 121

28. $(8, 7)$
a. 661
b. 957
c. 826
d. 824
e. 106

29. $(-11, 10)$
a. 812
b. 514
c. 320
d. 645
e. 137

30. $(-3, 5)$
a. 862
b. 512
c. 450
d. 837
e. 322

31. $(-2, -6)$
a. 859
b. 252
c. 601
d. 166
e. 787

32. $(-11, -5)$
a. 817
b. 934
c. 511
d. 780
e. 114

33. $(-7, 11)$
a. 150
b. 262
c. 886
d. 217
e. 558

34. $(10, 5)$
a. 866
b. 161
c. 678
d. 237
e. 401

35. $(3, 7)$
a. 139
b. 222
c. 548
d. 683
e. 913

36. $(7, 3)$
a. 710
b. 913
c. 701
d. 111
e. 613

37. $(0, 2)$
a. 595
b. 339
c. 438
d. 843
e. 483

38. $(2, 5)$
a. 441
b. 762
c. 253
d. 599
e. 713

39. $(6, -3)$
a. 344
b. 712
c. 738
d. 343
e. 434

40. $(10, -12)$
a. 610
b. 968
c. 986
d. 433
e. 440

Instrument Comprehension

1. Which of the answer choices represents the orientation of the plane?

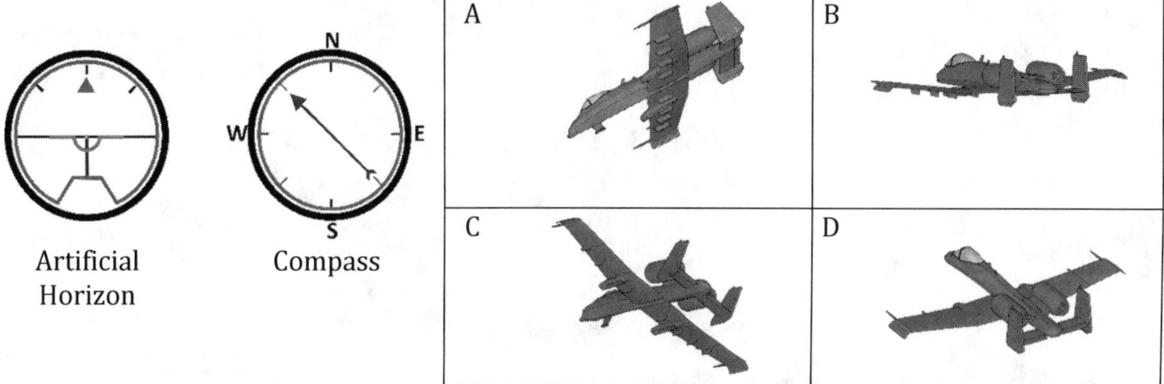

2. Which of the answer choices represents the orientation of the plane?

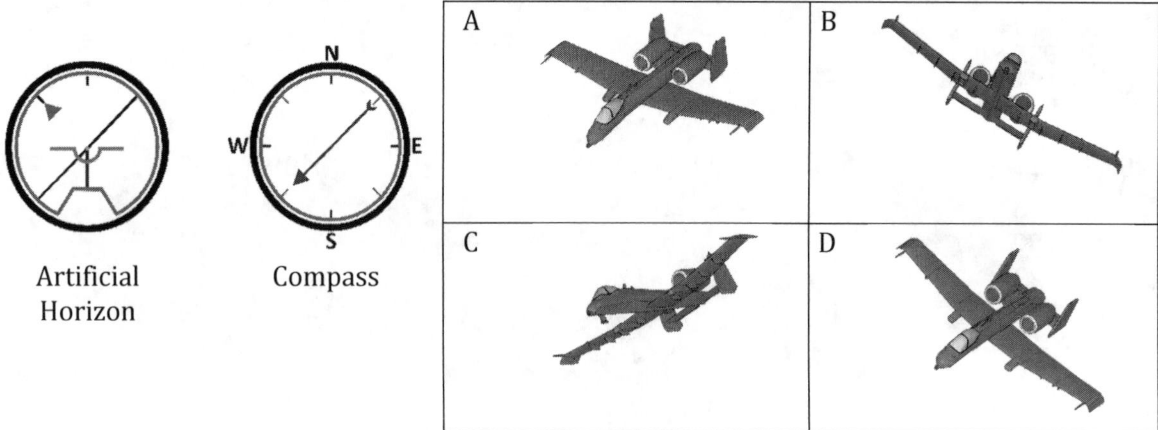

3. Which of the answer choices represents the orientation of the plane?

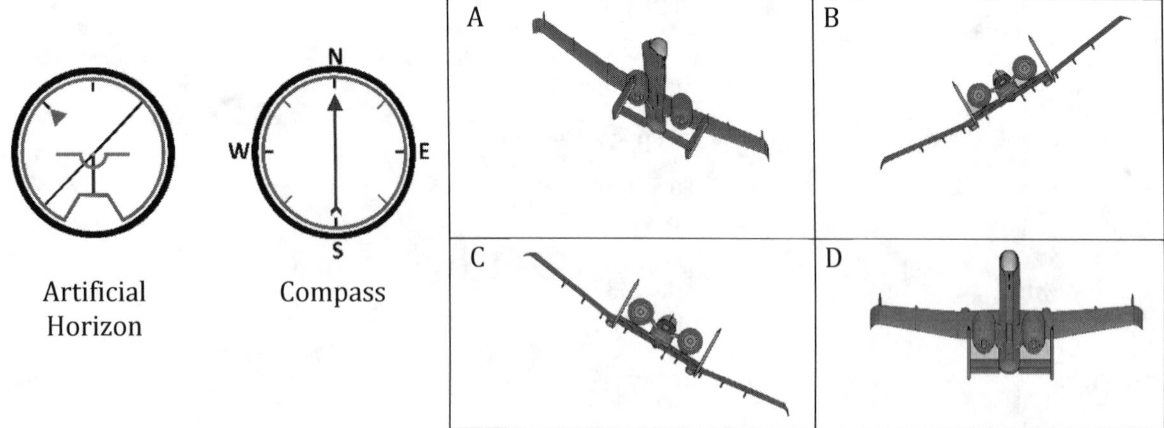

4. **Which of the answer choices represents the orientation of the plane?**

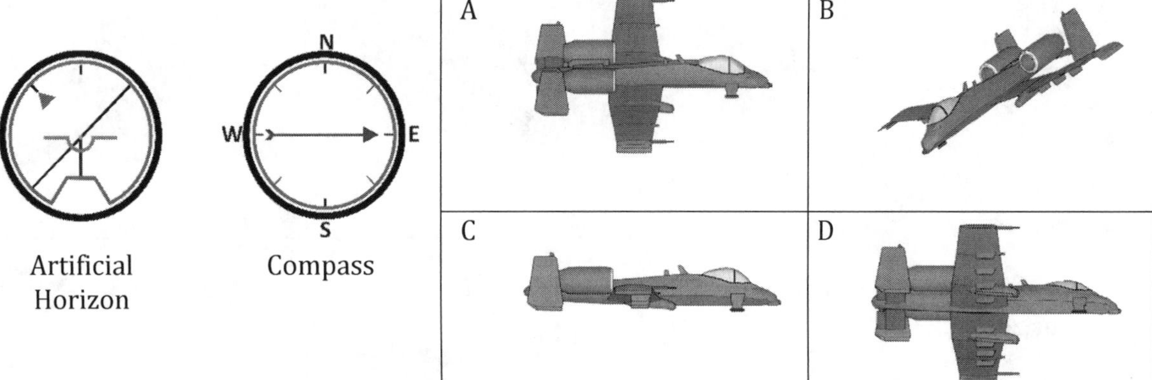

5. **Which of the answer choices represents the orientation of the plane?**

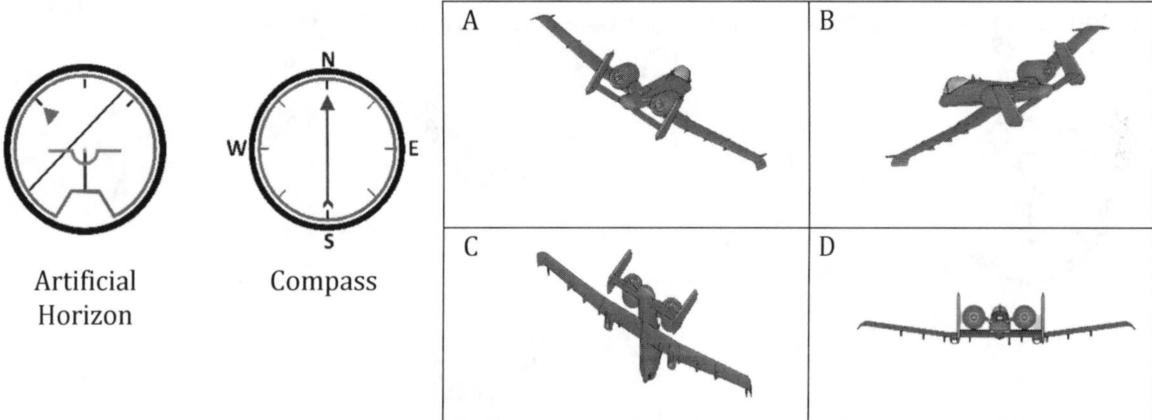

6. **Which of the answer choices represents the orientation of the plane?**

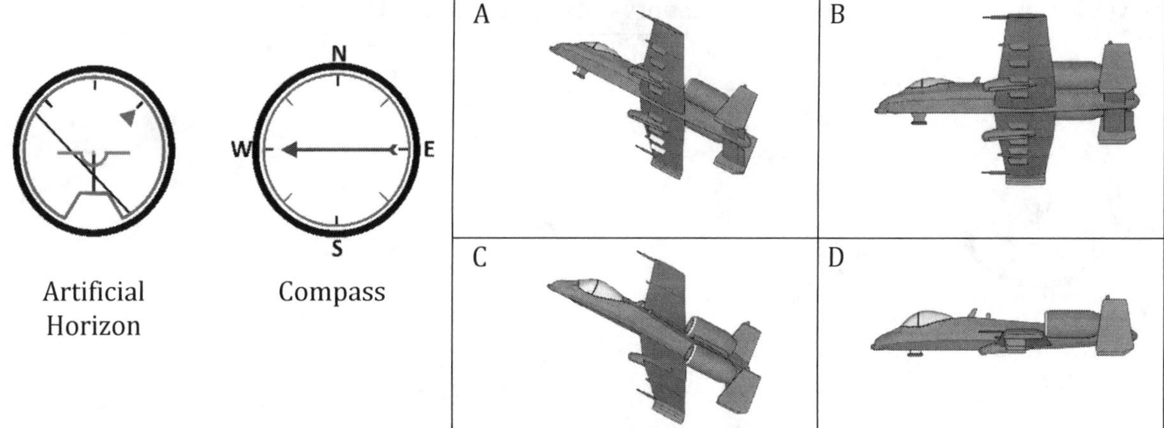

7. Which of the answer choices represents the orientation of the plane?

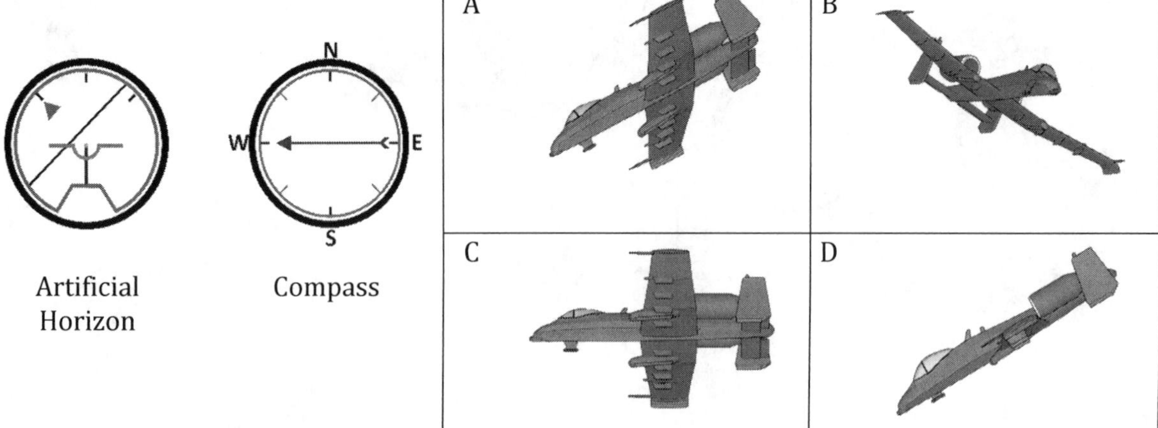

8. Which of the answer choices represents the orientation of the plane?

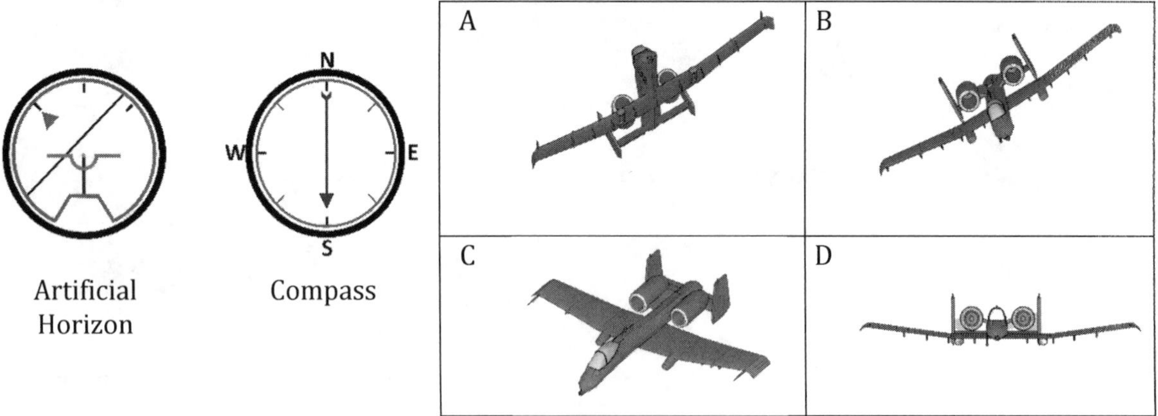

9. Which of the answer choices represents the orientation of the plane?

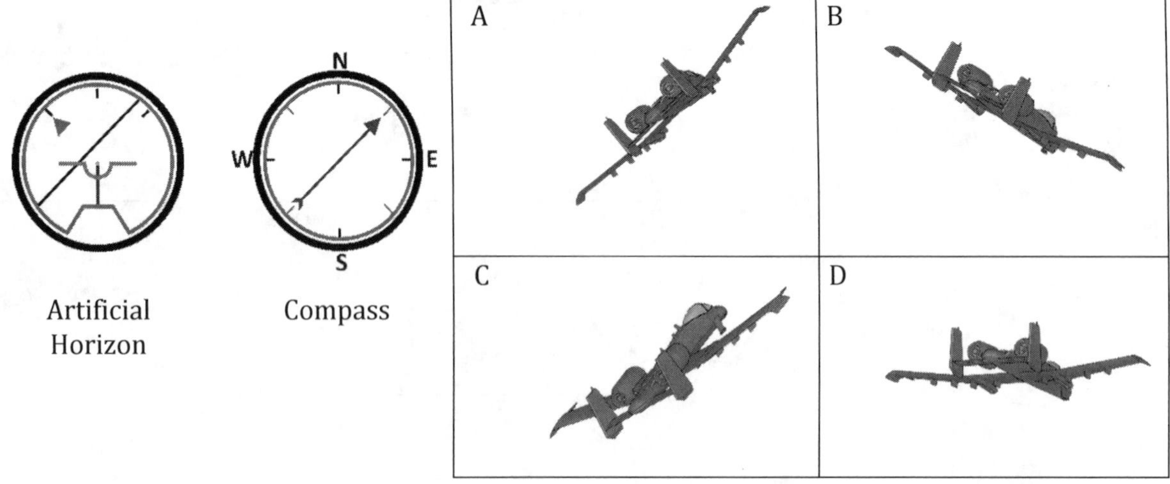

10. Which of the answer choices represents the orientation of the plane?

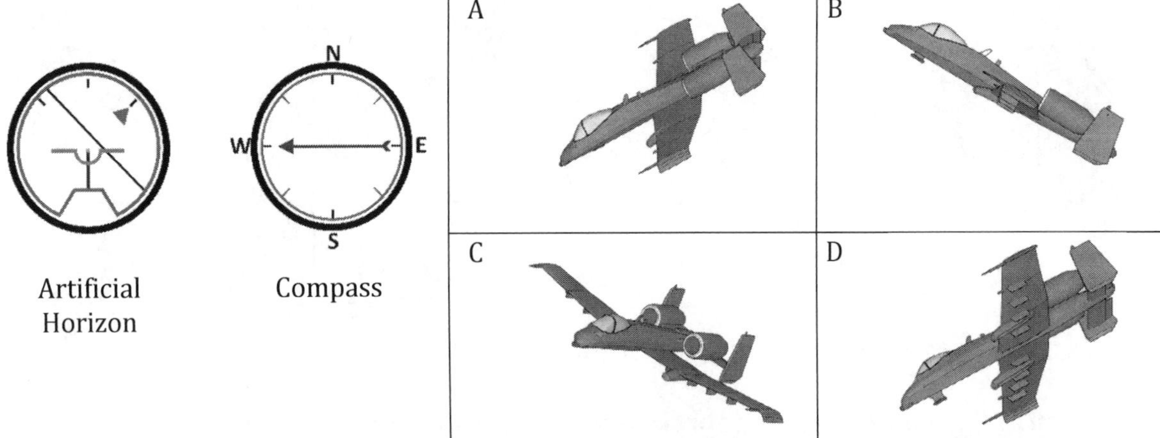

11. Which of the answer choices represents the orientation of the plane?

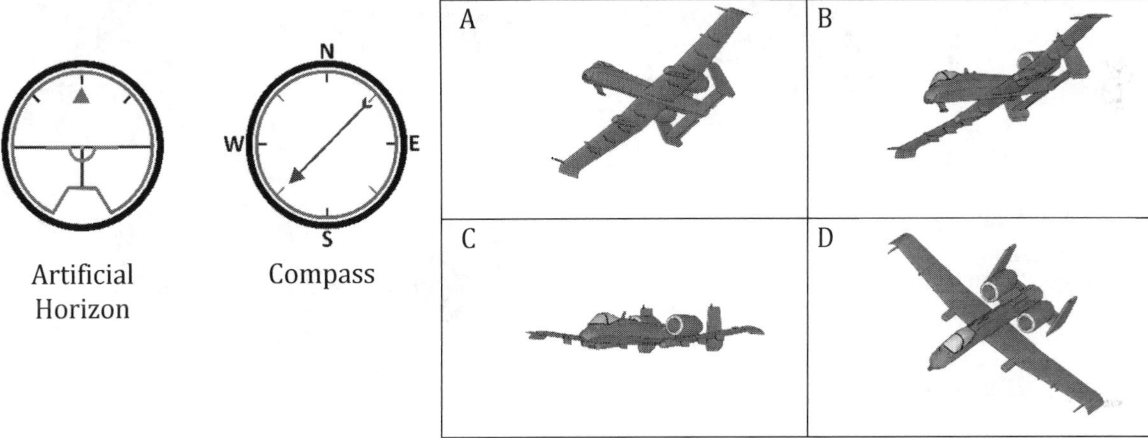

12. Which of the answer choices represents the orientation of the plane?

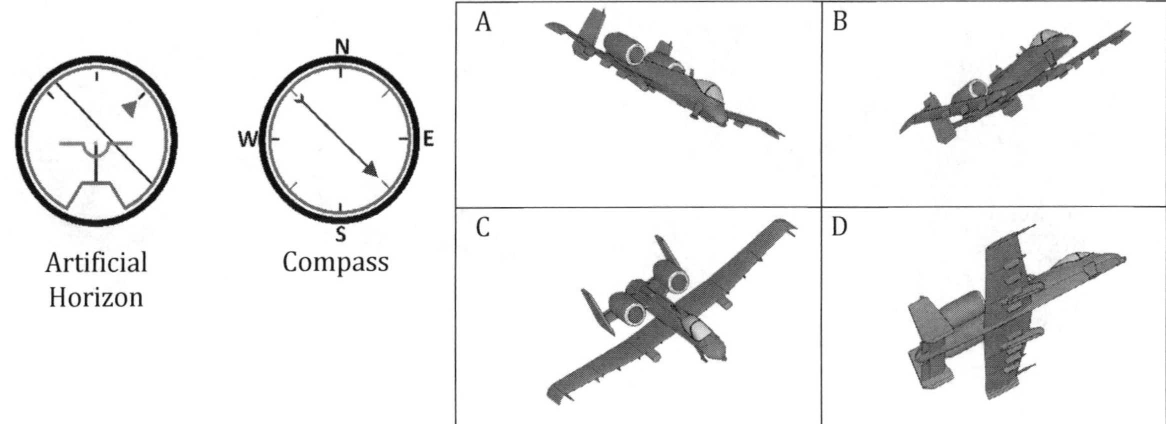

13. Which of the answer choices represents the orientation of the plane?

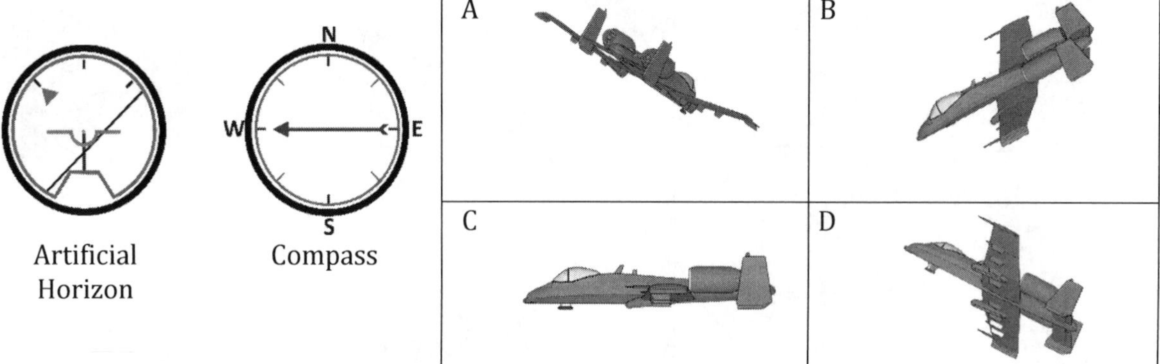

14. Which of the answer choices represents the orientation of the plane?

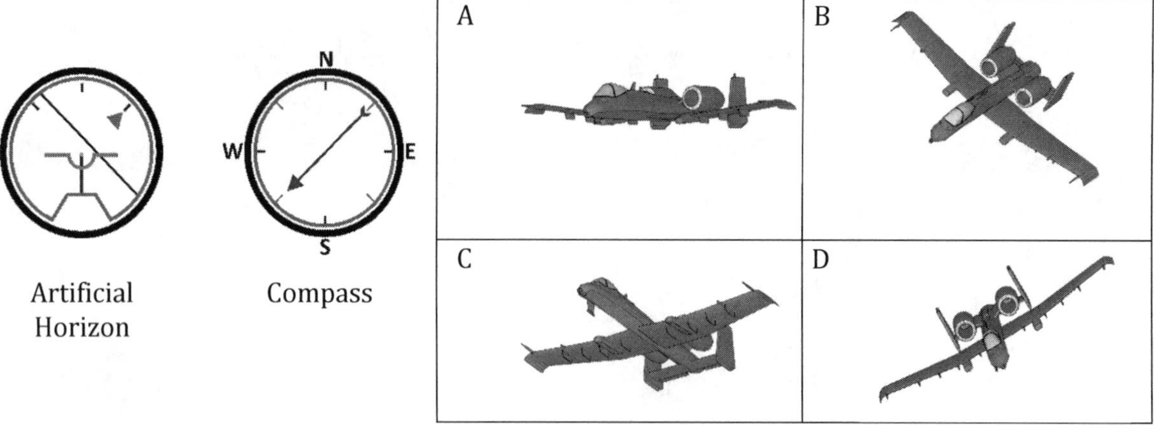

15. Which of the answer choices represents the orientation of the plane?

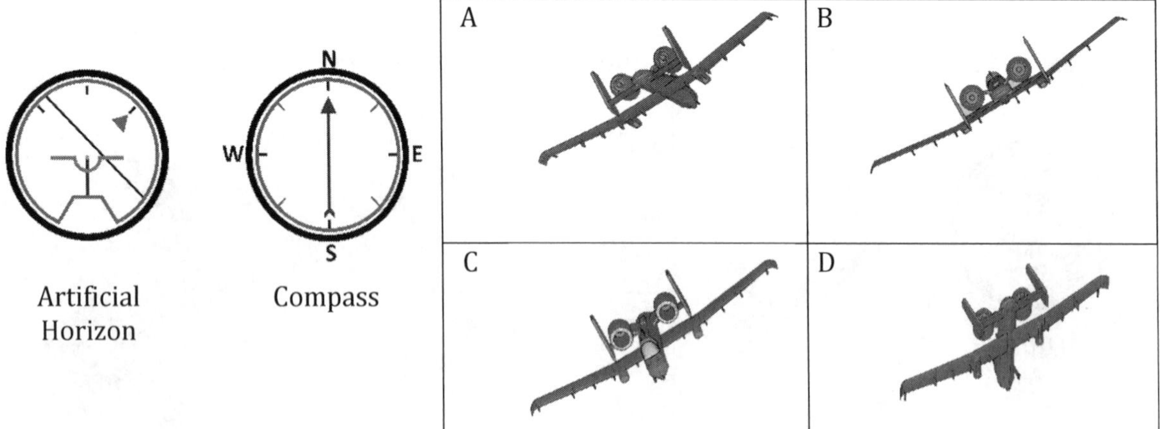

16. Which of the answer choices represents the orientation of the plane?

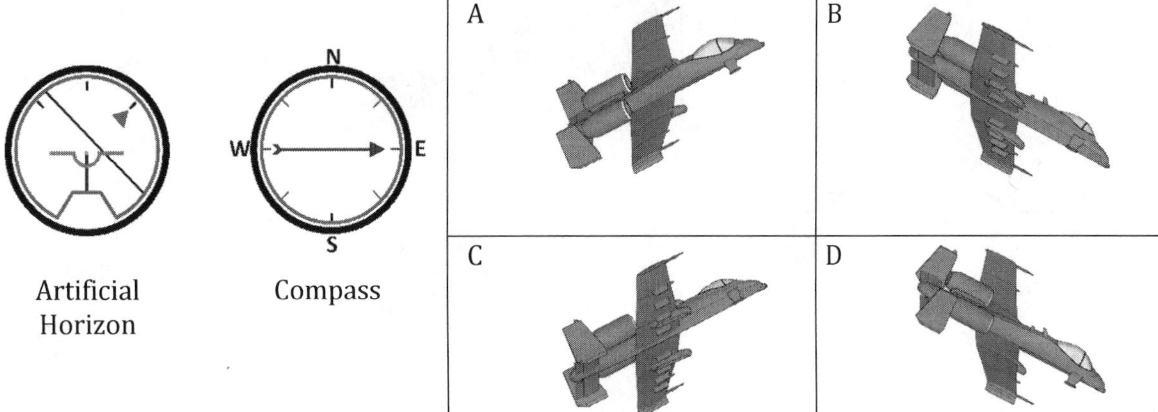

17. Which of the answer choices represents the orientation of the plane?

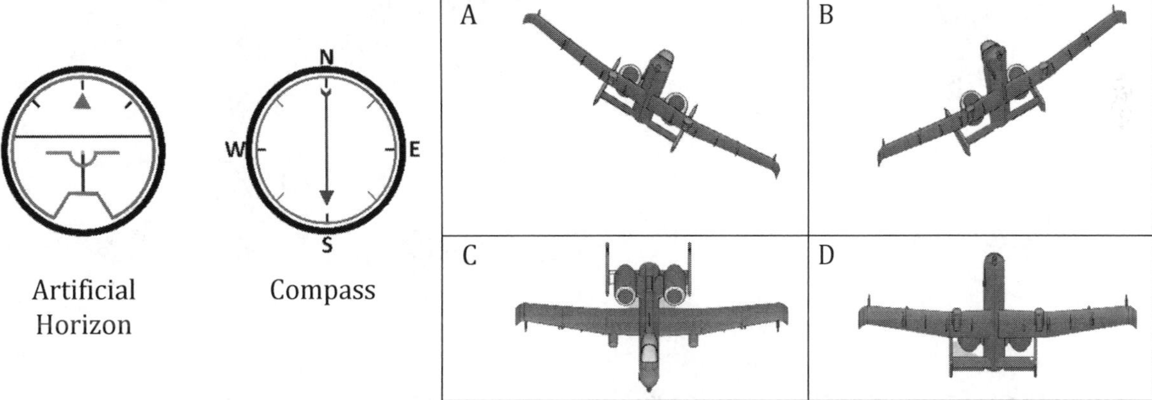

18. Which of the answer choices represents the orientation of the plane?

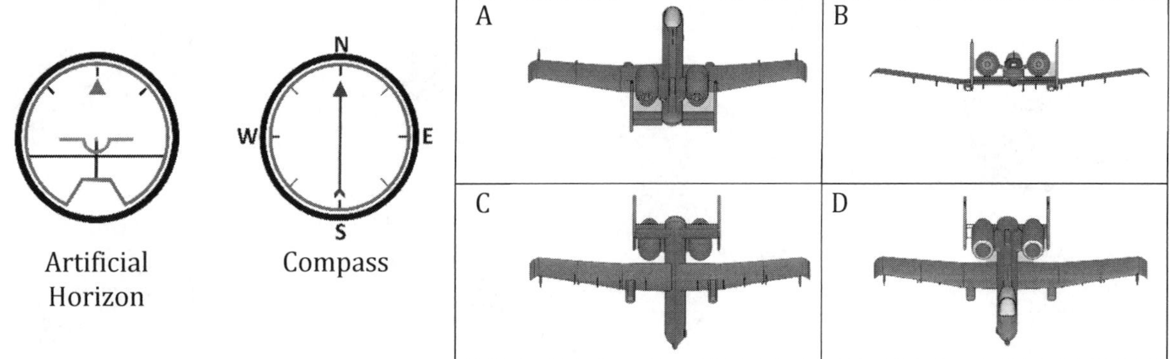

19. Which of the answer choices represents the orientation of the plane?

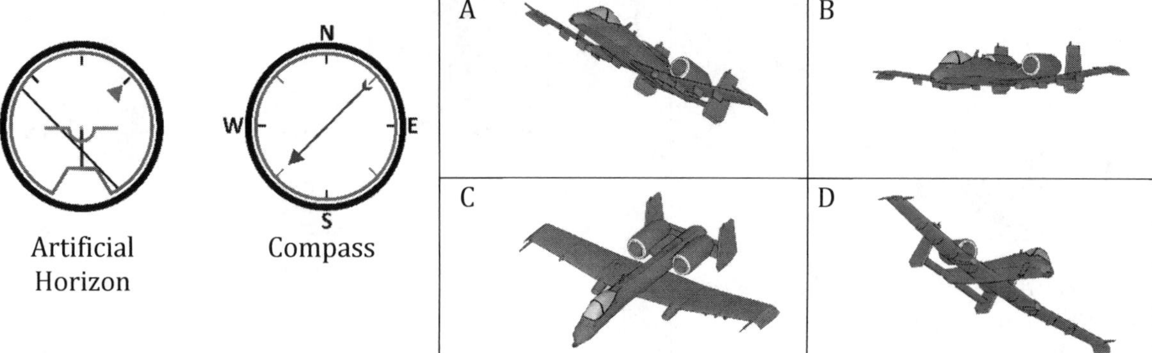

20. Which of the answer choices represents the orientation of the plane?

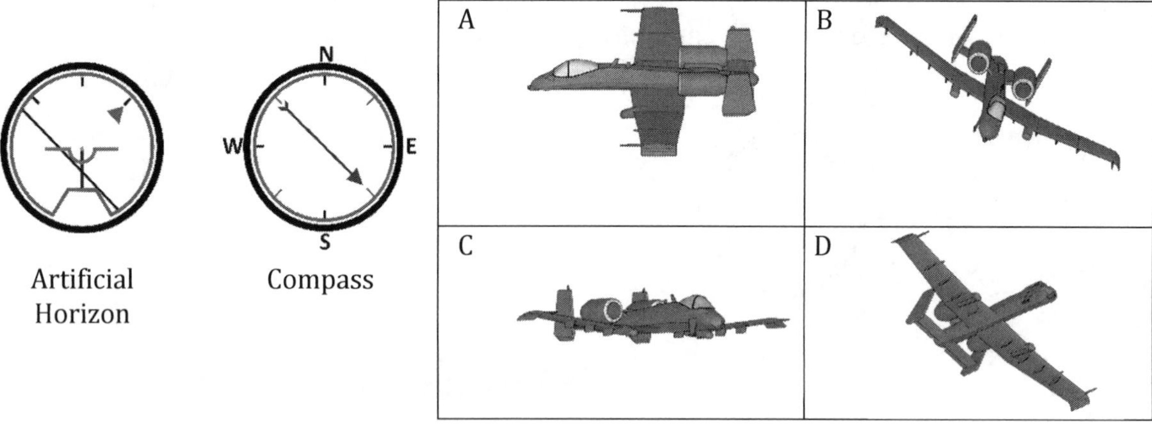

21. Which of the answer choices represents the orientation of the plane?

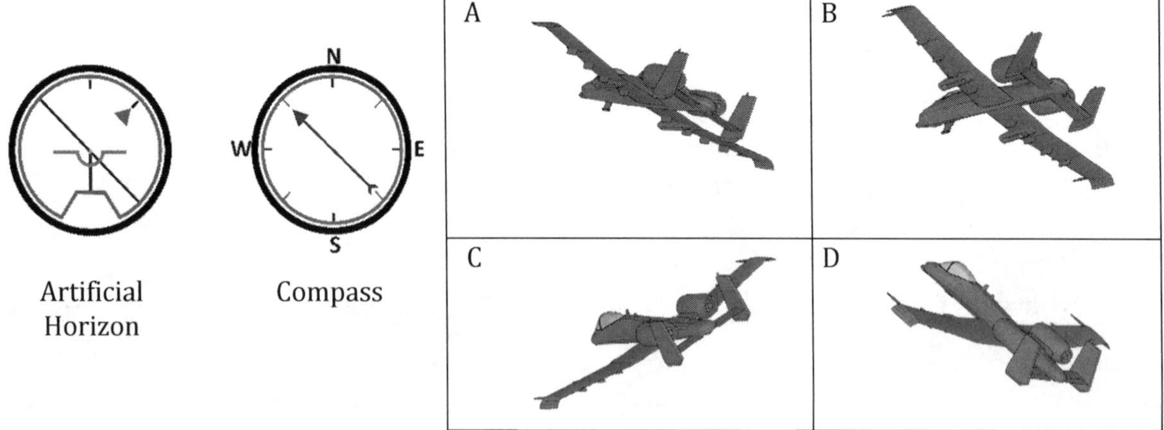

22. **Which of the answer choices represents the orientation of the plane?**

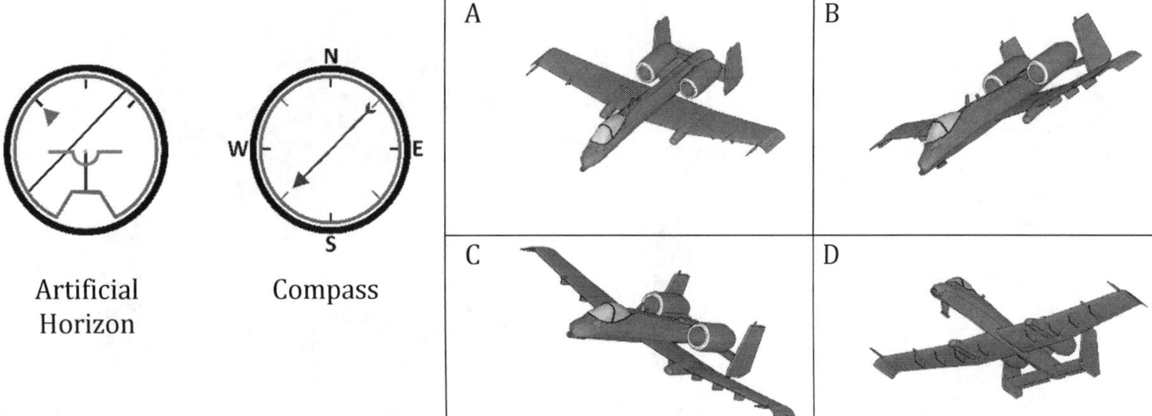

23. **Which of the answer choices represents the orientation of the plane?**

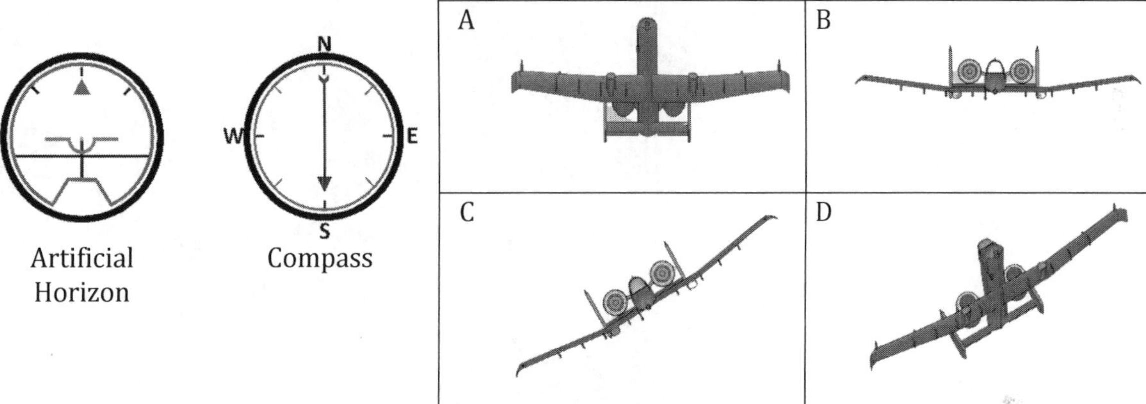

24. **Which of the answer choices represents the orientation of the plane?**

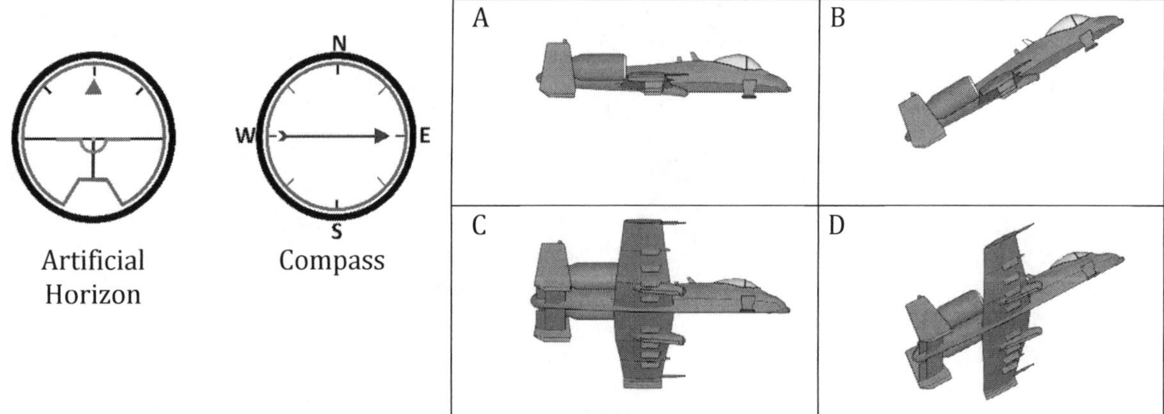

25. Which of the answer choices represents the orientation of the plane?

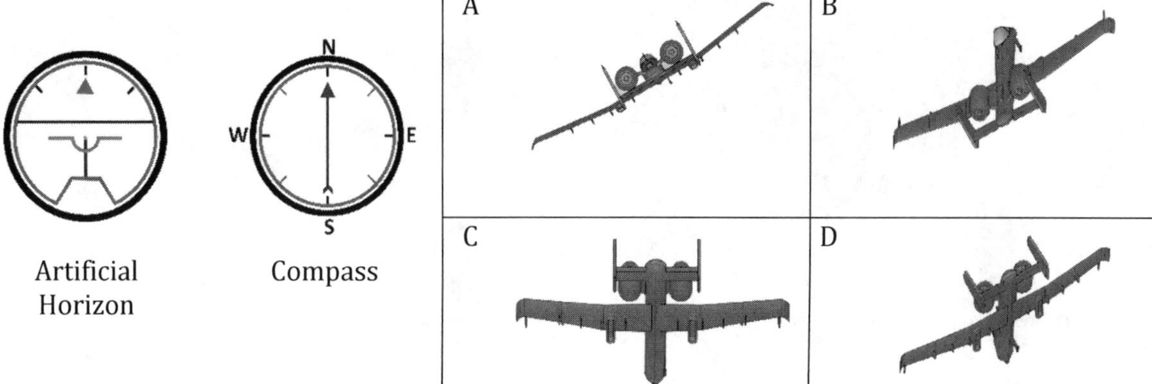

Artificial Horizon

Compass

Block Counting

The explanations to these problems use terms like "top," "left," and "front" to refer to the faces of the blocks. This terminology can be confusing due to the angled view of the block arrangements, so the illustration below is provided to help you keep these terms straight.

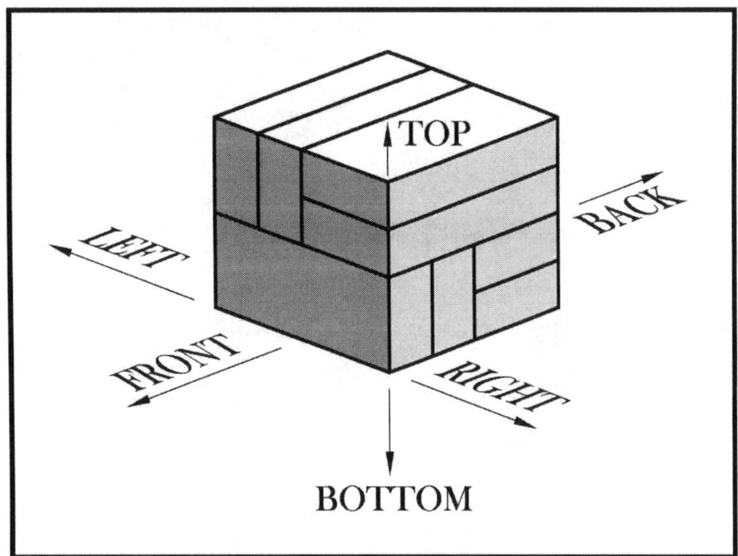

Once you understand these terms, proceed to the practice problems below. As a reminder, all the blocks in the images are intended to be the same size and shape, regardless of how much of each block is shown.

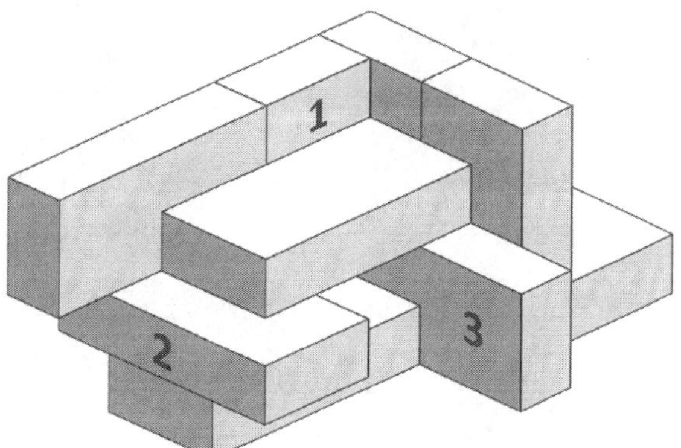

1. How many blocks are touching block 1 in the figure above?

2. How many blocks are touching block 2 in the figure above?

3. How many blocks are touching block 3 in the figure above?

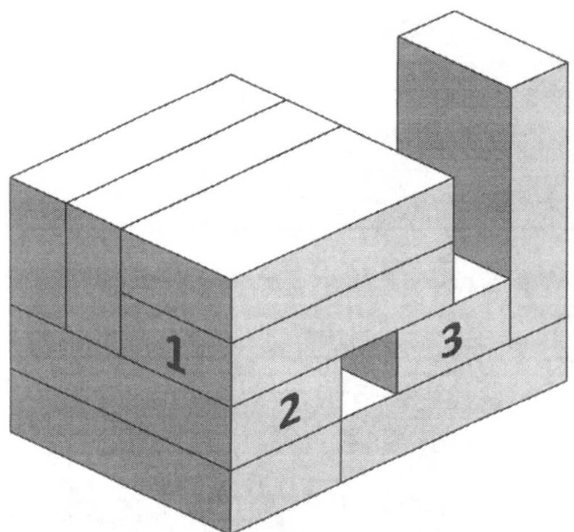

4. How many blocks are touching block 1 in the figure above?

5. How many blocks are touching block 2 in the figure above?

6. How many blocks are touching block 3 in the figure above?

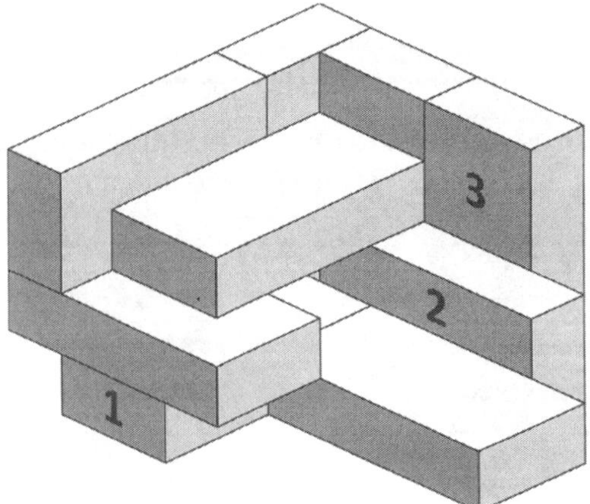

7. How many blocks are touching block 1 in the figure above?

8. How many blocks are touching block 2 in the figure above?

9. How many blocks are touching block 3 in the figure above?

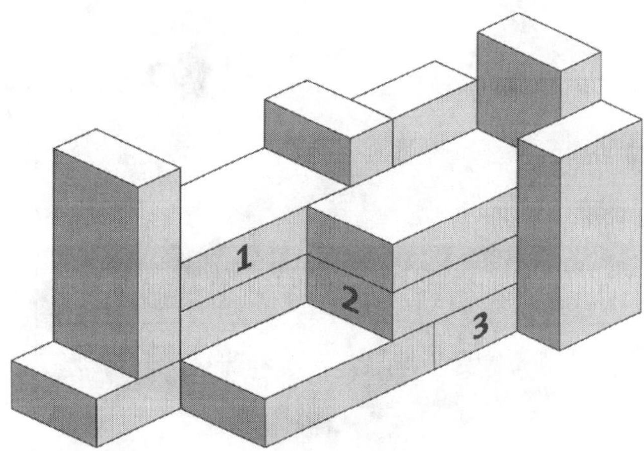

10. How many blocks are touching block 1 in the figure above?

11. How many blocks are touching block 2 in the figure above?

12. How many blocks are touching block 3 in the figure above?

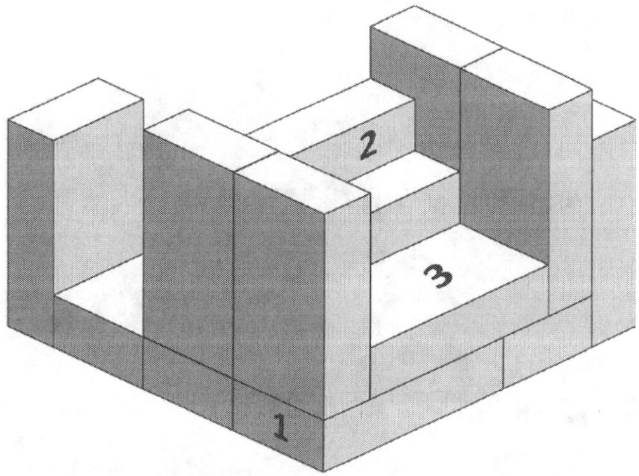

13. How many blocks are touching block 1 in the figure above?

14. How many blocks are touching block 2 in the figure above?

15. How many blocks are touching block 3 in the figure above?

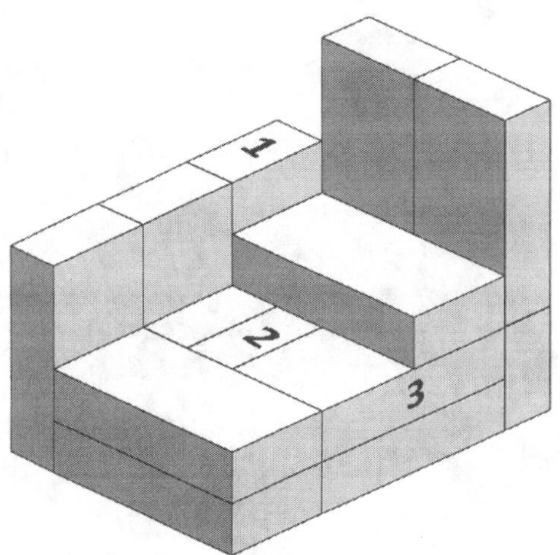

16. How many blocks are touching block 1 in the figure above?

17. How many blocks are touching block 2 in the figure above?

18. How many blocks are touching block 3 in the figure above?

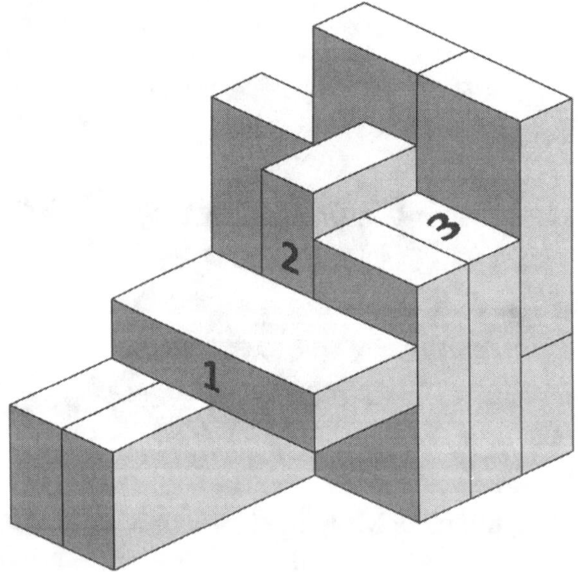

19. How many blocks are touching block 1 in the figure above?

20. How many blocks are touching block 2 in the figure above?

21. How many blocks are touching block 3 in the figure above?

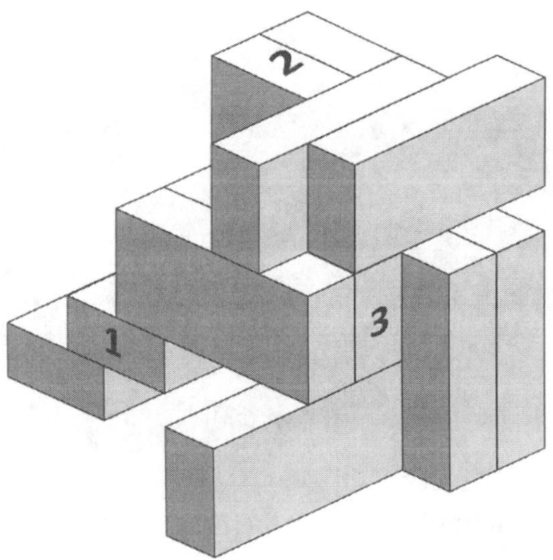

22. How many blocks are touching block 1 in the figure above?

23. How many blocks are touching block 2 in the figure above?

24. How many blocks are touching block 3 in the figure above?

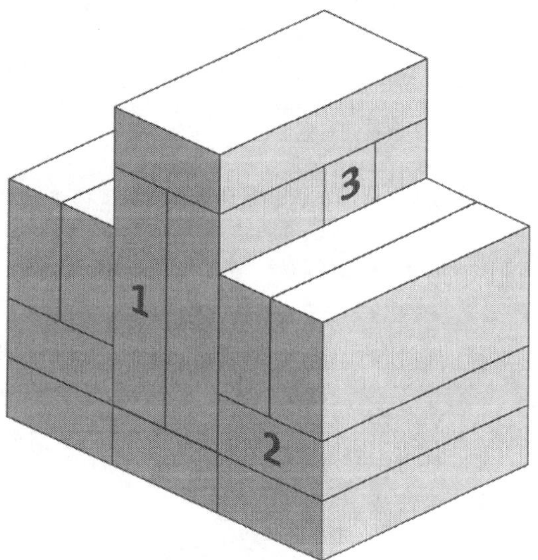

25. How many blocks are touching block 1 in the figure above?

26. How many blocks are touching block 2 in the figure above?

27. How many blocks are touching block 3 in the figure above?

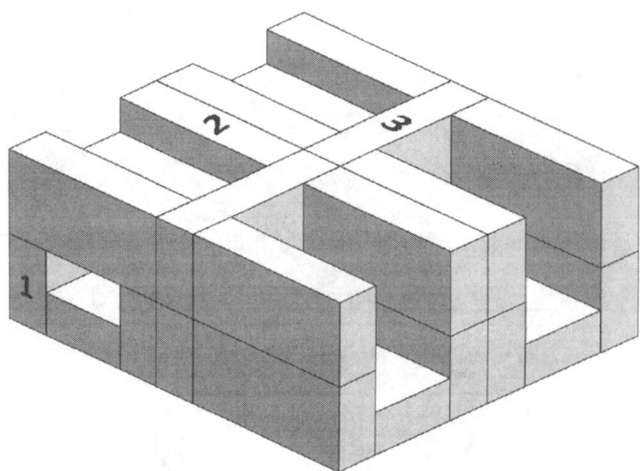

28. How many blocks are touching block 1 in the figure above?

29. How many blocks are touching block 2 in the figure above?

30. How many blocks are touching block 3 in the figure above?

Aviation Information

1. From approximately how far away should a Visual Approach Slope Indicator be visible at night?

a. Five miles
b. Ten miles
c. Twenty miles
d. Thirty miles
e. Fifty miles

2. Which of the following is NOT one of the forces a pilot must manage during flight?

a. Thrust
b. Gravity
c. Drag
d. Lift
e. Torque

3. Which control affects the angle of the main rotor blades of a helicopter?

a. Collective
b. Throttle
c. Cyclic
d. Directional control system
e. None of the above

4. What is the flight attitude?

a. The environment immediately around the plane
b. The morale of the flight crew
c. The position of the plane in motion
d. The inclination of the elevators
e. The positions of the ailerons

5. The curvature of an airfoil is known as the

a. Bank
b. Position
c. Camber
d. Angle
e. Attitude

6. Which of the following is considered one of the primary flight controls?

a. Elevators
b. Leading edge devices
c. Flaps
d. Spoilers
e. Trim tabs

7. What is the term in aviation for movement around the plane's longitudinal axis?

a. Stalling
b. Rolling
c. Pitching
d. Leaning
e. Yawing

8. What is the primary determinant of air pressure in the flight envelope?

a. The altitude at which the plane is flying
b. The camber of the wings
c. The amount of lift that the airfoils can create
d. The pitch of the elevators
e. The humidity of the air

9. A plane is said to have conventional landing gear when the third wheel is

a. Aligned with the second wheel
b. Under the tail
c. Directly behind the first wheel
d. Under the nose
e. Underneath the cockpit

10. Which of the following is NOT part of the empennage?

a. Rudder
b. Trim tab
c. Elevator
d. Aileron
e. Horizontal stabilizer

11. A glider would be most likely to have a

a. Delta wing
b. Triangular wing
c. Forward swept wing
d. Backward swept wing
e. Straight wing

12. Which of the following is NOT considered part of a plane's basic weight?

a. Crew
b. Fuel
c. External equipment
d. Internal equipment
e. Fuselage

13. The support structure that runs the length of the fuselage in a monocoque plane is called a

a. Counter
b. Former
c. Truss
d. Stringer
e. Bulkhead

14. Which control is used to manipulate the elevators on an airplane?

a. Throttle
b. Rudder
c. Joystick
d. Pedals
e. Collective

15. Which maneuver is appropriate when a pilot needs to descend quickly onto a shorter-than-normal runway?

a. Descent at minimum safe airspeed
b. Idle
c. Partial power descent
d. Glide
e. Stall

16. In aviation, which of the following is NOT one of the possible functions of a spoiler?

a. Diminishing lift
b. Raising the nose
c. Increasing drag
d. Reducing adverse yaw
e. Enabling descent without speed reduction

17. The vertical axis of a plane extends upward through the plane's

a. Cockpit
b. Tail
c. Landing gear
d. Center of mass
e. Geometric center

18. When is trimming necessary?

a. When the plane is ascending or descending
b. After the elevators have been deflected upwards
c. After the ailerons have been adjusted
d. After the elevators have been deflected downwards
e. After any change in the flight condition

19. How far away is an approaching plane when the Runway Centerline Lighting System lights become solid red?

a. Five hundred feet
b. One thousand feet
c. Three thousand feet
d. Five thousand feet
e. One mile

20. What is the Coriolis force?

a. The extra lift generated by a helicopter once it has exited its own downwash
b. The force that spins the rotors of a helicopter even when there is no power from the engine
c. The greater downwash at the rear half of the rotor disc, as compared with the front
d. The phenomenon in which the effects of a force applied to a spinning disc occur ninety degrees later
e. The change in rotational speed caused by the shift of the weight towards or away from the center of the spinning object

Answer Key and Explanations for Test #1

Verbal Analogies

1. B: Rash. Chastise and reprimand are synonyms. The answer choice synonym for impetuous is rash.

2. C: Femur. The humerus is a bone in the arm; the femur is a bone in the leg.

3. A: Quotient. A quotient is the result of division as a product is the result of multiplication.

4. C: Asparagus. As a sweater is something one wears, asparagus is something one eats.

5. A: Famished. As a person who is impecunious needs money, so a person who is famished needs food.

6. A: Protest. Denigrate and malign are synonyms. The answer choice synonym for demur is protest.

7. D: Generous. Obeisance and deference are synonyms. The answer choice synonym for munificent is generous.

8. D: Sow. A female goat is a nanny and a female pig is a sow.

9. B: Paucity. Cache and reserve are synonyms. The answer choice synonym for dearth is paucity.

10. E: Refuge. Arable and farmable are synonyms. The answer choice synonym for asylum is refuge.

11. A: Peripatetic. Myriad and few are antonyms. The answer choice antonym for stationary is peripatetic.

12. A: Flagon. As a mansion is a large house, so a flagon is a large bottle.

13. B: Synonyms. As a dictionary is a collection of definitions, so a thesaurus is a collection of synonyms.

14. B: Stubborn. Abstruse and esoteric are synonyms. The answer choice synonym for adamant is stubborn.

15. C: Herd. A group of bees is called a hive, and a group of cattle is called a herd.

16. E: Meridian. A parallel is a line of latitude, while a meridian is a line of longitude.

17. B: Provocation. Prevention and deterrence are synonyms. The answer choice synonym for incitement is provocation.

18. A: Gauge. Value and worth are synonyms. The answer choice synonym for measure is gauge.

19. A: Oppose. Enervate and energize are antonyms. The answer choice antonym for espouse is oppose.

20. D: The analogy is tool to worker. A carpenter uses a hammer, just as a doctor uses a stethoscope.

21. B: The analogy describes characteristic location. An armoire is usually kept in a bedroom, just as a desk is usually kept in an office.

22. C: This analogy describes a food source to animal relationship. Just as plankton is a food source for whales, so is bamboo a food source for pandas.

23. C: The analogy is geographic location. Just as the tundra is located in the Arctic regions, so are savannas located in tropic regions.

24. A: This is an analogy of relative degree. *Parched* is a more intense degree of *thirsty,* just as *famished* is a more intense degree of *hungry.*

25. E: This is an analogy based on antonyms. *Felicity,* or happiness, is the opposite of *sadness,* just as *ignominy,* or disgrace, is the opposite of *honor.*

Arithmetic Reasoning

1. B: First, find the total before taxes:

$$\$7.50 + \$3.00 = \$10.50$$

Then, calculate 6% of the total:

$$\$10.50 \times 0.06 = \$0.63$$

Finally, add the tax to find how much he pays in all:

$$\$10.50 + \$0.63 = \$11.13$$

2. D: There are 7 days in a week. Knowing that the chef can make 25 pastries in a day, the weekly number can be calculated:

$$25 \times 7 = 175$$

3. B: The woman has four days to earn $250. To find the amount she must earn each day, divide the amount she must earn ($250) by 4:

$$\frac{\$250}{4} = \$62.50$$

4. A: To find the number of cars remaining, subtract the number of cars that were sold from the original number:

$$476 - 36 = 440$$

5. B: Calculate 0.5% of $450:

$$\$450 \times 0.005 = \$2.25$$

This is the amount of interest she will earn.

6. C: First, figure out how much the second child contributed:

$$\$24.00 - \$15.00 = \$9.00$$

Then, calculate how much the first two children contributed in total:

$$\$24.00 + \$9.00 = \$33.00$$

Finally, figure out how much the third child will have to contribute:

$$\$78.00 - \$33.00 = \$45.00$$

7. C: First, figure out how many points the first woman will earn:

$$3 \times 5 = 15$$

Then, figure out how many points the second woman will earn:

$$6 \times 5 = 30$$

Then, add these two values together:

$$30 + 15 = 45 \text{ points total}$$

8. E: First, calculate 13% of 540:

$$540 \times 0.13 = 70.2 \text{ (round to 70)}$$

Then, add this value onto the original number of workers:

$$540 + 70 = 610$$

610 is the number of people that the company will employ after the expansion.

9. D: To find the number of apartments on each floor, divide the total number of apartments by the number of floors:

$$\frac{65}{13} = 5$$

10. C: First, find the total number of pens:

$$5 \times 3 = 15$$

Then, find the total number of pencils:

$$3 \times 7 = 21$$

Finally, express it as a ratio: 15: 21 which simplifies to 5: 7.

11. C: To calculate his new salary, add his raise to his original salary:

$$\$15.23 + \$2.34 = \$17.57$$

12. A: To find the total number of passengers, multiply the number of planes by the number of passengers each can hold:

$$6 \times 300 = 1{,}800$$

13. B: Currently, there are two men for every woman. If the number of women is doubled, then the new ratio is 2: 2. This is equivalent to 1: 1.

14. C: First, calculate 3% of 250 pounds:

$$250 \times 0.03 = 7.5 \text{ lb}$$

Calculate how much she weighs at the end of the first week:

$$250 - 7.5 = 242.5 \text{ lb}$$

Calculate 2% of 242.5:

$$242.5 \times 0.02 = 4.85 \text{ lb}$$

Add the two values together to get the total number of pounds she lost:

$$7.5 + 4.85 = 12.35 \text{ lb}$$

15. D: Divide the total distance she must travel (600 km) by the number of kilometers she drives each hour (80 km) to figure out how many hours it will take to reach her destination:

$$\frac{600 \text{ km}}{80 \text{ km/hr}} = 7.5 \text{ hours}$$

16. D: One gallon of paint can paint three rooms, so to find out how many rooms 28 gallons can paint, multiply that number by 3:

$$28 \times 3 = 84 \text{ rooms}$$

17. A: Each earns $135, so to find the total earned, that amount must be multiplied by the number of workers:

$$\$135 \times 5 = \$675$$

18. C: First, calculate her score on the second test:

$$99 - 15 = 84$$

Then, calculate her score on the third test:

$$84 + 5 = 89$$

19. A: To find out how much he has remaining, subtract both the amounts that he spent from the original amount ($50.00):

$$\$50.00 - \$15.64 - \$7.12 = \$27.24$$

20. E: Divide the number of students (600) by the number of classrooms they will share (20):

$$\frac{600}{20} = 30$$

21. C: To calculate this value, divide the number of dogs (48) by the number of workers that are available to care for them (4):

$$\frac{48}{4} = 12$$

22. C: First, calculate the length of the second office:

$$20 + 6 = 26 \text{ feet}$$

Then, add both values together to get a combined length:

$$26 + 20 = 46 \text{ feet}$$

23. C: Find the total cost of the items:

$$\$6.65 + \$159.23 = \$165.88$$

Then, calculate how much each individual will owe:

$$\frac{\$165.88}{4} = \$41.47$$

24. A: To answer this question, simply calculate half of 140 acres:

$$\frac{140}{2} = 70 \text{ acres}$$

25. C: First, calculate how many he has after selling 45:

$$360 - 45 = 315$$

Then, calculate how many he has after buying 85:

$$315 + 85 = 400$$

Word Knowledge

1. A: Spoiled has a number of meanings, and one of them is ruined. If you said somebody spoiled your fun, it would convey the same meaning as saying somebody ruined your fun.

2. B: An oath is a promise. For example, if you make an oath to keep a secret, you are promising to keep that secret.

3. B: When you inquire about something, you are asking about it or requesting more information. For example, if you told somebody you inquired about a job, it would mean you asked about it.

4. C: If you say that you comprehend something, it is the same as saying you understand it. For example, saying you comprehend what another person is saying is the same as saying you understand them.

5. A: To say that something is apparent implies that it is clear or obvious. For example, saying that it is apparent that somebody wants a job is the same as saying it is clear they want the job.

6. C: Silent or silence indicates quiet and calm. To enjoy the silence of the night is to enjoy the complete quiet of the night.

7. E: Absolutely, when used to describe a feeling or state of mind, means completely or totally. For example, saying you are absolutely certain that you made the right decision or saying you are completely certain you made the right decision conveys the same meaning.

8. D: Something that has been modified has been changed. Saying you modified your plans or saying that you changed them conveys the same meaning.

9. A: Something that is delicate can also be described as fragile. Saying that a crystal figurine is delicate or saying it is fragile conveys the same meaning.

10. B: Festivities are commonly known as celebrations. Attending festivities implies that you are attending a celebration or party.

11. B: To say that someone is exhausted or to say that they are tired conveys a similar meaning. Usually, exhausted is a word used to describe extreme tiredness.

12. B: To cleanse something is to clean or wash it. Saying you cleansed your face or clothes is the same as saying you washed them.

13. A: To battle something is to fight it. To say that two armies battled each other and to say they fought each other conveys the same meaning.

14. C: To wander is to roam. To say someone wandered around a mall is to say they roamed or walked around aimlessly, without a specific goal or destination in mind.

15. E: Something that is done abruptly is done suddenly and without warning. For example, saying the car stopped abruptly and saying it stopped suddenly conveys the same meaning.

16. A: Somebody who has been tricked has been conned. To trick somebody is to con them, which implies that dishonest methods are used to convince another to do something they wouldn't normally do.

17. C: When used as an adjective extremely has the same meaning as very. Saying somebody is extremely happy and saying they are very happy conveys the same meaning.

18. A: To have doubts is to have uncertainties or hesitations. To say that someone is doubtful about something means that they are uncertain.

19. D: To describe something as peculiar is to say it is strange or out of the ordinary. For example, saying you are in a strange situation or saying you are in a peculiar situation conveys the same meaning.

20. B: Describing somebody as courteous implies that they are polite and well-mannered. Polite and courteous both convey the same meaning.

21. C: When somebody says they are troubled by something, they mean that they are bothered by it.

22. A: Perspiration is another word for sweat. Saying somebody is perspiring is the same as saying they are sweating.

23. B: Tremble is another word for shake. To say somebody or something trembled means that it shook or shuddered.

24. A: Adhered is often used as another word for stuck. For example, to say a piece of tape adhered to the wall conveys the same meaning as saying the piece of tape stuck to the wall.

25. D: When something is described as tidy, it usually means that it is neat and that things are in their proper place. Saying a house is tidy and saying it is neat conveys the same meaning.

Mathematics Knowledge

1. B: The perimeter of a figure is the sum of all of its sides. Since a rectangle's width and length will be the same on opposite sides, the perimeter of a rectangle can be calculated by using the following formula:

$$P = 2w + 2l$$

Using the numbers given in the question:

$$P = 2(7) + 2(9)$$

$$P = 14 + 18 = 32 \text{ cm}$$

2. D: First, gather the like terms on opposite sides of the equation to make it easier to solve:

$$12 + 30 \geq 4q + 3q$$

$$42 \geq 7q$$

Then, divide both sides by 7 to solve for q:

$$\frac{42}{7} \geq \frac{7q}{7}$$

$$6 \geq q \text{ or } q \leq 6$$

3. C: To solve for x, simply add 6 to both sides:

$$x - 6 + 6 = 0 + 6$$

$$x = 6$$

4. A: To calculate the value of this expression, substitute -3 for x each time it appears in the expression:

$$3(-3)^3 + (3(-3) + 4) - 2(-3)^2$$

According to the order of operations, any operations inside of brackets must be done first:

$$3(-3)^3 + (-9 + 4) - 2(-3)^2$$

$$3(-3)^3 + (-5) - 2(-3)^2$$

Then, exponential operations may be performed:

$$3(-27) + (-5) - 2(9)$$

Next, multiplication:

$$-81 - 5 - 18$$

Finally, subtraction from left to right:

$$-81 - 5 - 18 = -104$$

5. C: First, combine like terms to make the equation easier to solve:

$$3x + 2x = 45 + 30$$

$$5x = 75$$

Then, divide both sides by 5 to solve for x:

$$\frac{5x}{5} = \frac{75}{5}$$

$$x = 15$$

6. A: First, add 25 to both sides to isolate x:

$$\frac{1}{4}x - 25 + 25 \geq 75 + 25$$

$$\frac{1}{4}x \geq 100$$

Then, multiply both sides by 4 to solve for x:

$$4 \times \frac{1}{4}x \geq 4 \times 100$$

$$x \geq 400$$

7. A: First, add 5 to both sides to isolate x:

$$x^2 - 5 + 5 = 20 + 5$$

$$x^2 = 25$$

Then, take the square root of both sides to solve for x:

$$\sqrt{x^2} = \sqrt{25}$$

$$x = \pm 5$$

8. B: First, we must calculate the length of one side of the square. Since we know the perimeter is 8 cm and that a square has 4 equal sides, the length of each side can be calculated by dividing the perimeter (8 cm) by 4:

$$\frac{8 \text{ cm}}{4} = 2 \text{ cm}$$

The formula for the area of a square is its side length squared:

$$A = (2 \text{ cm})^2 = 4 \text{ cm}^2$$

9. D: To find the value of this expression, substitute the given values for x and y into the expression and simplify:

$$3(4)(2) - 12(2) + 5(4) = 24 - 24 + 20 = 20$$

10. D: First, subtract 10 from both sides to isolate x:

$$\frac{2}{3}x + 10 - 10 = 16 - 10$$

$$\frac{2}{3}x = 6$$

Then, multiply both sides by the reciprocal of $\frac{2}{3}$ to solve for x:

$$\frac{3}{2} \times \frac{2}{3}x = 6 \times \frac{3}{2}$$

$$x = 9$$

11. B: Use the FOIL method (first, outside, inside, and last) to expand the polynomial:

$$12x^2 - 18x + 20x - 30$$

Then, combine like terms to simplify the expression:

$$12x^2 + 2x - 30$$

12. B: To simplify this expression, recall the law of exponents for division:

$$\frac{x^n}{x^m} = x^{n-m}$$

Apply to each variable in the expression:

$$\frac{x^{18}}{x^5} = x^{13}; \frac{t^6}{t^2} = t^4; \frac{w^3}{w^2} = w; \frac{z^{20}}{z^{19}} = z$$

Combine to simplify:

$$10x^{13}t^4wz$$

13. E: To calculate 4-factorial, take the product of all the integers between 1 and 4:

$$4! = 4 \times 3 \times 2 \times 1 = 24$$

14. D: Because it is a cube, we can find the volume by taking the cube of any side length:

$$5 \times 5 \times 5 = 125 \text{ cm}^3$$

15. A: First, factor this equation to make solving for x easier:

$$x^2 - 13x + 42 = (x - 6)(x - 7) = 0$$

The expression on the left side of the equation is equal to zero when either $(x - 6)$ or $(x - 7)$ equals zero. Thus:

$$x = 6, 7$$

16. C: The area of a triangle can be calculated by using the following formula:

$$A = \frac{1}{2}bh$$

Therefore, by using the values given in the question:

$$A = \frac{1}{2}(12)(12) = 72 \text{ cm}^2$$

17. D: To simplify this expression, recall the law of exponents for multiplication:

$$x^n x^m = x^{n+m}$$

Apply to each variable in the expression:

$$x^7 x^2 = x^9; y^{12} y^3 = y^{15}$$

$$(3x^2 7x^7) + (2y^3 9y^{12}) = 21x^9 + 18y^{15}$$

18. C: First, subtract 27 from both sides to isolate x:

$$\frac{x}{3} + 27 - 27 = 30 - 27$$

$$\frac{x}{3} = 3$$

Next, multiply both sides by 3:

$$\frac{x}{3} \times 3 = 3 \times 3$$

$$x = 9$$

19. B: The slope of a line can be calculated by dividing the change in the y-coordinate by the change in the x-coordinate:

$$y_{change} = 8 - 1 = 7$$

$$x_{change} = -13 - 4 = -17$$

$$Slope = \frac{y_{change}}{x_{change}} = -\frac{7}{17}$$

20. A: To solve for x, calculate the value of 20% of 200:

$$20\% \times 200 = 0.2 \times 200 = 40$$

$$x = 40$$

21. B: The odds of a black balloon being chosen at random from a bag of balloons is calculated as:

$$P = \frac{\text{\# black balloons}}{\text{\# total balloons}}$$

The total number of balloons is found by adding up the number of each color:

$$37 + 8 + 15 = 60$$

There are ten black balloons, so calculate the probability of selecting a black balloon:

$$P = \frac{15}{60} = 25\%$$

22. D: Each ticket has the same odds of being the winning ticket:

$$1 \text{ in } 500 \text{ or } \frac{1}{500}$$

If a man buys 25 tickets, his odds of winning are now multiplied by 25:

$$25 \text{ in } 500 \text{ or } \frac{25}{500}$$

We can reduce this ratio by dividing both numbers by 25:

$$\frac{25}{25} = 1; \frac{500}{25} = 20$$

$$1 \text{ in } 20 \text{ or } \frac{1}{20} = 5\%$$

23. E: To find the volume of a rectangular prism, the formula is $V = L \times W \times H$. For the prism described in this question:

$$V = 5 \text{ cm} \times 6 \text{ cm} \times 10 \text{ cm} = 300 \text{ cm}^3$$

24. C: To calculate the midpoint of a line, take the average of both the x- and y-coordinates. The x-coordinate of the midpoint can be calculated as follows:

$$\frac{6 + 10}{2} = 8$$

The y-coordinate of the midpoint can be calculated as follows:

$$\frac{20 + 40}{2} = 30$$

Therefore, the midpoint is $(8, 30)$.

25. A: First, subtract 60 from both sides:

$$5x + 60 - 60 = 75 - 60$$

Then divide both sides by 5:

$$\frac{5x}{5} = \frac{15}{5}$$

$$x = 3$$

Reading Comprehension

1. A: Explaining the qualities of air that may affect flight is the primary purpose of the passage.

2. C: The best definition for *inversely* as it is used in the second paragraph is *in the opposite direction*. The author is indicating that the density of air decreases as the temperature rises, and increases as the temperature falls.

3. D: A pilot can expect the air density to decrease as the plane gains altitude. At the end of the second paragraph, the author states that a gain in altitude will usually lead to a decrease in air density, no matter what changes there may be in the temperature.

4. B: The author would most likely agree that air density is more important than relative humidity. Though the passage states that humidity can have an effect on aircraft performance, the author admits that it is not considered an essential factor. Indeed, humidity is just one of three factors (along with pressure and temperature) that affect air density.

5. C: The most likely reason why there is no chart for assessing the effects of humidity on density altitude is that humidity does not affect flight performance very much. The author mentions several times that flight performance is not significantly affected by humidity, and so it is seems that a special chart for this purpose would be unnecessary.

6. D: *Influences on Climb Performance* would be the best title for this passage. The passage surveys the various factors that affect climb performance and the choices made by pilots as they gain altitude, both during take-off and while the aircraft is already in flight.

7. E: The best definition for *pronounced* as it is used in the second paragraph is *noticeable*. The author is stating that the weight of an aircraft has a significant impact on aircraft performance. In this sentence *pronounced* is being used as an adjective, but it can also be used as a verb, meaning *spoke* or *said*.

8. C: An increase in weight means that the angle of attack must be higher in order to maintain altitude. Greater weight diminishes reserve power, lowers the climb rate, diminishes the maximum rate of climb, and increases drag.

9. B: The author would most likely agree that at the end of a long journey a plane will have a higher maximum rate of climb. The maximum rate of climb of a plane increases as the weight decreases, and the weight of a plane will decrease as it burns off fuel over the course of a long journey.

10. A: A helicopter that weighs two tons and has rotor blades that cover five hundred square feet would have a disc loading measure of eight pounds per square foot. Pounds per square foot is the standard measure for disc loading. There are two thousand pounds in a ton. Disc loading is calculated by dividing the weight of the helicopter by the area covered by the rotor blades.

11. B: Discussing the interrelationships of airspeed, power, and pitch attitude is the primary purpose of the passage. Answer choices *C* and *D* are partially correct, but they leave out large sections of the passage and therefore do not comprehensively describe the purpose or the content of the passage.

12. A: *Inadvertently*, as it is used in the fifth paragraph, most nearly means *unintentionally*. The author is indicating that a pilot can enter the region of reversed command without meaning to, if he or she attempts to climb out of ground effect without first attaining normal climb pitch attitude and airspeed.

13. B: Most flight occurs in the region of normal command. In the region of normal command, increasing power increases the airspeed, and decreasing power decreases the airspeed. This information is given in the last sentence of the second paragraph.

14. E: The author would most likely agree that as the speed of flight decreases, the power required to maintain altitude increases. This inverse relationship between required power and airspeed is expressed in the last sentence of the first paragraph.

15. D: The best title for this passage would be *Power Requirements During Flight.* The passage discusses how the need for and effects of changes in power are influenced by factors such as airspeed, pitch attitude, and altitude.

16. E: The primary purpose of the passage is to describe the factors that influence landing distance. The passage begins by discussing the minimum and normal landing distances and goes on to cover influences on landing distance, as for instance gross weight, wind, and density altitude.

17. B: When making a normal landing, a pilot will rely on aerodynamic drag in order to avoid wearing down the brakes and tires. This point is made several times in the third paragraph of the passage.

18. A: The best definition for *principal* as it is used in the fifth paragraph is *most important.* The author is trying to make the point that gross weight has an enormous effect on landing distance.

19. C: A heavier plane must be landed at a higher airspeed to avoid hitting the runway with too much force. This idea is explored in the fourth paragraph. In order to generate an amount of lift sufficient for a smooth landing, a higher airspeed must be maintained.

20. C: The author would most likely agree that gross weight and minimum landing distance are positively correlated. The information in the passage makes it clear that as gross weight rises, minimum landing distance increases.

21. D: The primary purpose of the article is to discuss aeronautical decision making, or ADM. The article does give some examples of decision-making strategies, but these are given in the context of a description of ADM, not as the main body of the article.

22. D: The passage explains that aviation safety is distinct from other areas of safety because there is a much smaller margin for error. In other words, even small accidents in aviation can be catastrophic, because of the risks inherent in flight.

23. A: The closest definition for *conjunction* as it is used in the second paragraph is *combination.* The author is stating that the FAA manuals worked well when combined with the usual flight training.

24. A: The author would most likely agree that the body of knowledge about ADM is increasing, and this will have a positive effect on flight safety. The article details the efforts to improve ADM and suggests that these have already improved flight safety a great deal.

25. E: For a pilot, reading the account of a recent aviation accident is an opportunity for an indirect learning experience. The passage distinguishes between direct learning experiences, which are events in one's own life, and indirect learning experiences, which are things that happen to others.

Situational Judgment

1. C (Most effective)

2. A (Least effective)

3. A (Most effective)

4. C (Least effective)

5. E (Most effective)

6. B (Least effective)

7. D (Most effective)

8. A (Least effective)

9. E (Most effective)

10. C (Least effective)

11. B (Most effective)

12. C (Least effective)

13. A (Most effective)

14. B (Least effective)

15. E (Most effective)

16. B (Least effective)

17. C (Most effective)

18. A (Least effective)

19. A (Most effective)

20. B (Least effective)

21. B (Most effective)

22. D (Least effective)

23. A (Most effective)

24. C (Least effective)

25. B (Most effective)

26. E (Least effective)

27. D (Most effective)

28. A (Least effective)

29. B (Most effective)

30. C (Least effective)

31. E (Most effective)

32. B (Least effective)

33. A (Most effective)

34. D (Least effective)

35. D (Most effective)

36. C (Least effective)

37. A (Most effective)

38. D (Least effective)

39. E (Most effective)

40. A (Least effective)

41. B (Most effective)

42. C (Least effective)

43. E (Most effective)

44. A or C (Least effective)

45. A (Most effective)

46. D (Least effective)

47. A (Most effective)

48. B (Least effective)

49. B (Most effective)

50. D (Least effective)

Physical Science

1. B: A long nail or other type of metal, substance, or matter that is heated at one end and then the other end becomes equally hot is an example of conduction. Conduction is energy transfer by neighboring molecules from an area of hotter temperature to cooler temperature.

2. E: The measure of energy within a system is called heat.

3. B: They have a different number of neutrons. The distinguishing feature of an isotope is its number of neutrons. Two different isotopes of the same element will have the same number of protons but different numbers of neutrons.

4. A: Fission is a nuclear process where atomic nuclei split apart to form smaller nuclei. Nuclear fission can release large amounts of energy, emit gamma rays and form daughter products. It is used in nuclear power plants and bombs.

5. D: The process whereby a radioactive element releases energy slowly over a long period of time to lower its energy and become more stable is best described as decay. The nucleus undergoing decay spontaneously releases energy, most commonly through the emission of an alpha particle, a beta particle, or a gamma ray.

6. B: Light within a single medium travels in a straight line. When it changes to a different medium, however, the light rays bend according to the refractive index of each substance. Light coming from the submerged portion of the pencil is refracted as it passes through the air-water barrier, giving the perception of a bent pencil.

7. A: Hertz (Hz) is a unit of measure used for frequency, often described as 1 cycle/second. In the context of wave motion, it is the number of complete waves that pass a given point in one second.

8. B: A cyclist coasting up a hill is trading his speed for increased altitude. This is an example of kinetic energy being converted to potential energy. The other options are examples of potential energy being converted to kinetic, kinetic energy being dissipated, and conservation of kinetic energy.

9. E: Phase changes such as boiling, melting, and freezing are physical changes. No chemical reaction takes place when water is boiled.

10. A: The center of an atom is known as the nucleus. It is composed of protons and neutrons.

11. A: Sublimation is the process of a solid changing directly into a gas without entering the liquid phase.

12. D: Mendeleev was able to connect the trends of the different elements' behaviors and develop a table that showed the periodicity of the elements and their relationship to each other.

13. A: Density is mass per unit volume, typically expressed in units such as g/cm^3, or kg/m^3.

14. C: The closer the data points are to each other, the more precise the data. This does not mean the data is accurate, but rather that the results are reproducible.

15. E: Current is measured in units of amperes or amps.

16. C: In order for a solar eclipse to occur, the moon must come directly between the earth and the sun, blocking the sun's light from the earth.

17. B: Inertia is the tendency of objects that are in motion to continue moving in the same direction. The turning car initiates a change in direction, but the passengers' mass wants to continue going straight, causing them to feel a pull in that direction. This phenomenon is sometimes referred to as centrifugal force.

18. B: According to the ideal gas law, when volume is held constant, the temperature of a gas is directly proportional to the pressure of the gas. Thus, when the temperature is increased, the pressure will also increase.

19. B: The amplitude of a sound wave is what determines how loud the sound is perceived by the ear.

20. D: In all of the other examples, there is a person applying work to the book, either directly, by being picked up, pushed, or thrown, or indirectly, by being carried in a backpack. In the example of a book being released so that it falls, the only work being applied to the book is being done by gravity.

Table Reading

1. B
2. A
3. C
4. C
5. E
6. D
7. C
8. A
9. A
10. B
11. E
12. E
13. A
14. B
15. B
16. D
17. A
18. E
19. C
20. A
21. E
22. E
23. C
24. B
25. A
26. B
27. A
28. E
29. C
30. A
31. D
32. C
33. C
34. D
35. A
36. B
37. E
38. E
39. A
40. C

Instrument Comprehension

1. B

2. C

3. C

4. A

5. C

6. C

7. A

8. B

9. B

10. A

11. C

12. A

13. D

14. B

15. D

16. B

17. C

18. A

19. A

20. D

21. C

22. B

23. A

24. A

25. C

Block Counting

1. 5: 1 on the front, 1 on the back, 3 on the right.

2. 3: 2 on the top, 1 on the bottom.

3. 5: 1 on the front, 2 on the back, 1 on the left, 1 on the top.

4. 4: 1 on the left, 1 on the top, 2 on the bottom.

5. 4: 3 on the top, 1 on the bottom.

6. 5: 1 on the back, 3 on the top, 1 on the bottom.

7. 3: 1 on the back, 1 on the right, 1 on the top.

8. 5: 2 on the front, 2 on the back, 1 on top.

9. 2: 1 on the front, 1 on the left.

10. 4: 1 on the front, 1 on the back, 1 on the right, 1 on the bottom.

11. 8: 1 on the back, 3 on the left, 1 on the right, 1 on the top, 2 on the bottom,

12. 6: 1 on the front, 1 on the back, 2 on the left, 1 on the right, 1 on the top.

13. 4: 1 on the back, 1 on the left, 2 on the top.

14. 4: 1 on the front, 1 on the back, 1 on the right, 1 on the bottom.

15. 5: 1 on the front, 1 on the back, 1 on the left, 2 on the bottom.

16. 3: 1 on the front, 2 on the right.

17. 7: 2 on the front, 1 on the back, 1 on the left, 2 on the right, 1 on top.

18. 5: 1 on the front, 1 on the back, 1 on the left, 1 on the top, 1 on the bottom.

19. 4: 2 on the back, 2 on the bottom.

20. 6: 2 on the front, 2 on the back, 2 on the right.

21. 4: 1 on the front, 2 on the back, 1 on the left.

22. 5: 4 on the top, 1 on the bottom.

23. 4: 1 on the front, 1 on the back, 1 on the right, 1 on the bottom.

24. 7: 1 on the front, 2 on the back, 2 on the top, 2 on the bottom.

25. 6: 1 on the back, 2 on the left, 1 on the right, 1 on the top, 1 on the bottom.

26. 6: 3 on the left, 2 on the top, 1 on the bottom.

27. 9: 2 on the front, 1 on the back, 2 on the left, 2 on the right, 1 on the top, 1 on the bottom.

28. 5: 1 on the back, 1 on the right, 3 on top.

29. 5: 1 on the front, 1 on the back, 1 on the right, 2 on the bottom.

30. 7: 1 on the front, 3 on the left, 2 on the right, 1 on the bottom.

Aviation Information

1. C: A Visual Approach Slope Indicator should be visible from approximately twenty miles away at night. A Visual Approach Slope Indicator (VASI) is a common feature at large airports. This system helps guide the approaching pilot to the runway. The pilot will see white lights at the lower border of the glide path, and red lights at the upper border. In normal conditions, the lights of the VASI system should be visible for three to five miles during the day and for twenty miles at night. If the VASI system is working properly, the plane will be safe so long as it stays within ten degrees of the extended runway centerline and four nautical miles of the runway threshold.

2. E: Torque is not one of the forces a pilot must manage during flight. The four forces a pilot must manage are lift, gravity, thrust, and drag. Lift pushes the plane up, gravity pulls the plane down, thrust propels the plane forward, and drag holds the plane back. The overall admixture of these forces as they operate on the plane is called the flight envelope.

3. A: The collective affects the angle of the main rotor blades of a helicopter. It is a long tube that extends from the floor of the cockpit. In most helicopters, it is situated on the pilot's left. The collective has two parts: a handle that can be raised or lowered, to control the pitch of the blades; and a throttle, to control the torque of the engine. The handle is the part that affects the angle of the main rotor blades. When it is raised, the leading edge of the blade is raised higher than the trailing edge.

4. C: The flight attitude is the position of a plane in motion. The flight attitude is described in terms of its position with respect to three axes: vertical, lateral, and longitudinal. The vertical axis runs up through the plane's center of gravity. A plane's position with respect to this axis is known as its yaw. The lateral axis of a plane runs from wingtip to wingtip, and the motion of the plane around this axis is known as pitch. The longitudinal axis, finally, is an imaginary line extending from the nose of the plane to its tail. The position of the plane in relation to the longitudinal axis is called roll. The attitude of the plane is controlled with the joystick, rudder pedals, and throttle.

5. C: The curvature of an airfoil is known as the camber. An airfoil (wing) is considered to have a high camber if it is very curved. A related piece of wing terminology is the mean camber line, which runs along the inside of the wing, such that the upper and lower wings are equal in thickness.

6. A: The elevators are considered one of the primary flight controls. The elevators are responsible for the plane's pitch, or movement around the lateral axis. The other primary flight controls are the ailerons and the rudder. The ailerons control the roll, or movement around the longitudinal axis, while the rudder controls the yaw, or movement around the vertical axis. The secondary flight controls are the flaps, spoilers, leading edge devices, and trim systems.

7. B: In aviation, the term for movement around the plane's longitudinal axis is rolling. The longitudinal axis runs from the nose of the plane to its tail. For the most part, the plane's roll is controlled by the joystick. By moving the stick to the right or left, the pilot dips the wings.

8. A: The altitude at which the plane is flying is the primary determinant of air pressure in the flight envelope. The most important elements of the flight envelope are the temperature, air pressure, and humidity. The conditions in the atmosphere have a great deal of influence over the amount of lift created by the airfoils. Greater air pressure is the same as greater air density. A plane will generate greater lift when it is in cool air, because cool air is less dense than warm air.

9. B: A plane is said to have conventional landing gear when the third wheel is under the tail. Typically, a plane's landing gear will consist of three wheels or sets of wheels. Two of these are under either wing or on opposing sides of the fuselage. In the conventional arrangement, the third wheel, or wheel set, is under the tail, while in the tricycle arrangement it is under the nose. This third wheel can rotate, which will make it possible for the plane to turn while moving on the ground.

10. D: An aileron is not part of the empennage. The empennage, otherwise known as the tail assembly, includes the elevators, vertical and horizontal stabilizers, rudders, and trim tabs. A fixed wing aircraft will typically have both vertical and horizontal stabilizers, which are immobile surfaces that extend from the back of the fuselage. The horizontal stabilizers have mobile surfaces along their trailing edges; these surfaces are called the elevators. The elevators deflect up and down to raise or lower the nose of the plane. The rudder is a single, large flap connected by a hinge to the vertical stabilizer. The rudder's back-and-forth motion controls the motion of the plane with respect to its vertical axis. The trim tabs, finally, are connected to the trailing edges of one or more of the primary flight controls (i.e., ailerons, elevators, rudder).

11. E: A glider would be most likely to have a straight wing. A straight wing may be tapered, elliptical, or rectangular. This planform (wing shape) is common in aircraft that move at extremely low speeds. A straight wing is often found on sailplanes and gliders. The swept wing, on the other hand, is appropriate for high-speed aircraft. The wing may be swept forward or back. This will make the plane unstable at low speeds, but will produce much less drag. A swept wing requires high-speed takeoff and landing. The delta wing, which is also known as the triangular wing, has a straight trailing edge and a high angle of sweep. This allows the plane to take off and land at high speeds.

12. A: The crew is not considered part of a plane's basic weight. The basic weight is the aircraft plus whatever internal or external equipment will remain on the plane during its journey. The crew is not included in the basic weight, though it is a part of the operating weight (basic weight plus crew), gross weight (total weight of the aircraft at any particular time), landing gross weight (weight of the plane and its contents upon touchdown), and zero fuel weight (weight of the airplane when it has no usable fuel).

13. D: The support structure that runs the length of the fuselage in a monocoque plane is called a stringer. In a monocoque plane, the fuselage is supported by stringers, formers, and bulkheads. Stringers and formers are generally made out of the same material, though they run perpendicular to one another (that is, formers run in circles around the width of the fuselage). Bulkheads are the walls that divide the sections of the fuselage. The other style of fuselage, known as a truss, is composed of triangular groupings of aluminum or steel tubing.

14. C: The joystick is used to manipulate the elevators. When the stick is pulled back, the elevators deflect upwards. This decreases the camber of the horizontal tail surface, which moves the nose up and pushes the tail down. Pushing the joystick forward, on the other hand, pushes the elevators down, which creates an upward force on the tail by increasing the camber of the horizontal tail surface.

15. A: When a pilot needs to descend quickly onto a shorter-than-normal runway, he or she will descend at the minimum safe airspeed. A descent at the minimum safe airspeed is achieved by slightly lifting the nose and moving the plane into the landing configuration. During such a descent, the plane should not exceed 1.3 times the stall speed. This technique is appropriate for landing quickly on a short runway because the rate of descent is much faster. However, if the rate of descent should become too great, the pilot should be ready to increase power.

16. B: Raising the nose is not one of the possible functions of a spoiler. Spoilers can diminish lift and reduce drag, which enables the plane to descend without reducing its speed. However, spoilers also control the plane's roll, partly by reducing any adverse yaw. A pilot uses the spoiler in this way by raising the spoiler on the side of the turn. That side will thereby have less lift and more drag, making it drop. The plane will then bank and yaw in the intended direction. When the pilot raises both of the spoilers at the same time, the plane will descend without losing any speed. Another incidental benefit of spoilers is improved brake performance, which occurs because the plane has lift and is pushed down towards the ground.

17. D: The vertical axis of a plane extends up through the plane's center of gravity. Movement around this axis is called yawing. The position of a plane is also described with respect to the lateral and longitudinal axes. The lateral axis extends from wingtip to wingtip. The longitudinal axis runs from the nose of the plane to its tail.

18. E: Trimming is necessary after any change in the flight condition. Trimming is the adjustment of the trim tabs, which are small flaps that extend from the trailing edges of the elevators, rudder, and ailerons. Trimming generally occurs after the pilot has achieved the desired pitch, power, attitude, and configuration. The trim tabs are then used to resolve the remaining control pressures. A small plane may only have a single tab, which is controlled with a small wheel or crank.

19. B: When the Runway Centerline Lighting System lights become solid red, an approaching plane is one thousand feet away. A Runway Centerline Lighting System is a line of white lights every fifty feet or so along the centerline. The lights change their color and pattern as the plane nears the runway. When the plane gets within 3,000 feet of the runway, the lights blink red and white. Within a thousand feet, the lights will turn solid red.

20. E: The Coriolis force is the change in rotational speed caused by the shift of the weight towards or away from the center of the spinning object. This phenomenon has an important application for helicopters, in which the rotor will move faster or will require less power to maintain its speed when the weight is closer to the base of the blade. The other answer choices are similarly related to helicopters. The extra lift generated by a helicopter once it has exited its own downwash is known as translational lift. The force that spins the rotors of a helicopter even when there is no power from the engine is autorotation. Greater downwash at the rear half of the rotor disc, as compared to the front half, is the result of applying the lateral cyclic. The phenomenon in which the effects of a force applied to a spinning disc occur ninety degrees later is called gyroscopic precession.

AFOQT Practice Test #2

Verbal Analogies

1. VIVACIOUS is to ANIMATED as BOISTEROUS is to

a. SERENE
b. LOUD
c. SUBDUED
d. BELLIGERENT
e. CONFLATED

2. BEE is to APIOLOGY as FOSSIL is to

a. ANTHROPOLOGY
b. GENEALOGY
c. HISTORY
d. ARCHAEOLOGY
e. BIOLOGY

3. STALACTITE is to CAVE as a TOOTH is to

a. MOUTH
b. DENTIST
c. FACE
d. TOOTHBRUSH
e. CAVITIES

4. ORBIT is to SPACE as CIRCUMNAVIGATE is to

a. CITIES
b. CAMPUS
c. LAKES
d. OCEANS
e. CONTINENTS

5. PLANETARIUM is to ASTRONOMER as ARBORETUM is to

a. BIOLOGIST
b. FARMER
c. HORTICULTURIST
d. CHEMIST
e. DIETICIAN

6. CHRONOMETER is to TIME as BAROMETER is to

a. HUMIDITY
b. TEMPERATURE
c. VELOCITY
d. PRECIPITATION
e. PRESSURE

7. MAKEUP BRUSH is to BLUSH as HAMMER is to

a. SAW
b. SCREWDRIVER
c. CARPENTER
d. BOARD
e. NAIL

8. SMOKE is to FIRE as FROST is to

a. RAIN
b. COLD
c. SNOW
d. TEMPERATURE
e. STORMS

9. FATIGUE is to EXHAUSTION as FEAR is to

a. JOY
b. TERROR
c. SCARED
d. UNEASE
e. WORRY

10. DRILL is to TOOL as PEPPER is to

a. SALT
b. TASTE
c. CARROT
d. SPICE
e. FRUIT

11. PETROLOGY is to ROCKS as CARTOGRAPHY is to

a. WRITING
b. ARCHITECTS
c. MAPS
d. ENGINEERS
e. SAILORS

12. MARATHON is to RUN as RECITAL is to:

a. DANCE
b. SWIM
c. BALLET
d. JAZZ
e. HIP HOP

13. SWIM is to DROWN as FLY is to

a. SOAR
b. FLOAT
c. LAND
d. CRASH
e. GLIDE

14. EMANCIPATE is to FREE as SUBJUGATE is to

a. PERMIT
b. ENSLAVE
c. BURY
d. UNCOVER
e. RELEASE

15. CORPULENT is to THIN as MOROSE is to

a. OBESE
b. CORRUPT
c. SULLEN
d. CHEERFUL
e. ROUGH

16. NIAGARA is to WATERFALL as HURON is to

a. OCEAN
b. RIVER
c. TRIBUTARY
d. LANDMARK
e. LAKE

17. BIRTHDAY is to JOY as GRADUATION is to

a. REGRET
b. MOROSE
c. PRIDE
d. AFFABLE
e. EXCORIATION

18. BRAG is to BOAST as INSULT is to

a. RIDICULE
b. LAUD
c. PUMMEL
d. AUGMENT
e. RECONCILE

19. WATER is to WELL as GRAIN is to

a. BARN
b. TROUGH
c. BREAD
d. SILO
e. FIELD

20. CLEAVER is to BUTCHER as AWL is to

a. TAILOR
b. BAKER
c. MASON
d. FARMER
e. LEATHER WORKER

21. INFINITESIMAL is to MICROSCOPIC as PRODIGIOUS is to

a. COLOSSAL
b. MINUTE
c. AWAY
d. ABREAST
e. MINISCULE

22. SCULPT is to STATUE as WRITE is to

a. PRESCRIPTION
b. NOVEL
c. LIBRARY
d. LEARN
e. STUDENT

23. ITCH is to SCRATCH as FATIGUE is to

a. DREAM
b. WAKE
c. NIGHTMARE
d. SLEEP
e. ACTIVATE

24. FRUIT is to VINE as LEAF is to

a. FLOWER
b. BRANCH
c. GROWTH
d. TREE
e. AUTUMN

25. MURDER is to CROWS as FLOCK is to

a. DOGS
b. CATS
c. SHEEP
d. PARROTS
e. FISH

Arithmetic Reasoning

1. A preschooler spent 2 hours on the playground, 1 hour doing arts and crafts, and $2\frac{1}{2}$ hours napping. What percentage of her time was spent napping?

a. 45%
b. 36%
c. 18%
d. 55%
e. 50%

2. Find the volume of a rectangular tissue box that is 9 inches long by 4 inches wide and 5 inches tall.

a. 180 square inches
b. 180 cubic inches
c. 36 square inches
d. 45 cubic inches
e. 45 square inches

3. In a drawing that contains both circles and squares, there are 16 more circles than squares. The total number of circles and squares is 36. How many squares are there in the drawing?

a. 16
b. 26
c. 10
d. 24
e. 18

4. At the gym, 30% of the equipment consists of cardio machines. Of the cardio machines, 40% are treadmills. What percentage of the equipment at the gym consists of treadmills?

a. 67%
b. 1.2%
c. 70%
d. 12%
e. 10%

5. A car travels 135 miles at 45 miles per hour and then travels 165 miles at 55 miles per hour. What is the average speed of the car over the entire duration?

a. 55 mph
b. 50 mph
c. 60 mph
d. 49.5 mph
e. 45 mph

6. Snack boxes are taken on a school field trip. Each snack box holds either pretzels, chips, or a granola bar. If $\frac{1}{3}$ of the snack boxes contain pretzels and $\frac{1}{4}$ contains chips, which fraction of the snack boxes contain granola bars?

a. $\frac{7}{12}$
b. $\frac{1}{12}$
c. $\frac{5}{7}$
d. $\frac{1}{2}$
e. $\frac{5}{12}$

7. A sloth travels 110 feet in 15 minutes. What is the sloth's average speed? Round to the nearest tenth if necessary.

a. 7 ft/min
b. 7.3 ft/min
c. 27.5 ft/min
d. 15 ft/min
e. 45.8 ft/min

8. Solve $15x + 80 = 110$ for x.

a. 3
b. 12.7
c. 2
d. 1.2
e. 10

9. If a car can travel 210 miles in 3.5 hours, how far can it travel in 40 minutes (assuming it travels at the same speed)?

a. 45 miles
b. 55 miles
c. 35 miles
d. 40 miles
e. 60 miles

10. $(15) - (-13) =$

a. 2
b. 28
c. -28
d. -2
e. 13

11. 70 is 80% of what number?

a. 56
b. 87.5
c. 1.1
d. 112.5
e. 52.5

12. A car travels 55 mph to its first destination, 52 mph to its second destination, and 58 mph to its third destination. If each segment of the trip took 1 hour, what is the average of its three speeds?

a. 53.5 mph
b. 51 mph
c. 52 mph
d. 56.5 mph
e. 55 mph

13. Katie needs envelopes for her party invitation business. She has $50 budgeted for envelopes, and they cost $0.03 each. What is the maximum number of envelopes she can purchase?

a. 1,600
b. 1,666
c. 1,500
d. 150
e. 1,800

14. While playing the lottery, Kevin won $47.50 but then lost $12 on scratch-offs. The next day, he lost $27 more playing another game. How much money does he have left?

a. $86.50
b. $62.50
c. $8.50
d. $0.00
e. $12.50

15. Approximately how long does it take a car traveling at 57 mph to go 33 miles?

a. 34.8 hours
b. 34.8 minutes
c. 1.72 hours
d. 1.72 minutes
e. 45.4 minutes

16. A restaurant has 160 servings of chicken to be cooked tonight that will either be fried or grilled. 45% of the servings will be fried, and the rest will be grilled. How many servings will be grilled?

a. 88
b. 72
c. 80
d. 100
e. 90

17. Sam purchases a backpack and a water bottle. The backpack costs $39, and the water bottle costs $11. If an 8% sales tax is added, what is the final cost of Sam's purchase?

a. $50
b. $54
c. $40
d. $50.08
e. $50.80

18. Which of the following is NOT a way to write 50% of x?

a. $0.50x$
b. $\frac{50}{100}x$
c. $\frac{1}{2}x$
d. $50x$
e. $\frac{2}{4}x$

19. $(-4) - 9 =$

a. -13
b. -5
c. 13
d. 5
e. -12

20. 40 is what percent of 85?

a. 47%
b. 34%
c. 43%
d. 65%
e. 40%

21. Krystal spent 32 minutes answering emails, 25 minutes on a phone call, and 45 minutes in a meeting this morning at work. Approximately what percentage of the total time did she spend on the phone call?

a. 32%
b. 36%
c. 44%
d. 25%
e. 31%

22. At the drugstore today, a pack of tissues containing three boxes of tissues was \$6.25, and a pack of paper towels containing four rolls of paper towels was \$5.75. You ended up purchasing 12 boxes of tissues and 16 rolls of paper towels. How much was your total?

a. \$48
b. \$41.75
c. \$28
d. \$42.25
e. \$54

23. A total of \$240 was spent on apples and oranges. Each apple cost \$2, each orange cost \$4, and an equal number of each type of fruit was purchased. How many apples were purchased?

a. 20
b. 30
c. 40
d. 50
e. 60

24. What is 35% of 200?

a. 25
b. 35
c. 571
d. 70
e. 140

25. What is the perimeter of a rectangular room that is 35 feet long and 88 feet wide?

a. 3,080 feet
b. 158 feet
c. 246 feet
d. 1,540 square feet
e. 3,080 square feet

Word Knowledge

Select the answer choice that is closest in meaning to the given word.

1. ABERRATION

a. Obtuse
b. Intricate
c. Oddity
d. Conformity
e. Obsolete

2. FORTITUDE

a. Fear
b. Nerve
c. Anger
d. Lucky
e. Grateful

3. OPULENT

a. Bright
b. Meager
c. Heavy
d. Morose
e. Extravagant

4. MUNDANE

a. Dull
b. Creative
c. Dramatic
d. Courageous
e. Solitary

5. BRAZEN

a. Aflame
b. Huge
c. Curious
d. Bold
e. Timid

6. DISDAIN

a. Separate
b. Different
c. Dislike
d. Retrieve
e. Dull

7. PROSPEROUS

a. Destitute
b. Expansive
c. Beautiful
d. Languid
e. Flourishing

8. REVERE

a. Condemn
b. Respect
c. Condone
d. Recalcitrant
e. Repudiate

9. CAPITULATE

a. Conquer
b. Elevate
c. Rename
d. Surrender
e. Sink

10. ARROGANT

a. Pompous
b. Considerate
c. Affluent
d. Brave
e. Meek

11. MITIGATE

a. Aggravate
b. Console
c. Alleviate
d. Adjudicate
e. Mediate

12. PETULANT

a. Floral
b. Pleasant
c. Patient
d. Diligent
e. Irritable

13. FEASIBLE

a. Equitable
b. Attainable
c. Immeasurable
d. Irreconcilable
e. Impossible

14. BOLSTER

a. Strengthen
b. Obstruct
c. Neglect
d. Sanitize
e. Frighten

15. AMBIGUOUS

a. Underwater
b. Interchangeable
c. Determined
d. Equivocal
e. Explicit

16. BENEVOLENT

a. Merciless
b. Compassionate
c. Philanthropic
d. Malevolent
e. Capricious

17. TENTATIVE

a. Bold
b. Conclusive
c. Influential
d. Cautious
e. Commensurate

18. PERISH

a. Thrive
b. External
c. Decline
d. Berate
e. Cease

19. ERRATIC

a. Unpredictable
b. Abolish
c. Stable
d. Construct
e. Incorrect

20. CANDOR

a. Deception
b. Honesty
c. Quizzical
d. Humorous
e. Devious

21. OUST

a. Surround
b. Fight
c. Remove
d. Freeze
e. Shine

22. SQUALID

a. Filthy
b. Large
c. Daring
d. Sterile
e. Gaunt

23. AVID

a. Airborne
b. Dry
c. Enthusiastic
d. Thick
e. Weak

24. UNADORNED

a. Free
b. Embellished
c. Poor
d. Plain
e. Crowded

25. INCITE

a. Bring in
b. Offer advice
c. Soothe
d. Urge
e. Instigate

Mathematics Knowledge

1. What are the factors of $16x^2 - 64$?

a. $(4x + 4), (4x + 4)$
b. $(4x - 4), (4x + 8)$
c. $(4x + 8), (4x - 8)$
d. $(8x + 8), (2x - 8)$
e. $(2x + 4), (8x + 16)$

2. Evaluate the following expression: $\frac{1}{16}\sqrt{64}$.

a. 1
b. 2
c. $\frac{1}{4}$
d. 4
e. $\frac{1}{2}$

3. Simplify the following: $\frac{41}{80} + \frac{5}{20} + \frac{7}{40}$.

a. $\frac{53}{80}$
b. $\frac{53}{140}$
c. $\frac{75}{80}$
d. $\frac{15}{16}$
e. $\frac{14}{15}$

4. If $x + y = 9$ and $x + 2y = 13$, what is the simultaneous solution?

a. $x = 4, y = 5$
b. $x = 8, y = 1$
c. $x = -4, y = -5$
d. $x = 5, y = 4$
e. $x = -1, y = -9$

5. Which statement is true?

a. A triangle can have three obtuse angles.
b. A triangle can have three acute angles.
c. A triangle can have three right angles.
d. A triangle can have four acute angles.
e. A triangle can have a 200-degree angle.

6. What is $\frac{1}{9}$ is equal to?

a. 0.99
b. 0.11
c. 0.12
d. 0.19
e. 0.09

7. On a map, 1 centimeter represents 100 miles. The distance between two airports is $7\frac{1}{2}$ centimeters. How many miles separate the airports?

a. 700
b. 650
c. 750
d. 75
e. 550

8. Calculate the following: $(5 - (3 - 5(6 + 2)) - 1) + 9$.

a. 50
b. 49
c. 53
d. 41
e. 32

9. What is $1.75 + 1.75 + 2.25 - 2.25 + 5.5$ equal to?

a. 8
b. 9.5
c. 13.5
d. 3.5
e. 9

10. Solve the following equation for x:

$$72 \div 8 = x - 17$$

a. 8
b. 17
c. 26
d. 9
e. 27

11. Solve the following equation for x:

$$7x - 9 = 47$$

a. 7
b. 8
c. 9
d. 6
e. 5

12. Simplify $4 + 2 \times 9$.

a. 54
b. 44
c. 22
d. 15
e. 36

13. Which of the following is an equivalent expression to $(14 \times 5) + (4 \times 5)$?

a. (10×5)
b. (56×5)
c. (5×5)
d. (18×5)
e. (12×5)

14. If Kirsten spends $320 a month on her total grocery bill, and $150 on produce, what percentage of her monthly grocery bill is spent on produce?

a. 45%
b. 27%
c. 31%
d. 53%
e. 47%

15. Simplify the following and write the answer as a mixed number: $\frac{7}{8} + \frac{2}{3}$.

a. $1\frac{11}{24}$
b. $\frac{35}{24}$
c. $\frac{37}{24}$
d. $1\frac{13}{24}$
e. $1\frac{3}{4}$

16. Simplify $10 \times 5 - 3$.

a. 35
b. 53
c. 20
d. 23
e. 47

17. Which of the following is a solution for x?

$$41 - 14 = 3x^2$$

a. 3
b. 1
c. 18
d. 9
e. 12

18. Three angles have measures of 88 degrees, 75 degrees, and 45 degrees. By how many (total) degrees would the angles have to be adjusted in order to create a triangle from these three angles?

a. 45 degrees
b. 28 degrees
c. 38 degrees
d. 24 degrees
e. 12 degrees

19. Kendall purchased a scarf for \$25 and had to pay 12% sales tax. What was her total bill when she checked out?

a. \$26
b. \$27
c. \$28
d. \$37
e. \$25

20. Solve the following for x:

$$5x - 9 \leq 4x - 2$$

a. $x \leq 2$
b. $x \geq 7$
c. $x < 11$
d. $x \leq 7$
e. $x \leq 2$

21. Simplify the following and write the answer as a mixed number:

$$\frac{17}{3} - \frac{1}{5}$$

a. $\frac{82}{15}$
b. $5\frac{7}{15}$
c. $1\frac{7}{15}$
d. $\frac{98}{15}$
e. $\frac{16}{5}$

22. Simplify the following expression:

$$4x^2 - 5x + x^2 - 9x + x^3$$

a. $4x^2 - 14x + x^3$
b. $5x^2 - 14x + x^3$
c. $5x^2 + 14x + x^3$
d. $6x^2 - 14x$
e. $3x^2 - 14x + x^3$

23. What does $|-11| \times \frac{1}{11}$ equal?

a. 11
b. −1
c. 121
d. 1
e. $\frac{1}{11}$

24. Solve the following for x:

$$\frac{x}{63} = \frac{1}{7}$$

a. 5
b. 6
c. 7
d. 8
e. 9

25. If $2x + 2y = 8$ and $-3x + y = 12$, what is the simultaneous solution?

a. $x = -2, y = 5$
b. $x = 6, y = -2$
c. $x = 2, y = 6$
d. $x = -2, y = 6$
e. $x = 1, y = -9$

Reading Comprehension

Questions 1–5 are about the following passage:

Circumambulate the city of a dreamy Sabbath afternoon. Go from Corlears Hook to Coenties Slip, and from thence, by Whitehall, northward. What do you see?—Posted like silent sentinels all around the town, stand thousands upon thousands of mortal men fixed in ocean reveries. Some leaning against the spiles; some seated upon the pier-heads; some looking over the bulwarks of ships from China; some high aloft in the rigging, as if striving to get a still better seaward peep. But these are all landsmen; of week days pent up in lath and plaster—tied to counters, nailed to benches, clinched to desks. How then is this? Are the green fields gone? What do they here?

But look! here come more crowds, pacing straight for the water, and seemingly bound for a dive. Strange! Nothing will content them but the extremest limit of the land; loitering under the shady lee of yonder warehouses will not suffice. No. They must get just as nigh the water as they possibly can without falling in. And there they stand—miles of them—leagues. Inlanders all, they come from lanes and alleys, streets and avenues—north, east, south, and west. Yet here they all unite. Tell me, does the magnetic virtue of the needles of the compasses of all those ships attract them thither?

Once more. Say you are in the country; in some high land of lakes. Take almost any path you please, and ten to one it carries you down in a dale, and leaves you there by a pool in the stream. There is magic in it. Let the most absent-minded of men be plunged in his deepest reveries—stand that man on his legs, set his feet a-going, and he will infallibly lead you to water, if water there be in all that region. Should you ever be athirst in the great American desert, try this experiment, if your caravan happen to be supplied with a metaphysical professor. Yes, as every one knows, meditation and water are wedded for ever.

But here is an artist. He desires to paint you the dreamiest, shadiest, quietest, most enchanting bit of romantic landscape in all the valley of the Saco. What is the chief element he employs? There stand his trees, each with a hollow trunk, as if a hermit and a crucifix were within; and here sleeps his meadow, and there sleep his cattle; and up from yonder cottage goes a sleepy smoke. Deep into distant woodlands winds a mazy way, reaching to overlapping spurs of mountains bathed in their hill-side blue. But though the picture lies thus tranced, and though this pine-tree shakes down its sighs like leaves upon this shepherd's head, yet all were vain, unless the shepherd's eye were fixed upon the magic stream before him. Go visit the Prairies in June, when for scores on scores of miles you wade knee-deep among Tiger-lilies—what is the one charm wanting?—Water—there is not a drop of water there! Were Niagara but a cataract of sand, would you travel your thousand miles to see it?

Excerpt from Moby Dick by Herman Melville

1. What is the purpose of this passage?

a. To describe the landscape and setting
b. To reveal information about the townspeople
c. To put the reader in the narrator's shoes
d. To draw a contrast between the countryside and the city
e. To establish the pull that draws men to water

2. What is the meaning of the first word in the passage, *circumambulate*?

a. To fly around
b. To walk around
c. To look for work
d. To look around
e. To meet people

3. Based on the passage, what does the narrator think of landsmen?

a. The narrator would like to recruit them to the sea.
b. The narrator would like to be captured by an artist like them.
c. The narrator is jealous of their access to the woods.
d. The narrator sees them as chained to the structures of the city.
e. The narrator believes they are absent-minded and naïve.

4. Which statement would the narrator most agree with?

a. All people would venture to the sea if able.
b. The sea is the only important body of water.
c. Some people are satisfied as landsmen.
d. Prairies are enjoyable without water.
e. The only thing better than the sea is the city.

5. In the final paragraph, what is the purpose of describing all the elements of the scene as "sleepy?"

a. It reflects the autumnal season.
b. The narrator believes nothing comes alive until water is introduced.
c. The narrator is drawing a contrast between the fields of tiger lilies and Niagara Falls.
d. The narrator is drawing a contrast to the bustle of the city.
e. It is only significant because he is attempting to draw something "dreamy."

Questions 6–10 are based on the following passage:

Several kinds of assessments are conducted in child welfare, such as assessments of safety, risk and development. All serve distinct purposes and may be used at one or more points in the casework process, but they are not all comprehensive. For the purposes of these guidelines, "comprehensive" means that the assessment incorporates information Comprehensive Family Assessment Guidelines collected through other assessments and addresses the broader needs of the child and family that are affecting a child's safety, permanency, and well-being—the "big picture"—not just a set of symptoms.

The focus of a comprehensive family assessment is not only the presenting issues at a specific time, but also the underlying causal factors for behaviors and conditions affecting children. A comprehensive family assessment also includes evaluation of contributing factors such as family history, domestic violence, substance abuse, mental health, chronic health problems, and poverty. In addition, the family's strengths and protective factors are assessed to identify resources that can support the family's ability to meet its needs and better protect the children.

Different types of assessments are used in child welfare: assessments of safety, risk assessments, and special assessments of particular needs such as developmental assessments. A comprehensive family assessment incorporates information collected through other assessments— particularly safety and risk assessments.

Those conducting comprehensive family assessment need to consider the family's history and the passage of time—what led to the current problems as well as the likely impact of both the maltreatment and the response on the child and family. Comprehensive means moving beyond the "here and now."

The purpose of a comprehensive family assessment is to develop a service plan or a strategy for intervention that addresses the major factors affecting a child's well-being, safety, and permanency over time. This plan should aim at helping the family get on the right track for improved functioning.

In short, a comprehensive family assessment involves recognizing patterns of parental behavior over time in the broad context of needs and strengths, rather than focusing only on the incident that brought the family to the attention of the child welfare agency.

Gathering valid and useful information is critical for appropriate and adequate intervention with children, youth, and families who enter the child welfare system. If comprehensive family assessment is not undertaken as part of developing the service plan, we often miss the opportunity to develop interventions that contribute to lasting change. Moreover, comprehensive assessment helps us to prioritize what can change through interventions. ASFA (Adoption and Safe Families Act) timelines for intervention make the comprehensive assessment critical as the foundation for developing an effective plan with the family. An early and well-conducted comprehensive assessment increases the likelihood of matching services to the real needs and addressing the key issues within the limited timeframes prescribed by the law.

Most jurisdictions use safety and risks assessments to gather information to guide and structure initial decision-making, predict future harm, and develop service plans. It is not clear, however, how caseworkers gain a full understanding of family strengths, needs, and resources with just these assessments or how this information is incorporated into ongoing service planning and decision-making.

Excerpt from "Comprehensive Family Assessment Guidelines for Child Welfare" prepared by Patricia Schene

6. According to the passage, a comprehensive assessment includes:

a. Safety, risk, development assessments
b. Assessments and analysis of the bigger picture
c. Identifying all symptoms
d. A full welfare assessment
e. Evaluating causal factors

7. Based on the passage, what appears to be a shortcoming of these assessments?

a. Consideration of future actions
b. Assessment of contributing factors
c. Understanding familial strengths
d. Impact of poverty on welfare
e. Implications of foster care

8. What is one of the biggest factors in assessing the big picture?

a. Mental health
b. Physical health
c. Poverty
d. Patterns over time
e. Substance abuse

9. What is the purpose of these comprehensive plans?

a. To prepare for termination of parental rights
b. To develop a strategy for intervention
c. To prepare a child for foster care
d. To identify potential threats to a child
e. To incarcerate parents for neglect

10. What appears to be the trigger for these assessments?

a. Self-reported need
b. Parental drug addiction and substance abuse
c. Childhood poverty
d. Domestic violence arrests
e. Children entering the welfare system

Questions 11–15 are based on the following passage:

Drought is a lack of water. This simple wording implies potentially complex stories. The most important implication is that drought is characteristic of time, not of place. A place can be dry or wet, but droughts occur in given locations over time. For example, the Sonoran Desert may have a lack of water for many purposes, but conceptually it has just the right amount of water for the Sonoran Desert, and it occasionally experiences droughts. Wet places, like the coastal rain forests in Washington State, also experience droughts when there is an unusually dry summer. Consistently dry seasons would not merit the designation of "drought" in and of themselves; however, variations in how dry or long the dry season is from year to year are relevant. In places like the Western United States, where there is a coincidence of the dry season with the growing season every year, it does not make sense to frame summer as a "drought" so much as to note the seasonal aridity of the location (Seneviratne and others 2012, Wilhite and Buchanan-Smith 2005).

Although drought is generally defined from a climatic perspective (precipitation levels that are much lower than the annual average), short-term moisture fluctuations also provide important ecological context. A wet period leading to a vegetation flush, followed by a long dry spell, for instance, may not constitute a "drought" relative to long-term averages, but the inability to meet the temporarily increased water demand would nonetheless represent a meaningful drought. From the perspective of a plant, it may look like a temporary enhancement of seasonal aridity contrasts. An example of this is seen in fire risks in rangeland ecosystems where wet springs can produce an overabundance of fine fuels from invasive annual grasses (Littell and others 2009, Swetnam and Betancourt 1998, Westerling and others 2003). Similarly, such fluctuations have been tied to forest mortality, with timing having an important influence on outcomes (Anderegg and others 2013).

This descriptive definition also speaks to a purpose for water. Lack of water is most relevant when water requirements for sustaining terrestrial and aquatic ecosystems or providing for human uses cannot be met. In natural ecosystems, those requirements broadly relate to climatological expectations (in a statistical sense) for water supply. Similarly, in rational agricultural management, climatological expectations should still provide a basic norm for distinguishing drought conditions, although sometimes drought is claimed when slightly dry conditions endanger marginally suited crops. Generally, drought is perceived as a concern during the growing season or warm season, as these are when there is a demand for water. However, droughts can have substantial ecological consequence related to lack of snow cover, particularly for wildlife (McKelvey and others 2011) or plants that are protected from cold extremes by a layer of snow.

Excerpt from Effects of Drought on Forests and Rangelands in the United States: A Comprehensive Science Synthesis edited by James M. Vose, J.S. Clark, C.H. Luce, and T. Patel-Weynand.

11. Which statement best summarizes this passage?

a. Droughts happen mostly in arid climates.
b. Droughts are defined by their impact.
c. Drought is an issue of prolonged water shortage.
d. Droughts are a serious problem throughout the world.
e. The worst droughts occur during summer.

12. Where do droughts occur, according to the passage?

a. In wetlands that need a lot of water
b. In deserts and dry areas
c. Predominantly inland
d. In any location
e. In the arctic

13. What is caused by wet periods that are followed by flourishing vegetation?

a. Potential fuel in case of subsequent drought
b. Decrease in chance of drought
c. Increase in water demand that leads to drought
d. Nothing but normal fluctuations
e. Wetlands that replenish arid landscapes

14. What is water's primary purpose, according to the passage?

a. To sustain crops and vegetation
b. To facilitate climatological cycles
c. To replenish aquatic systems
d. To complete the water cycle
e. To provide for humans and ecosystems

15. Dry seasons alone do not meet the definition of drought. What does drought depend on?

a. Whether the dry season coincides with a growing season
b. How long the dry season persists
c. Which meteorological season the dry season occurs in
d. Whether the dry season creates problems for the ecosystem
e. Whether wetlands can be replenished

Questions 16–20 are based on the following passage:

A rover trundles over rocky terrain, its four metal wheels clattering along until they encounter a seemingly insurmountable hazard: a steep slope. Down below is a potential trove of science targets. With a typical rover, the operators would need to find another target, but this is DuAxel, a robot built for situations exactly like this.

The rover is actually made of a pair of two-wheeled rovers, each called Axel. To divide and conquer, the rover stops, lowers its chassis and anchors it to the ground before essentially splitting in two. With the rear half of DuAxel (short for "dual-Axel") firmly in place, the forward half undocks and rolls away on a single axle. All that connects the two halves now is a tether that unspools as the lead axle approaches the hazard and rappels down the slope, using instruments stowed in its wheel hub to study a scientifically attractive location that would normally be out of reach.

This scenario played out last fall during a field test in the Mojave Desert, when a small team of engineers from NASA's Jet Propulsion Laboratory in Southern California put the modular rover through a series of challenges to test the versatility of its design.

"DuAxel performed extremely well in the field, successfully demonstrating its ability to approach a challenging terrain, anchor, and then undock its tethered Axel rover," said Issa Nesnas, a robotics technologist at JPL. "Axel then autonomously maneuvered down steep and rocky slopes, deploying its instruments without the necessity of a robotic arm."

The idea behind creating two single-axle rovers that can combine into one with a central payload is to maximize versatility: The four-wheeled configuration lends itself to driving great distances across rugged landscapes; the two-wheeled version offers a nimbleness that larger rovers cannot.

"DuAxel opens up access to more extreme terrain on planetary bodies such as the Moon, Mars, Mercury, and possibly some icy worlds, like Jupiter's moon Europa," added Nesnas.

The flexibility was built with crater walls, pits, scarps, vents, and other extreme terrain on these diverse worlds in mind. That's because on Earth, some of the best locations to study geology can be found in rocky outcrops and on cliff faces, where many layers of the past are neatly exposed. They're hard enough to reach here, let alone on other celestial bodies.

The rover's mobility and ability to access extreme locations is an enticing combination to Laura Kerber, a planetary geologist at JPL. "This is why I find the Axel rover to be quite delightful," she said. "Instead of always trying to safeguard itself against dangers such as falling or flipping over, it is designed to withstand them."

The radical concept of two robotic vehicles functioning as one has roots in the late 1990s, when NASA began exploring ideas for modular, reconfigurable, self-repairing rovers. This inspired Nesnas and his team at JPL to develop the robust, flexible two-wheeled robot that would come to be known as Axel.

They envisioned a modular system: Two Axels could dock to either side of a payload, for example, or three Axels could dock to two payloads, and so on, creating a "train" of Axels capable of transporting many payloads. This concept also fulfilled the "self-repairing" requirement of NASA's challenge: Should one Axel fail, another could take its place.

"This Transforming Rover Can Explore the Toughest Terrain." NASA article, edited by Tony Greicius.

16. What is the primary principle behind the design of the DuAxel rover?

a. To increase payload capacity
b. To increase durability
c. To increase speed
d. To increase versatility
e. To create power redundancy

17. According to the passage, what type of previously inaccessible place does the design enable exploration of?

a. Large areas of land mass
b. Deep craters and crevasses
c. Important geological features
d. Subterranean spaces
e. The Mojave Desert

18. Which type of terrain does the passage suggest has not been tested yet?

a. Mountains and craters
b. Ice and snow
c. Dry and rocky
d. Sandy and dusty
e. Wet and muddy

19. Based on the passage, why was the rover tested in the Mojave Desert?

a. It is near the Jet Propulsion Laboratory.
b. It features geological layers.
c. They need to know if it can handle heat exposure.
d. It is the home of all tests for Mars exploration.
e. The terrain best replicates the environments where it would be used.

20. Per the passage, which statement about DuAxel is correct?

a. DuAxel will be modular and scalable.
b. DuAxel will be retired after this mission.
c. DuAxel will be used on Jupiter's moons.
d. DuAxel will be equipped with robotic arms.
e. DuAxel will be used for underwater exploration.

Questions 21–25 are based on the following passage:

There's no greater challenge facing our nation and our planet than the climate crisis—and the writing on the wall is that in order to avoid its worst effects, we need to do everything we can to achieve President Biden's goal of net-zero carbon emissions by 2050.

Currently, nearly 40% of all carbon dioxide pollution comes from power plants burning fossil fuels to create the energy we use every day. That means we need to revolutionize how we generate and use electricity, by making renewable energy sources like wind and solar more abundant, more affordable, and more accessible to everyone.

That's why last month the Department of Energy (DOE) announced two bold goals: to deploy 30 gigawatts of offshore wind within the decade, and cut the current cost of solar energy by 60% by 2030. These announcements are a big deal for combating the climate crisis, recovering from the economic slowdown caused by the pandemic, and addressing energy justice.

These visionary upgrades for the wind and solar sector will create millions of good-paying union jobs for American workers—maybe even you—building and scaling the technologies that will power American homes, support community development, and cut carbon dioxide emissions.

In partnership with the Departments of Interior, Commerce, and Transportation, DOE's new offshore wind goal would generate enough clean electricity to power over 10 million homes, and keep 78 million metric tons of carbon dioxide out of the atmosphere. It would also create tens of thousands of good-paying jobs like staffing up wind turbine manufacturing plants, to building and piloting new ships to install turbines, to constructing and maintaining ports.

While we work on scaling up new offshore wind projects and making them cheaper, DOE is also funding research efforts like the Northeast Sea Grant program, which will study the impacts of ocean-based renewable energy—such as offshore wind, wave, current, and tidal energy—on the fishing industry and Northeastern coastal communities.

Meanwhile, DOE's new solar cost goal is a key step towards making solar—which is already one of the most affordable forms of renewable energy—even cheaper, and therefore even easier for Americans to take advantage of. That starts by funding projects that explore new and advanced solar technologies, so we can speed up their deployment.

DOE is also committed to doing its part to ensure that more Americans have access to these rewarding careers and research opportunities, which is why we're requiring applicants to also submit plans to increase the participation of underrepresented groups on their teams.

"How We're Moving to Net-Zero by 2050" by Annemarie Horowitz.

21. Based on the passage, which action would have the biggest impact on climate change?

a. Invest in green vehicles.
b. Reduce greenhouse gases.
c. Fund scientific research.
d. Create jobs in green industries.
e. Reduce reliance on fossil fuels for electricity.

22. Per the passage, what is one primary goal of research into off-shore wind projects?

a. To study their impact on power consumption
b. To learn about job creation
c. To make them cheaper
d. To catch up to the solar industry
e. To study the impact on shipping

23. Which statement best summarizes the passage?

a. Solar energy is one of our best solutions to power production.
b. The investment in wind energy means it will surpass solar in a few years.
c. A green economy will be robust across multiple sectors.
d. Combating the climate crisis will take a significant shift in our power production.
e. The Department of Energy will play a key role in our climate solutions.

24. According to the passage, what will happen within the next ten years?

a. We will have greater access to renewable energy.
b. We will increase solar energy and cut costs of wind energy.
c. We will invest in tidal energy collection.
d. We will diversify our renewable energy production.
e. We will increase wind energy and cut solar costs.

25. In the passage, the sixth paragraph includes the phrase "scaling up." Based on context, what does that phrase mean?

a. Research in depth.
b. Increase at a reasonable rate.
c. Grow in size or stature.
d. Provide financing or funding.
e. Make extensive plans.

Situational Judgment

SITUATION 1:

You are approached by a senior officer who informs you that she has received transfer requests from a significant number of subordinates you directly oversee and believes this reflects poorly on your management style. However, none of the requests indicate any negligence or malpractice on your account.

Possible actions:

a. Investigate the matter yourself by talking with each of your subordinates personally.
b. Ask the senior officer for resources to set up an anonymous messaging system to allow the subordinates to speak as freely as possible.
c. Contrive a scenario in which you claim the transfers were your idea because you thought that would be the most beneficial for your subordinates.
d. Discuss the transfers with fellow officers to see if they are experiencing similar situations.
e. Excuse yourself from the discussion to brainstorm possible explanations.

1. Select the MOST EFFECTIVE action in response to the situation.

2. Select the LEAST EFFECTIVE action in response to the situation.

SITUATION 2:

A subordinate in your unit has informed you that he is being considered for a promotion that will make him equal in rank with you. Up to this point, he has been a proficient and diligent worker with no behavioral problems, and you expect he will receive the advancement. Since this announcement, you have noticed that he has been slacking in his efforts and more vocal about his disagreements with your practices.

Possible actions:

a. Send an email to the unit, reminding everyone that they are obligated to perform their duties as assigned regardless of any possible promotions they may receive.
b. Go to fellow officers to ask for advice about handling the situation.
c. Let the behavior slide because he is likely to become equal in rank with you in the near future.
d. Make senior officers aware of the behavior being presented so that they can make the most informed decision about whether to award the promotion to your subordinate.
e. Give him the most difficult or tedious assignments to help him learn some humility while you still outrank him.

3. Select the MOST EFFECTIVE action in response to the situation.

4. Select the LEAST EFFECTIVE action in response to the situation.

SITUATION 3:

You have begun to notice that your superior officer has been having episodes of memory loss and lapses in judgment. She dismisses your concerns and claims to have everything under control, but you strongly suspect that this behavior is a medical issue.

Possible actions:

a. Ask fellow officers if they agree with you about the superior officer.
b. Write a list of concrete examples of the superior officer's lapses and forgetfulness to present to the base commander.
c. Ask the superior officer for more responsibility to try and decrease her current workload.
d. Ignore the behavior because you are not qualified to make those kinds of medical determinations.
e. Respectfully ask to be reassigned until she has received a medical evaluation.

5. Select the MOST EFFECTIVE action in response to the situation.

6. Select the LEAST EFFECTIVE action in response to the situation.

SITUATION 4:

During a training exercise, you overhear two fellow officers who are conversing privately make disparaging remarks of a racial nature about another officer.

Possible actions:

a. Immediately confront the officers and demand that they apologize to the disparaged officer.
b. Ignore the comments because they were not directed at you.
c. Meet with the two officers as soon as the training exercise is over and remind them that comments like those you overheard have no place in the military.
d. Later email each of the officers who made the comments and let them know you will report them if they do not report their behavior themselves.
e. Speak with the officer who was disparaged and let him know what you heard, making sure you express that you are disgusted by the other officers' behavior.

7. Select the MOST EFFECTIVE action in response to the situation.

8. Select the LEAST EFFECTIVE action in response to the situation.

Situation 5:

While working on a report, you recognize that you will require the assistance of a senior officer in order to finish. The senior officer responds that she is very busy and emails you a large file that contains all of the information that you need to finish the report. You are nearly done with the report when you realize that some of the material you've reviewed is classified beyond your security clearance.

Possible actions:

a. Contact the senior officer to let her know what you have seen and ask how she wishes to proceed.
b. Do not say anything to anyone because you did not know the information was classified at the time.
c. Delete the report you were working on and report the incident to the security officer.
d. Ask an officer you trust if he has experience with this kind of situation and what he might do in your place.
e. Report the senior officer for her negligence in sending you classified material.

9. Select the MOST EFFECTIVE action in response to the situation.

10. Select the LEAST EFFECTIVE action in response to the situation.

Situation 6:

While working in a field office, you notice that one of the older male officers is physically affectionate with the female staff members. By listening to discussions among the staff members, you learn that none of them feel he has crossed a line into impropriety, but they give a general sense of being uncomfortable with his overfamiliarity with them.

Possible actions:

a. Speak with the senior officer privately to let him know how the female staff members feel about his behavior.
b. Email the senior officer the policy on physical contact in the workspace.
c. Email the senior officer about the feelings the female staff expressed.
d. Trust that the female staff are capable of handling the situation themselves and will report any behavior they deem unacceptable.
e. Ask some of the female staff members to come with you to discuss their feelings about the male officer's behavior in person.

11. Select the MOST EFFECTIVE action in response to the situation.

12. Select the LEAST EFFECTIVE action in response to the situation.

SITUATION 7:

You have been assigned to a task that will involve two other officers from your unit, as well as three from another unit. You have already had two meetings with the five other involved officers, and both have devolved into chaos, with no consensus being reached on how to proceed with the assignment. You will be required to present a plan of action regarding the assignment to your commanding officer immediately after the third meeting next week. All of the officers have raised valid points, but you believe the solutions you've presented are the most sensible.

Possible actions:

a. Ask your commanding officer for an extension on the assignment to try and gain a greater consensus on the plan.
b. Ask each officer to bring a written list of their proposed solutions to be voted on at the next meeting.
c. Work out a solution that favors the officers in your unit, as you will have to deal with them the most.
d. Work out a solution that favors the officers in the other unit so as not to show favoritism.
e. Present only your solutions because you are responsible for the assignment.

13. Select the MOST EFFECTIVE action in response to the situation.

14. Select the LEAST EFFECTIVE action in response to the situation.

SITUATION 8:

A subordinate offers to complete the report from your team's last mission because he believes that he had the greatest view of the overall situation. Since you are currently swamped with other work, you agree on the condition that you will review the report before it is submitted. Upon reading the report, you notice that he has presented the team exceptionally well, even beyond your own judgment of their proficiency. However, he has portrayed you as aloof and largely uninvolved.

Possible actions:

a. Meet with the subordinate to understand why he has portrayed you this way before submitting the report.
b. Accept the report as is because the team is portrayed well and that matters more than your personal leadership.
c. Ask the other team members if they agree with the report as it is written.
d. Rewrite the report to reflect better upon yourself without letting your subordinate know about your changes.
e. Accept the report, but ask the airman to make you look better if he ever writes another report for you.

15. Select the MOST EFFECTIVE action in response to the situation.

16. Select the LEAST EFFECTIVE action in response to the situation.

Situation 9:

An officer that you are close with is transferred to a different unit. A few weeks later, she contacts you asking to speak in private. She shares with you that she has evidence that seems to indicate that a senior officer has been altering budget numbers. However, she recognizes the possibility that someone else may be responsible for the discrepancies or there may be another explanation, and she asks for your help on how to proceed.

Possible actions:

a. Since she admits she might be mistaken, urge her not to pursue the investigation further.
b. Ask your commanding officer for time to look into the matter personally.
c. Ask your commanding officer to verify the officer's suspicions.
d. Tell her you can't get involved since it does not directly affect you or your unit.
e. Advise her to consult with the security officer so an investigation can be quietly conducted.

17. Select the MOST EFFECTIVE action in response to the situation.

18. Select the LEAST EFFECTIVE action in response to the situation.

Situation 10:

You observe an airman from another unit improperly utilizing specialized equipment for obviously unsanctioned purposes while in the company of a group of other airmen. Both the airmen and the equipment appear presently to be unharmed.

Possible actions:

a. Reprimand the instigating airman privately and issue pursuant discipline.
b. Step in to immediately issue a verbal warning to the airman and to the group for not stopping the behavior.
c. Decline to get involved because no one is hurt and they are not from your unit.
d. Ask for the airman's name to speak with his commanding officer about the situation later.
e. Put an immediate stop to the improper behavior and inform the airman's commanding officer of the situation.

19. Select the MOST EFFECTIVE action in response to the situation.

20 Select the LEAST EFFECTIVE action in response to the situation.

Situation 11:

Upon arrival to the base in the morning, you are met with the sound of an altercation that has escalated to violence. One airman has accused the other of stealing. This is the second time this airman has been accused of theft, but there was no evidence to prove any wrongdoing in the previous incident. The airman in this instance has no concrete evidence to validate his claims either. Neither airman is in your unit and the accused denies the allegations.

Possible actions:

a. Issue discipline to the accusing airman because he has no evidence to support his claim.
b. Issue discipline to both airmen for engaging in violence and begin the process of initiating a formal investigation into the matter.
c. Separate the airmen and have another airman search through the accused's belongings to determine if the theft took place.
d. Try to avoid a formal investigation by examining the evidence of the alleged crime yourself to determine culpability.
e. Separate the airmen and inform their commanding officer of the situation.

21. Select the MOST EFFECTIVE action in response to the situation.

22. Select the LEAST EFFECTIVE action in response to the situation.

Situation 12:

After years of dedicated service, you find that you have been passed up for a promotion once again. You believe that your record is adequate and that you do not possess any flagrant character flaws.

Possible actions:

a. Contact the officer who was promoted instead of you to ask if she engaged in any under-the-table dealing to receive the promotion.
b. Investigate the promotion process yourself to determine the role that office politics or favoritism played in the promotion decision.
c. Request a meeting with your superior officer to discuss why you have not advanced beyond your current rank.
d. Ask your superior officer for extra responsibility in order to try to improve your record.
e. Request a transfer to a new unit in the hopes you will find better success there.

23. Select the MOST EFFECTIVE action in response to the situation.

24. Select the LEAST EFFECTIVE action in response to the situation.

Situation 13:

A new recruit joins your unit. Within two months, he comes to you with a complaint that he is being treated harshly by the other airmen in the unit and held to unfair standards. You have not personally witnessed any behavior that seems out of line.

Possible actions:

a. Assure the airman that you have received the complaint but cannot take any action until you witness it firsthand.
b. Interview the other members of the team to better understand their side of the situation.
c. Ask the airman to write down specific instances of mistreatment so you can investigate them.
d. Suggest that the airman may be overreacting to the team's attempts to help him grow.
e. Inform your senior officer of the situation.

25. Select the MOST EFFECTIVE action in response to the situation.

26. Select the LEAST EFFECTIVE action in response to the situation.

Situation 14:

A fellow flight commander comes to you asking for help. She says she is drowning in late reports and cannot get ahead of training requirements and other work tasks. You are also barely managing to stay ahead of the work you have been given. She mentions that another flight commander is performing very well and making her look bad in front of her superiors. You have heard a few of the superiors mention her poor performance. She is considering asking the other flight commander to stop working so hard so she will not look as bad by comparison.

Possible actions:

a. Offer to help the poorly performing commander at the risk of falling behind yourself.
b. Encourage the poorly performing commander to ask the other commander to not work as hard, as this will make her performance look better as well as your own.
c. Encourage the poorly performing commander to request a leave of absence to work on her management skills.
d. Ask to meet with both commanders to discuss different management styles and organizational successes to maximize everyone's efficiency.
e. Tell the poorly performing worker to delegate some of her lower priority tasks to her subordinates to help relieve her workload.

27. Select the MOST EFFECTIVE action in response to the situation.

28. Select the LEAST EFFECTIVE action in response to the situation.

SITUATION 15:

A scheduling error mistakenly forces your squadron into a direct time conflict with another squadron for a monthly training. If this training is not completed today, your squadron will not meet their monthly requirements.

Possible actions:

a. Notify your supervisor of the mistake and ask her to resolve the situation.
b. Coordinate with the training officer to see if your squadron can combine with the other group that is scheduled for the same time.
c. Insist that your squadron be given the spot because they need it to meet monthly training requirements.
d. Ask the officer in charge of scheduling to reserve the next available session for your squadron and then report the incident to your supervisor.
e. Request that the training officer speak with your supervisor because the issue was outside of your control.

29. Select the MOST EFFECTIVE action in response to the situation.

30. Select the LEAST EFFECTIVE action in response to the situation.

SITUATION 16:

You wake up in the morning, after experiencing significant sinus congestion since yesterday evening. You had been hoping the congestion would go away overnight, but it has not lessened at all. Your unit is scheduled for a flight exercise in less than 2 hours, and there is already a shortage of aviators available to fill the schedule. You recognize that if you take several hours to be examined by the flight physician, you will leave the operations office in a bind. You also recognize the possibility of severe sinus damage if you fly while congested, but you don't want to let your unit down or cause any issues for the operations office.

Possible actions:

a. Speak to the operations officer, making sure to sneeze and cough loudly in his presence, so he will actually believe your congestion is real and let you go see the doctor.
b. Take medicine for your congestion and then perform the flight, as it's just a stuffy nose.
c. Ask a fellow officer if she can take your spot this morning, and you will pay her back by filling in for her if she ever needs it.
d. Apologize for the inconvenient timing to the scheduler, but go ahead and take yourself off available flight status.
e. Ask your commanding officer what he would do in your situation.

31. Select the MOST EFFECTIVE action in response to the situation.

32. Select the LEAST EFFECTIVE action in response to the situation.

SITUATION 17:

You have been assigned by your commanding officer to lead a survival skills training to prepare airmen before they deploy. He informs you that many senior ranking officers will be observing you and encourages you to perform at your best.

Possible actions:

a. Be as authoritative as possible to impress the officers with your leadership skills.
b. Make sure to be as harsh as possible to the airmen since the course is about surviving in harsh conditions.
c. Ask another officer to lead the training to prove that you do not require the senior officers' approval.
d. Be as thorough and focused on the teaching as you can be because that matters more than impressing your superiors.
e. Frequently confer with the senior officers during the training to make sure you are doing everything correctly.

33. Select the MOST EFFECTIVE action in response to the situation.

34. Select the LEAST EFFECTIVE action in response to the situation.

SITUATION 18:

Your facility has recently issued numerous revisions to longstanding policies and procedures. While trying to manage an equipment delivery, you recognize that some checklist items involving various other personnel have now been added to the procedure. Rather than wait for those personnel to arrive, your commander orders you to forgo the new procedure and receive the equipment the way it had always been done before. As a result of not following these new procedures, a team member ends up seriously injured, and an investigation into the incident is initiated. Your commander orders your squadron not to cooperate with the team who is investigating.

Possible actions:

a. Answer the investigating team's questions without incriminating yourself.
b. Blame your commander as the sole source of wrongdoing to deflect any responsibility from yourself.
c. Inform the investigating team that the injury was just an act of human error because the team member did not listen to the commander's orders.
d. Inform the team that is investigating about the order that was given by the commander in exchange for reduced penalties.
e. Ignore the order from your superior, and answer any and all questions you are asked to the best of your ability.

35. Select the MOST EFFECTIVE action in response to the situation.

36. Select the LEAST EFFECTIVE action in response to the situation.

SITUATION 19:

Two months ago, you joined a new unit. The supervisor of this unit was very welcoming to you, and she made sure to give you as much assistance as you needed in learning your new duties and responsibilities. Annual evaluations arrive, and you prepare your list of awards, trainings, and accomplishments you have acquired as you used to do for your evaluations in your old unit. However, your new supervisor instead asks you to draft a full written evaluation of yourself. She explains that this process is a useful technique for understanding her team better. However, you are fairly certain this is against standing guidelines.

Possible actions:

a. Request a meeting with the base commander to verify your suspicion and voice your concerns.
b. Share your concerns related to Air Force evaluations guidelines with your supervisor to see if she understands them differently.
c. Contact your supervisor from your old unit to discuss your new supervisor's directive.
d. Ask other members of the unit if this is how this supervisor typically conducts evaluations.
e. Write the evaluation as requested regardless of standing guidelines.

37. Select the MOST EFFECTIVE action in response to the situation.

38. Select the LEAST EFFECTIVE action in response to the situation.

SITUATION 20:

A junior officer has come to you expressing frustration that his career is not advancing as quickly as he would like. He works very hard, but he has some particular character flaws that other officers have also noticed and made mention of.

Possible actions:

a. Do not mention any details about his character, and instead, say he will likely achieve his goals if he continues to work hard.
b. Gently explain that his work efforts will have a hard time surpassing his character flaws, and that he should work on addressing them if he wants to advance.
c. Ask your senior officer to overlook the junior officer's character flaws and offer him a promotion.
d. Provide the junior officer with sympathy, but take no action, as his promotion is not directly in your control.
e. Convince the junior officer that he might have better success if he transfers to a different unit.

39. Select the MOST EFFECTIVE action in response to the situation.

40. Select the LEAST EFFECTIVE action in response to the situation.

Situation 21:

You and another junior officer are candidates for a promotion. The two of you have never particularly gotten along, and you frequently hear that he talks poorly about you behind your back. You are interviewed by a senior officer who asks you for your candid opinion on the other officer as a potential candidate.

Possible actions:

a. Dodge the senior officer's question by saying that you don't really know much about him.
b. Do not give any indications about your real feelings about the junior officer, and redirect the conversation toward your own accomplishments instead.
c. Describe in detail your distaste for the junior officer so that the senior officer will more fully understand what he is really like.
d. Intently describe how great of an officer he is, so you will seem extraordinarily humble.
e. Briefly mention your shared history, but do not let it be the major focus of your response.

41. Select the MOST EFFECTIVE action in response to the situation.

42. Select the LEAST EFFECTIVE action in response to the situation.

Situation 22:

Upon arrival for your shift in the control center, the exiting crew informs you that instruments had not been shut down properly and doors were left unlocked when they arrived after the last shift you were in charge of. These represent large breaches of protocol and potential security issues. You remember that you were called away early for an emergency during the last shift and left the shutdown procedure to your colleague.

Possible actions:

a. Apologize for the mishap and take responsibility for the mistake because you were in charge of that shift.
b. Accept the responsibility in front of the exiting crew, but reprimand your colleague the next time you share the same shift.
c. Apologize for the unprofessional break in procedure, and explain the extenuating circumstances behind the lack of professionalism.
d. Call the incident a fluke that will never happen again and move on as if nothing happened.
e. Report your colleague to your commanding officer for breaking protocol after you were pulled away.

43. Select the MOST EFFECTIVE action in response to the situation.

44. Select the LEAST EFFECTIVE action in response to the situation.

SITUATION 23:

While waiting to meet some fellow airmen in a bar near your base, you overhear a man bragging to a group of patrons about being a senior officer stationed there, but you do not recognize him. You hear him relating a story about something that took place on the base recently—nothing that could remotely be construed as confidential—but it doesn't sound like anything that you can recall happening lately.

Possible actions:

a. Join the group and announce that you are also an officer on the base and that you believe the man is lying.
b. Wait for your friends to arrive and then confront the man together.
c. Report the man to the local police for impersonating a military officer.
d. Approach the group and casually begin asking the man questions to try to trap him in a lie.
e. Leave the man alone since it would be unwise to risk a false accusation when there is no danger of a security breach.

45. Select the MOST EFFECTIVE action in response to the situation.

46. Select the LEAST EFFECTIVE action in response to the situation.

SITUATION 24:

In recent months, budget cuts and transfers have left you completely overwhelmed with work. Despite your best efforts, numerous deadlines have been missed or barely reached, and you know your commanding officer has been displeased with your performance. Starting earlier and staying later still does not seem to be enough to get everything done.

Possible actions:

a. Request a leave of absence to try and come up with a new strategy for how to approach the workload.
b. Accept your limitations and ask other officers for advice about completing your workload.
c. Express your frustration with the situation to your commanding officer and demand additional support.
d. Begin delegating as many tasks as possible to your subordinates.
e. Temporarily reduce the quality of your work in order to meet the increased quantity of work assigned.

47. Select the MOST EFFECTIVE action in response to the situation.

48. Select the LEAST EFFECTIVE action in response to the situation.

Situation 25:

A fellow officer approaches you for help concerning a new junior officer who transferred into her command. She reports that the junior officer did extremely well in all of his academic tests, but he seems relatively inept when it comes to actual flight exercises. This is not the first time you have heard about this junior officer's poor performance.

Possible actions:

a. Advise her to try to be more relaxed during the exercises since she might be making the junior officer more nervous.
b. Issue an order to your unit prohibiting them from flying with the junior officer.
c. Volunteer to fly with the junior officer to see if you are able to pinpoint what his problem might be.
d. Request a meeting with the junior officer to let him know about his supervisor's concerns and the consequences of continued deficiency.
e. Recommend that she meet with the junior officer to gauge his commitment to being a flight officer.

49. Select the MOST EFFECTIVE action in response to the situation.

50. Select the LEAST EFFECTIVE action in response to the situation.

Physical Science

1. The rate of a chemical reaction depends on all of the following EXCEPT

a. Temperature
b. Surface area
c. Presence of catalysts
d. Amount of mass lost
e. Quantity of reactants

2. What is the oxidation number of hydrogen in CaH_2?

a. +1
b. −1
c. 0
d. −2
e. +2

3. Which of the following does NOT exist as a diatomic molecule?

a. Boron
b. Fluorine
c. Oxygen
d. Nitrogen
e. Iodine

4. What is the name for the reactant that is entirely consumed by the reaction?

a. Limiting reactant
b. Reducing agent
c. Reaction intermediate
d. Reagent
e. Reaction composite

5. What is the mass (in grams) of 7.35 mol water?

a. 10.7 g
b. 18 g
c. 73.5 g
d. 132 g
e. 180.6 g

6. Which of the following orbitals is the last to fill?

a. 1s
b. 3s
c. 4p
d. 6s
e. 4f

7. Which of the following is NOT one of the five major physical properties of minerals?

a. Chemical composition
b. Hardness
c. Luster
d. Streak
e. Form

8. Which of these minerals would have the lowest score on the Mohs scale?

a. Gypsum
b. Fluorite
c. Talc
d. Diamond
e. Quartz

9. When water changes directly from a solid to a gas, skipping the liquid state, this is called

a. Evapotranspiration
b. Condensation
c. Sublimation
d. Runoff
e. Transpiration

10. Which of the following techniques is NOT a radiometric dating process?

a. Potassium-argon dating
b. Stratigraphic dating
c. Uranium-lead dating
d. Chlorine-36 dating
e. Uranium-thorium dating

11. Which law of classical thermodynamics states that energy can neither be created nor destroyed?

a. Zeroth
b. First
c. Second
d. Third
e. Fourth

12. The formula for calculating kinetic energy is

a. $\frac{1}{2}mv^2$
b. $\frac{1}{2}mv$
c. mgh
d. mgv
e. mv^2

13. What is most likely the pH of a solution containing many hydroxide ions (OH^-) and few hydrogen ions (H^+)?

a. 1
b. 2
c. 6
d. 7
e. 9

14. Which of the following cannot be found on the periodic table?

a. Bromine
b. Magnesium oxide
c. Phosphorous
d. Chlorine
e. Yttrium

15. What law describes the electric force between two charged particles?

a. Ohm's law
b. Coulomb's law
c. The Doppler effect
d. Kirchhoff's current law
e. Charles's law

16. What is the mass (in grams) of 1.0 mol oxygen gas?

a. 12 g
b. 16 g
c. 22 g
d. 28 g
e. 32 g

17. Which kind of radiation has no charge?

a. Beta
b. Alpha
c. Delta
d. Gamma
e. Zeta

18. What is 119 Kelvin in degrees Celsius?

a. 32 °C
b. –154 °C
c. 154 °C
d. –32 °C
e. 0 °C

19. What is the SI unit of energy?

a. Ohm
b. Joule
c. Henry
d. Newton
e. Tesla

20. What is the name of the device that separates gaseous ions by their mass-to-charge ratio?

a. Mass spectrometer
b. Interferometer
c. Magnetometer
d. Gas chromatograph
e. Capacitance meter

Table Reading

For each question, select the number that appears in the table at the given coordinates. Recall that the first number in the ordered pair gives the column number, and the second gives the row number. For instance, the ordered pair $(2, -1)$ refers to the number in column 2, row -1, which is 439 in the table.

Use the table below to answer questions 1-40.

	-12	-11	-10	-9	-8	-7	-6	-5	-4	-3	-2	-1	0	1	2	3	4	5	6	7	8	9	10	11	12
-12	738	220	346	348	699	732	234	302	365	105	173	219	223	582	737	760	541	802	540	654	795	827	512	231	271
-11	506	600	301	458	712	379	824	153	918	324	508	956	335	213	932	189	259	358	602	861	698	734	333	589	389
-10	321	701	213	441	798	957	122	692	381	127	327	666	392	874	979	350	753	997	929	778	836	433	194	407	436
-9	983	850	605	517	712	795	959	704	485	383	234	537	886	165	318	546	318	331	223	486	887	154	105	620	109
-8	220	658	675	222	437	873	414	245	222	434	150	132	365	762	293	602	858	253	606	755	838	867	531	630	714
-7	566	133	429	476	329	885	630	463	255	998	666	858	722	914	423	868	122	747	859	907	394	104	193	426	939
-6	890	822	978	800	917	556	333	728	780	438	764	298	515	171	579	583	239	426	607	507	444	233	313	995	937
-5	462	282	189	598	538	583	766	746	590	992	782	206	127	318	705	390	629	621	467	550	329	735	109	199	980
-4	170	851	136	312	979	167	661	866	398	915	463	329	483	246	117	957	539	644	312	492	658	168	127	501	328
-3	643	686	640	664	686	241	789	338	177	759	880	752	786	755	892	713	771	782	766	520	866	454	792	235	778
-2	544	425	243	260	542	133	605	178	552	149	699	339	716	391	754	471	888	358	165	486	248	142	282	999	344
-1	703	735	631	508	560	723	470	925	255	704	862	465	719	431	439	583	752	873	692	758	807	550	108	716	631
0	547	836	594	149	711	745	175	601	169	161	106	500	715	910	709	715	348	120	162	778	309	585	344	470	460
1	873	962	110	566	657	692	891	222	747	750	280	427	884	696	462	219	646	447	347	973	672	400	677	316	903
2	868	563	699	265	791	129	411	472	962	637	481	317	330	633	414	807	311	141	989	227	641	959	708	788	638
3	364	502	511	673	128	864	869	779	567	490	546	242	170	848	964	716	339	873	405	207	409	932	400	993	508
4	894	592	515	371	698	571	861	657	618	426	468	320	230	676	134	842	579	999	996	106	377	839	535	815	423
5	359	603	985	740	318	461	662	316	832	277	872	457	421	902	117	888	540	237	981	573	163	990	763	653	601
6	683	750	823	295	778	104	572	526	951	526	275	637	689	875	528	791	950	816	208	535	281	438	192	852	561
7	822	430	534	426	736	110	563	529	963	390	697	478	559	412	867	101	119	388	775	675	271	606	531	642	279
8	673	388	207	597	980	777	559	548	190	696	382	964	265	378	581	142	527	993	284	990	571	643	143	458	392
9	866	218	740	592	862	498	427	417	678	354	272	950	356	409	489	521	599	778	237	430	288	125	837	527	396
10	676	934	915	513	581	573	473	360	880	879	488	585	504	461	414	491	552	152	435	301	850	477	911	442	881
11	917	828	837	635	748	618	339	179	377	189	374	583	418	490	547	804	429	814	397	434	719	768	726	956	580
12	512	287	134	245	954	140	276	994	456	591	481	129	104	569	435	976	480	394	935	556	651	584	398	580	839

1. $(\mathbf{7}, \mathbf{3})$
a. 207
b. 409
c. 405
d. 868
e. 520

2. $(\mathbf{-5}, \mathbf{11})$
a. 339
b. 360
c. 179
d. 814
e. 197

3. $(\mathbf{1}, \mathbf{-4})$
a. 246
b. 318
c. 426
d. 755
e. 329

4. $(\mathbf{11}, \mathbf{1})$
a. 470
b. 344
c. 788
d. 316
e. 361

5. $(\mathbf{-3}, \mathbf{11})$
a. 879
b. 198
c. 819
d. 189
e. 324

6. $(\mathbf{4}, \mathbf{-6})$
a. 629
b. 122
c. 780
d. 239
e. 950

7. $(\mathbf{-11}, \mathbf{-8})$
a. 685
b. 586
c. 388
d. 658
e. 712

8. $(\mathbf{-1}, \mathbf{7})$
a. 637
b. 559
c. 478
d. 858
e. 723

9. $(\mathbf{8}, \mathbf{-10})$
a. 863
b. 836
c. 887
d. 798
e. 850

10. $(\mathbf{-8}, \mathbf{6})$
a. 736
b. 778
c. 295
d. 917
e. 787

11. $(\mathbf{6}, \mathbf{1})$
a. 162
b. 347
c. 989
d. 374
e. 437

12. $(\mathbf{-1}, \mathbf{-11})$
a. 735
b. 962
c. 589
d. 956
e. 213

13. $(\mathbf{1}, \mathbf{-10})$
a. 847
b. 213
c. 165
d. 392
e. 874

14. $(\mathbf{12}, \mathbf{6})$
a. 651
b. 516
c. 279
d. 601
e. 561

15. $(\mathbf{10}, \mathbf{9})$
a. 143
b. 837
c. 911
d. 477
e. 513

16. $(\mathbf{-5}, \mathbf{7})$
a. 526
b. 548
c. 463
d. 550
e. 529

17. $(\mathbf{1}, \mathbf{6})$
a. 857
b. 347
c. 875
d. 902
e. 412

18. $(\mathbf{-4}, \mathbf{-8})$
a. 255
b. 222
c. 434
d. 190
e. 979

19. $(\mathbf{2}, \mathbf{11})$
a. 547
b. 414
c. 574
d. 788
e. 932

20. $(\mathbf{-7}, \mathbf{0})$
a. 723
b. 692
c. 754
d. 722
e. 745

21. $(\mathbf{-3}, \mathbf{-11})$
a. 324
b. 189
c. 686
d. 342
e. 105

22. $(-10, -1)$
a. 243
b. 631
c. 613
d. 260
e. 508

23. $(4, -3)$
a. 539
b. 888
c. 782
d. 771
e. 426

24. $(9, -4)$
a. 168
b. 735
c. 678
d. 312
e. 485

25. $(-9, 4)$
a. 673
b. 740
c. 317
d. 312
e. 371

26. $(-4, 7)$
a. 951
b. 190
c. 963
d. 390
e. 255

27. $(9, -9)$
a. 867
b. 517
c. 125
d. 154
e. 433

28. $(3, 6)$
a. 888
b. 719
c. 791
d. 405
e. 528

29. $(-6, 12)$
a. 276
b. 140
c. 994
d. 935
e. 234

30. $(-9, 7)$
a. 736
b. 426
c. 462
d. 476
e. 486

31. $(-2, 2)$
a. 280
b. 546
c. 418
d. 754
e. 481

32. $(9, -12)$
a. 872
b. 348
c. 866
d. 584
e. 827

33. $(5, 0)$
a. 120
b. 873
c. 601
d. 421
e. 447

34. $(10, -9)$
a. 194
b. 150
c. 105
d. 154
e. 513

35. $(-1, -2)$
a. 329
b. 752
c. 339
d. 393
e. 862

36. $(3, -12)$
a. 760
b. 737
c. 706
d. 643
e. 364

37. $(-2, -8)$
a. 234
b. 132
c. 542
d. 150
e. 510

38. $(6, 4)$
a. 996
b. 989
c. 405
d. 999
e. 950

39. $(7, -10)$
a. 957
b. 534
c. 957
d. 778
e. 861

40. $(-12, -10)$
a. 701
b. 321
c. 738
d. 312
e. 346

Instrument Comprehension

1. Which of the answer choices represents the orientation of the plane?

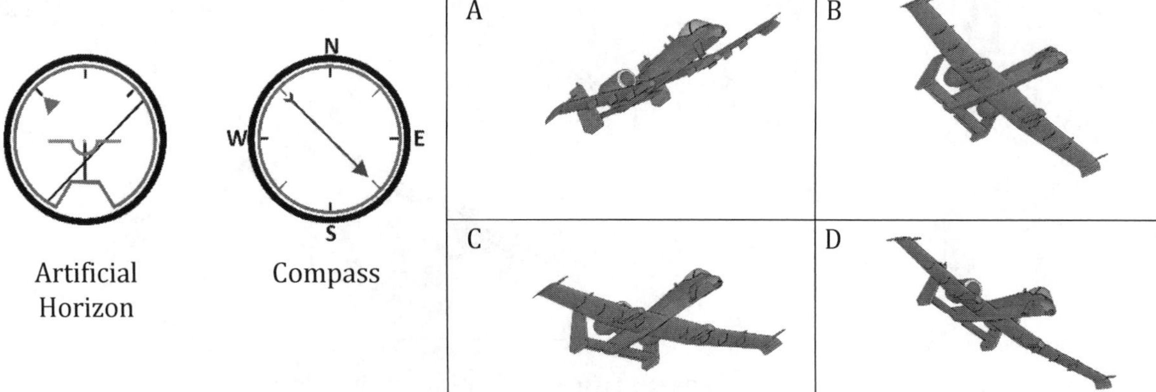

2. Which of the answer choices represents the orientation of the plane?

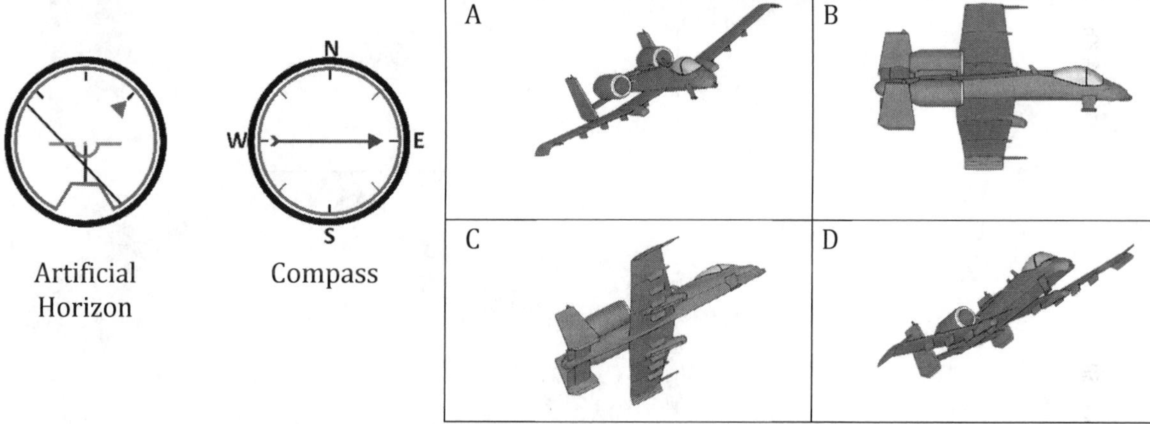

3. Which of the answer choices represents the orientation of the plane?

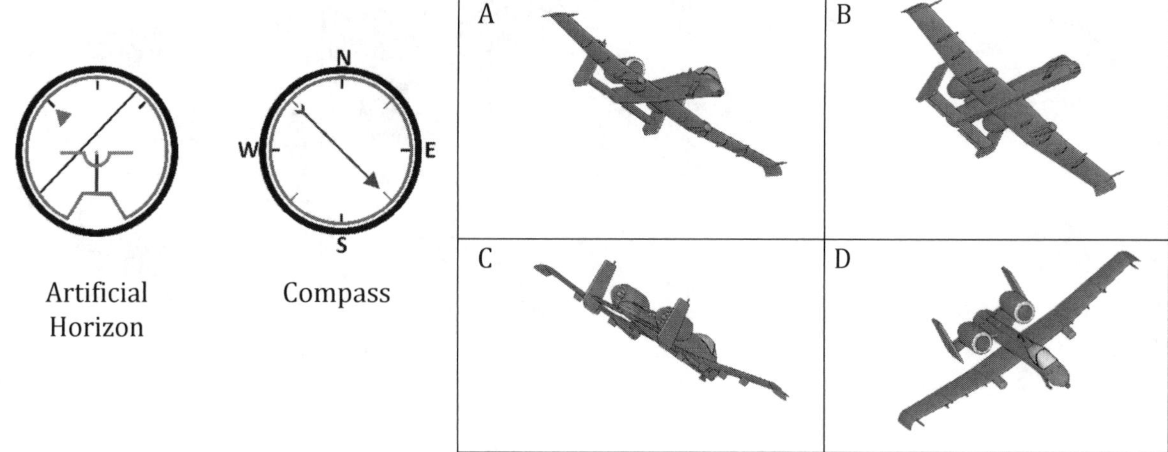

4. **Which of the answer choices represents the orientation of the plane?**

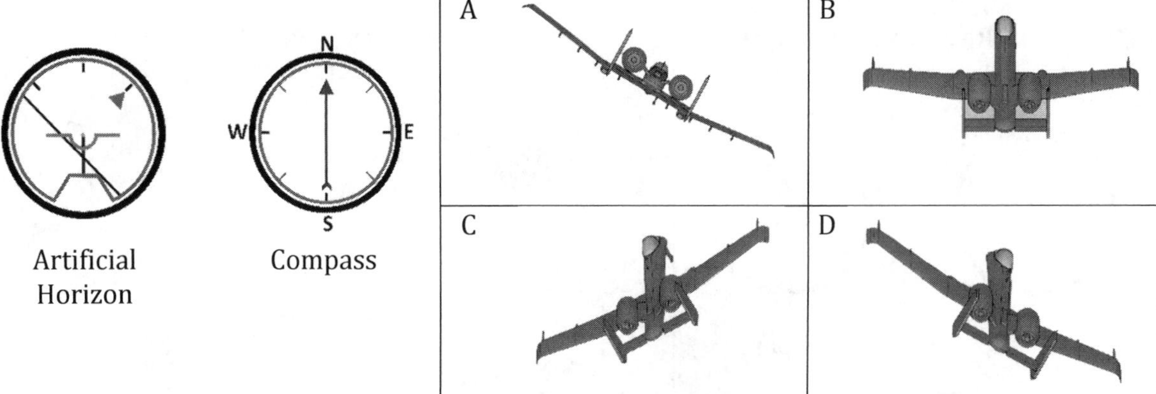

5. **Which of the answer choices represents the orientation of the plane?**

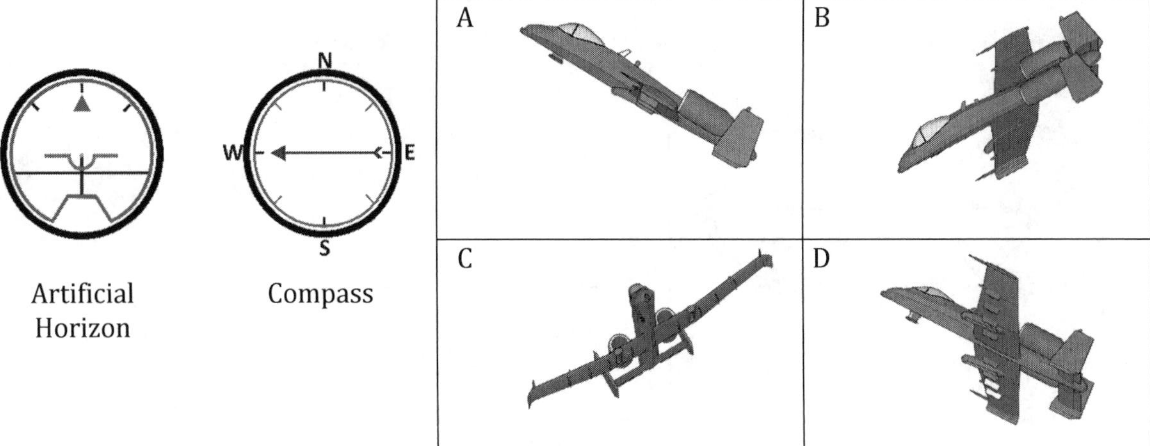

6. **Which of the answer choices represents the orientation of the plane?**

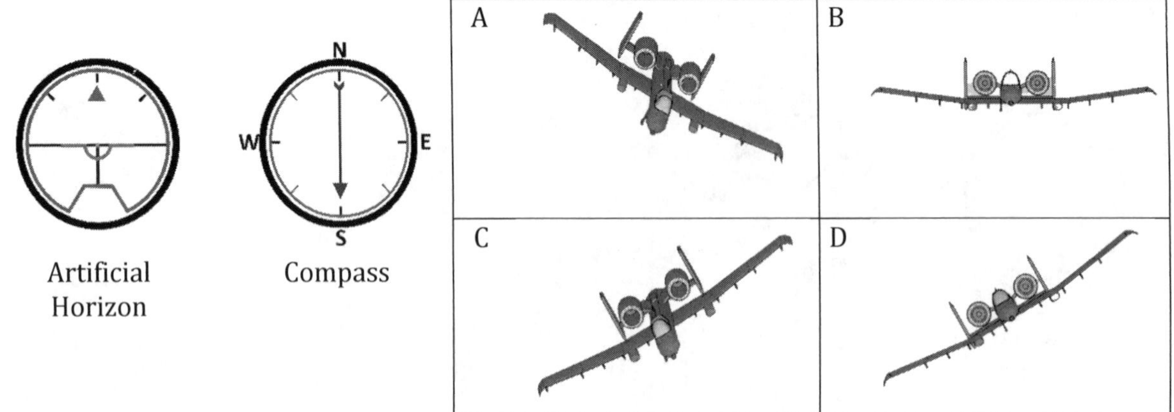

7. Which of the answer choices represents the orientation of the plane?

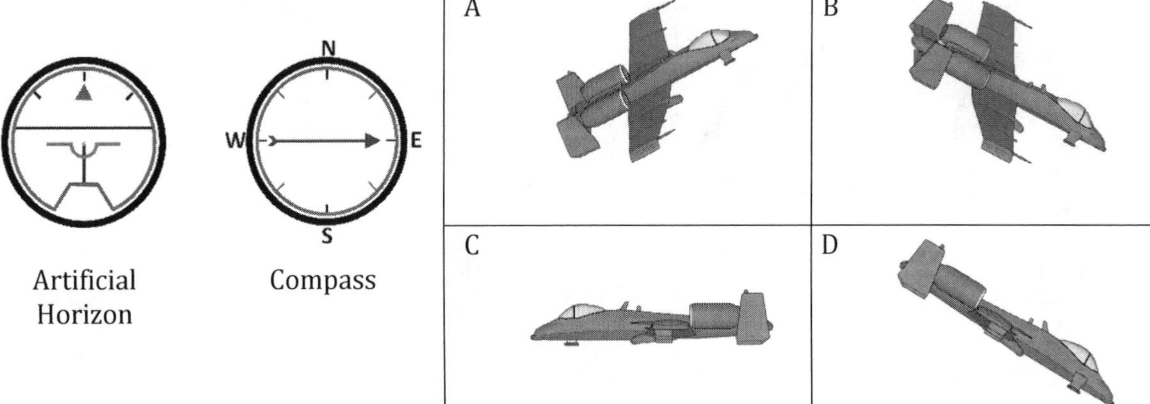

8. Which of the answer choices represents the orientation of the plane?

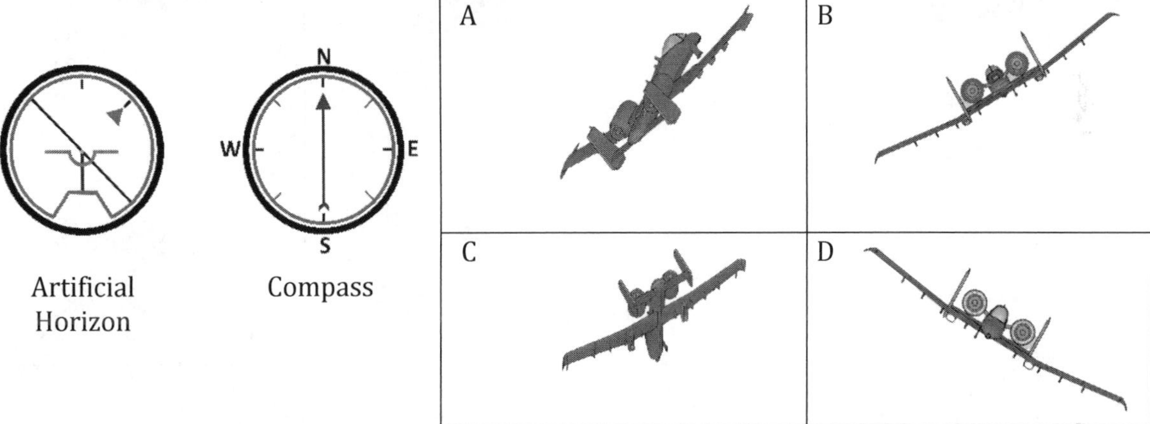

9. Which of the answer choices represents the orientation of the plane?

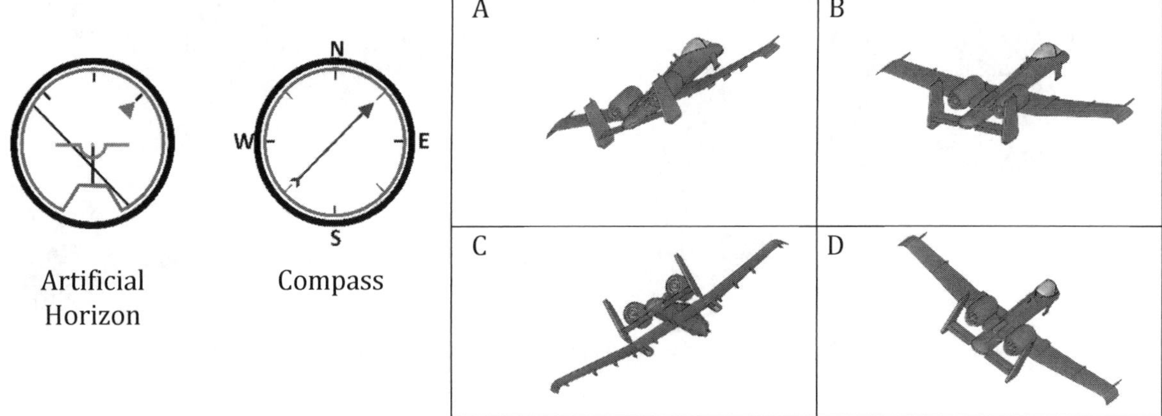

10. Which of the answer choices represents the orientation of the plane?

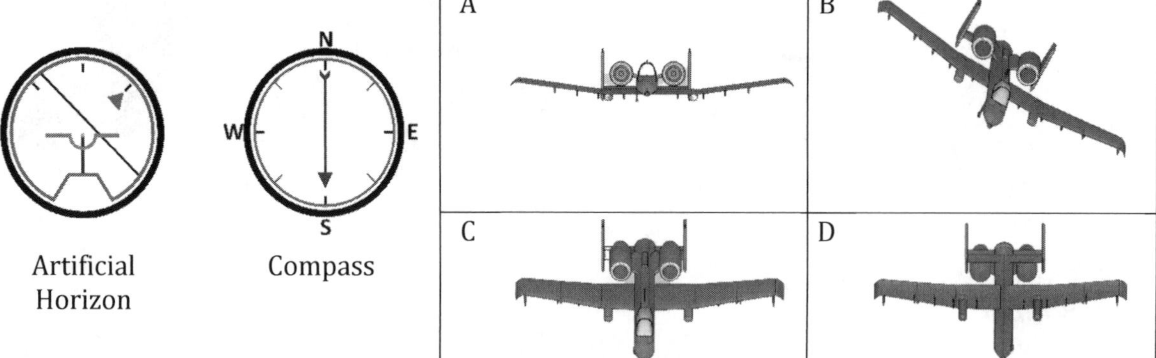

11. Which of the answer choices represents the orientation of the plane?

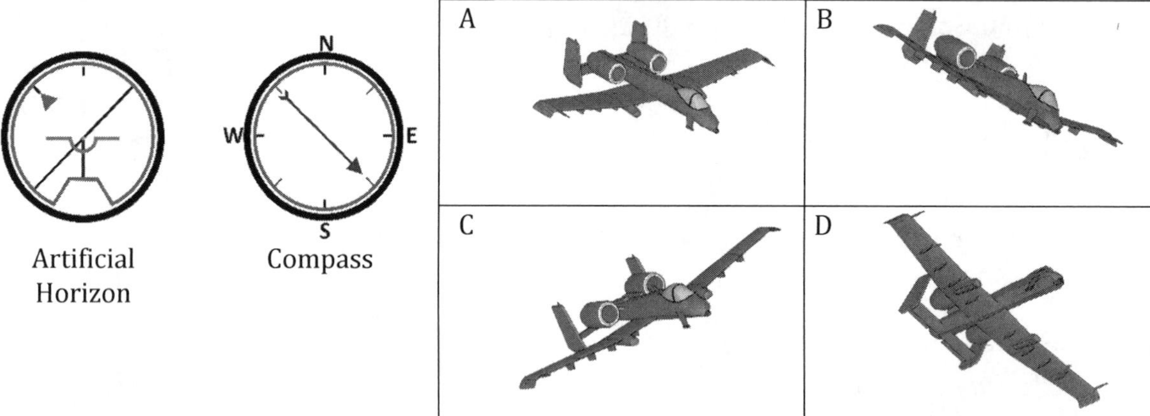

12. Which of the answer choices represents the orientation of the plane?

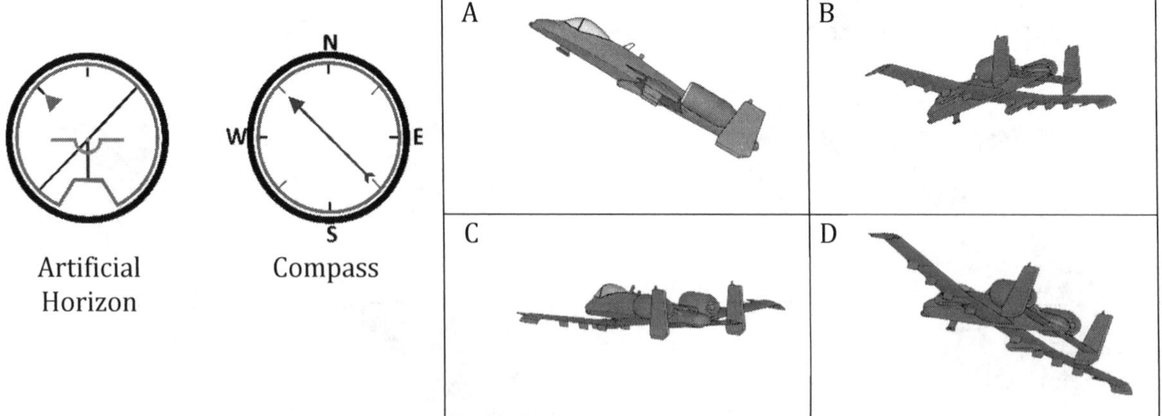

13. Which of the answer choices represents the orientation of the plane?

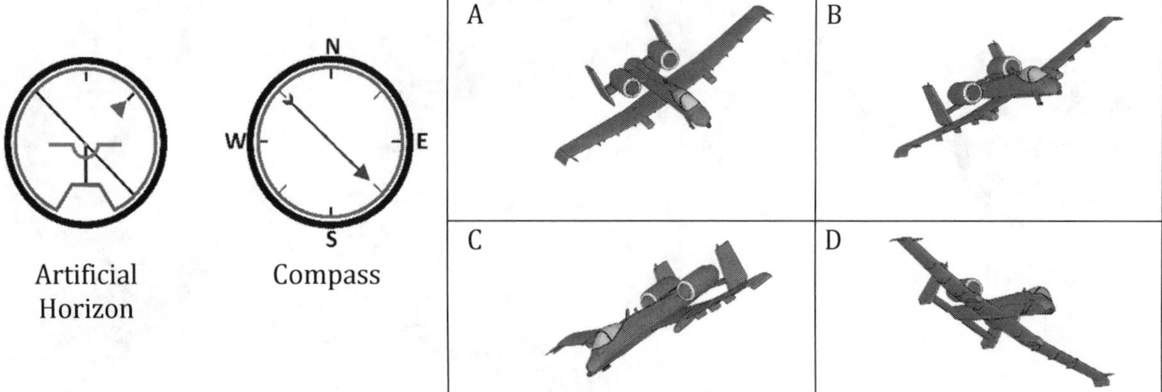

14. Which of the answer choices represents the orientation of the plane?

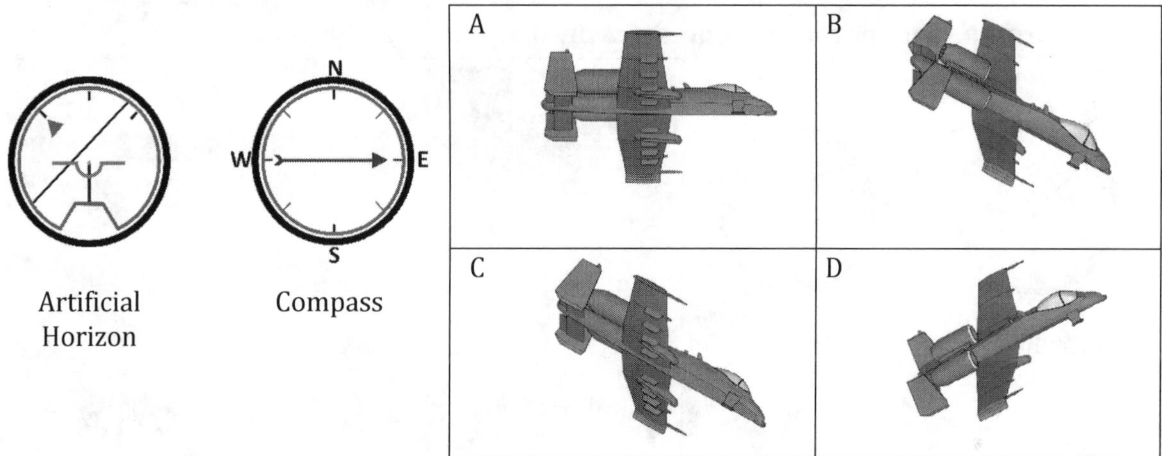

15. Which of the answer choices represents the orientation of the plane?

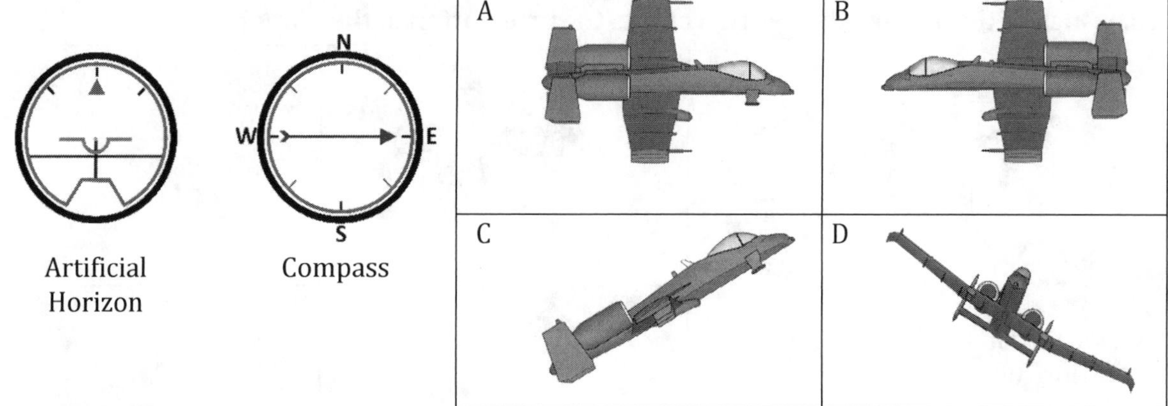

16. Which of the answer choices represents the orientation of the plane?

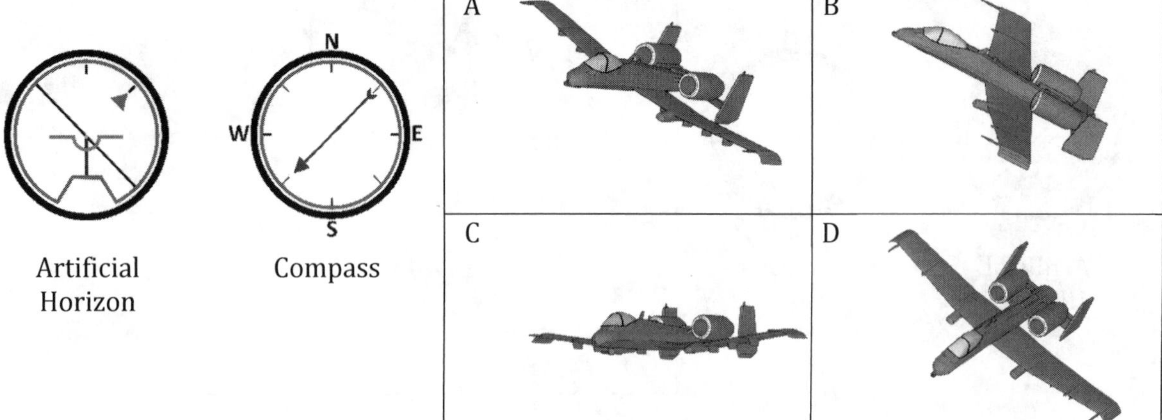

17. Which of the answer choices represents the orientation of the plane?

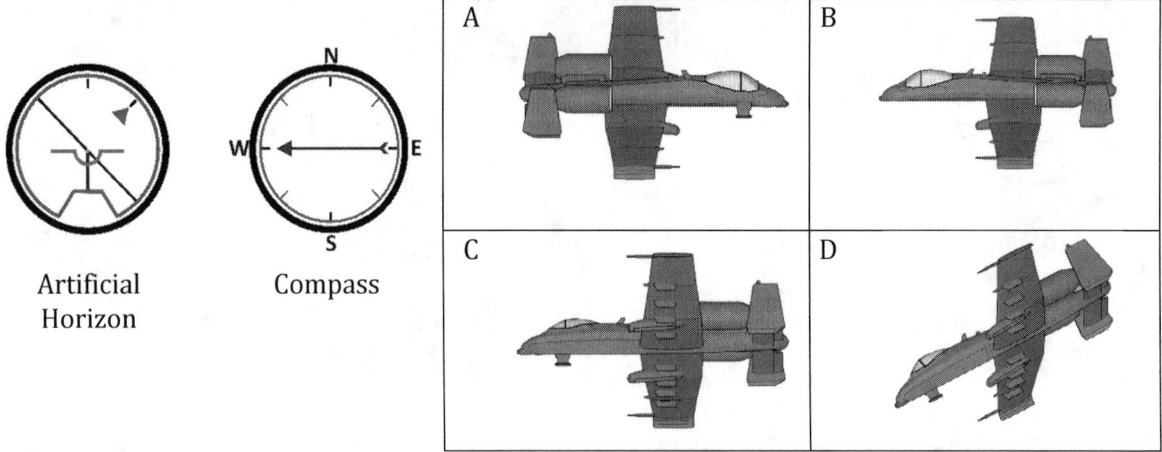

18. Which of the answer choices represents the orientation of the plane?

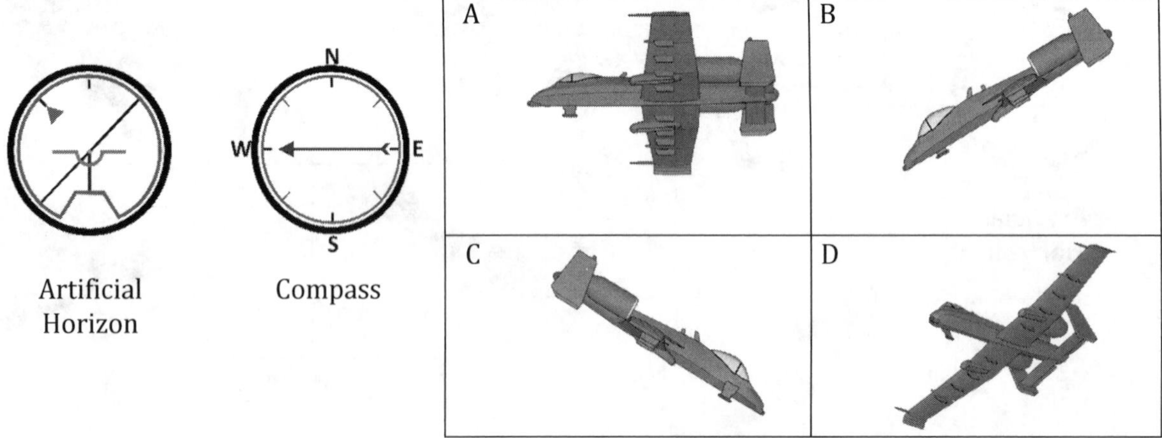

19. Which of the answer choices represents the orientation of the plane?

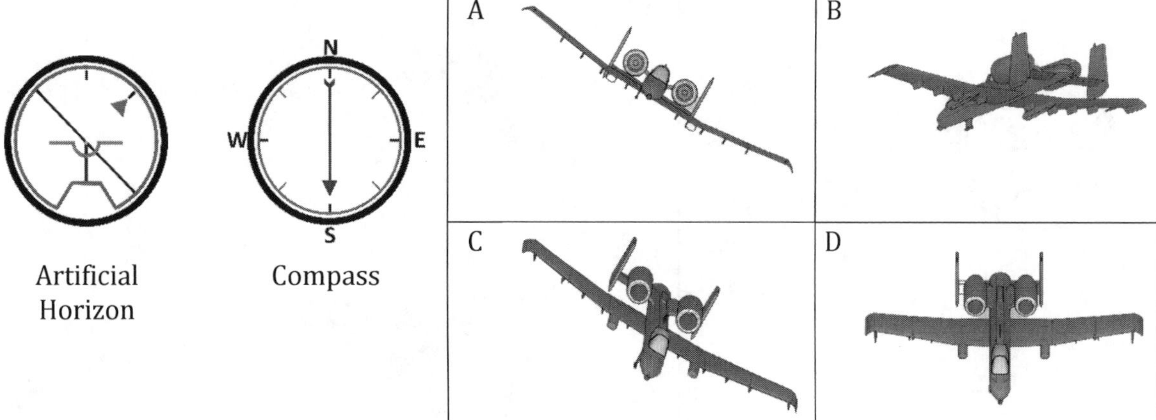

20. Which of the answer choices represents the orientation of the plane?

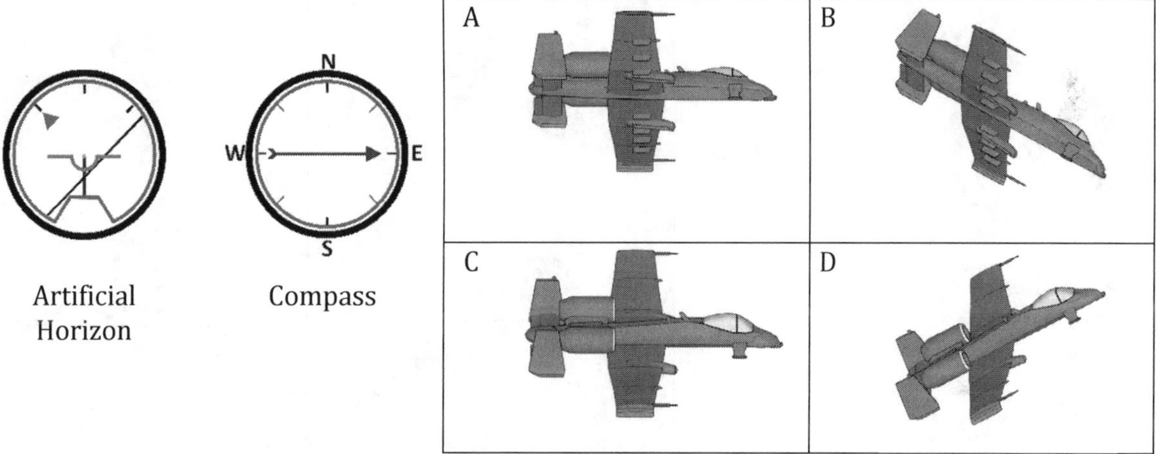

21. Which of the answer choices represents the orientation of the plane?

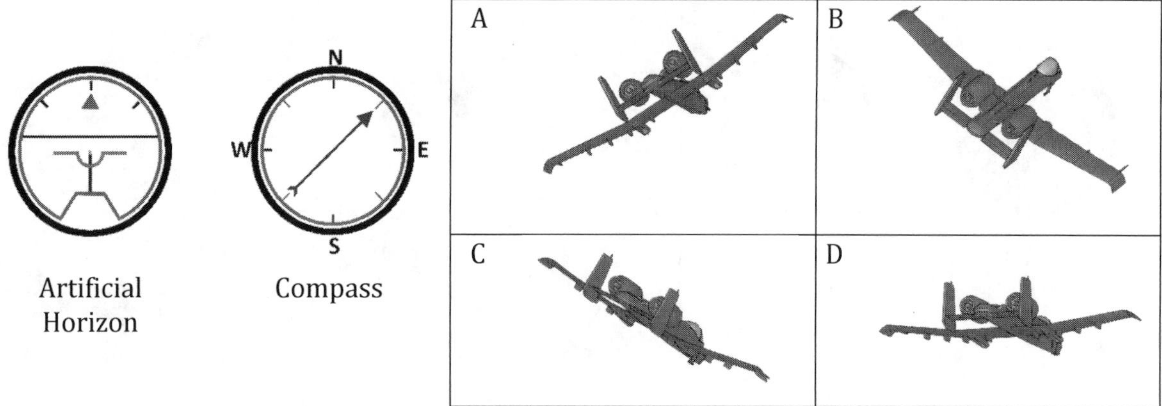

22. Which of the answer choices represents the orientation of the plane?

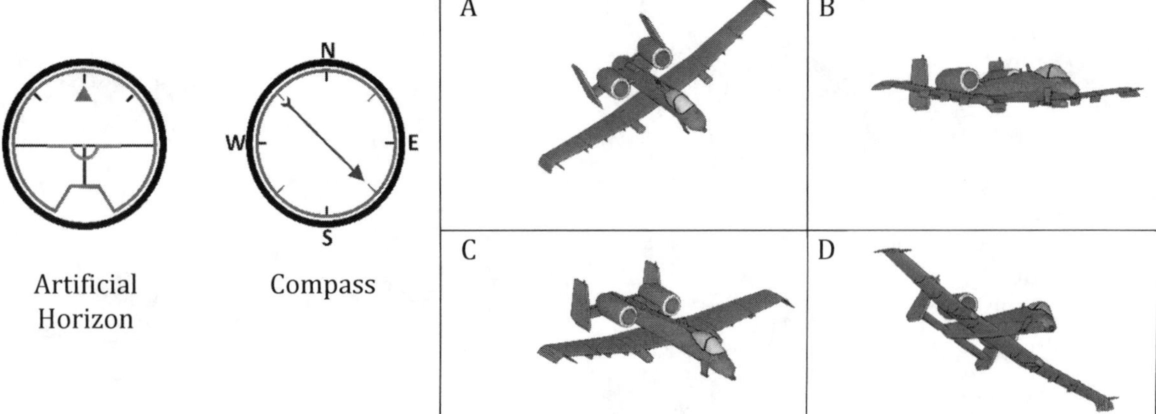

23. Which of the answer choices represents the orientation of the plane?

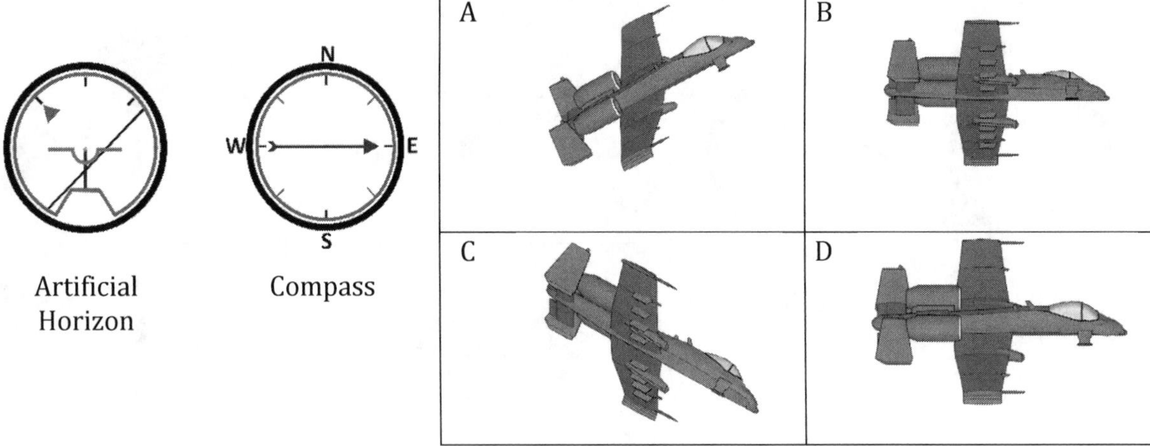

24. Which of the answer choices represents the orientation of the plane?

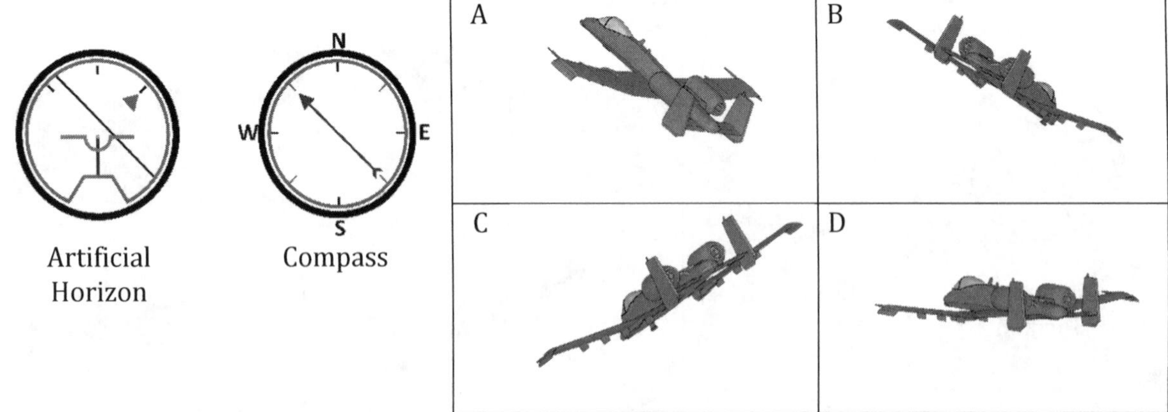

25. Which of the answer choices represents the orientation of the plane?

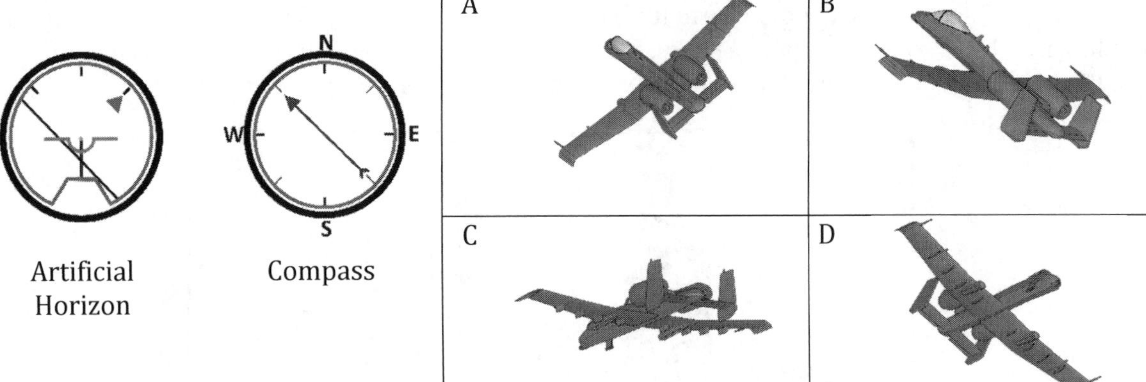

Block Counting

The explanations to these problems use terms like "top," "left," and "front" to refer to the faces of the blocks. This terminology can be confusing due to the angled view of the block arrangements, so the illustration below is provided to help you keep these terms straight.

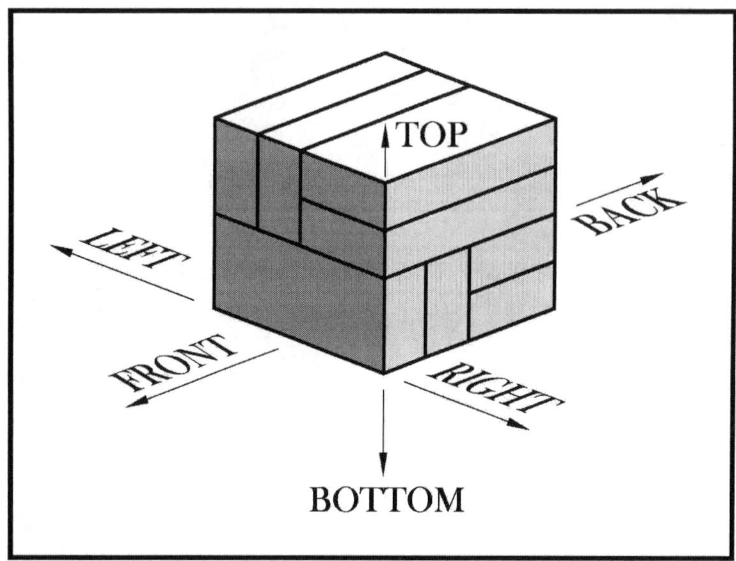

Once you understand these terms, proceed to the practice problems below. As a reminder, all the blocks in the images are intended to be the same size and shape, regardless of how much of each block is shown.

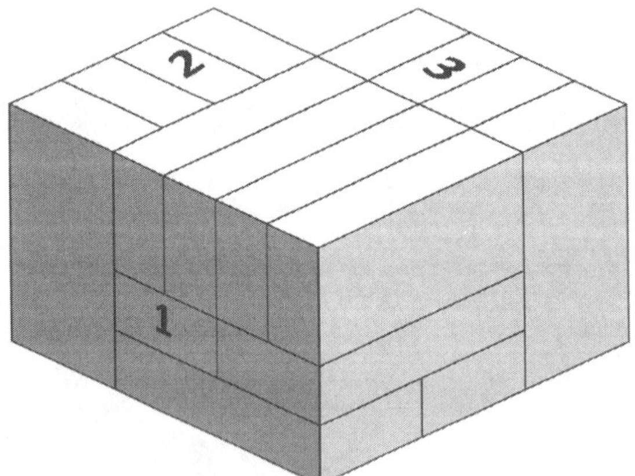

1. How many blocks are touching block 1 in the figure above?

2. How many blocks are touching block 2 in the figure above?

3. How many blocks are touching block 3 in the figure above?

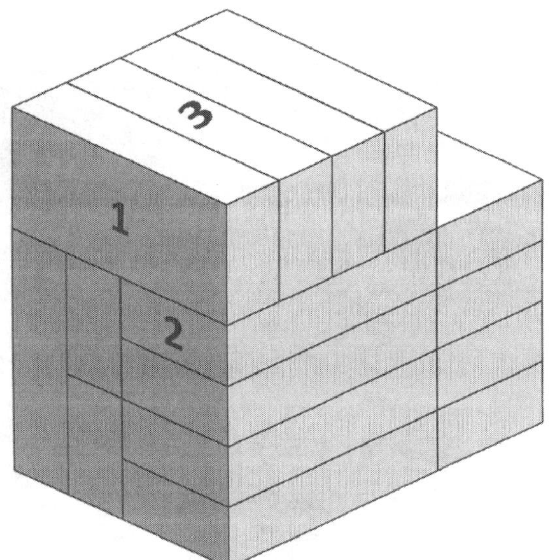

4. How many blocks are touching block 1 in the figure above?

5. How many blocks are touching block 2 in the figure above?

6. How many blocks are touching block 3 in the figure above?

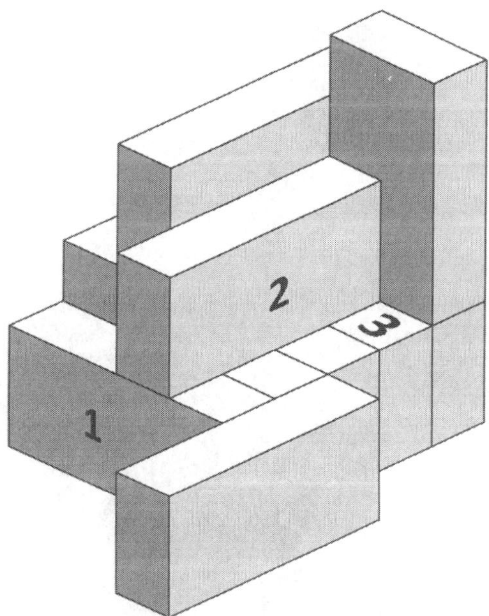

7. How many blocks are touching block 1 in the figure above?

8. How many blocks are touching block 2 in the figure above?

9. How many blocks are touching block 3 in the figure above?

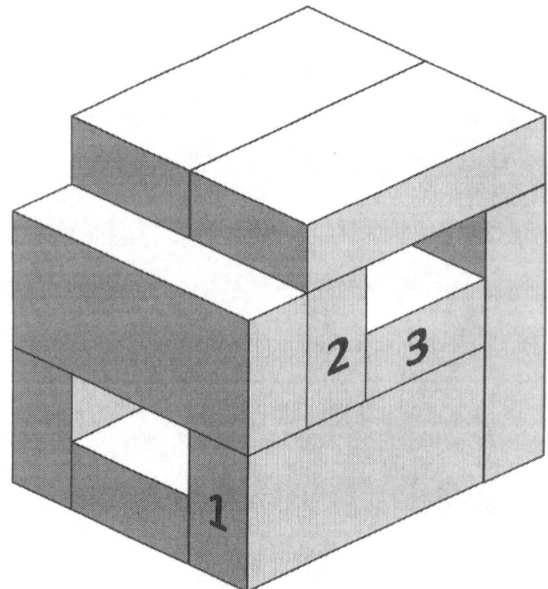

10. How many blocks are touching block 1 in the figure above?

11. How many blocks are touching block 2 in the figure above?

12. How many blocks are touching block 3 in the figure above?

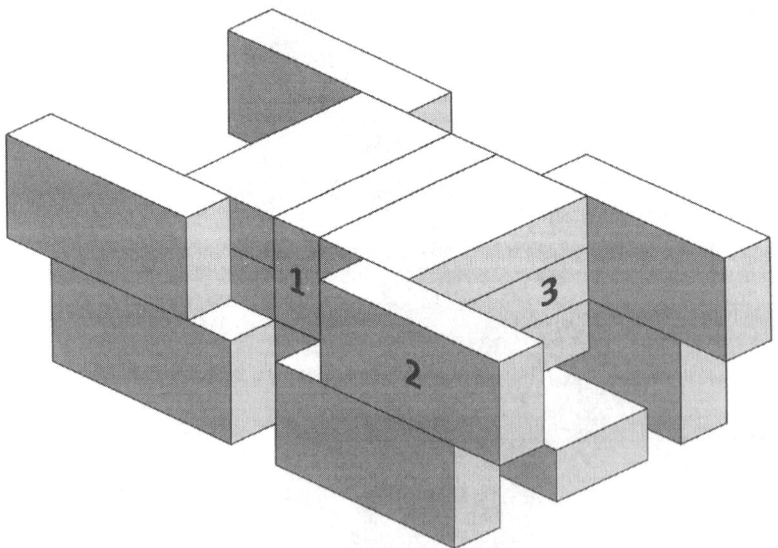

13. How many blocks are touching block 1 in the figure above?

14. How many blocks are touching block 2 in the figure above?

15. How many blocks are touching block 3 in the figure above?

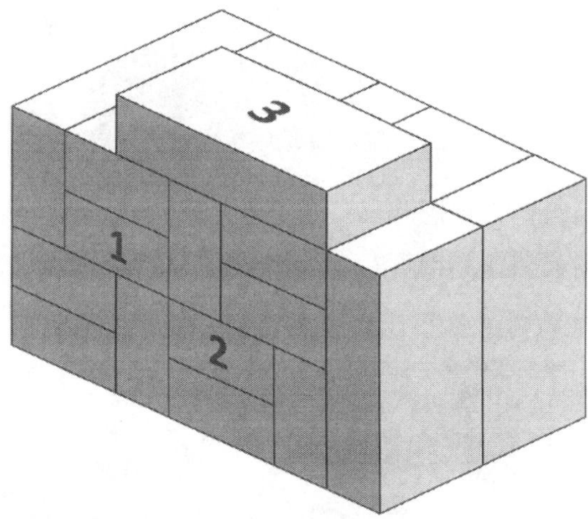

16. How many blocks are touching block 1 in the figure above?

17. How many blocks are touching block 2 in the figure above?

18. How many blocks are touching block 3 in the figure above?

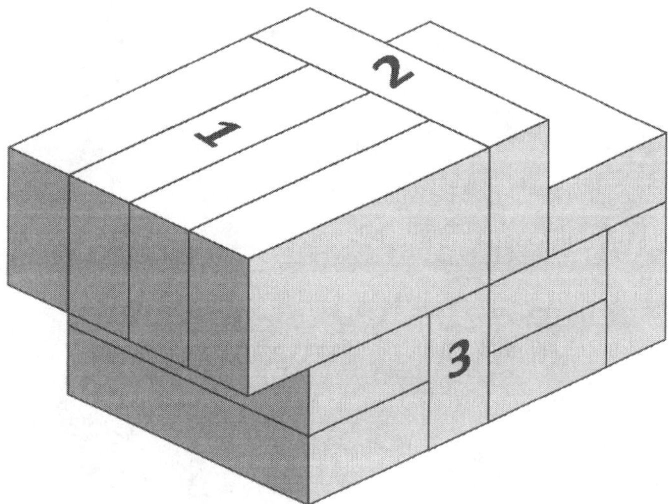

19. How many blocks are touching block 1 in the figure above?

20. How many blocks are touching block 2 in the figure above?

21. How many blocks are touching block 3 in the figure above?

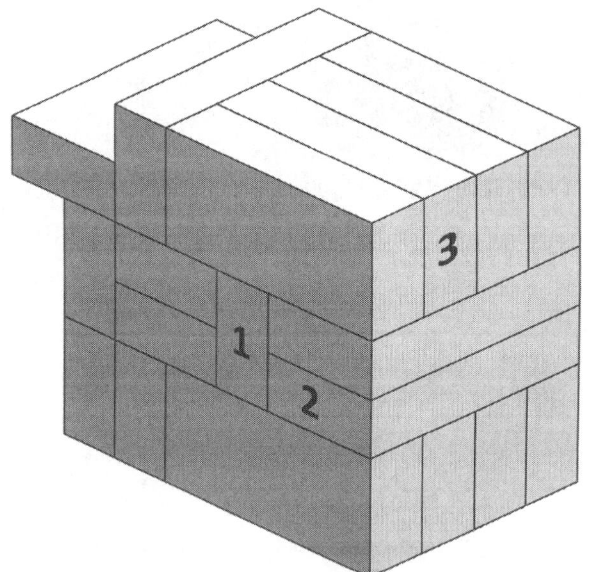

22. How many blocks are touching block 1 in the figure above?

23. How many blocks are touching block 2 in the figure above?

24. How many blocks are touching block 3 in the figure above?

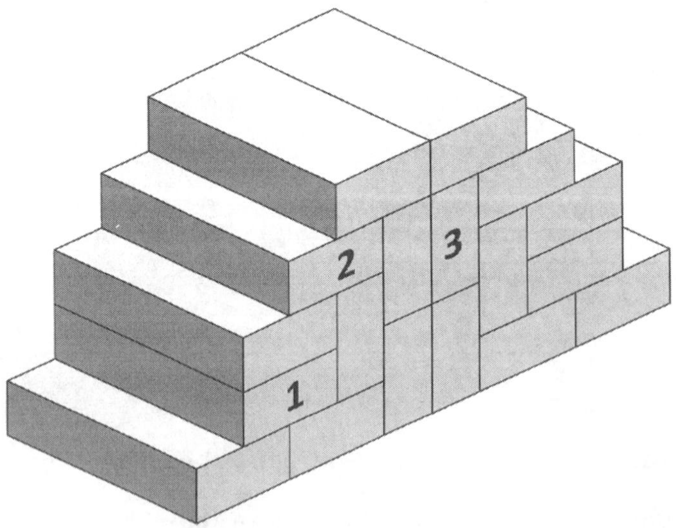

25. How many blocks are touching block 1 in the figure above?

26. How many blocks are touching block 2 in the figure above?

27. How many blocks are touching block 3 in the figure above?

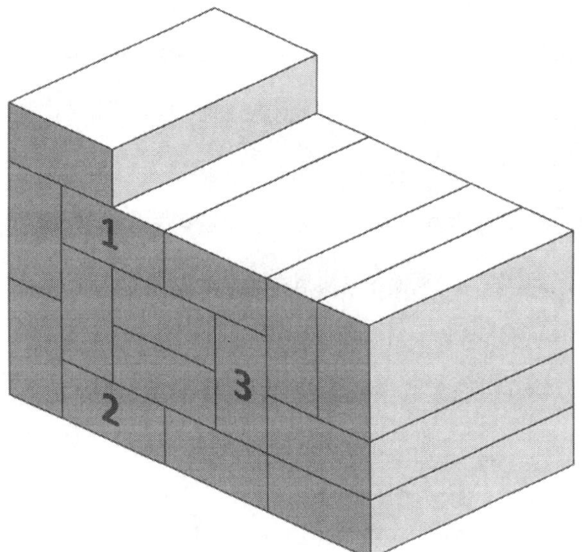

28. How many blocks are touching block 1 in the figure above?

29. How many blocks are touching block 2 in the figure above?

30. How many blocks are touching block 3 in the figure above?

Aviation Information

1. Which of the following is NOT a basic component of a fixed-wing aircraft?

a. Powerplant
b. Landing gear
c. Fuselage
d. Flight envelope
e. Tail assembly

2. Which of the following forces is unique to helicopter flight?

a. Thrust
b. Translational lift
c. Gravity
d. Operating weight
e. Induced drag

3. When the Runway Centerline Lighting System is blinking red and white, the plane is within what range of the runway?

a. 500-3,000 ft
b. 1,000-1,500 ft
c. 1,000-3,000 ft
d. 1,000-4,000 ft
e. 100-300 ft

4. The yaw of a plane is mainly controlled by the

a. Elevators
b. Throttle
c. Flaps
d. Rudder
e. Ailerons

5. Which of the following is a quality of higher density air?

a. Lower altitude
b. Lower pressures
c. Higher humidity
d. Higher temperatures
e. Higher altitude

6. Which flight control is controlled by pedals?

a. Aileron
b. Elevator
c. Rudder
d. Cyclic
e. Collective

7. When executing a landing of a plane, the nose of the plane should be

a. Angled to the pilot's left
b. Angled upward
c. Level
d. Angled downward
e. Angled to the pilot's right

8. Which of the following is NOT used to describe wings on an aircraft?

a. Cantilever, semi-cantilever
b. Dihedral, anhedral
c. High-, mid-, low-wing
d. Straight, sweep, delta
e. Shallow, medium, steep

9. When experiencing stalling, the best course of action includes

a. Angling the nose upward and increasing the throttle
b. Angling the nose upward and decreasing the throttle
c. Increasing the throttle only
d. Angling the nose downward and decreasing the throttle
e. Angling the nose downward and increasing the throttle

10. A turn with a 30-degree bank is considered a

a. Shallow turn
b. Glide
c. Deep turn
d. Medium turn
e. Descent

11. The ailerons are located

a. Along the trailing edge of the wing, from the middle to the tip
b. Along the trailing edge of the wing, from the fuselage to the middle
c. Along the trailing edges of the horizontal stabilizers in the tail assembly
d. Along the trailing edge of the vertical stabilizer in the tail assembly
e. Along the length of the fuselage

12. What type of runway usually has no markings and requires the pilot to see the runway in order to use it?

a. Flight line
b. Precision instrument runway
c. Visual runway
d. Taxiway
e. Non-precision instrument runway

13. Which lights run along the length of the runway on both sides?

a. Approach Lighting System
b. Runway edge lights
c. Taxiway edge lights
d. Visual Approach Slope Indicators
e. Runway end lights

14. What happens to the aircraft when the joystick is pushed to the right?

a. The left aileron rises.
b. The right aileron lowers.
c. The rudder swings to the right.
d. The right aileron rises.
e. The elevators lower.

15. The line that runs along the inside of the wing, such that the parts of the wing above and below it are equal in thickness is called the

a. Chord
b. Chord line
c. Mean camber line
d. Planform
e. Dihedral angle

16. "Truss" and "monocoque" are terms that are used to describe the

a. Fuselage
b. Empennage
c. Flight envelope
d. Landing gear
e. Flight attitude

17. The force that is resistance to forward movement that is caused by the wings generating lift is known as

a. Thrust
b. Induced drag
c. Translational lift
d. Profile drag
e. Transverse flow effect

18. A runway named "20L" runs

a. North and south
b. SE and NW
c. WSW and ENE
d. East and west
e. SSW and NNE

19. Why is the rudder used when making a smooth turn?

a. It is used to achieve a suitable speed.
b. It banks the wings.
c. It raises the nose to establish the rate of turn.
d. It counters any undesired yaw resulting from the effects of the other controls or to introduce desired yaw.
e. It eases the work of the pilot by resolving remaining control pressures after the pilot has achieved desired pitch, power, attitude, and configuration.

20. Which of the following is NOT a secondary flight control surface?

a. Flaps
b. Fixed or moveable slats
c. Spoilers
d. Collective
e. Trim systems

Answer Key and Explanations for Test #2

Verbal Analogies

1. B: This question is an example of a synonym analogy; the words *vivacious* and *animated* are synonyms. Similarly, *boisterous* and *loud* are synonyms, so choice B is the correct answer. Choice A and choice C are both incorrect as they represent antonyms, or words opposite in meaning, to *boisterous*. Choice D is incorrect as it means argumentative and while *boisterous* means loud, it doesn't necessarily mean itching to fight as *belligerent* does. Finally, choice E means to *consolidate* and so it does not have a clear connection to *boisterous*.

2. D: In this question, the connection is object and classification. The study of *bees* and *beekeeping* is *apiology*. Therefore, choice D is correct because it establishes *archaeology* as the study of fossils. Choice A is incorrect because while *anthropology* is the study of humans, it is more the study of culture and behavior rather than anatomy/bones. Further, *fossils* covers a wide range of flora and fauna and is not limited to humans as *anthropology* is. Choice B is incorrect as *genealogy* is the study of ancestry and lineage, not *fossils*. Choice C is incorrect; history covers events from the past rather than the fossilized remains of flora and fauna. Finally, choice E is incorrect. While fossils are the remains of biological materials, biology is much larger in scope.

3. A: This is an analogy of object and group, meaning that we would find stalactites in a cave. Therefore, the best match for a tooth, or where we might find it, is choice A, *mouth*. While choices B, D, and E are all related to teeth, the relationship between the two words does not reflect or match the same relationship as the one between *stalactite* and *cave*. Choice C is incorrect; while the mouth is found on the face, teeth themselves are not. There is a relationship here, but it's not specific or clear enough for it to be the best fit.

4. D: To orbit is to move through space, and one meaning of circumnavigate is to travel around the globe by water. Therefore, oceans are where circumnavigation would occur. Choices A, B, and C, although they are locations, do not encompass the whole planet, so they are incorrect. Choice E would include land masses where one could travel around the globe, but it is not the best match because *circumnavigate* includes the meaning of travelling by water.

5. C: The connection in this analogy is the person who works in the field and a workplace related to that field. As an astronomer might work at a planetarium, so a horticulturist might work at an arboretum. Choice A is too general since there are too many fields of biology for this to fit the specificity of the original comparison. While a farmer, choice B, works with plants, they do not work at an arboretum. While chemists and dieticians (Choices D and E) are scientists, they do not work at an arboretum.

6. E: This is an object and function analogy. So, if a chronometer measures time, then the best answer is choice E, a barometer measures air pressure. While choices A, B, and D are also aspects of weather and the environment, they are not measured by a barometer. Similarly, a speedometer would measure velocity, not a barometer, so choice C is incorrect as well.

7. E: This analogy looks at the relationship between tools and the objects they are used with. When looking at what goes best with a hammer, choice E, a nail, is best, as they need one another to function. In the same way, a person would need a makeup brush in order to apply blush. While choice A and choice B are also tools, they aren't used in conjunction with a hammer. Similarly, a carpenter, choice C, might use a hammer, but a carpenter is a person, not an object. Finally, choice D is incorrect as a hammer isn't normally applied directly to a board as it is to a nail.

8. B: Smoke typically indicates that there is a fire in the same way that frost indicates it is cold. Choice A is incorrect as frost does not indicate rain. Similarly, choice C is incorrect because, although frost indicates cold, it does not necessarily mean snow is inevitable. Choice D is too vague because frost indicates a particular type of temperature. Finally, frost does not indicate storms are inevitable, either.

9. B: Fatigue is tiredness, and exhaustion is extreme tiredness. Similarly, fear is the feeling of being afraid, and terror is magnified fear. Choice A is the opposite of fear and so is incorrect. Choices C and D are similar in magnitude to fear; they don't amplify the meaning. Choice E actually decreases the intensity and so is incorrect as well.

10. D: This is an analogy of category. A drill is a type of tool, just as pepper is a type of spice. Choice A, salt, is something that goes with pepper; it is not a category and is therefore incorrect. Choice B is similarly incorrect. Pepper does have a taste, but the analogy doesn't match. Choices C and E are incorrect; they can be eaten, but they aren't the categories that pepper belongs to.

11. C: Petrology is the study of rocks, and cartography is the study of maps. Choice A is incorrect as cartography doesn't include the study of writing. Choice B and choice D are incorrect as architects and engineers have no connection to maps, though both professions rely on detailed drawings. Finally, choice E is incorrect. While sailors have always relied upon cartographers, the two are not connected.

12. A: A person runs in a marathon. Likewise, a person dances in a recital. Choice B, swim, is also a verb, but there is no swimming in a recital. Choices C, D, and E, ballet, jazz, and hip hop, are types of dances, but they do not complete the analogy of an action done within an event.

13. D: A failure to swim in water means one will drown in the same way that a failure to fly in the air means one will crash. Choices A, B, and E are all incorrect as they are associated with successful flights. Choice C is similarly incorrect; landing happens at the end of a successful flight, but the analogy is about failing to swim or fly.

14. B: *Emancipate* means to free in the same way that *subjugate* means to enslave. Choice A is incorrect as *permit* means the opposite of emancipate, and the analogy is between similar meanings. Choice C is incorrect. While *sub* implies under, the meaning of the word *subjugate* is to "keep under" or enslave, not bury. Choice D and choice E would also be incorrect as they mean the opposite of *subjugate*.

15. D: *Corpulent* means fat, so *thin* is the opposite. *Morose* means sad and so choice D, *cheerful*, is the opposite. Choice A is incorrect as it means the same as *corpulent* and is not connected to *morose*. Choice C means the same as *morose* and so is incorrect. Finally, choice E is incorrect as it has no clear connection to the word *morose*.

16. E: Niagara is a very specific waterfall in the same way that Huron is a very specific lake. Choices A, B, and C are all incorrect; while they are bodies of water, they are not lakes. Finally, choice D is incorrect. While both Niagara and Huron are landmarks, the analogy offers up a more specific comparison than landmark.

17. C: At a birthday, which marks a specific moment in one's life, one typically feels joy. Similarly, at a graduation, a specific moment in one's life, one typically feels pride. Choice A and choice B are incorrect as they have negative connotations. One does not typically regret graduation nor does one feel sullen or sad. Choice D is incorrect; while it means friendly, that feeling doesn't best capture a milestone event. Choice E is incorrect as *excoriation* means chastisement and so is not the best fit for a graduation, either.

18. A: *Brag* is another word for *boast*, and *insult* is another word for *ridicule*. Choice B is incorrect as to *laud* means to praise and is the opposite of bragging. Choice C, *pummel*, means beat and typically refers to a physical beating. Choice D is incorrect as *augment* means to make greater, which insults do not do. Finally, choice E is incorrect as *reconcile* means to make up and typically is required after an insult has occurred.

19. D: Water is collected in a well for later use. The same is true of a silo and grain. Choice A and choice E are incorrect; although you'll find a barn and fields on a farm where one might also find grain, there is no other connection. Choice B is incorrect; while a trough may have grain in it, its function is not to store grain. Finally, choice C is incorrect. While bread is made from grain, it is not where grain is stored, and the connection is not the same.

20. E: Butchers use cleavers as tools and leather workers use awls. Choices A, B, C, and D are all incorrect, as the tool is not used by any of those other professions.

21. A: Infinitesimal and microscopic are synonyms. Prodigious and colossal are also synonyms, so choice A is the correct answer. Choice B and choice E are incorrect as they mean the opposite of *prodigious*. Choice C, *away*, has no relation to the analogy. Choice D means to stay on top of, like news, and so does not align with the comparison either.

22. B: To sculpt is to make a statue. To write is to make a novel. Choice A, *prescription*, is incorrect; while that is written, it is simply a few words and not artistic in nature. Choice C, *library*, is incorrect because while libraries are full of the written word, a library is not crafted through writing the way a statue is crafted through sculpting. Choice D, *learn*, is incorrect because while learning is an action, it does not always follow writing. Writing does not create learning. Finally, choice E, *student*, is incorrect as writing does not create students.

23. D: A person who has an itch scratches it. Likewise, a person who has fatigue sleeps. Choice A, *dream*, and choice C, *nightmare*, are incorrect because they go further than just satiating the condition. They are experiences within sleep, so they go too far for the analogy. Choice B is incorrect because one who has fatigue does not solve it by waking. Finally, choice E, *activate*, is incorrect because it's not necessarily related to *fatigue* or *sleep*.

24. B: Fruit is part of the vine it grows on as leaves are part of the branches they grow on. Choice A is incorrect as leaves do not grow on flowers. Choice C, *growth*, is incorrect; fruit, vines, and leaves are all themselves growth. Choice D, *tree*, is incorrect because it moves further away from the specific connection of a leaf to a branch. The fruit and the vine are directly contiguous, while the leaf is immediately connected to a branch, not a tree. Choice E, *autumn*, is incorrect; while leaves change in autumn, leaves do not grow "on" autumn.

25. C: A group of crows is called a murder. A group of sheep is called a flock. Choice A is incorrect as a group of dogs is called a pack. Choice B is incorrect as a group of cats is called a clowder. Choice D is incorrect as a group of parrots is called a pandemonium. Choice E is incorrect as a group of fish is called a shoal.

Arithmetic Reasoning

1. A: The total number of hours is $2 + 1 + 2\frac{1}{2} = 5\frac{1}{2} = 5.5$. Then, we take the ratio of napping hours to total hours and convert it to a percentage: $\frac{2.5}{5.5} \approx 0.45 = 45\%$.

2. B: Volume is equal to length times width times height. Therefore, $V = 9 \text{ in} \times 4 \text{ in} \times 5 \text{ in} = 180$ cubic inches.

3. C: If there are x squares in the drawing, there are $x + 16$ circles. Therefore, $x + (x + 16) = 2x + 16 = 36$. Solving this for x, $x = 10$. Therefore, there are 10 squares and 26 circles.

4. D: 40% of 30% is $0.4(0.3) = 0.12 = 12\%$.

5. B: Average speed is found by dividing the total distance traveled by the total time taken to travel that distance. The total distance traveled is 135 miles + 165 miles = 300 miles. Next, we have to determine the total amount of time the trip took. We can determine this by finding the sum of the times for each portion of the trip. The first portion is described by the equation $\frac{135 \text{ miles}}{45 \text{ miles per hour}} = 3$ hours, and the second portion by $\frac{165 \text{ miles}}{55 \text{ miles per hour}} = 3$ hours. Therefore, the average speed for the entire trip is $\frac{300 \text{ miles}}{6 \text{ hours}} = 50$ mph.

6. E: We start by adding together the total fraction of pretzels or chips. $\frac{1}{3} + \frac{1}{4} = \frac{4}{12} + \frac{3}{12} = \frac{7}{12}$. Therefore, $\frac{7}{12}$ of the boxes contain pretzels and chips. Therefore, $1 - \frac{7}{12} = \frac{12}{12} - \frac{7}{12} = \frac{5}{12}$ contain granola bars.

7. B: Average speed is found by dividing the total distance traveled by the total time taken to travel that distance. Therefore, the sloth's average speed is $\frac{110 \text{ feet}}{15 \text{ minutes}} = 7.3$ ft/min, rounded to the nearest tenth.

8. C: First, subtract 80 from both sides of the equation to obtain $15x = 30$. Then, divide both sides by 15 to obtain the solution $x = 2$.

9. D: The car is traveling at a speed of $\frac{210 \text{ miles}}{3.5 \text{ hours}} = 60$ mph. Therefore, the car is traveling at a rate of 60 miles per 60 minutes. We set up a proportion to find the answer. Let x be the number of miles traveled in 40 minutes. $\frac{x \text{ miles}}{40 \text{ minutes}} = \frac{60 \text{ miles}}{60 \text{ minutes}}$ or $\frac{x \text{ miles}}{40 \text{ minutes}} = \frac{1 \text{ mile}}{1 \text{ minute}}$. The car will travel 40 miles in 40 minutes.

10. B: This expression can be changed to $15 + 13 = 28$, since the opposite of a negative number is a positive number.

11. B: Let x be the unknown quantity. Therefore, $70 = 0.8x$. Dividing both sides by 0.8, we obtain that $x = 87.5$.

12. E: Because each segment lasted for the same amount of time, we can find the average by adding the three speeds and dividing that sum by 3. Therefore, the average of the car's three speeds was $\frac{55+52+58}{3} = 55$ mph.

13: B: To find out how many envelopes she can buy, we divide \$50 by \$0.03, obtaining approximately 1,666.6. Therefore, she can buy 1,666 envelopes.

14. C: Kevin has $\$47.50 - \$12.00 - \$27.00 = \$8.50$ left.

15. B: We can use the distance formula $d = rt$, where d is the distance, r is the rate or speed, and t is the time. In this case, $33 \text{ miles} = \frac{57 \text{ miles}}{1 \text{ hour}}(t)$. Dividing both sides by 57, we find that $t \approx 0.58$ hrs. Since this is not an answer choice, we must convert hours to minutes by multiplying by 60, which gives us 34.8 minutes.

16. A: If 45% of the servings will be fried, that means the rest, or 55%, will be grilled. Therefore, $0.55(160 \text{ servings}) = 88$ servings will be grilled.

17. B: The total before tax is $\$39 + \$11 = \$50$. We apply an 8% tax rate to obtain the sales tax of $\$50(0.08) = \$4$. Therefore, the total is $\$50 + \$4 = \$54$.

18. D: $50x$ is equal to 50 times x, which is not equivalent to 50% of x, or 50% times x. The other four responses are different ways to write 50% times x, including the fractions, which are different ways to write $\frac{50}{100}$ or $\frac{1}{2}$.

19. A: $(-4) - 9$ is equivalent to $(-4) + (-9)$. The sum of two negative numbers is negative. Therefore, $(-4) - 9 = -13$.

20. A: To find what percent 40 is of 85, divide 40 by 85 and convert to a percentage. Therefore, $\frac{40}{85} \approx 0.471 = 47\%$.

21. D: First, we find the total number of minutes Krystal worked this morning: $32 \text{ min} + 25 \text{ min} + 45 \text{ min} = 102 \text{ min}$. Then, we find the ratio of the time spent on her phone call to the total time: $\frac{25 \text{ min}}{102 \text{ min}} \approx 0.245$. Converting this to a percent, we have approximately 25%.

22. A: Because you are buying 12 boxes of tissues, you need four of the 3-packs of tissues. Also, because you are buying 16 rolls of paper towels, you need four of the 4-packs of paper towels. Therefore, your total is $4(\$6.25) + 4(\$5.75) = \$25 + \$23 = \$48$.

23. C: Let x represent the number of apples *or* oranges purchased. Because an equal number of each type of fruit was purchased, they can be represented by the same variable, x. Therefore $\$2x + \$4x = \$6x = \$240$. Dividing both sides by \$6, we find that $x = 40$. Therefore, 40 apples and 40 oranges were purchased.

24. D: 35% converted to a decimal is 0.35. Therefore, we find that 35% of 200 is $0.35(200) = 70$.

25. C: The perimeter of a rectangle is $P = 2L + 2W$, where L is the length and W is the width. Therefore, the perimeter of this room is $P = 2(35 \text{ ft}) + 2(88 \text{ ft}) = 70 \text{ ft} + 176 \text{ ft} = 246 \text{ ft}$.

Word Knowledge

1. C: *Aberration* means something out of the norm, so *oddity* is the best fit. Choice A, *obtuse*, means slow to understand and so isn't the best fit, nor is choice B, *intricate*, which means detailed. Choice D, *conformity*, means compliance with norms and so is the opposite of aberration. Finally, choice E, *obsolete*, means no longer used or out of date, so it isn't the best match.

2. B: *Fortitude* means nerve in the sense of courage. *Fear* is the opposite of fortitude, so choice A is not correct. *Anger* is also not the same as courage, so choice C is incorrect. Similarly, *lucky* and *grateful*, which are adjectives, have little to do with *courage*, a noun, and so choices D and E are incorrect as well.

3. E: *Opulent* means extravagant or lavish. Choice A is incorrect as *bright* is not the same as extravagant. *Meager* means lacking in quality or quantity and is, therefore, the opposite of opulent, and so choice B is incorrect. Choice C, *heavy*, has nothing to do with lavishness and so is incorrect. Choice D, *morose*, means gloomy or sulky and so is not the best match.

4. A: One meaning of *mundane* is *dull*; it comes from a Latin root meaning world, and so it can also refer to the ordinary, everyday things of this world in contrast to a sublime or dramatic spiritual realm. Choices B and C, *creative* and *dramatic*, would both be opposites of mundane, so they aren't the best fit. Choice D, *courageous*, means adventurous or bold, and it is not a match with mundane. Finally, choice E, *solitary*, means alone or by oneself and is not a match.

5. D: To be *brazen* means to be *bold.* Choice A, *aflame*, means to be on fire and is not the same as brazen. Neither choice B, *huge*, nor choice C, *curious*, are good matches. Finally, choice E, *timid*, is the opposite of bold and is incorrect.

6. C: To *disdain* something means to *dislike* it. Choice A, *separate*, choice B, *different*, and choice D, *retrieve*, are not good matches as they don't share the meaning or fit the definition. Finally, choice E, *dull*, may be a reason to disdain something, but it is not a definition of the word.

7. E: Someone who is *prosperous* thrives or is successful, so *flourishing* is the best match. Choice A, *destitute*, is the opposite of prosperous and is not a match. Choice B, *expansive*, refers to something broad or sweeping and is not the best match. Choice C, *beautiful*, is not a match for the word *prosperous*. Finally, choice D, *languid*, describes a state of sluggishness or relaxation; someone who is prosperous might be relaxed, but the concepts are unrelated.

8. B: choice B, *respect*, is correct. To *revere* means to hold in esteem, honor, or respect. Choice A and choice E are both opposites of respect and are therefore incorrect. Choice C, *condone*, means to accept, which is not the same as to respect. Choice D, *recalcitrant*, is an adjective that means uncooperative or oppositional.

9. D: To *capitulate* means to *surrender*. Choice A, *conquer*, and choice B, *elevate*, suggest opposite meanings and are not correct. Choice C, *rename*, is incorrect. Finally, choice E, *sink*, means to descend or submerge and is therefore incorrect.

10. A: To be *arrogant* is to exaggerate one's worth or to be *pompous*. Choice B, *considerate*, and choice E, *meek*, are nearly opposites of arrogant in that they refer to one who is thoughtful of others and timid, respectively. Choice C, *affluent*, refers to someone who is wealthy and so is incorrect. Finally, choice D, *brave*, is not a good match either because the characteristics of bravery and arrogance are not similar.

11. C: To *mitigate* something means to make it somewhat less harsh or harmful, and to *alleviate* means to partially remove something painful or unpleasant, so it is the best choice. Choice A, *aggravate*, means to make worse and so is the opposite. Choice B, *console*, means comfort. One might console someone to mitigate their grief, but the meaning isn't the same. Choice D, *adjudicate*, means to judge and choice E, *mediate*, means to act as an intermediary or go-between, so these aren't good matches either.

12. E: choice E is correct as someone who is *petulant* is bad-tempered, often in a childish way, so *irritable* is the best fit. Choice A, *floral*, has nothing to with being petulant and so is not correct. Someone who is petulant would probably be unpleasant and impatient, so choice B, *pleasant*, and choice C, *patient*, are incorrect. Finally, choice D, *diligent*, describes someone who is hardworking and so is not a match either.

13. B: choice B, *attainable*, is correct. *Feasible* means possible or attainable. Choice A, *equitable*, means fair and so is not a match. Choice C, *immeasurable*, describes something so large it cannot be measured, so it is not the best match. Choice D, *irreconcilable*, means incompatible so is not a match. Choice E, *impossible*, is the opposite of feasible and so is also incorrect.

14. A: choice A is correct since *bolster* means reinforce or *strengthen*. Choice B, *obstruct*, means to get in the way or block, so this is incorrect. Similarly, choice C, *neglect*, means to not take care of and so does not match. *Sanitize*, choice D, means to clean and choice E, *frighten*, means to scare; therefore, neither is a correct match.

15. D: Something that is *ambiguous* can be interpreted in more than one way, and this is true of *equivocal* also. The word *underwater*, choice A, might suggest *amphibious*, which means to be acclimated to both land and water, but underwater is not a synonym for ambiguous. Choice B, *interchangeable*, is not correct, though again, one might think of *ambidextrous*, which uses a similar prefix as well. Choice C, *determined*, and choice E, *explicit*, are not good matches because they mean nearly the opposite of ambiguous.

16. B: Someone who is *benevolent* shows good will; the word comes from Latin roots meaning good and will. So, the benevolent person is kind or *compassionate*. Choice A, *merciless*, is incorrect, as it means the opposite of benevolent. Choice C is incorrect; while being *philanthropic* is benevolent, one can be benevolent without being philanthropic. Choice D is incorrect, as someone who is *malevolent* exhibits ill will or evil. Choice E, *capricious*, is incorrect; it means to be very changeable in mood or behavior. Someone capricious exercises their will randomly and not necessarily as good will.

17. D: choice D, *cautious*, is correct. To be *tentative* means to be hesitant or uncertain. Choices A, B, and C are incorrect as they all mean the opposite of tentative. People who are *bold*, *conclusive*, or *influential* act with certainty. Choice E is incorrect as it means corresponding to.

18. E: To *perish* means to end or *cease*. Choice A, *thrive*, is incorrect because it means the opposite of perish. Choice B, *external*, is incorrect because it means outside. Choice C, *decline*, is incorrect because it means to move downward or to grow worse, but something can decline without perishing. Choice D, *berate*, is incorrect because it means to criticize.

19. A: To be *erratic* means to be *unpredictable*. Choice B, *abolish*, means to get rid of, so it is incorrect. Choice C, *stable*, is incorrect because it's the opposite in meaning of *erratic*. Choice D, *construct*, is incorrect because it means to build. And choice E, *incorrect*, is not the right answer choice. It might sound like the word error, but it does not have the same meaning as erratic.

20. B: choice B, *honesty*, is correct. *Candor* means honesty or frankness. Choice A, *deception*, is incorrect because it is the opposite of honesty. Choice C is incorrect because someone who looks *quizzical* is puzzled. Choice D, *humorous*, is incorrect because it means funny. Choice E, *devious*, is incorrect as it means sneaky.

21. C: choice C, *remove*, is correct. To *oust* is to remove. Choice A, *surround*, is incorrect; surrounding is not the same as removal. Choices B, D, and E are all incorrect as they do not have the same meaning as oust.

22. A: *Squalid* means *filthy*. Choice B, *large*, and choice C, *daring*, are incorrect because they don't match the definition. Choice D, *sterile*, is the opposite of squalid and so is incorrect. Choice E is incorrect because *gaunt* means thin.

23. C: *Avid* means *enthusiastic*. Choice A, *airborne*, is incorrect because it does not have anything to do with avid, though it does sound like *aviary*. Similarly, another word for dry is arid, not avid, and so choice B is incorrect. Choice D, *thick*, and choice E, *weak*, are both incorrect as well because they are not the same as enthusiastic.

24. D: *Unadorned* means *plain*. Choice A, *free*, is incorrect because unadorned does not mean free. Choice B, *embellished*, is the opposite of unadorned and so is incorrect. Choice C, *poor*, and choice E, *crowded*, are not suitable definitions either.

25. E: To *incite* means to encourage something violent or illegal; for example, to provoke a crowd so that it riots. Choice A, *bring in*, is incorrect, although incite contains the prefix *-in*. Choice B, *offer advice*, is incorrect because it has nothing to do with encouraging something illegal. Choice C, *soothe*, is the opposite of incite and so is incorrect. Choice D, *urge*, has other meanings that do not relate to inciting violence. Therefore, choice D is incorrect.

Mathematics Knowledge

1. C: $16x^2 - 64$ is a difference of squares, which factors into $(4x + 8)(4x - 8)$. We can check our answer by using the FOIL method to obtain the product. $(4x + 8)(4x - 8) = 16x^2 - 32x + 32x - 64 = 16x^2 - 64$.

2. E: $\sqrt{64} = 8$. Therefore, this expression is equal to $\frac{1}{16}(8) = \frac{8}{16} = \frac{1}{2}$.

3. D: To add fractions, we must convert them so that they have the same denominator. Therefore, we have $\frac{41}{80} + \frac{5}{20} + \frac{7}{40} = \frac{41}{80} + \frac{5}{20}\left(\frac{4}{4}\right) + \frac{7}{40}\left(\frac{2}{2}\right) = \frac{41}{80} + \frac{20}{80} + \frac{14}{80}$. Then, we add the numerators over the same denominator to obtain $\frac{75}{80}$. This is not the final answer, since it is not expressed in lowest terms. The numerator and the denominator have a common factor of 5. Dividing a 5 out of both the numerator and the denominator yields $\frac{15}{16}$.

4. D: The correct solution can be found using substitution. Solving the first equation for x, we obtain $x = 9 - y$. Substituting this expression into the second equation for x, we obtain $(9 - y) + 2y = 9 + y = 13$. Therefore, $y = 4$. Plugging this value into the first equation, we find that $x + 4 = 9$, so $x = 5$.

5. B: A triangle has three angles that add up to 180 degrees. An acute angle is less than 90 degrees, so the sum of three acute angles could equal 180 degrees. For instance, they could all be 60 degrees. An obtuse angle is more than 90 degrees, so the sum of three obtuse angles would be more than 180 degrees. Therefore, choice A is incorrect. Right angles are 90 degrees, so the sum of three right angles would be 270 degrees. Therefore, choice C is incorrect. A triangle cannot have four angles. Therefore, choice D is incorrect. Finally, a triangle cannot have a 200-degree angle, since 200 degrees is more than 180 degrees. Therefore, choice E is incorrect.

6. B: To convert a fraction to a decimal, divide the numerator by the denominator. Therefore, $\frac{1}{9} = 1 \div 9 \approx 0.1111$, which rounds to 0.11.

7. C: Because there are $7\frac{1}{2}$ centimeters between the two airports on the map, we convert this amount to a decimal (7.5) and then multiply it by 100. Using this scale, we have $7.5 \times 100 = 750$ miles.

8. A: Following order of operations, we compute the operations in the innermost parentheses first, working our way to the outermost parentheses. Therefore:

$$\begin{aligned}\big(5 - (3 - 5(6 + 2)) - 1\big) + 9 &= \big(5 - (3 - 5(8)) - 1\big) + 9 \\ &= (5 - (3 - 40) - 1) + 9 \\ &= (5 - (-37) - 1) + 9 \\ &= (5 + 37 - 1) + 9 \\ &= (42 - 1) + 9 \\ &= 41 + 9 \\ &= 50\end{aligned}$$

9. E: Following order of operations, we can compute the addition and subtraction from left to right. Therefore:

$$\begin{aligned} 1.75 + 1.75 + 2.25 - 2.25 + 5.5 &= 3.5 + 2.25 - 2.25 + 5.5 \\ &= 5.75 - 2.25 + 5.5 \\ &= 3.5 + 5.5 \\ &= 9 \end{aligned}$$

10. C: First, compute the division on the left side to obtain $9 = x - 17$. Then, add 17 to both sides of the equation to obtain the solution $x = 9 + 17 = 26$.

11. B: First, add 9 to both sides of the equation to obtain $7x = 56$. Then, divide both sides by 7 to obtain the solution: $x = 8$.

12. C: Following order of operations, multiplication must be computed first. Therefore, we have $4 + 2 \times 9 = 4 + 18$. Adding, we obtain the answer of 22.

13. D: Each expression has a common factor of 5, which can be factored out to obtain $5(14 + 4)$. This expression is equivalent to $5(18)$, which can be written as (18×5).

14. E: We find the ratio of produce to the total grocery bill and then convert the value to a percentage, rounding to the nearest percent. Therefore, the percentage of her monthly grocery bill that she spends on produce is $\frac{150}{320} = 0.46875 \approx 47\%$.

15. D: Rewriting the fractions with a common denominator, we have $\frac{7}{8} + \frac{2}{3} = \frac{7}{8}\left(\frac{3}{3}\right) + \frac{2}{3}\left(\frac{8}{8}\right) = \frac{21}{24} + \frac{16}{24} = \frac{37}{24}$. This expression is an improper fraction. To write the answer as a mixed number, divide the denominator into the numerator and place the remainder over the denominator. Therefore, $37 \div 24 = 1R13 = 1\frac{13}{24}$.

16. E: We must follow the order of operations. Therefore, compute the multiplication first. We obtain $10 \times 5 - 3 = 50 - 3$. Finally, subtracting gives the final answer of 47.

17. A: First, simplify the left-hand side to obtain $27 = 3x^2$. Dividing both sides by 3 results in $9 = x^2$. In order to find x, we must find the value for which its square is equal to 9. Therefore, $x = \pm 3$. Since only positive 3 is listed as one of the answer choices, this is the correct answer.

18. B: Every triangle is composed of 3 angles that sum to 180 degrees. These three angles have a sum of $88 + 75 + 45 = 208$ degrees. Therefore, their total must be adjusted down from 208 to 180. To find this: $208 - 180 = 28$ degrees.

19. C: Because the sales tax is 12%, we convert the amount to a decimal to obtain 0.12. Multiplying the price of the scarf by 1.12 gives her a total bill of $25(1.12) = \$28$.

20. D: First, we subtract $4x$ from both sides of the inequality to obtain $x - 9 \leq -2$. Then, adding 9 to both sides, we find the solution $x \leq -2 + 9$. Simplifying gives us $x \leq 7$.

21. B: Rewriting the fractions with a common denominator, we have $\frac{17}{3} - \frac{1}{5} = \frac{17}{3}\left(\frac{5}{5}\right) - \frac{1}{5}\left(\frac{3}{3}\right) = \frac{85}{15} - \frac{3}{15} = \frac{82}{15}$. This expression is an improper fraction. To write it as a mixed number, divide the denominator into the numerator and place the remainder over the denominator. Therefore, $82 \div 15 = 5R7 = 5\frac{7}{15}$.

22. B: In order to simplify this expression, we add or subtract the coefficients with the same variable term. Therefore, $4x^2 - 5x + x^2 - 9x + x^3 = (4 + 1)x^2 + (-5 - 9)x + x^3 = 5x^2 - 14x + x^3$.

23. D: The absolute value of -11 is equal to 11. Also, 11 and $\frac{1}{11}$ are reciprocals. The product of reciprocals is 1. Therefore, $|-11| \times \frac{1}{11} = 11 \times \frac{1}{11} = 1$.

24: E: This is a proportion that can be solved using cross-multiplication, yielding $7x = 63$. Dividing both sides of the equation by 7, we obtain the solution $x = 9$.

25. D: The solution can be found by using substitution. First, the second equation can be solved for y as $y = 3x + 12$. Substituting this expression into the first equation results in $2x + 2(3x + 12) = 8$ which simplifies to $8x + 24 = 8$. Thus, $8x = -16$ and $x = -2$. Plugging this value into the second equation results in $-3(-2) + y = 12$. Therefore, $6 + y = 12$ and $y = 6$.

Reading Comprehension

1. E: Throughout the passage, the writer focuses on how people are pulled to the ocean or the water. Choice A is incorrect. While the passage discusses different landscapes, it does not settle on any specific setting for the larger story. Choice B is incorrect; while we get a few hints of what the townspeople may be like, they only make a brief appearance and are not the focus. Choice C is incorrect; while the narrator is speaking, we don't have a clear sense from this passage about who they are or what they're doing. There is no real insight, other than a draw to the water (Choice E). Choice D is incorrect because while both areas are discussed, what is of larger importance is the presence of water in both of those locations. The contrast is less significant and is not the focus.

2. B: *Circum* means around and *ambulate* means to walk, so the literal translation is *to walk around*. However, a reader can also infer from the next few sentences, which constitute a "walk" around an area of the city, that the meaning of the word is to walk around. Choice A is incorrect because there is no mention of flight. Choice C is incorrect; although the narrator moves from location to location and suggests some of the roles the men play in town, there is no mention of seeking work. Choice D is incorrect. Though one is looking around, the vantage points and sights are only available if one is walking and moving about town rather than remaining stationary. Choice E is incorrect; while the narrator mentions many "landsmen," there are no interactions with any of them. There is no conversation. There are no names given. As such, one cannot infer that the meaning of the word is to meet people.

3. D: In several instances, the narrator refers to the men as "landsmen." More specifically, however, at the end of the first paragraph, they are referred to as "pent up," "tied," and "nailed" to their stations. It is mentioned, as well, that many of them look out to sea, with the inference being that they never go. Therefore, choice D is the best answer. Choice A is incorrect; while the narrator notes that many of them seem enthralled by the sea, the passage makes no mention of recruiting them to sea. Choice B is incorrect. There is mention of an artist, but the artist is focused on landscapes, not on men. Choice C is incorrect as the narrator clearly has an affinity for the sea, and though they admire the beauty of the woods, they are focused more on the water that appears in such landscapes than on the woods themselves. Choice E is incorrect; although the narrator notes absent-minded men, it is in reference to what happens when men are able to clear their minds. The narrator believes their focus is on the sea. There is not a generalization that "landsmen" are absent-minded or naïve.

4. A: As the writer describes people traveling from all over, coming out from everywhere, across the city and seeking water in every landscape imaginable, it is likely that the narrator, feeling pulled by the water, believes everyone is enchanted by the sea and would venture there if possible. Choice B is incorrect because, in the paragraph about the painting, it is clear that the stream is important. This suggests that the writer, while valuing the sea perhaps above all, still believes water to be the most important element of any landscape. Choice C is incorrect; the description of all people flocking to the sea suggests the writer wouldn't be confident in that statement. Choice D is incorrect; in reference to the prairie, the narrator notes that the one thing the prairie is "wanting" is water. Choice E is incorrect; in the passage, the city seems not to have value beyond its proximity to water. There is no language describing the city and no focus on the city itself in the way the narrator focuses on the water.

5. B: The writer describes everything as sleepy until getting to the enchanted water. Even the path meanders and has movement, as do the shaking leaves. Everything moves from hollow and sleepy to alive and moving, suggesting the water is what makes things come alive. Choice A is incorrect because there is no reference to the season, though the "hollow" trees and smoke suggest autumn or winter. Choice C is incorrect; the description of the sleepy scene comes well before the narrator gets to the prairie and Niagara Falls. Choice D is incorrect because while there is a contrast between those fields and the city, they are too far separated for that connection to be clear, and, again, the focus is on how the water brings life and enchantment, not on elements of the city. Finally, choice E is incorrect because while the artist's goal is to create something dreamy, the magic element is the water, not sleep. The language is figurative, not literal.

6. B: The passage notes that a comprehensive assessment includes a battery of standard assessments as well as consideration of history and extenuating or aggravating circumstances (like poverty, drug abuse etc.). Choice A includes only some of the standard assessments and so is incorrect. The passage notes that choice C, analyzing just the symptoms, should be avoided so that is incorrect. Choice D includes only part of the assessments without attention to history and other concerns that should be evaluated. Finally, as the passage notes, choice E is only part of the equation so that is also incorrect.

7. C: As the passage notes at the end, there does not seem to be, at this time, a clear way to assess what strengths a family may bring to the table, and this is a shortcoming considering that that should be part of the overall evaluation. Choice A is incorrect because that is a factor that is currently considered, as are choice B and choice D. Finally, choice E is not noted in the passage, though children's welfare is discussed as well as a child's ability to stay with a family.

8. D: The passage notes, in particular, that a comprehensive assessment must look beyond the here and now and consider patterns of behavior over time. Therefore, time is one of the biggest factors in understanding the full picture. Choice A, choice B, choice C, and choice E are all noted in the passage as contributing factors and therefore, in and of themselves, they could not be considered the biggest factor in assessment.

9. B: According to the passage, the primary goal of these assessments is to determine the best intervention strategy to support the child. Choice A is incorrect; while child welfare may dictate foster care or another solution, this is not necessarily preparation for parental termination. Choice C is incorrect as well. While foster care may be an option, it is not the only one. In fact, the passage seems to stress solutions that would enable a child to stay in the home. Choice D is incorrect. This is part of the assessment, but not part of the comprehensive plan. Finally, choice E is incorrect. Though the assessment may find neglect, the comprehensive plan is designed to find the best solution.

10. E: According to the passage, the assessments begin when the child enters the welfare system. Choice A is not noted as a cause, although signing up for services is a self-report of need. Choice B, choice C, and choice D, similarly, may trigger entrance into a child welfare system; however, they are not the only triggers and are therefore too narrow as answers.

11. C: According to the passage, time is the biggest factor in determining what constitutes a drought. Choice A is contradicted by the passage, which notes that some natural wetlands experience droughts as well. Choice B is incorrect because although it is hinted at, there isn't much discussion about the potential long-term impact of droughts on regions. Choice D may be implied by the passage as it refers to drought not being a regional problem, but it is not the focus of the passage. Choice E is incorrect as the passage contradicts the idea of seasonal causes for droughts.

12. D: The passage notes, in particular, that the concept of droughts being relegated to regions is incorrect. They occur everywhere, over periods of time. Choice A, choice B, choice C, and choice E are incorrect as the passage specifically notes that all regions are susceptible.

13. A: The passage notes that some areas are further endangered by wet periods prior to a drought because the growth of vegetation creates fuel for potential fires once there is a lack of sufficient water. Choice B is incorrect as vegetation is not a determining factor for drought. Choice C is incorrect as this correlation is not noted. The growth occurs because of the abundance of water at the present time and the passage notes time as the most important factor. Therefore, a short period of water shortages or abundance does not impact droughts. Choice D is incorrect; that conclusion cannot be drawn given the information. Some areas may experience those fluctuations, some may not. It depends on the region and that is not specified. Finally, choice E is incorrect. While periods of rain and abundant water may create wetlands, it may have little long-term impact on arid landscapes.

14. E: The passage notes, in the final paragraph, that water's primary purpose is to sustain the ecosystem or provide for human use. Choice A is incorrect. While crops are noted in the passage for their water consumption, it is not a complete answer. Choice B and choice D are both processes that water is involved in, but they are not its purpose, according to the passage. Finally, choice C may be a role water fulfills, but it is only part of its function, so that is incorrect.

15. B: A dry season is not enough. A drought is defined as a prolonged period without water. Dry seasons occur naturally, but when they continue for extended periods, beyond normal fluctuations, that is when a drought occurs. Choice A is incorrect. While the damage and risk of effects are more severe during a growing season that requires rain, that is not what defines a drought. Choice C is incorrect, as season has little impact on occurrence. Choice D is incorrect; the consequences do not determine the drought, though certainly amplifies the impact. Finally, choice E is incorrect; droughts do not always happen in or near wetlands.

16. D: The primary principle behind the design is to increase versatility. Choice A and choice E are both incorrect. While these are noted in the final paragraphs as added benefits, the primary goal of the DuAxel is to enable the rover to traverse difficult terrain. Choice B and choice C are incorrect as well. While these may be inferred, they are not explicitly noted as benefits and, therefore, not the primary principle behind the design.

17. C: The passage specifically notes that the advantages of this rover design enable it to explore and gather data from important geological features that may have previously been inaccessible with the single-axle design. Choice A is incorrect as other rovers are also able to traverse large areas. Choice B is incorrect as it is an incomplete answer. Craters and crevasses are only two of the geological features the design gives access to. Choice D is incorrect. There is no specific mention of subterranean spaces, though it can be inferred that those spaces would also be accessible. Finally, choice E is incorrect. The Mojave is where the design was tested, not what it was designed for.

18. B: The passage describes a variety of environmental landscapes the rover has already been exposed to, but it notes that it has not yet been cleared for use on icy landscapes. Choice A, choice C, and choice D are all landscapes that the rover has been tested on or has been exposed to. Choice E is incorrect; this is the one landscape not mentioned in the passage.

19. E: The Mojave Desert is the region that best resembles the surface of Mars and so is best suited for testing. Choice A is incorrect because, although the JPL is mentioned in the article, proximity doesn't appear to be a factor. Choice B is incorrect; while that is true, it is not the complete reason. In fact, other areas of the U.S. have visible geological layers, yet they were not selected. Choice C is incorrect. While the rover may be exposed to significant environmental temperatures, that isn't noted as reasoning in the passage. Choice D is incorrect. While this could be true due to its suitability, that conclusion is not clear in the passage provided.

20. A: The final paragraph notes that part of the design includes the ability to scale with additional axles to provide even more versatility and functionality. Choice B is incorrect. While outside knowledge might reveal that the rover will not return from the Mars trip, it's not discussed in this passage. Choice C is incorrect because, although it is suggested, that's not clearly determined here, nor is the rover's ability to handle that environment. Choice D is incorrect. Though the passage discusses ways to increase versatility and functionality, there is no discussion of adding robotic arms. Similarly, choice E is not noted as an option for future use.

21. E: The passage notes that 40% of carbon dioxide pollution comes from energy production. Therefore, reducing our reliance on fossil fuels for energy production would have the biggest impact on climate change. Choice A is incorrect. While vehicles are a contributor to carbon emissions, they're not identified in the article. Choice B is incorrect. While carbon dioxide is a greenhouse gas, the others aren't discussed in this passage. Choice C is incorrect. While funding research will have an impact, the research must deliver actionable solutions. Research is not enough. Choice D is incorrect. Though the article discusses the impact of this research on green jobs, green jobs are an outcome of our efforts, not an active solution.

22. C: According to the passage, one of the primary goals of research is to make off-shore wind production more affordable and, as a result, a more viable solution. Choice A is incorrect. The passage notes the impact they will have on power production; it does not suggest power consumption data. Choice B is incorrect because the passage already presents data suggesting that research has been completed. Choice D is incorrect. While the passage discusses the success of solar in comparison to wind, the goal of the research is not to have wind surpass solar. Choice E is incorrect. While research will be conducted regarding how off-shore wind may impact fishing and coastal communities, shipping is not mentioned.

23. D: The primary assertion of the passage is that combatting the climate crisis will take a significant shift in how we produce power in the U.S. Choice A is incorrect. The passage presents both solar and wind options but does not argue that either is necessarily superior. Instead, they are part of the larger solution. Choice B is incorrect. While there is significant investment in wind right now, it is unclear how it will compete with solar in the coming years. Choice C is incorrect. Though job creation is discussed as a benefit of investment in green solutions, it's not the primary focus of the passage. Choice E is incorrect because even though the DOE is playing a big role in funding research, there is no indication of the larger role they will play.

24. E: The passage focuses on the fact that, over the next decade, wind energy will increase and solar costs will decrease and be more affordable. Choice A is incorrect. Though this idea is hinted at, there is no detailed discussion of greater access. Choice B is incorrect because it is the opposite of the facts stated in the passage. Choice C is mentioned, but not given a timeline and so is incorrect. Choice D is also incorrect. While many options for research are discussed, there is no timeline given for their inclusion.

25. B: Scaling up means to increase at a reasonable, typically incremental, and manageable rate. Choice A, choice D, and choice E are incorrect because they don't reflect the true meaning. Choice C is incorrect because it would imply physical growth, such as the height of windmills, rather than their proliferation.

Situational Judgment

1. A (Most effective)

2. C (Least effective)

3. D (Most effective)

4. C (Least effective)

5. B (Most effective)

6. D (Least effective)

7. C (Most effective)

8. B (Least effective)

9. A (Most effective)

10. E (Least effective)

11. A (Most effective)

12. D (Least effective)

13. B (Most effective)

14. E (Least effective)

15. A (Most effective)

16. D (Least effective)

17. E (Most effective)

18. D (Least effective)

19. E (Most effective)

20. C (Least effective)

21. B or E (Most effective)

22. A (Least effective)

23. C (Most effective)

24. A (Least effective)

25. C (Most effective)

26. D (Least effective)

27. D (Most effective)

28. B (Least effective)

29. B (Most effective)

30. A (Least effective)

31. C or D (Most effective)

32. B (Least effective)

33. D (Most effective)

34. C (Least effective)

35. E (Most effective)

36. B (Least effective)

37. B (Most effective)

38. A (Least effective)

39. B (Most effective)

40. C (Least effective)

41. E (Most effective)

42. C (Least effective)

43. A (Most effective)

44. D (Least effective)

45. E (Most effective)

46. A or C (Least effective)

47. B (Most effective)

48. A or E (Least effective)

49. C (Most effective)

50. B (Least effective)

Physical Science

1. D: The rate at which a chemical reaction occurs does not depend on the amount of mass lost, since the law of conservation of mass (or matter) states that in a chemical reaction there is no loss of mass.

2. B: The oxidation number of the hydrogen in CaH_2 is –1. One of the general rules for determining oxidation states applies specifically to hydrogen: when hydrogen is bonded to a nonmetal, its oxidation state is +1, but when hydrogen is bonded to a metal, its oxidation state is –1. An ion is a charged version of an element. The oxidation number for an atom is also referred to as the oxidation state. It can be used to describe the number of electrons that must be added or removed from an atom in order to convert the atom to its elemental form.

3. A: Boron does not exist as a diatomic molecule. The other possible answer choices, fluorine, oxygen, and nitrogen, all exist as diatomic molecules. A diatomic molecule always appears in nature as a pair: the word *diatomic* means "having two atoms." With the exception of astatine, all of the halogens are diatomic. Chemistry students often use the mnemonic BrINClHOF (pronounced "brinkelhoff") to remember all of the diatomic elements: bromine, iodine, nitrogen, chlorine, hydrogen, oxygen, and fluorine. Note that not all of these diatomic elements are halogens.

4. A: A limiting reactant is entirely used up by the chemical reaction. Limiting reactants control the extent of the reaction and determine the quantity of the product. A reducing agent is a substance that reduces the amount of another substance by losing electrons. A reagent is any substance used in a chemical reaction. Some of the most common reagents in the laboratory are sodium hydroxide and hydrochloric acid. The behavior and properties of these substances are known, so they can be effectively used to produce predictable reactions in an experiment.

5. D: The mass of 7.35 mol water is 132 grams. You should be able to find the mass of various chemical compounds when you are given the number of moles. The information required to perform this function is included on the periodic table. To solve this problem, find the molecular mass of water by finding the respective weights of hydrogen and oxygen. Remember that water contains two hydrogen molecules and one oxygen molecule. The molecular mass of hydrogen is roughly 1, and the molecular mass of oxygen is roughly 16. A molecule of water, then, has approximately 18 grams of mass. Multiply this by 7.35 mol, and you will obtain the answer 132.3, which is closest to answer choice C.

6. E: Of these orbitals, the last to fill is 4f. Orbitals fill in the following order: 1s, 2s, 2p, 3s, 3p, 4s, 3d, 4p, 5s, 4d, 5p, 6s, 4f, 5d, 6p, 7s, 5f, 6d, and 7p. The number is the orbital number, and the letter is the sublevel identification. Sublevel s has one orbital and can hold a maximum of two electrons. Sublevel p has three orbitals and can hold a maximum of six electrons. Sublevel d has five orbitals and can hold a maximum of 10 electrons. Sublevel f has seven orbitals and can hold a maximum of 14 electrons.

7. A: Chemical composition is not one of the physical properties used to classify minerals. The five major physical properties used to classify minerals are luster, hardness, cleavage, streak, and form. There is a separate classification system based on the chemical composition of minerals.

8. C: On the Mohs scale of mineral hardness, talc has the lowest possible score (a one). Diamond is a ten, which is the highest possible score, and gypsum and fluorite have a score of two and four, respectively. Quartz has a score of seven. Minerals can always scratch minerals that have a Mohs score lower than their own.

9. C: When water changes directly from a solid to a gas, skipping the liquid state, it is known as sublimation. It typically occurs when snow or ice is exposed to direct sunlight, and it is possible at unusually low atmospheric pressure points.

10. B: Stratigraphic dating is not a radiometric dating process because it does not consider the radioactive properties of materials to estimate their dates. Instead, it relies on the Law of Superposition to estimate relative ages by comparing the relative depths of materials.

11. B: The first law of classical thermodynamics states that energy can neither be created nor destroyed. The zeroth law is concerned with thermodynamic equilibrium, and the second and third laws discuss entropy. There is no fourth law of thermodynamics.

12. A: The formula for calculating kinetic energy is $\frac{1}{2}mv^2$, where m = mass and v = velocity. Kinetic energy is defined as the energy of an object in motion. Potential energy, or stored energy, is measured using the formula mgh, where m = mass, g = gravity, and h = height.

13. E: A solution that contains more hydroxide ions than hydrogen ions is a base, and bases have a pH greater than 7, so the only possible answer is E, 9.

14. B: Magnesium oxide cannot be found on the periodic table because it is a compound of two elements.

15. B: Coulomb's law describes the electric force between two charged particles. It states that like charges repel and opposite charges attract, and the greater their distance, the less force they will exert on each other.

16. E: The mass of 1.0 mol oxygen gas is 32 grams. The molar mass of oxygen can be obtained from the periodic table. In most versions of the table, the molar mass of the element is directly beneath the full name of the element. There is a little trick to this question. Oxygen is a diatomic molecule, which means that it always appears in pairs. In order to determine the mass in grams of 1.0 mol of oxygen gas, then, you must double the molar mass. The listed mass is 16, so the correct answer to the problem is 32.

17. D: Gamma radiation has no charge. This form of electromagnetic radiation can travel a long distance and can penetrate the human body. Sunlight and radio waves are both examples of gamma radiation. Alpha radiation has a 2+ charge. It only travels short distances and cannot penetrate clothing or skin. Radium and uranium both emit alpha radiation. Beta radiation has a 1– charge. It can travel several feet through the air and is capable of penetrating the skin. This kind of radiation can be damaging to health over a long period of exposure. There is no such thing as delta or zeta radiation.

18. B: To convert degrees Kelvin to degrees Celsius, simply subtract 273. To convert degrees Celsius to degrees Kelvin, simply add 273. Thus, 119 K is equivalent to –154 degrees Celsius.

19. B: The *joule* is the SI unit of energy. Energy is the ability to do work or generate heat. In regard to electrical energy, a joule is the amount of electrical energy required to pass a current of one ampere through a resistance of one ohm for one second. In physical or mechanical terms, the joule is the amount of energy required for a force of one newton to act over a distance of one meter. The *ohm* is a unit of electrical resistance. The *henry* is a unit of inductance. The *newton* is a unit of force. The *tesla* is a unit of magnetic field intensity.

20. A: A *mass spectrometer* separates gaseous ions according to their mass-to-charge ratio. This machine is used to distinguish the various elements in a piece of matter. An *interferometer* measures the wavelength of light by comparing the interference phenomena of two waves: an experimental wave and a reference wave. A *magnetometer* measures the direction and magnitude of a magnetic field. A *gas chromatograph* separates compounds by injecting a mixture with a carrier gas into a mobile phase and a stationary phase. Finally, a *capacitance meter* measures the capacitance of a capacitor. Some sophisticated capacitance meters may also measure inductance, leakage, and equivalent series resistance.

Table Reading

1. A
2. C
3. A
4. D
5. D
6. D
7. D
8. C
9. B
10. B
11. B
12. D
13. E
14. E
15. B
16. E
17. C
18. B
19. A
20. E
21. A
22. B
23. D
24. A
25. E
26. C
27. D
28. C
29. A
30. B
31. E
32. E
33. A
34. C
35. C
36. A
37. D
38. A
39. D
40. B

Instrument Comprehension

1. A

2. C

3. D

4. C

5. A

6. B

7. D

8. B

9. A

10. B

11. C

12. D

13. D

14. B

15. C

16. A

17. B

18. A

19. A

20. D

21. D

22. B

23. A

24. C

25. A

Block Counting

1. 11: 2 on the back, 4 on the left, 1 on the right, 2 on the top, 2 on the bottom.

2. 5: 1 on the front, 1 on the back, 3 on the right.

3. 5: 3 on the front, 1 on the left, 1 on the right.

4. 4: 1 on the back, 3 on the bottom.

5. 7: 1 on the back, 1 on the left, 4 on the top, 1 on the bottom.

6. 5: 1 on the front, 1 on the back, 3 on the bottom.

7. 3: 1 on the back, 1 on the right, 1 on the top.

8. 7: 1 on the back, 2 on the left, 4 on the bottom.

9. 4: 1 on the front, 1 on the back, 2 on the top.

10. 5: 1 on the back, 1 on the left, 3 on the top.

11. 6: 1 on the front, 1 on the back, 2 on the top, 2 on the bottom.

12. 5: 1 on the front, 2 on the back, 2 on the bottom.

13. 5: 2 on the left, 2 on the right, 1 on the bottom.

14. 3: 2 on the back, 1 on the bottom.

15. 5: 1 on the front, 1 on the back, 1 on the left, 1 on the top, 1 on the bottom.

16. 5: 1 on the left, 1 on the right, 1 on the top, 2 on the bottom.

17. 5: 1 on the left, 1 on the right, 2 on the top, 1 on the bottom.

18. 3: 3 on the bottom.

19. 5: 1 on the back, 1 on the left, 1 on the right, 2 on the bottom.

20. 6: 4 on the front, 1 on the back, 1 on the bottom.

21. 8: 2 on the front, 2 on the back, 4 on the top.

22. 12: 2 on the left, 2 on the right, 4 on the top, 4 on the bottom.

23. 6: 1 on the left, 1 on the top, 4 on the bottom.

24. 6: 1 on the front, 1 on the back, 1 on the left, 3 on the bottom.

25. 4: 1 on the back, 1 on the top, 2 on the bottom.

26. 4: 1 on the back, 1 on the top, 2 on the bottom.

27. 5: 1 on the front, 2 on the back, 1 on the top, 1 on the bottom.

28. 5: 1 on the left, 1 on the right, 1 on the top, 2 on the bottom.

29. 4: 1 on the left, 1 on the right, 2 on the top.

30. 6: 2 on the left, 2 on the right, 1 on the top, 1 on the bottom.

Aviation Information

1. D: The basic components of a fixed-wing aircraft include: wings, fuselage, tail assembly, landing gear, power plant, and flight controls and control surfaces. The flight envelope is not a component of an aircraft. The flight envelope is the collective input of forces that a pilot experiences in flight: lift, gravity, thrust, and drag.

2. B: Both planes and helicopters experience the four fundamental forces: lift, weight, thrust, and drag. Operating weight is a type of weight force, and induced drag is a type of drag. However, translational lift, the extra lift a helicopter experiences when traveling in a forward direction, is a force specific to helicopters.

3. C: When the plane is first approaching the runway, the Runway Centerline Lighting System lights are white. Once the plane gets within 3,000 feet of the runway, the lights start to blink white and red. Once the plane gets within 1,000 feet of the runway, the lights become solid red. Therefore, the range at which the lights are blinking white and red is 1,000 to 3,000 feet.

4. D: The rudder controls the yaw, or motion of the plane around its vertical axis, by swinging to the right or the left. The elevators control the plane's pitch, or movement around the lateral axis. The throttle is a primary flight control that manipulates the amount of thrust being produced by the engines. The flaps are a secondary flight control that are raised or lowered to adjust the lift or drag. Ailerons extend from the trailing edges of the wings and can be manipulated to control the roll or motion around the longitudinal axis.

5. A: Lower temperatures and lower humidity are associated with higher density air. Higher pressures are also a quality of higher density air, and pressure decreases as altitude increases. Therefore, a lower altitude will result in higher density air, and a higher altitude will result in less density in the surrounding air.

6. C: The rudders are controlled with left and right pedals. A joystick controls the ailerons and elevators. Both the cyclic and collective are helicopter controls. The cyclic is a stick that tilts the main rotor. The collective is a tube with a handle and throttle that controls the angle of the main rotor blades.

7. B: Unlike a descent, the nose should be angled upwards. The pilot continues to pull back on the throttle in order to reduce the amount of generated thrust and the air speed of the plane.

8. E: Shallow, medium, and steep are the three different classes for turns and are not used to describe the wings of an aircraft. Cantilever and semi-cantilever are used to describe the internal support structures of the wing. Dihedral and anhedral describe the angle the wings make with the horizontal plane. High-, mid-, and low-wing describe where the wings are attached to the fuselage. Straight, sweep, and delta describe the shape of the wings.

9. E: A stall is commonly caused by an insufficient amount of thrust to maintain air speed. Angling the nose downward and increasing the throttle helps to generate enough airspeed so that the control surfaces are effective and can be used to pull out of the dive.

10. D: A medium turn has a bank of roughly 20 to 45 degrees. Since 30 is in between 20 and 45, a turn with a 30-degree bank would be considered a medium turn. A shallow turn describes a turn with a bank of less than 20 degrees. A steep turn has a bank greater than 45 degrees. Glides and descents are other maneuvers and do not describe types of turns.

11. A: Ailerons are attached to the trailing edge of a wing and run from the middle of the wing to the tip. Flaps are attached to the trailing edge of a wing and run from the fuselage to the middle of the wing. The elevator is a part of the tail assembly that is positioned along the trailing edges of the horizontal stabilizers. The rudders are connected to the trailing edge of the vertical stabilizer. The stringer is a support structure that runs the length of the fuselage.

12. C: Visual runways are typical of small airports and have no markings. Because of this, the pilot must be able to see the ground in order to land. Flight lines, or aprons, are not runways. They are areas where aircraft are parked for servicing. A precision instrument runway includes markings and gives the pilot feedback on both horizontal and vertical position. A taxiway is not a runway but a path for aircraft that connects to runways. A non-precision instrument runway has aiming points along the center of the runway and may be able to be approached using instruments.

13. B: Runway edge lights run the length of the runway on both sides. An Approach Lighting System is a set of lights that indicate the end of the runway from which descending aircraft should arrive. Taxiway edge lights run the length of the taxiway on both sides. Visual Approach Slope Indicators indicate the lower and upper glide path limits and keep planes clear of obstructions, to an extent. Runway end lights run the width of both ends of the runway.

14. D: Pushing the joystick to the right raises the right aileron and lowers the left aileron. Similarly, pushing the joystick to the left raises the left aileron and lowers the right aileron. The rudder is not usually controlled by the joystick but by left and right pedals. Pressing the right pedal swings the rudder to the right. The elevator lowers when the joystick is pushed forward.

15. C: The mean camber line runs along the inside of the wing, dividing it into top and bottom halves of equal thickness. The chord is the distance from the leading edge of a wing to the trailing edge. The chord line runs through the wing from leading edge to trailing edge, dividing it into upper and lower surfaces. The planform is the shape of the wings when viewed from overhead. The dihedral angle is the angle the wings make with the horizontal plane if they are not parallel to it.

16. A: "Truss" and "monocoque" are used to describe the fuselage's structural integrity, whether by triangular arrangements of steel or aluminum tubing or by bulkheads, stringers, and formers. The empennage is also known as the tail assembly. The flight envelope consists of the four forces relevant to flight: lift, gravity, thrust, and drag. The landing gear can either have a tricycle arrangement or a conventional arrangement. The flight attitude consists of roll, pitch, and yaw.

17. B: Induced drag is a drag force (resistance to forward movement) that results from the wings generating lift. As the wings redirect oncoming wind downward, this causes induced drag. Thrust is the forward movement of the aircraft, not the resistance to forward movement. Translational lift is the lift a helicopter experiences when traveling in a forward direction. Profile drag is the drag a plane experiences as it moves through the air. The transverse flow effect is an effect specific to helicopters. If the main rotor increases the flow of air over the rear part of the main rotor disc, then the rear part will have a smaller angle of attack. There will be less lift in the rear part of the rotor disc as a result.

18. E: Runways are named according to their direction on the compass, ranging from 01 to 36. 20 is in between 18 and 27, which are due south and due west respectively. Since 20 is closer to 18 than 27, the direction of the runway runs closer to south than west. This means it runs south-southwest and north-northeast (SSW and NNE respectively). The "L" in the name indicates that this runway is located on the left but is not relevant to its direction.

19. D: The rudder is employed to counter any undesired yaw or to introduce desired yaw. The throttle is set to achieve a speed suitable to the desired type of turn. The ailerons bank the wings, and the elevators raise the nose to establish the rate of turn. Trim systems exist mainly to ease the work of the pilot. Typically, a pilot first will achieve the desired pitch, power, attitude, and configuration, and then use the trim tabs to resolve the remaining control pressures.

20. D: The collective is not a secondary flight control surface. The collective is a tube running up from the cockpit floor to the left of the pilot. It is used to control the angle of the main rotor blades. Flaps are a secondary flight control surface located on the trailing edges of the wings. They are used to adjust the lift or drag. Fixed and moveable slats are leading-edge devices, which is another secondary flight control surface. Spoilers are secondary flight control surfaces that are attached to the wings to diminish lift and increase drag. Trim systems are attached to the trailing edges of one or more of the primary control surfaces and help to resolve the remaining control pressures a pilot experiences while trimming.

How to Overcome Test Anxiety

Just the thought of taking a test is enough to make most people a little nervous. A test is an important event that can have a long-term impact on your future, so it's important to take it seriously and it's natural to feel anxious about performing well. But just because anxiety is normal, that doesn't mean that it's helpful in test taking, or that you should simply accept it as part of your life. Anxiety can have a variety of effects. These effects can be mild, like making you feel slightly nervous, or severe, like blocking your ability to focus or remember even a simple detail.

If you experience test anxiety—whether severe or mild—it's important to know how to beat it. To discover this, first you need to understand what causes test anxiety.

Causes of Test Anxiety

While we often think of anxiety as an uncontrollable emotional state, it can actually be caused by simple, practical things. One of the most common causes of test anxiety is that a person does not feel adequately prepared for their test. This feeling can be the result of many different issues such as poor study habits or lack of organization, but the most common culprit is time management. Starting to study too late, failing to organize your study time to cover all of the material, or being distracted while you study will mean that you're not well prepared for the test. This may lead to cramming the night before, which will cause you to be physically and mentally exhausted for the test. Poor time management also contributes to feelings of stress, fear, and hopelessness as you realize you are not well prepared but don't know what to do about it.

Other times, test anxiety is not related to your preparation for the test but comes from unresolved fear. This may be a past failure on a test, or poor performance on tests in general. It may come from comparing yourself to others who seem to be performing better or from the stress of living up to expectations. Anxiety may be driven by fears of the future—how failure on this test would affect your educational and career goals. These fears are often completely irrational, but they can still negatively impact your test performance.

Review Video: 3 Reasons You Have Test Anxiety
Visit mometrix.com/academy and enter code: 428468

Elements of Test Anxiety

As mentioned earlier, test anxiety is considered to be an emotional state, but it has physical and mental components as well. Sometimes you may not even realize that you are suffering from test anxiety until you notice the physical symptoms. These can include trembling hands, rapid heartbeat, sweating, nausea, and tense muscles. Extreme anxiety may lead to fainting or vomiting. Obviously, any of these symptoms can have a negative impact on testing. It is important to recognize them as soon as they begin to occur so that you can address the problem before it damages your performance.

Review Video: 3 Ways to Tell You Have Test Anxiety
Visit mometrix.com/academy and enter code: 927847

The mental components of test anxiety include trouble focusing and inability to remember learned information. During a test, your mind is on high alert, which can help you recall information and stay focused for an extended period of time. However, anxiety interferes with your mind's natural processes, causing you to blank out, even on the questions you know well. The strain of testing during anxiety makes it difficult to stay focused, especially on a test that may take several hours. Extreme anxiety can take a huge mental toll, making it difficult not only to recall test information but even to understand the test questions or pull your thoughts together.

Review Video: How Test Anxiety Affects Memory
Visit mometrix.com/academy and enter code: 609003

Effects of Test Anxiety

Test anxiety is like a disease—if left untreated, it will get progressively worse. Anxiety leads to poor performance, and this reinforces the feelings of fear and failure, which in turn lead to poor performances on subsequent tests. It can grow from a mild nervousness to a crippling condition. If allowed to progress, test anxiety can have a big impact on your schooling, and consequently on your future.

Test anxiety can spread to other parts of your life. Anxiety on tests can become anxiety in any stressful situation, and blanking on a test can turn into panicking in a job situation. But fortunately, you don't have to let anxiety rule your testing and determine your grades. There are a number of relatively simple steps you can take to move past anxiety and function normally on a test and in the rest of life.

Review Video: How Test Anxiety Impacts Your Grades
Visit mometrix.com/academy and enter code: 939819

Physical Steps for Beating Test Anxiety

While test anxiety is a serious problem, the good news is that it can be overcome. It doesn't have to control your ability to think and remember information. While it may take time, you can begin taking steps today to beat anxiety.

Just as your first hint that you may be struggling with anxiety comes from the physical symptoms, the first step to treating it is also physical. Rest is crucial for having a clear, strong mind. If you are tired, it is much easier to give in to anxiety. But if you establish good sleep habits, your body and mind will be ready to perform optimally, without the strain of exhaustion. Additionally, sleeping well helps you to retain information better, so you're more likely to recall the answers when you see the test questions.

Getting good sleep means more than going to bed on time. It's important to allow your brain time to relax. Take study breaks from time to time so it doesn't get overworked, and don't study right before bed. Take time to rest your mind before trying to rest your body, or you may find it difficult to fall asleep.

Review Video: The Importance of Sleep for Your Brain
Visit mometrix.com/academy and enter code: 319338

Along with sleep, other aspects of physical health are important in preparing for a test. Good nutrition is vital for good brain function. Sugary foods and drinks may give a burst of energy but this burst is followed by a crash, both physically and emotionally. Instead, fuel your body with protein and vitamin-rich foods.

Also, drink plenty of water. Dehydration can lead to headaches and exhaustion, especially if your brain is already under stress from the rigors of the test. Particularly if your test is a long one, drink water during the breaks. And if possible, take an energy-boosting snack to eat between sections.

Review Video: How Diet Can Affect your Mood
Visit mometrix.com/academy and enter code: 624317

Along with sleep and diet, a third important part of physical health is exercise. Maintaining a steady workout schedule is helpful, but even taking 5-minute study breaks to walk can help get your blood pumping faster and clear your head. Exercise also releases endorphins, which contribute to a positive feeling and can help combat test anxiety.

When you nurture your physical health, you are also contributing to your mental health. If your body is healthy, your mind is much more likely to be healthy as well. So take time to rest, nourish your body with healthy food and water, and get moving as much as possible. Taking these physical steps will make you stronger and more able to take the mental steps necessary to overcome test anxiety.

Mental Steps for Beating Test Anxiety

Working on the mental side of test anxiety can be more challenging, but as with the physical side, there are clear steps you can take to overcome it. As mentioned earlier, test anxiety often stems from lack of preparation, so the obvious solution is to prepare for the test. Effective studying may be the most important weapon you have for beating test anxiety, but you can and should employ several other mental tools to combat fear.

First, boost your confidence by reminding yourself of past success—tests or projects that you aced. If you're putting as much effort into preparing for this test as you did for those, there's no reason you should expect to fail here. Work hard to prepare; then trust your preparation.

Second, surround yourself with encouraging people. It can be helpful to find a study group, but be sure that the people you're around will encourage a positive attitude. If you spend time with others who are anxious or cynical, this will only contribute to your own anxiety. Look for others who are motivated to study hard from a desire to succeed, not from a fear of failure.

Third, reward yourself. A test is physically and mentally tiring, even without anxiety, and it can be helpful to have something to look forward to. Plan an activity following the test, regardless of the outcome, such as going to a movie or getting ice cream.

When you are taking the test, if you find yourself beginning to feel anxious, remind yourself that you know the material. Visualize successfully completing the test. Then take a few deep, relaxing breaths and return to it. Work through the questions carefully but with confidence, knowing that you are capable of succeeding.

Developing a healthy mental approach to test taking will also aid in other areas of life. Test anxiety affects more than just the actual test—it can be damaging to your mental health and even contribute to depression. It's important to beat test anxiety before it becomes a problem for more than testing.

Review Video: Test Anxiety and Depression
Visit mometrix.com/academy and enter code: 904704

Study Strategy

Being prepared for the test is necessary to combat anxiety, but what does being prepared look like? You may study for hours on end and still not feel prepared. What you need is a strategy for test prep. The next few pages outline our recommended steps to help you plan out and conquer the challenge of preparation.

Step 1: Scope Out the Test

Learn everything you can about the format (multiple choice, essay, etc.) and what will be on the test. Gather any study materials, course outlines, or sample exams that may be available. Not only will this help you to prepare, but knowing what to expect can help to alleviate test anxiety.

Step 2: Map Out the Material

Look through the textbook or study guide and make note of how many chapters or sections it has. Then divide these over the time you have. For example, if a book has 15 chapters and you have five days to study, you need to cover three chapters each day. Even better, if you have the time, leave an extra day at the end for overall review after you have gone through the material in depth.

If time is limited, you may need to prioritize the material. Look through it and make note of which sections you think you already have a good grasp on, and which need review. While you are studying, skim quickly through the familiar sections and take more time on the challenging parts. Write out your plan so you don't get lost as you go. Having a written plan also helps you feel more in control of the study, so anxiety is less likely to arise from feeling overwhelmed at the amount to cover.

Step 3: Gather Your Tools

Decide what study method works best for you. Do you prefer to highlight in the book as you study and then go back over the highlighted portions? Or do you type out notes of the important information? Or is it helpful to make flashcards that you can carry with you? Assemble the pens, index cards, highlighters, post-it notes, and any other materials you may need so you won't be distracted by getting up to find things while you study.

If you're having a hard time retaining the information or organizing your notes, experiment with different methods. For example, try color-coding by subject with colored pens, highlighters, or post-it notes. If you learn better by hearing, try recording yourself reading your notes so you can listen while in the car, working out, or simply sitting at your desk. Ask a friend to quiz you from your flashcards, or try teaching someone the material to solidify it in your mind.

Step 4: Create Your Environment

It's important to avoid distractions while you study. This includes both the obvious distractions like visitors and the subtle distractions like an uncomfortable chair (or a too-comfortable couch that makes you want to fall asleep). Set up the best study environment possible: good lighting and a comfortable work area. If background music helps you focus, you may want to turn it on, but otherwise keep the room quiet. If you are using a computer to take notes, be sure you don't have any other windows open, especially applications like social media, games, or anything else that could distract you. Silence your phone and turn off notifications. Be sure to keep water close by so you stay hydrated while you study (but avoid unhealthy drinks and snacks).

Also, take into account the best time of day to study. Are you freshest first thing in the morning? Try to set aside some time then to work through the material. Is your mind clearer in the afternoon or evening? Schedule your study session then. Another method is to study at the same time of day that you will take the test, so that your brain gets used to working on the material at that time and will be ready to focus at test time.

Step 5: Study!

Once you have done all the study preparation, it's time to settle into the actual studying. Sit down, take a few moments to settle your mind so you can focus, and begin to follow your study plan. Don't give in to distractions or let yourself procrastinate. This is your time to prepare so you'll be ready to fearlessly approach the test. Make the most of the time and stay focused.

Of course, you don't want to burn out. If you study too long you may find that you're not retaining the information very well. Take regular study breaks. For example, taking five minutes out of every hour to walk briskly, breathing deeply and swinging your arms, can help your mind stay fresh.

As you get to the end of each chapter or section, it's a good idea to do a quick review. Remind yourself of what you learned and work on any difficult parts. When you feel that you've mastered the material, move on to the next part. At the end of your study session, briefly skim through your notes again.

But while review is helpful, cramming last minute is NOT. If at all possible, work ahead so that you won't need to fit all your study into the last day. Cramming overloads your brain with more information than it can process and retain, and your tired mind may struggle to recall even previously learned information when it is overwhelmed with last-minute study. Also, the urgent nature of cramming and the stress placed on your brain contribute to anxiety. You'll be more likely to go to the test feeling unprepared and having trouble thinking clearly.

So don't cram, and don't stay up late before the test, even just to review your notes at a leisurely pace. Your brain needs rest more than it needs to go over the information again. In fact, plan to finish your studies by noon or early afternoon the day before the test. Give your brain the rest of the day to relax or focus on other things, and get a good night's sleep. Then you will be fresh for the test and better able to recall what you've studied.

Step 6: Take a practice test

Many courses offer sample tests, either online or in the study materials. This is an excellent resource to check whether you have mastered the material, as well as to prepare for the test format and environment.

Check the test format ahead of time: the number of questions, the type (multiple choice, free response, etc.), and the time limit. Then create a plan for working through them. For example, if you have 30 minutes to take a 60-question test, your limit is 30 seconds per question. Spend less time on the questions you know well so that you can take more time on the difficult ones.

If you have time to take several practice tests, take the first one open book, with no time limit. Work through the questions at your own pace and make sure you fully understand them. Gradually work up to taking a test under test conditions: sit at a desk with all study materials put away and set a timer. Pace yourself to make sure you finish the test with time to spare and go back to check your answers if you have time.

After each test, check your answers. On the questions you missed, be sure you understand why you missed them. Did you misread the question (tests can use tricky wording)? Did you forget the information? Or was it something you hadn't learned? Go back and study any shaky areas that the practice tests reveal.

Taking these tests not only helps with your grade, but also aids in combating test anxiety. If you're already used to the test conditions, you're less likely to worry about it, and working through tests until you're scoring well gives you a confidence boost. Go through the practice tests until you feel comfortable, and then you can go into the test knowing that you're ready for it.

Test Tips

On test day, you should be confident, knowing that you've prepared well and are ready to answer the questions. But aside from preparation, there are several test day strategies you can employ to maximize your performance.

First, as stated before, get a good night's sleep the night before the test (and for several nights before that, if possible). Go into the test with a fresh, alert mind rather than staying up late to study.

Try not to change too much about your normal routine on the day of the test. It's important to eat a nutritious breakfast, but if you normally don't eat breakfast at all, consider eating just a protein bar. If you're a coffee drinker, go ahead and have your normal coffee. Just make sure you time it so that the caffeine doesn't wear off right in the middle of your test. Avoid sugary beverages, and drink enough water to stay hydrated but not so much that you need a restroom break 10 minutes into the test. If your test isn't first thing in the morning, consider going for a walk or doing a light workout before the test to get your blood flowing.

Allow yourself enough time to get ready, and leave for the test with plenty of time to spare so you won't have the anxiety of scrambling to arrive in time. Another reason to be early is to select a good seat. It's helpful to sit away from doors and windows, which can be distracting. Find a good seat, get out your supplies, and settle your mind before the test begins.

When the test begins, start by going over the instructions carefully, even if you already know what to expect. Make sure you avoid any careless mistakes by following the directions.

Then begin working through the questions, pacing yourself as you've practiced. If you're not sure on an answer, don't spend too much time on it, and don't let it shake your confidence. Either skip it and come back later, or eliminate as many wrong answers as possible and guess among the remaining ones. Don't dwell on these questions as you continue—put them out of your mind and focus on what lies ahead.

Be sure to read all of the answer choices, even if you're sure the first one is the right answer. Sometimes you'll find a better one if you keep reading. But don't second-guess yourself if you do immediately know the answer. Your gut instinct is usually right. Don't let test anxiety rob you of the information you know.

If you have time at the end of the test (and if the test format allows), go back and review your answers. Be cautious about changing any, since your first instinct tends to be correct, but make sure you didn't misread any of the questions or accidentally mark the wrong answer choice. Look over any you skipped and make an educated guess.

At the end, leave the test feeling confident. You've done your best, so don't waste time worrying about your performance or wishing you could change anything. Instead, celebrate the successful completion of this test. And finally, use this test to learn how to deal with anxiety even better next time.

Review Video: 5 Tips to Beat Test Anxiety
Visit mometrix.com/academy and enter code: 570656

Important Qualification

Not all anxiety is created equal. If your test anxiety is causing major issues in your life beyond the classroom or testing center, or if you are experiencing troubling physical symptoms related to your anxiety, it may be a sign of a serious physiological or psychological condition. If this sounds like your situation, we strongly encourage you to seek professional help.

How to Overcome Your Fear of Math

Not again. You're sitting in math class, look down at your test, and immediately start to panic. Your stomach is in knots, your heart is racing, and you break out in a cold sweat. You're staring at the paper, but everything looks like it's written in a foreign language. Even though you studied, you're blanking out on how to begin solving these problems.

Does this sound familiar? If so, then you're not alone! You may be like millions of other people who experience math anxiety. Anxiety about performing well in math is a common experience for students of all ages. In this article, we'll discuss what math anxiety is, common misconceptions about learning math, and tips and strategies for overcoming math anxiety.

What Is Math Anxiety?

Psychologist Mark H. Ashcraft explains math anxiety as a feeling of tension, apprehension, or fear that interferes with math performance. Having math anxiety negatively impacts people's beliefs about themselves and what they can achieve. It hinders achievement within the math classroom and affects the successful application of mathematics in the real world.

Symptoms and Signs of Math Anxiety

To overcome math anxiety, you must recognize its symptoms. Becoming aware of the signs of math anxiety is the first step in addressing and resolving these fears.

Negative Self-Talk

If you have math anxiety, you've most likely said at least one of these statements to yourself:

- "I hate math."
- "I'm not good at math."
- "I'm not a math person."

The way we speak to ourselves and think about ourselves matters. Our thoughts become our words, our words become our actions, and our actions become our habits. Thinking negatively about math creates a self-fulfilling prophecy. In other words, if you take an idea as a fact, then it will come true because your behaviors will align to match it.

Avoidance

Some people who are fearful or anxious about math will tend to avoid it altogether. Avoidance can manifest in the following ways:

- Lack of engagement with math content
- Not completing homework and other assignments
- Not asking for help when needed
- Skipping class
- Avoiding math-related courses and activities

Avoidance is one of the most harmful impacts of math anxiety. If you steer clear of math at all costs, then you can't set yourself up for the success you deserve.

Lack of Motivation

Students with math anxiety may experience a lack of motivation. They may struggle to find the incentive to get engaged with what they view as a frightening subject. These students are often overwhelmed, making it difficult for them to complete or even start math assignments.

Procrastination

Another symptom of math anxiety is procrastination. Students may voluntarily delay or postpone their classwork and assignments, even if they know there will be a negative consequence for doing so. Additionally, they may choose to wait until the last minute to start projects and homework, even when they know they need more time to put forth their best effort.

Physiological Reactions

Many people with a fear of math experience physiological side effects. These may include an increase in heart rate, sweatiness, shakiness, nausea, and irregular breathing. These symptoms make it difficult to focus on the math content, causing the student even more stress and fear.

Strong Emotional Responses

Math anxiety also affects people on an emotional level. Responding to math content with strong emotions such as panic, anger, or despair can be a sign of math anxiety.

Low Test Scores and Performance

Low achievement can be both a symptom and a cause of math anxiety. When someone does not take the steps needed to perform well on tests and assessments, they are less likely to pass. The more they perform poorly, the more they accept this poor performance as a fact that can't be changed.

Feeling Alone

People who experience math anxiety feel like they are the only ones struggling, even if the math they are working on is challenging to many people. Feeling isolated in what they perceive as failure can trigger tension or nervousness.

Feeling of Permanency

Math anxiety can feel very permanent. You may assume that you are naturally bad at math and always will be. Viewing math as a natural ability rather than a skill that can be learned causes people to believe that nothing will help them improve. They take their current math abilities as fact and assume that they can't be changed. As a result, they give up, stop trying to improve, and avoid engaging with math altogether.

Lack of Confidence

People with low self-confidence in math tend to feel awkward and incompetent when asked to solve a math problem. They don't feel comfortable taking chances or risks when problem-solving because they second-guess themselves and assume they are incorrect. They don't trust in their ability to learn the content and solve problems correctly.

Panic

A general sense of unexplained panic is also a sign of math anxiety. You may feel a sudden sense of fear that triggers physical reactions, even when there is no apparent reason for such a response.

Causes Of Math Anxiety

Math anxiety can start at a young age and may have one or more underlying causes. Common causes of math anxiety include the following:

The Attitude of Parents or Guardians

Parents often put pressure on their children to perform well in school. Although their intentions are usually good, this pressure can lead to anxiety, especially if the student is struggling with a subject or class.

Perhaps your parents or others in your life hold negative predispositions about math based on their own experiences. For instance, if your mother once claimed she was not good at math, then you might have incorrectly interpreted this as a predisposed trait that was passed down to you.

Teacher Influence

Students often pick up on their teachers' attitudes about the content being taught. If a teacher is happy and excited about math, students are more likely to mirror these emotions. However, if a teacher lacks enthusiasm or genuine interest, then students are more inclined to disengage.

Teachers have a responsibility to cultivate a welcoming classroom culture that is accepting of mistakes. When teachers blame students for not understanding a concept, they create a hostile classroom environment where mistakes are not tolerated. This tension increases student stress and anxiety, creating conditions that are not conducive to inquiry and learning. Instead, when teachers normalize mistakes as a natural part of the problem-solving process, they give their students the freedom to explore and grapple with the math content. In such an environment, students feel comfortable taking chances because they are not afraid of being wrong.

Students need teachers that can help when they're having problems understanding difficult concepts. In doing so, educators may need to change how they teach the content. Since different people have unique learning styles, it's the job of the teacher to adapt to the needs of each student. Additionally, teachers should encourage students to explore alternate problem-solving strategies, even if it's not the preferred method of the educator.

Fear of Being Wrong

Embarrassing situations can be traumatic, especially for young children and adolescents. These experiences can stay with people through their adult lives. Those with math anxiety may experience a fear of being wrong, especially in front of a group of peers. This fear can be paralyzing, interfering with the student's concentration and ability to focus on the problem at hand.

Timed Assessments

Timed assessments can help improve math fluency, but they often create unnecessary pressure for students to complete an unrealistic number of problems within a specified timeframe. Many studies have shown that timed assessments often result in increased levels of anxiety, reducing a student's overall competence and ability to problem-solve.

Debunking Math Myths

There are lots of myths about math that are related to the causes and development of math-related anxiety. Although these myths have been proven to be false, many people take them as fact. Let's go over a few of the most common myths about learning math.

Myth: Men Are Better at Math Than Women

Math has a reputation for being a male-dominant subject, but this doesn't mean that men are inherently better at math than women. Many famous mathematical discoveries have been made by women. Katherine Johnson, Dame Mary Lucy Cartwright, and Marjorie Lee Brown are just a few of the many famous women mathematicians. Expecting to be good or bad at math because of your gender sets you up for stress and confusion. Math is a skill that can be learned, just like cooking or riding a bike.

Myth: There Is Only One Good Way to Solve Math Problems

There are many ways to get the correct answer when it comes to math. No two people have the same brain, so everyone takes a slightly different approach to problem-solving. Moreover, there isn't one way of problem-solving that's superior to another. Your way of working through a problem might differ from someone else's, and that is okay. Math can be a highly individualized process, so the best method for you should be the one that makes you feel the most comfortable and makes the most sense to you.

Myth: Math Requires a Good Memory

For many years, mathematics was taught through memorization. However, learning in such a way hinders the development of critical thinking and conceptual understanding. These skill sets are much more valuable than basic memorization. For instance, you might be great at memorizing mathematical formulas, but if you don't understand what they mean, then you can't apply them to different scenarios in the real world. When a student is working from memory, they are limited in the strategies available to them to problem-solve. In other words, they assume there is only one correct way to do the math, which is the method they memorized. Having a variety of problem-solving options can help students figure out which method works best for them. Additionally, it provides students with a better understanding of how and why certain mathematical strategies work. While memorization can be helpful in some instances, it is not an absolute requirement for mathematicians.

Myth: Math Is Not Creative

Math requires imagination and intuition. Contrary to popular belief, it is a highly creative field. Mathematical creativity can help in developing new ways to think about and solve problems. Many people incorrectly assume that all things are either creative or analytical. However, this black-and-white view is limiting because the field of mathematics involves both creativity and logic.

Myth: Math Isn't Supposed To Be Fun

Whoever told you that math isn't supposed to be fun is a liar. There are tons of math-based activities and games that foster friendly competition and engagement. Math is often best learned through play, and lots of mobile apps and computer games exemplify this.

Additionally, math can be an exceptionally collaborative and social experience. Studying or working through problems with a friend often makes the process a lot more fun. The excitement and satisfaction of solving a difficult problem with others is quite rewarding. Math can be fun if you look for ways to make it more collaborative and enjoyable.

Myth: Not Everyone Is Capable of Learning Math

There's no such thing as a "math person." Although many people think that you're either good at math or you're not, this is simply not true. Everyone is capable of learning and applying mathematics. However, not everyone learns the same way. Since each person has a different learning style, the trick is to find the strategies and learning tools that work best for you. Some people learn best through hands-on experiences, and others find success through the use of visual aids. Others are auditory learners and learn best by hearing and listening. When people are overwhelmed or feel that math is too hard, it's often because they haven't found the learning strategy that works best for them.

Myth: Good Mathematicians Work Quickly and Never Make Mistakes

There is no prize for finishing first in math. It's not a race, and speed isn't a measure of your ability. Good mathematicians take their time to ensure their work is accurate. As you gain more experience and practice, you will naturally become faster and more confident.

Additionally, everyone makes mistakes, including good mathematicians. Mistakes are a normal part of the problem-solving process, and they're not a bad thing. The important thing is that we take the time to learn from our mistakes, understand where our misconceptions are, and move forward.

Myth: You Don't Need Math in the Real World

Our day-to-day lives are so infused with mathematical concepts that we often don't even realize when we're using math in the real world. In fact, most people tend to underestimate how much we do math in our everyday lives. It's involved in an enormous variety of daily activities such as shopping, baking, finances, and gardening, as well as in many careers, including architecture, nursing, design, and sales.

Tips and Strategies for Overcoming Math Anxiety

If your anxiety is getting in the way of your level of mathematical engagement, then there are lots of steps you can take. Check out the strategies below to start building confidence in math today.

Focus on Understanding, Not Memorization

Don't drive yourself crazy trying to memorize every single formula or mathematical process. Instead, shift your attention to understanding concepts. Those who prioritize memorization over conceptual understanding tend to have lower achievement levels in math. Students who memorize may be able to complete some math, but they don't understand the process well enough to apply it to different situations. Memorization comes with time and practice, but it won't help alleviate math anxiety. On the other hand, conceptual understanding will give you the building blocks of knowledge you need to build up your confidence.

Replace Negative Self-Talk with Positive Self-Talk

Start to notice how you think about yourself. Whenever you catch yourself thinking something negative, try replacing that thought with a positive affirmation. Instead of continuing the negative thought, pause to reframe the situation. For ideas on how to get started, take a look at the table below:

Instead of thinking...	Try thinking...
"I can't do this math." "I'm not a math person."	"I'm up for the challenge, and I'm training my brain in math."
"This problem is too hard."	"This problem is hard, so this might take some time and effort. I know I can do this."
"I give up."	"What strategies can help me solve this problem?"
"I made a mistake, so I'm not good at this."	"Everyone makes mistakes. Mistakes help me to grow and understand."
"I'll never be smart enough."	"I can figure this out, and I am smart enough."

Practice Mindfulness

Practicing mindfulness and focusing on your breathing can help alleviate some of the physical symptoms of math anxiety. By taking deep breaths, you can remind your nervous system that you are not in immediate danger. Doing so will reduce your heart rate and help with any irregular breathing or shakiness. Taking the edge off of the physiological effects of anxiety will clear your mind, allowing your brain to focus its energy on problem-solving.

Do Some Math Every Day

Think about learning math as if you were learning a foreign language. If you don't use it, you lose it. If you don't practice your math skills regularly, you'll have a harder time achieving comprehension and fluency. Set some amount of time aside each day, even if it's just for a few minutes, to practice. It might take some discipline to build a habit around this, but doing so will help increase your mathematical self-assurance.

Use All of Your Resources

Everyone has a different learning style, and there are plenty of resources out there to support all learners. When you get stuck on a math problem, think about the tools you have access to, and use them when applicable. Such resources may include flashcards, graphic organizers, study guides, interactive notebooks, and peer study groups. All of these are great tools to accommodate your individual learning style. Finding the tools and resources that work for your learning style will give you the confidence you need to succeed.

Realize That You Aren't Alone

Remind yourself that lots of other people struggle with math anxiety, including teachers, nurses, and even successful mathematicians. You aren't the only one who panics when faced with a new or challenging problem. It's probably much more common than you think. Realizing that you aren't alone in your experience can help put some distance between yourself and the emotions you feel about math. It also helps to normalize the anxiety and shift your perspective.

Ask Questions

If there's a concept you don't understand and you've tried everything you can, then it's okay to ask for help! You can always ask your teacher or professor for help. If you're not learning math in a traditional classroom, you may want to join a study group, work with a tutor, or talk to your friends. More often than not, you aren't the only one of your peers who needs clarity on a mathematical concept. Seeking understanding is a great way to increase self-confidence in math.

Remember That There's More Than One Way To Solve A Problem

Since everyone learns differently, it's best to focus on understanding a math problem with an approach that makes sense to you. If the way it's being taught is confusing to you, don't give up. Instead, work to understand the problem using a different technique. There's almost always more than one problem-solving method when it comes to math. Don't get stressed if one of them doesn't make sense to you. Instead, shift your focus to what does make sense. Chances are high that you know more than you think you do.

Visualization

Visualization is the process of creating images in your mind's eye. Picture yourself as a successful, confident mathematician. Think about how you would feel and how you would behave. What would your work area look like? How would you organize your belongings? The more you focus on something, the more likely you are to achieve it. Visualizing teaches your brain that you can achieve whatever it is that you want. Thinking about success in mathematics will lead to acting like a successful mathematician. This, in turn, leads to actual success.

Focus on the Easiest Problems First

To increase your confidence when working on a math test or assignment, try solving the easiest problems first. Doing so will remind you that you are successful in math and that you do have what it takes. This process will increase your belief in yourself, giving you the confidence you need to tackle more complex problems.

Find a Support Group

A study buddy, tutor, or peer group can go a long way in decreasing math-related anxiety. Such support systems offer lots of benefits, including a safe place to ask questions, additional practice with mathematical concepts, and an understanding of other problem-solving explanations that may work better for you. Equipping yourself with a support group is one of the fastest ways to eliminate math anxiety.

Reward Yourself for Working Hard

Recognize the amount of effort you're putting in to overcome your math anxiety. It's not an easy task, so you deserve acknowledgement. Surround yourself with people who will provide you with the positive reinforcement you deserve.

Remember, You Can Do This!

Conquering a fear of math can be challenging, but there are lots of strategies that can help you out. Your own beliefs about your mathematical capabilities can limit your potential. Working toward a growth mindset can have a tremendous impact on decreasing math-related anxiety and building confidence. By knowing the symptoms of math anxiety and recognizing common misconceptions about learning math, you can develop a plan to address your fear of math. Utilizing the strategies discussed can help you overcome this anxiety and build the confidence you need to succeed.

Tell Us Your Story

We at Mometrix would like to extend our heartfelt thanks to you for letting us be a part of your journey. It is an honor to serve people from all walks of life, people like you, who are committed to building the best future they can for themselves.

We know that each person's situation is unique. But we also know that, whether you are a young student or a mother of four, you care about working to make your own life and the lives of those around you better.

That's why we want to hear your story.

We want to know why you're taking this test. We want to know about the trials you've gone through to get here. And we want to know about the successes you've experienced after taking and passing your test.

In addition to your story, which can be an inspiration both to us and to others, we value your feedback. We want to know both what you loved about our book and what you think we can improve on.

The team at Mometrix would be absolutely thrilled to hear from you! So please, send us an email at tellusyourstory@mometrix.com or visit us at mometrix.com/tellusyourstory.php and let's stay in touch.

Additional Bonus Material

Due to our efforts to try to keep this book to a manageable length, we've created a link that will give you access to all of your additional bonus material:

mometrix.com/bonus948/afoqt